the Human Project

FOURTH EDITION

Readings on

the Individual,

Society,

and Culture

Edited by
Clive Cockerton
Humber College Institute of
Technology and Advanced Learning

Melanie Chaparian
Humber College Institute of
Technology and Advanced Learning

StudyDesk Program by
George Byrnes
Humber College Institute of
Technology and Advanced Learning

Editorial Committee
Steve Boev, George Bragues, George Byrnes,
Naomi Couto, Brian Doyle, John Elias, Guy Letts,
Greg Narbey, Milos Vasic, and William Walcott

PEARSON
Prentice
Hall

Toronto

National Library of Canada Cataloguing in Publication

The human project : readings on the individual, society, and culture / edited by Clive Cockerton, Melanie Chaparian.—4th ed.

Includes index.
ISBN 0-13-130708-8

1. Humanities. I. Cockerton, Clive II. Chaparian, Melanie, 1958–

AZ221.H85 2005   001.3   C2004-905250-0

0-13-130708-8

Vice President, Editorial Director: Michael J. Young
Acquisitions Editor: Christine Cozens
Sponsoring Editor: Carolin Sweig
Marketing Manager: Ryan St. Peters
Developmental Editor: John Polanszky
Production Editor: Richard di Santo
Copy Editor: Susan Marshall
Proofreader: Heather Bean
Production Coordinator: Janis Raisen
Page Layout: B. J. Weckerle
Art Director: Julia Hall
Cover and Interior Design: Dave Mckay
Cover Image: Jan (Johannes) Vermeer, *The Astronomer* (oil on canvas, 1668); courtesy of Erich Lessing/Art Resource, NY

1 2 3 4 5   09 08 07 06 05

Printed and bound in the United States of America.

Additional Credits
Page 1: Ackerman, Diane, excerpt from *The Moon by Whalelight* (New York: Random House, Inc., 1991), reprinted with permission from Random House, Inc.
Additional literary credits appear on the first page of every reading, and photo credits appear on page 363, thus constituting an extension of the copyright page.

CONTENTS

UNIT 1

THE INDIVIDUAL: REFLECTIONS ON THE SELF   1

UNIT 2

CHANGE AND THE SOCIAL WORLD   51

UNIT 3

THE INDIVIDUAL AND THE COLLECTIVE: CONFLICT AND COOPERATION   129

UNIT 4

SCIENCE AND THE NATURAL WORLD   203

Unit 5
Arts and Culture   293

Appendix

PREFACE FOR INSTRUCTORS

The Human Project is an issues-based reader for colleges, designed to introduce students to the Humanities and Social Sciences. It is organized around the fundamental questions asked by a liberal education— questions of personal identity, social change, politics, science and the arts. Students are challenged to grapple with issues that don't have easy answers, to develop the higher level thinking skills that such complex questions require, and to acquire a tolerance for the fundamental ambiguities that many of life's basic problems engender. Those who meet this challenge not only become more valuable, flexible and reflective workers and citizens, but they have also started down the path of discovery, making them wiser and more fully rounded individuals.

Features The text includes a number of features designed to make the book both approachable for students and useful to instructors. The readings included in this text present a nice balance between commissioned articles written by experienced college teachers that are specifically geared toward the college audience, and previously published articles written by journalists or academics that are geared toward the wider Canadian and international community. Throughout the text, there are boldfaced key terms with marginal definitions as well as quotations related to the text discussion.

StudyDesk CD-ROM StudyDesk is a computer-based companion guide to the text that runs on the internet browser of any Pentium-level PC or Mac computer with an OS X or Unix operating system. StudyDesk provides a rich bank of supplementary material including point-form summaries of every textbook article, definitions and commentary on over 150 terms and concepts, biographical sketches of over 80 historical figures discussed in the textbook, and a selection of representative works from a number of authors cited in the textbook.

New to the Fourth Edition In the fourth edition of *The Human Project,* we have continued to present multidimensional issues that encourage students to explore different perspectives and compare theoretical views with their own experience. New articles have been included to ensure that current issues are addressed and an array of views represented.

Tim Adam's "The Skin We're In" and B. F. Skinner's "Can Science Help?" serve to complement and deepen the issues of personal identity and free will raised in Unit 1. An extensive revision of Unit 2 has rendered it more reflective of contemporary issues. In "The Economics of Social Change," George Bragues offers an interesting economic explanation of the political and cultural changes that transform society. Arlie Hochschild's "Exploring the Managed Heart," meanwhile, analyses the ways in which employers try to manage employees' emotions on the job in a bid to promote the financial viability of their business. The challenges faced by the family in response to the rapid pace of contemporary societal change, furthermore, are explored by Michael Ignatieff in "Rights, Intimacy, and Family Life" and by Laura Kipnis in "Marriage Is Made in Hell." Greg Narbey's "Can We All Just Get Along?" and Bhiku Parekh's "Diversity vs. Solidarity" address the complex struggles faced by pluralistic societies such as Canada. Turning to Unit 3, George Bragues's "A Game We Call Politics: A Primer" outlines the Canadian political process as it compares with the U.S. and other countries. "Righting the Ship of Democracy" by Bruce Ackerman and James Fishkin and "Smooth Sailing" by Richard Posner introduce a spirited debate on how—or even if—Americans (and, by implication, Canadians, too) should be encouraged not only to vote but to do so on the basis of an understanding of the issues at hand. Unit 4 has been extensively revised. Suzanne Senay's "Making Sense of the Universe" analyses the nature of the scientific enterprise by way of a historical account of the field of cosmology. A complementary account of scientific methodology is offered by Carl Sagan in "Can We Know the Universe? Reflections on a Grain of Sand." Meanwhile, Kenneth R. Miller, in "Finding Darwin's God," contends that the theory of evolution does not eradicate faith in a higher being. Bjorn Lomborg's "The Truth about the Environment" and E. O. Wilson's "Is Humanity Suicidal?" introduce an intriguing debate about the state of the natural environment and, on that basis, what measures need to be taken to preserve it. In "When Doctors Make Mistakes," Atul Gawande shares his experiences as a surgeon to explore the complexities that can lead even the most experienced, well trained, and careful doctors to make sometimes fatal mistakes in the operating room. Unit 5 also boasts some compelling new additions. Ian Baird's "One More Time: Our Ongoing Dialogue with Popular Music" offers an engaging account of the role of popular music in the 20th century. "Us or Me"—the first chapter of Ian McEwan's *Enduring Love*—provides the reader with a page-turner of a narrative that demonstrates the special kind of insight that fiction can offer. Noteworthy, too, is the new collection of poems—thoughtfully analyzed by George Byrnes in "Poems: An Introduction"—that represents a variety of styles: Philip Larkin's "This Be the Verse" and Walt Whitman's "A Noiseless Patient Spider."

Organization: The perspectives are drawn from various disciplines, including psychology, philosophy, sociology, anthropology, political theory, science, medicine and the arts. They are organized into units that begin with the individual and extend to the social, political, physical and cultural realms where the individual operates. This organization, going from the individual outwards, allows the student to approach the complexities of the world from familiar ground. Students are encouraged to arrive at an appreciation of the inter-connectedness of things and of how the world is inter-related by starting with themselves.

We have been eager to show that contemporary problems have their roots in the past and their solutions in a rich diversity of theoretical perspectives. At least in some measure, the text reflects the following goals of general education: aesthetic appreciation, civic life, cultural understanding, personal development, science, technology, work and the economy. It is only when students become engaged with such issues that real intellectual stretching occurs and they are able to arrive at their own, unique conclusions. We hope that our book, based on classroom experience and inspired by much of the animated debate on general education that has taken place over the last decade, contributes in a real and practical way to the ongoing discussion about what students need to know to face an ever-changing, complex reality.

Acknowledgements: The editors wish to thank the team that gave their time and effort so generously to the task of creating a new text. Our editorial committee—Steve Boev, George Bragues, George Byrnes, Naomi Couto, Brian Doyle, John Elias, Guy Letts, Greg Narbey, Milos Vasic, and William Walcott—made the evolution of this text an object lesson in collaborative effort.

The editors would also like to thank the team at Pearson Education Canada—including sponsoring editor, Carolin Sweig; developmental editor, John Polanszky; production editor Richard di Santo; photo researcher Sandy Cooke; and copy editor Susan Marshall. Special thanks go to our Humber writers who used their understanding of students to translate difficult issues in a way that has relevance to students' lives.

INTRODUCTION FOR THE STUDENT

Everyone, it seems, wants to be an individual, to be recognized as a unique and special person. Most people also relish the notion of freedom, the idea that they hold the reins, at least some of the time, in determining the course of their lives. Yet, as desirable as individuality and freedom are, very few of us want to live alone. Indeed, most of us need a community of others if we are to live well and flourish. However, the cost of living in a community is usually some sacrifice (in theory anyway) of our individuality and freedom.

Our family expects us to behave in certain ways, our friends demand a code of behaviour, and all the institutions of society, our schools, businesses, churches and government, influence and control our behaviour on many levels. So to live with others is to live with constraint, and yet if we submit to everyone's expectations of us, we run the danger of losing ourselves, our sense of who we are. A natural tension exists in every healthy life and this tension between individual and larger goals doesn't ever finally resolve itself. It is not something you grow out of; it doesn't go away. Just when you're being most dutiful, you can be haunted by the temptation to be wild. Just when you think that indulging your every whim is the answer, the heart responds to a larger call and a need greater than the self.

What do you do with a tension that cannot be resolved, that resists easy answers? You can pretend it doesn't exist and be blown about by the forces of change in an unconscious way. Or you can seek to understand the great tensions and problems of our day and hopefully gain not only awareness, but also some influence on how your life evolves.

This book attempts to grapple with some of the difficult problems that confront everyone, from questions of our basic human nature, to social change, to politics, to technology, and to arts and culture. This is frequently a dark and complex world, and modern students need all the information, all the understanding, and all the light they can get if they are to find their own way in this world. Grappling with these questions will most probably give your grey cells a good workout, and thinking skills can be developed that will be useful in all your courses at college and, even more importantly, in your place of work. The possibility of developing your high-level thinking skills through the study of this text is of real and obvious practical benefit. But along the way, not in every section, but perhaps in some area, we hope you find some personal revelation and acquire some understanding that is unique to you.

UNIT 1

The Individual: Reflections on the Self

After all, mind is such an odd predicament for matter to get into. I often marvel how something like hydrogen, the simplest atom, forged in some early chaos of the universe, could lead to us and the gorgeous fever we call consciousness. If a mind is just a few pounds of blood, dream, and electric, how does it manage to contemplate itself, worry about its soul, do time-and-motion studies, admire the shy hooves of a goat, know that it will die, enjoy all the grand and lesser mayhems of the heart? What is mind, that one can be *out of one's?* How can a neuron feel compassion? What is a self? Why did automatic, hand-me-down mammals like our ancestors somehow evolve brains with the ability to consider, imagine, project, compare, abstract, think of the future? If our experience of mind is really just the simmering of an easily alterable chemical stew, then what does it mean to know something, to want something, *to be?* How do you begin with hydrogen and end up with prom dresses, jealousy, chamber music?

Diane Ackerman

The gods do not die, only take new forms, new names. There is something in us that will not let them go, not a longing for redemption, though we do long for it, or even a fear of the dark though we do go in terror of it, but an unquenchable need to have ourselves and our mundane doings reflected and exalted, to see the saga of ourselves written across the sky.

John Banville

Introduction

Toward the Examined Life

You have likely already noticed that the scope of *The Human Project* is quite broad—encompassing issues drawn from the entire spectrum of the liberal arts, including the humanities, social sciences and natural sciences. But unless you are preparing for a career that draws heavily upon one or more of these academic areas, you may have also questioned the value of this textbook and the course for which it is required reading. In other words, you may have asked yourself the question: *Why should I care about all this?*

As you will read later, in Unit 3, "Whether we care or not, politics matters." The same may be said of all the disciplines introduced in this text: Whether we care or not, developments in psychology, sociology, biology, medicine, art, philosophy—as well as politics—matter. Why? Because they shape the world in which we live, study, love, hate, work, play, buy, parent, socialize, vote, worship, etc. The latest theories in psychology, for example, may very well influence the way teachers teach—via lectures, or group work, or experiential exercises—in our college or university courses as well as in our children's elementary-school and high-school classes. And the conditions in which we work—at the office or at home, full time or part time, long term or by contract—may be significantly affected by the current views of those sociologists, political scientists and economists who study and comment on the business world. On an even more personal level, relatively unobtrusive cutting-edge medical treatments offer us the promise of longer, healthier, more comfortable lives, but also present the chance, however remote, that human error in the application of these treatments may unexpectedly cut our lives short. So to truly understand our world and have some real control over our lives, it is necessary to have a familiarity with the ideas that matter. As the old adage says, "The unexamined life is not worth living." A study of the ideas introduced in this reader is a good beginning for an examination of timely issues in contemporary life. This is precisely why you should care about all this!

And the "this" that we should, must and actually do (although perhaps unwittingly) care about is nothing less than the "human project"—the world as it has been and continues to be constructed, transformed and explained by the accumulated efforts of humankind. This may sound like too lofty a subject of study until we recognize that this "project" is manifest in the various spheres of the everyday world in which we live today. A selected survey of the issues presented in *The Human Project* reflects this perspective: Is the "self" nothing more than a naturally occurring, albeit sophisticated, piece of "software" that is haphazardly "designed" and "redesigned" by the rewards and punishments we encounter in our social and natural environments? What might this mean about the personal decisions we make in life? Are big changes in society best understood as the result of the economic development that technological innovation makes possible? What might this imply about the growing incidence of alternative family structures or the increasingly multicultural composition of contemporary society? Is conflict among individuals and violence between nations inevitable? How might this question affect the way federal governments and international coalitions are structured? Do the conclusions of the physical sciences always trump explanations drawn from social science, philosophy, art and religion? How might this influence the working relationship between scientists and others? Do the arts offer nothing more than pleasant entertainment or do they also contain a special kind of serious insight? What impact might this have on the required curriculum not only in elementary schools and high schools but also in professional and technical programs in colleges and universities?

As this list of issues reveals, the human project is—and always has been, and always will be—a work in progress. As such, it can be seen as the largest public works project ever, since every individual, in every society, in every era—including you, in Canada, during the first decade of the twenty-first century—plays a part in modifying, maintaining and interpreting this project. The part we play as individuals depends on the responses we make to the timely issues of our day. And our responses, in turn, are greatly enhanced by a familiarity with some of the theories proposed by those thinkers who have wrestled with similar, and even different, issues in the past. It is for this reason that *The Human Project* invites us to think through contemporary issues in consultation with works constructed in the near-to-distant past in the fields of psychology, sociology, politics, science, art and philosophy.

Ultimately, all theories about the world—even scientific theories seemingly unconcerned with humanity—make assumptions, if not statements, about human nature. (The very idea that we are capable of transcending our human perspective and understanding the world objectively is itself a bold assumption about human nature.) Thus, we are led to the question of questions: What is human nature? What makes humans human? Any answer to these questions must account both for the qualities that make us all human as well as the characteristics that make each of us different.

"Know Thyself"

Every man bears the whole stamp of the human condition.

Michel de Montaigne, Essays, Bk. II, Ch. 12.

Since the abstract concept of "human nature" is brought to life in each individual human being, perhaps this is the best place to begin our investigation. In other words, the first step toward the examined life may be to "know thyself." Thus, Unit 1 in *The Human Project* is entitled "The Individual."

So what is the "individual"? Is it the same as the "self"? And what is the "self"? When you refer to "your*self*," who is the "you" that speaks? Is it the same as your "soul" or "mind"? Clearly, these are important to your understanding of "self" if you take pride in your spirituality or your intellect. But is not your body also essential to your understanding of "self"? It certainly seems so if you take any pride in your physical appearance and abilities. If so, is the significance of the body—in particular, the brain—equal to that of the mind? Contemporary neurology suggests that the brain is essential to all mental processes. That said, what is the relationship between the mental and physical qualities of the individual?

These are but a few of the difficult questions that arise when a serious attempt is made to understand the meaning of our life experience as human beings, as individuals, as minds, as bodies. This quest is even more difficult because our subjective experience may stand in the way of a fully objective self-investigation. But unless we accept the prospect of living the *un*examined life, we are compelled at least to attempt such an investigation.

Fortunately, we can benefit from the previous investigations of others. In the first article in Unit 1—"From Biology to Biography: A Brief History of the Self"—Wendy O'Brien explores the theories of self offered by the French philosopher René Descartes (1596–1650), the Austrian psychologist Sigmund Freud (1856–1939) and the German philosopher Friedrich Nietzsche (1844–1900) as well as contemporary approaches informed by the practice of behaviourism and the research of the Human Genome Project. In her discussion of these different theories and views, O'Brien touches upon three issues fundamental to the study of self: 1) the mind-body problem, 2) the nature-nurture question and 3) the free will-determinism debate.

The Mind-Body Problem

The mind-body problem stems from the "dualism" proposed by Descartes. This is the theory that human beings consist of two essentially different and distinct "substances": mind—a thinking entity that is purely mental in nature, and body—a physical thing that is completely material in nature. Although both of these substances are important to human nature, Descartes argues that the mind is not only the more knowable but also the more essential of the two. Most of us find that common sense confirms the Cartesian view of the dualistic self: We tend to think of ourselves as mind—our true, lasting, "inner" self—on the one hand, and body—our less true, changing, "outer" self—on the other. As Tim Adams explains in "The Skin We're In," we nonetheless spend a good deal of time, effort and money on our less essential "outward selves." In contemporary Western culture, for example, people go to great lengths to modify their bodies: they "make up" their faces; they cut, dye, curl, straighten and iron their hair; they pierce and tattoo various parts of their bodies; they diet to slim down their waists; they undergo plastic surgery to attain bigger breasts, smaller thighs and younger faces. The point of all this, Adams suggests, is to make our bodies more accurately reflect the internal selves we believe we are or want to become.

This phenomenon points to a problem that dualists like Descartes have yet to answer convincingly: How is it possible for a purely mental, non-physical mind to interact with an entirely material, physical body? In other words, is it really possible to move physical objects with your (purely mental) mind alone? When put this way, it is less obvious that dualism conforms to common sense.

Of course, not everyone agrees with Descartes that the mind is distinct from, and more significant than, the body. As O'Brien explains, the scientists involved in the Human Genome Project take a very different approach to the study of human nature; in fact, this impressive research project is limited in scope to a physical investigation of human beings through study of our genetic makeup. This does not mean that geneticists necessarily deny the existence of the mind. But when they propose, as O'Brien notes some do, that personality traits are determined by genetics, they are in effect claiming that the mind is at most the creation of, and, as such, less essential than, the body.

Perhaps Richard Restak has the most convincing solution to the mind-body problem. In "My Brain and I Are One," Restak, a practising neurologist, states in no uncertain terms that the brain's "temporal lobe is responsible for . . . our personal identity." But he also acknowledges how difficult it is, even for him, to really believe that who he is—an individual, a mind, a self—is determined by his brain. So Restak proposes an interesting compromise: namely, that mind and body really reflect different perspectives of the same reality—with mind existing in time and body existing in space. Both perspectives are real, but we can't understand one in terms of the other. So the mind-body problem remains just that—an unsolved problem.

The Nature-Nurture Question

Behaviourists such as B. F. Skinner (1904–1990) skirt the mind-body problem either by ignoring the mind—since it is not an observable entity and, therefore, is not amenable to scientific study—or by simply denying its existence. Nonetheless, behaviourists do have a very clear position on another big issue in the study of human nature: the nature-nurture question. This question asks whether the self is more the result of nature—qualities we are born with, such as genetics or instincts or even innate "drives"—or more the result of nurture—influences stemming from our environment, such as upbringing, schooling, socioeconomic status, culture, etc. Behaviourism is the theory that we are not what we think but rather what we do, i.e., how we behave, and that what we do is determined by rewards and punishments in our environment. But, as O'Brien argues, these environmental influences do not seem to have the lasting effect that behaviourists claim they do.

The Human Genome Project will provide evidence for the nature side of this debate if it does indeed discover that personality traits are determined by genetic makeup. But, as O'Brien notes, our understanding of genetics to date only points to probabilities, not certainties. Environmental factors may ultimately explain why certain genetic dispositions develop into realities while others do not.

Indeed, most if not all serious thinkers acknowledge that both nature and nurture are significant factors in understanding human nature. And this is the position of Sigmund Freud: while the *id* consists of irresistible innate instincts, the *superego* contains socially constructed rules and expectations, forcing the *ego* to try to mediate between the two in a realistic way. For Freud, nature (id) has a greater impact on the self than nurture (superego and ego), but both are strong and essential forces in human nature.

The Free Will–Determinism Debate

The id has the stronger hand in Freud's model of the self because it is part of the unconscious mind; after all, it is hard to control something if we are not aware of it. This leads us to the debate over whether or not we are truly free to make choices between alternative courses of action. This issue, summarized in "Am I Free or Determined?" by Melanie Chaparian, hinges on the debate between determinists—those who argue that all our actions are caused by forces beyond our control—and libertarians—those who argue that at least some of our actions are the result of our free will.

This debate is informed by the investigation into the nature of self. In other words, our view of the nature of the individual has a direct bearing on our position on free will. If you agree with Freud, for example, that the self is inalterably created by natural and environmental forces over which we have no control, you will have little hope that human beings can exercise true freedom. Or if, alternatively, you are persuaded by the behaviourist thesis that we are unendingly shaped by rewards and punishments in our environment, you will see no trace of free will in human behaviour. If, however, you are convinced by Nietzsche's understanding of the self as a personally styled work of art, you will find the theory of libertarianism not only probable, but likely evident.

Indeed, the American philosopher and psychologist William James (1842–1910) invites us to view both the determinist and the libertarian positions through introspective lenses to discern which makes the most sense of reality as we experience it in our daily lives. He suggests that although objective explanations of reality may be useful at times, they do not successfully account for our subjective experience of our lived lives in which we frequently feel free to make choices and often regret the choices we and others make. Restak's medical understanding of his epileptic patients helps him to treat them effectively, for instance, but at the same time he finds it difficult to convince himself that his patients as well as he, himself, are ultimately determined by the (mis)functions of the body and the brain—a "three-pound mass of protoplasm with the consistency of an overripe avocado." In "Can Science Help?" Skinner counters these kinds of arguments by pointing out that just because something is hard to believe does not mean that it is not true. He argues, moreover, that the subjective experience of freedom to which James and other libertarians appeal is a culturally created concept that seems to reflect a natural feeling only because of how prevalent the myth of free will is in our everyday lives.

From Biology to Biography: A Brief History of the Self

Wendy O'Brien

René Descartes

What do you mean when you say: "I'm so sorry, I'm just not myself today"? Do you mean that somehow you have inadvertently deviated from your essential being? If you aren't yourself, then who or what have you become? When you sit back and think about it for a minute, this simple phrase, one you hear people use all the time, raises important questions about the nature of identity. Who or what is this self that we refer to, this presence that provides continuity and perspective to our experience? Many great minds such as Descartes, Freud, Skinner and Nietzsche have asked themselves similar questions; while they have all contributed to our understanding of the self, they would also acknowledge that even after careful reflection and analysis there still remain many unanswered questions about the nature of personal identity.

The modern search to understand the self has its origin in the writings of the 17th-century philosopher René Descartes. Descartes was writing during the scientific revolution, a time of great hope and belief in the possibility of progress. It was, as well, a time marked by insecurity, as science began to challenge existing theories about the natural world, and consequently called into question long-held beliefs about human beings—about their innate qualities and characteristics, their place in nature and their relationship to God.

In raising these questions, the new science dispelled many myths about the natural world and challenged many traditional beliefs about humanity. Most importantly, it also changed the way people thought. No longer could they rely on authority figures to explain how the world worked and how they should act. People were left on their own to discover for themselves the answers to these questions. Reason replaced faith as the source of knowledge and humankind was forever changed as a result. While many of his contemporaries, including Galileo, were busy applying the principles of science to the natural world, Descartes used these principles to study human beings. His methodology consisted of four basic rules:

1. Do not accept any statement as true without evidence.

"From Biology to Biography: A Brief History of the Self" is by Wendy O'Brien of the Humber College Institute of Technology and Advanced Learning. Used by permission.

2. Divide every problem into its simplest parts.

3. Start with what is simple and build your way up to more complex ideas.

4. Be thorough: carefully record and analyze data in order to ensure that nothing is left out.

Why try to study human beings from a scientific perspective rather than accept the teachings of the church or rely upon tradition? As noted earlier, Descartes lived through a time when it seemed that the whole world was being turned upon its head. In this regard, perhaps he had a lot in common with people today living at the dawn of the 21st century. Even if you are as young as 20 or 25, you know how many things have changed throughout your lifetime. And with the current advances in science and technology, you know that things aren't likely to slow down any time soon. Descartes responded to change by trying to find one thing, just one thing that he could hold onto, one thing that he could know was true and would always be so. If he could find one thing that he could know for certain, then maybe he could make sense of the changes that were taking place.

In order to accomplish this goal, Descartes adopted the method of "radical doubt." For a claim to be true, for it to be certain, it had to be literally beyond doubt. So he began doubting everything that he had once taken for granted as true. He began by doubting the teachings of authority. Descartes was a rebel in his time. He dared to ask if politicians, religious leaders, teachers and other experts could be relied on to tell the truth. He quickly realized that while authorities often knew a lot about one thing, they tended to extend their claims beyond the area of their expertise.

Well, if you can't rely on others to tell you what is true, surely you can rely on your own experiences, your own sense perceptions, to provide you with knowledge. As you sit reading this, you see the words on the page. You feel the textbook in your hands. You smell the coffee that sits in the cup beside you. Given what your senses tell you, you can claim that these things—the book and the cup—are real. Or can you? You only have to think for a minute about how even great food can taste flavourless when you have a cold or how you can feel chilly even when you have a high fever to understand why Descartes concluded that even your own experiences cannot be trusted to lead you to the truth.

Moreover, how do you know that you aren't dreaming that you are reading this page? Haven't you ever had a dream that was so "real" that you thought that you had really lived it? If you have, then you can understand Descartes's point. How can you prove that what you are experiencing now isn't the same sort of a dream? Descartes questioned whether everything that you have known to date is part of a long and elaborate dream and, thus, he put into question all those things that you readily take for granted as real.

But even if the claims of authorities, the knowledge gained from sense perceptions and our assumptions about what is real are all possibly false, certainly such abstract truths as mathematical formulas must be true. It seems that 2+2 has always been, and will always be, 4. But how do you know that this is the right answer? What if there is some supreme being who, rather than being benevolent as portrayed in many religious teachings, is, in fact, an evil demon? What if he/she/it gets his/her/its kicks out of playing mind games with you and has indeed tricked you into believing that 2+2 is 4 when in reality it is 27?

True, this argument may seem far-fetched; however, if you have seen the movie *The Matrix*, you have a good idea of what Descartes had in mind here. In this film, robotic bugs have tricked human beings into believing that their everyday lives are real. The humans think that they live in New York City, that they work, that they socialize and that they fall in love, when, in fact, they are living inside of pods, having their energy sucked out of them to fuel a complex computer system known as the Matrix. How can you prove that even the most obvious truths aren't, in fact, illusions? Can you conclusively put aside any and all doubt that Descartes's evil demon or the Matrix may be real? If even the smallest doubt remains in your mind, you are left to conclude that you can't even be certain of the most basic mathematical equations.

At this point, it may seem like Descartes's search for one thing to believe in, for one thing that he could know for certain, had failed: there was nothing in the world that he could unquestioningly accept as true. Quite to the contrary, however, Descartes was on the verge of discovering the foundation on which he was to base all knowledge. For it was at this point that he realized that there *was* one thing that he could know for certain. In order to be sitting there doubting everything that exists, there was one thing that he was unable to doubt: he couldn't doubt that he was doubting, for if he doubted that he was doubting, he would nonetheless be doubting. (Don't worry if this sounds confusing the first time you read it. Read the sentence over a few times. Now sit back and doubt whether the book in front of you is real. Now doubt that you are doubting that the book is real. It is impossible, for in doubting that you are doubting you are still doubting.) But proving the existence of doubting alone didn't make much sense to Descartes. How can doubting exist on its own? This was impossible. Indeed, in order for there to be doubting, there must be some thing that is doing the doubting.

What is this thing that, according to the logic of the argument, you can know is true? Descartes concluded that it is the self. But what is the self? For Descartes it was "a thing that thinks"—a thing that understands, affirms, knows, imagines and doubts. In other words, the self is synonymous with what many of us would describe as the mind. This means that the minute you begin to doubt that you exist, you prove your own existence—for to doubt your existence is to think and, thus, to affirm the reality of the self. "*Cogito ergo sum*," Descartes concluded: "I think, therefore I am."

In making this claim, Descartes made the self the grounding concept of modern philosophy. The one thing that you can know for certain, the one thing that will provide a foundation for the knowledge that you gain about the world, about other people, about the existence of God, is your knowledge of the self. But in making this claim, Descartes really only began his investigation of identity. For, while he had proven the existence of the mind, he found himself with a new problem.

Recall that the method of radical doubt led Descartes to question the **veracity** of information gained through the body. In discrediting the body as a source of knowledge and locating the self in the mind, Descartes advocated a form of "dualism." According to this theory, you are composed of two different substances: mind and body. The mind has an immaterial and internal existence that only it can know. It is not available for public scrutiny. It cannot be located in space nor is it divisible. The body, on the other hand, exists in space and therefore is divisible. You can clearly distinguish between its various parts, for example, your hand, your finger and your thumb. Moreover, the body exists in the external world and, as such, is open to public appraisal. For Descartes, it was critical to distance the mind from the body in such a manner, as this ensured that the uncertainty associated with bodily perceptions would not infect the perfect knowledge that we could have of the mind.

veracity
truth

Descartes's descriptions of the mind and the body seem fairly accurate. You don't experience yourself as a disembodied, dislocated and lonely mind. When you talk about your "self," you are referring to your body too. Descartes himself seemed to recognize this fact when he defined the self as a "*thing* that thinks." But how is this possible? How can the self be two such different kinds of things, different substances, at one and the same time?

Descartes resolved this dilemma by acknowledging the existence of the body but giving it a secondary role. The mind was the "pilot of the vessel." It controlled and directed the body. Indeed, this is the view that many of us continue to hold regarding the self. How many times have you heard someone say that looks aren't everything and that what really matters is what kind of person an individual is? In doing so, they are claiming, along with Descartes, that when push comes to shove, the body really isn't all that important. It is the mind that makes you who you are.

But this account of the self has raised as many questions as it has provided answers. Can you be so certain that the self exists as Descartes described it? Descartes thought that it was impossible to disprove the existence of the self, but you might counter that it isn't all that clear that there is an essential self inside of you directing and guiding your actions. How many times have you been asked "what are you thinking?" and your response has been "I dunno"? It seems like the mind may not be easy to access after all. Indeed, it may be one of the hardest things to know. Think of how difficult it is sometimes to know what you are thinking, what you are feeling or what is motivating your actions. Further, the mind and the body are not isolated aspects of the self. Somehow they manage to work together to create your identity. Consider, for example, how the body affects the mind just as the mind affects the body. If you have ever drunk too much alcohol or have been with someone who is drunk, you have first- or at least second-hand experience of how powerful this influence can be. It is not so clear who or what is the "pilot of the vessel."

Questions such as these convinced Sigmund Freud that there is more to the self than his predecessors had appreciated. Theories that grounded the self in the thinking mind seemed to him too simplistic. They attempted to make the self a thing that is in control and relatively easy to understand. Listening to people describe their experiences, however, Freud realized that the self was mysterious, messy and complicated. More specifically, the mind seemed to be divided against itself—pulled and pushed in different directions by unknown forces.

Consider, for example, what could happen when you attempt to do something as simple as buying a pair of shoes. Suppose you get to the shoe department and immediately notice that the sales clerk is cute. You remind yourself that you are there to buy shoes, not to look for a date. You begin looking through the displays. You find the perfect pair. They look good on you. The only thing is that they cost about three times more than you had planned to spend. There are other shoes more in keeping with your budget, but, well, they just aren't *those* shoes. As you are standing there still checking out the clerk, a debate rages on in your head: "Buy them." "Don't buy them." "Buy them." "Go for a walk and think about it." "Buy them." "No, don't."

How often do such conversations take place in your head? Sometimes they may concern shoes, while at other times they might be

Sigmund Freud

about whether to ask that certain someone out or merely what to watch on television. It seems that you are often divided against yourself. Why? Why can't you be clear and decisive? Why is it so hard to make decisions about even the simplest things? What is it that pulls and pushes you in so many directions? Freud abandoned Descartes's project of trying to find one thing to believe in and, instead, in attempting to be more true to our lived experiences, he tried to explain why the self seems uncertain of everything—including its own workings.

The self, as described by Freud, could be compared to an iceberg. If you saw *Titanic*, you know that the ice formations that you see looming above the water compose only a small portion of the complete size of an iceberg. The same holds true for human beings. A large part of the self, for Freud, is an intricate web of conflicting desires and dictates of which you remain virtually unaware. His goal was to chart this unknown territory, to provide a map of the psyche. His analysis divided the self into three parts: the id, the superego and the ego.

Go back to the shoe example. Why do you want the expensive shoes? Is it really because they are comfortable, or do you have some ulterior motive? Why shoes, of all things? To answer these questions, Freud would suggest that you have to explore your id. This part of the self is housed in your unconscious—that mysterious part of yourself of which you are unaware but which, nonetheless, has a powerful effect on everything that you do, say, feel and think. The id contains two instincts—thanatos and eros—that constantly nag at you, wanting immediate satisfaction, pressuring you to act irrationally. And, if you think about it, you may be surprised to discover how often you succumb to such urges.

Thanatos is the drive toward death, aggression and violence. It is that part of the self that is willing to pull "your" pair of shoes out of the hands of another customer if they dare to pick them up. Most often, however, it takes more subtle forms and is expressed in feelings of envy and arrogance. While thanatos directs our feelings of aggression, eros concerns our desire for pleasure. According to Freud, the id operates according to the pleasure principle: it constantly tries to maximize pleasure, particularly the pleasure associated with our bodily desires for sex and food. If it *feels* good, it *is* good. Think about the shoes. Why is it that you want those shoes and you want those shoes now? Isn't it because they are a source of pleasure? They are not only comfortable; they might also serve to attract attention from others, which could lead to a date or to something even more. But if eros and thanatos are always unconsciously working toward fulfilling your desires, why aren't your closets full of shoes and your VISA bills permanently at your credit limit?

While it is true that the unconscious contains our basic instincts and desires, it also must wrestle with that part of our self that is constantly telling us "*Don't.*" Think of the lists of *do*s and *don't*s that you have been subjected to throughout your lifetime. Friends, religious leaders, politicians, the media and, above all, others in your family are constantly telling you what you should do and how you should do it. An integral part of the psyche, the superego, has been internalizing these lists to make sure that you obey them. Remember going to the store with your parents and being told "NO" you can't have a new toy? Don't you hear that same "NO" reverberating in your head when you go to buy a new pair of shoes? And when you ask yourself why you can't have them, you get the line that you heard a million times as a teenager: "*Don't* waste your money." The superego demands that you adhere to each and every social rule; it demands perfect and complete obedience at all times.

But it doesn't get such obedience, and the battle rages on. The id and the superego attempt to alter the structure of the self by denying the reality or the importance of the other. It is the role of the ego, of the conscious part of the self, to try to referee between your unending desires and your internalized social rules. No one can live according to the pleasure principle alone. If you tried, you would quickly find yourself in jail. Similarly, if you tried to live according to every existing social rule, you would quickly find yourself immobilized. It would be impossible to act if you tried to adhere to them all. The role of the ego is to balance between reality, your desires and your lists of *do*s and *don't*s. This is the part of the self that tells you to "Chill," that is, to slow down and think things through before you do something that you will regret later. Sometimes the ego is successful, and sometimes it isn't.

According to Freud, the self is the arena in which these three forces confront each other—making it hard to know what you are thinking, let alone why. To help identify these psychic forces, Freud developed a series of techniques to make the unconscious mind reveal itself. If you know what desires are directing your behaviour and if you know what rules you have stored away in your memory, then you might be able to devise a means for reconciling them with the realities of your daily life. His famous talking cure, "psychoanalysis," is one such technique. By talking about your past experiences, particularly about your childhood, Freud thought that the unconscious would come to the surface and reveal unresolved conflicts that inhibit your progress. Similarly, he found clues to what lies beneath the surface of the self in analyzing slips of the tongue, jokes, word associations, dreams, and memories recovered using hypnosis.

Freud's view of the self has had an enormous effect on modern conceptions of identity. He complicated our understanding of the self with his introduction of the unconscious mind. He also recognized that the mind and the body are more intricately intertwined than had been previously acknowledged. Indeed, Freud offered explanations of how biology can affect the mind—when, for example, desires direct thought—as well as how the mind can affect biology—as demonstrated, for instance, through hysteria and psychosomatic illness. In short, he showed how the self can be divided against itself. And Freud's account of the self has led to a new appreciation of the complexity of relationships. If you don't know what you are doing or why, and I don't know what I'm doing or why, and the two of us are engaged in an intimate relationship, well, needless to say, we've got trouble. Freud's theories helped to explain why relationships, particularly with those whom you most love, are so difficult. And he made evident that you need to sit back and reflect on your actions and beliefs, preferably before acting, in order to avoid doing things that will ultimately be self-destructive. Reflecting on these contributions, it's hard for us to really imagine how people thought about the self before Freud.

Like Descartes, however, Freud was left at the end of his life with more questions about the self than he had answers, questions that continue to be raised about his theory. Critics have questioned Freud's claim that the self is constantly at war with itself. Sure, there are times when you may feel internally conflicted, but for the most part things are pretty peaceful. This has led other commentators to speculate that the self is not so mysterious. You know what the self is and how it works, but it just isn't all that interesting compared to discussions of thanatos and eros. So, to liven up the story of your life, you accept Freud's notion of the unconscious mind. To relieve yourself of boredom, you convince yourself that there are such things as the id and the superego, and go on to ascribe to your actions all sorts of complicated and intriguing motivations.

Perhaps the most important criticism of Freud's theory of the self, however, concerns the very existence of the mind itself. To make this point clear, think for a minute about unicorns. Do you believe in unicorns? Most people don't. You may believe that if you can't see it or touch it, it just isn't real. Well, have you seen your mind? If you were shown a picture of your brain, would you be satisfied that you had seen your mind? Freud and Descartes put their faith in something as intangible as unicorns. They believed in a mind that you can't see or study or, for the most part, understand. It seems clear to many that the mind simply doesn't exist.

The search for alternative explanations of identity has led many theorists to return to that part of the self that Descartes had discarded as unreliable and unworthy of our attention and that Freud just began to explore, namely, the body. Most contemporary theories of the self emphasize that if there is such a thing as the mind, it must be located in a body that exists in time and space. Indeed, who you are is largely a consequence of your body. It seems that Descartes and Freud were too quick to focus on the mind and, as a result, underestimated the extent to which the body is the self.

Explanations of the self that centre on the body aren't new. Early attempts to explain behaviour and personality in terms of biology and physiology focused on the circulation of blood and on the shape and structure of the skull. Why did we turn to the body for information about the self? It seems pretty clear. The body is tangible. It can be observed and examined. You can study the body, quantify your results, use your findings to predict future outcomes, and perhaps even intervene. The body is knowable and predictable and, therefore, it seems to provide a more reliable foundation on which to build a theory of identity.

Clearly the most significant development in this school of thought was the discovery of DNA (deoxyribonucleic acid). While the chemical itself was first identified in 1869, it was not until 1953 that James Watson and Francis Crick were able to unlock the structure of DNA. In so doing, they initiated the genetic revolution—a revolution that would put into question some of the most cherished beliefs about the self much in the same way as scientific revolutions did centuries before.

DNA is a genetic code found in every cell in your body. It is most often represented by a double helix—that is, by two lines or polymers that intertwine with each other. The helix is divided into 24 distinct and separate units known as chromosomes. Along these chromosomes lie genes that hold within them a blueprint for how a person is predisposed to grow and to develop. Just as Morse code is composed of messages translated into a series of dots and dashes, the messages in our genes are encoded in the form of four basic acids known as nucleotides: adenine, guanine, cytosine and thymine. Various combinations of these acids within genes contain information that predispose you to develop certain physical traits, particular diseases and syndromes and, according to some researchers, specific aspects of your personality.

The Human Genome Project was initiated in 1990 with the goal of mapping the human genome—the complete map of human genetics— that consists of approximately 30,000 genes. With researchers in over 15 countries and a yearly budget that exceeded 30 billion dollars (U.S.), the project completed its first draft in 2000—when the dispositions associated with every chromosonal, single, human gene had been identified. The genes for over 500 hereditary diseases, including ALS, multiple sclerosis, Alzheimer's disease and breast cancer were located, and, based on this knowledge, scientists are beginning to develop new treatment procedures and therapies. But this was just the beginning.

Genetics has often been misinterpreted as the science that concerns itself simply with identifying causal relationships between single genes and human physiology and/or behaviour. In reality, however, this new science is far more complicated. It might be telling to ask why the complexity of this new science has been overlooked. Perhaps there is something appealing about a model of behaviour that seems to be so straightforward. Instead of trying to decipher the logic of Descartes's thinking mind or the irrationality of Freud's unconscious, it can be reassuring to think that humanity can be described and explained in a much more mechanistic and uncomplicated manner. Indeed, simplifying genetics does make it possible to sidestep some of the more challenging questions about human behaviour that are raised by this research. Paradoxically, genetics, as it has been popularized, is an easy target for criticism precisely due to its supposed failure to take into account the complexities raised by environmental influences and the role of free will. Dispelling this misleading view of genetics, then, is key to facing the important issues that it raises with regard to human behaviour.

Far from completing its task with the mapping of the human genome, the Human Genome Project has just begun its work. For instance, researchers are now looking at the effects of *combinations* of genes. They are trying, moreover, to better understand the complex relationships that exist not only among genes, but also among combinations of genes, biochemical events, the environment and the individual's responses to these variables. That is, they are attempting to map webs of *influence*, rather than causal relationships, in order to better understand the evolution and development of human physiology and behaviour. Adopting this approach, researchers do not expect to uncover simple, universal truths about human nature but rather hope, at best, to find statistically relevant patterns.

Genetic research is not a study of certainties. It deals in probabilities rather than with truths and laws of nature. Scientists acknowledge that, at most, genetic markers can tell us about dispositions, about the *likelihood* that a person will develop a particular physical characteristic, disease or personality trait. But dispositions are not certainties. This leaves room for the environment to play a role in shaping the self. Looking at your DNA, geneticists can make, at best, informed predictions as to what your future will hold. Studying your DNA, therefore, is not like looking into a crystal ball. It requires more interpretation and guess work than is often recognized. This is not to downplay the incredible potential that genetics holds. Combining this research with increasingly complex methods, such as in vitro and soma therapy, medicine now affords us opportunities that were only dreamed about even a decade ago. These discoveries have been miraculous. However, with such revolutionary findings also comes controversy.

Debates have emerged as researchers speculate on the existence of a gay gene, a serial-killer gene and an intelligence gene. Just how much of who you are is pre-programmed by your genes? While advocates of this school of thought admit that the environment and free will play a role in shaping behaviour, without a pre-existing genetic disposition, you would never have had the chance to act the way you do. Genetics thus seems to support arguments for fate and/or destiny. Your life may not be written in the stars, but it *is* encoded in your DNA. And if your behaviour and attitudes are the result of genetic encoding, how is it possible for you to be held responsible for your actions?

Further questions have been raised as to what should be done with the findings of this genetic research. While the Human Genome Project was mapping the genetic code, other scientists were developing the techniques necessary to alter DNA patterning. A whole series of ethical issues has arisen around genetic screening and the treatment of patients for diseases and syndromes that they might acquire in future. What are we going to do with this new knowledge of the self? What, if any, limits should be placed upon its use? The questions raised by this field of study centre on our very understanding of what it means to be human.

Perhaps as researchers continue to study genes, a clearer picture of the self and its workings will appear. Or maybe it will be discovered that the more we try to explain the self in scientific terms, the more such an account escapes us. Just as Descartes found himself unable to discuss the mind without referring to the body, maybe geneticists will discover that they are unable to discuss the body without referring to the mind.

For clearly there seems to be something missing from this account of the self. What even the most sophisticated geneticist cannot account for, or even predict, is the effect that others will have on the self. Think of how someone, maybe even a stranger, can just look at you in a particular way and change the way you see yourself. You may have changed for the better or for the worse, but you cannot deny that you have changed. The theories of the self offered by Descartes, Freud and contemporary geneticists do not adequately account for this effect. They underestimate the extent to which the self is constructed by other people.

Relying on the works of Ivan Pavlov and B. F. Skinner, behaviourists argue that the self is shaped or conditioned by the feedback it receives in response to its actions (or lack of action). Think for a minute about the fact that on even the coldest mornings, when you are exhausted and want nothing more than to stay in your nice, warm, cozy bed, you nonetheless get up at a ridiculously early hour, brave the cold and spend hours parked on the highway, just to get to work. Why do you do this? Clearly you are motivated by your desire and need for money. Not only do you go to work every day, you also wear uncomfortable work clothes and do work tasks that you might find boring, unnecessary or even reprehensible. In other words, money reinforces your behaviour. Reinforcement involves pairing something that an individual desires with a particular action or response. Most often, positive reinforcements are tools for shaping behaviour; that is, "rewards" can encourage certain actions. Rewards may take the form of money, material goods or more subtle stimulants such as reputation, social acceptance or friendship. Why do businesses post pictures of the employee of the month? Why do companies and corporations take their staff to baseball games? In these ways, employers clearly try to offer their employees the non-material things they desire as a consequence for good workplace performance. Conditioning also incorporates negative reinforcement. A negative reinforcement eliminates some existing annoyance or negative stimulant from the environment when the person acts in the desired manner. What happens, for example, when you first wake up in the morning? You hear that annoying buzz of your alarm clock. How do you get it to stop? Not only must you wake up, but you have to also reach over and turn the alarm off. This is an example of how your behaviour is modified using negative reinforcement.

While many employers rely on reinforcement to get their workers to work harder and longer hours, others rely on the second principle of conditioning—punishment—to achieve this goal. In order to ensure that you are punctual, your boss may deduct wages from your paycheque, give you a lousy schedule or delegate the worst work assignment to you. When you punish someone, you try to change his or her behaviour by pairing a particular action (or non-action) with something that the person wishes to avoid.

Using these two principles of conditioning, behaviourists argue that you can explain how the self is moulded or constructed by the environment. Think about all the subtle and not-so-subtle ways you are reinforced and punished for your behaviour. Consider how your workplace environment as well as other social forces such as family, peers, religious organizations, government institutions, media and even the physical space in which you live manipulate how you act as well as what you say and how you think.

It is hard to deny the success that behaviourism has had in explaining and, even more so, in controlling behaviour. When you sit back and think about it, it really does seem that who you are is to a great extent the consequence of the history of reinforcements and punishments to which you have been subjected. You not only get up in the morning and go to work but you also pay taxes and you buy Nike shoes. You can quit smoking and stop biting your nails to a great extent because these principles work. In institutions, these principles have been used to successfully manage large populations. Prison systems, for instance, often work on a merit system. If you are a good inmate, you receive cigarettes, television time and even conjugal visits. If you break the rules, you are not only denied such things, you may also be given the worst work detail or placed in solitary confinement.

Despite this success, behaviourism has its limitations. It has a hard time explaining, for example, why people living and working in exactly the same environment can come to act and behave differently. Co-workers who live in the same city, the same neighbourhood and sometimes even the same household can have entirely different work habits. Furthermore, if the environment is key to shaping identity, how is it possible that workers in as diverse cultural settings as Japan, Canada and India all seem to want basically the same things for themselves and their families? Maybe it is the result of globalization: everyone everywhere wears Nike, drinks Coke and watches CNN. Or, maybe, regardless of the culture you live in, the work you do or the families that you are part of, there remain some features of human nature that stubbornly assert themselves no matter what the environmental influences.

Yet further questions have been raised about the effectiveness of reinforcement and punishment. It is hard to determine what constitutes reinforcement and punishment because the things that people value and dislike vary greatly from group to group and from person to person. Something that I consider desirable, you may consider detestable. Business travel provides a good example. Your boss may think that sending you on a trip is a great opportunity, but you might not like the idea because you have tickets to see a basketball game that you have been looking forward to all season. Your boss thinks that she is reinforcing your performance when, in fact, she is punishing you.

Moreover, reinforcements only seem to work for a relatively short period of time before the person expects more in order to act in the desired manner. You might accept a fifty-cent-per-hour raise when you first start working, but over time, you will want more and more money to maintain the same level of performance. Eventually you may even decide that the money is just not worth getting out of bed for on cold winter mornings.

Similar studies have shown that punishment is not a particularly successful means for modifying behaviour. If you threaten to fire an employee if he or she arrives late again for work and then you don't go through with it, don't expect that tactic to work again in the future. Even if you do follow through with your threat, you need to recognize that punishment extinguishes quickly. If you punish someone over and over again, eventually they will rebel and will challenge you to "come and get them." What this suggests is that the self is not as malleable or as easily manipulated as behaviourists claim. It seems that people do not always want reinforcement and do not always fear punishment. Nonetheless, these techniques continue to be used in an attempt to try to understand and control this thing called the self.

Despite the best efforts of the thinkers described herein, it is still not clear what constitutes the self. In fact, as social scientists and medical researchers delve into increasingly complicated and minute factors intent on explaining identity, they seem to drift further and further away from everyday experiences. Consider, for example, how the self, as described by these theorists, is relatively stable across time. If you sit back and think about all the changes that you have gone through over your lifetime, over the past month or during the time that it has taken you to read this article, it seems pretty clear that the self is in constant flux. Rather than being a static entity, the self is a dynamic and creative force. And it is marked by incredible uncertainty. The theorists discussed so far all assume that the self—be it mind, body or environmental by-product—is knowable. In your everyday life, how often is this the case? How many times have you been asked why you acted in a particular way or made a particular comment and have been at a loss for an answer? It seems that you can only know your self in hindsight. Even then, your motivations and drives, to a great extent, remain a mystery.

Focusing on our experiences, the philosopher Friedrich Nietzsche devised yet another account of the self. Nietzsche was living at the end of the 19th century—when the effects of the Industrial Revolution were taking hold. It was a time marked by great optimism. With the development of new means of transportation, the mass production of goods and the remarkable technological advancements that marked this age, people put their faith in the future. They believed in progress. Things were getting better and better. And there was no sign of that trend ending any time soon. Nietzsche challenged this perceived view. He saw in his time not the ascent of humankind but rather its descent.

Friedrich Nietzsche

Far from things getting better and better, he saw them getting worse and worse. To reverse this trend, it was necessary to shake people up—to remind them of just who and what they were. This required a careful examination of the self—not of the self that you might wish you were, but of the self that you are.

A good starting point for looking at Nietzsche's notion of the self is his account of the "myth of the eternal recurrence of the same." This thought experiment asks you to imagine that you had to live your life over again and again and again, in all of its details—including both the big things and the small. How would you respond to this news? Would you jump for joy at the thought, or would you think that you had been cursed by some demon? Nietzsche noted that most people would gnash their teeth and say that they had never heard anything so horrible. Why this response? Why, Nietzsche asks, aren't people living lives that they would choose to repeat over and over again?

To answer this question, it is necessary to take a bit of a detour and discuss, of all things, sheep. Sheep are best known for the fact that they flock together. It is rare to see a single sheep standing alone, away from its herd. These animals seem to take comfort in numbers and constantly seek the companionship of their species. Along with flocking, sheep are also noted for their blind ability to follow. If one sheep goes over a cliff, the entire herd will follow suit. They will follow despite the dangers at hand. That means that sheep are easy prey.

Thinking about sheep may seem an unusual way to analyze the concept of the self. However, for Nietzsche it was necessary. Consider how much like sheep human beings have become. Like these docile animals, humans take comfort in numbers. Even after telling others that you "just want to be left alone," how often do you go into your bedroom, shut the door and turn on the television or log onto MSN? It seems that despite your words, you don't really want to be left alone with yourself. This may help to explain why it is that humans, like sheep, love to follow. For as much as you might think that you want to be different, don't you, in fact, work very hard to be the same as everyone else? Do you really want to risk being "original"? Think of all that you might lose if you stood out in a crowd. No wonder human beings have become easy prey. No wonder we are susceptible to fads and trends—in everything from clothing to ideas—that are painful, self-destructive and/or harmful to others. Clearly, humans have devolved to what Nietzsche calls herd mentality. But this is not the way that they have to be. It does not have to be human destiny.

Nietzsche envisioned human beings becoming more than what they are—both individually and collectively. A human being, according to

Nietzsche, is like a rope over an abyss, that is, a rope between beast and something more, something greater—an "Übermensch" or "overman." It is, then, your choice to determine which end of the rope you wish to head toward. You are a tightrope walker. But you can't be sure which way is which. Looks can be deceiving. The best you can do is to try. Try to be something more.

What exactly being something more entails is hard to say. Like most people, you may be so wedded to your present way of being that it may be hard to think of what else you could be if you dared to leave behind your conformist (that is, sheep-like) behaviour. Nietzsche was cautious in describing the life of the overman. Old habits die hard and he worried that if he told you what this new kind of self would look like, you could end up following again.

Instead, Nietzsche draws an analogy between the self and a work of art. He asks you to consider what it would mean to try to exercise the same kind of creativity in your life as an artist applies to an artwork. What if, rather than striving to lead a perfectly "normal" life, you tried to create a masterpiece out of your life—through your thoughts and your actions? What if, rather than following current fashion trends in everything from clothing to thought, you dared "to give style to your character"? What if, instead of settling for the predictable familiarity of the herd, you created a life for your self that you would be happy to live over and over again? What would your life be like if, in other words, you exercised "will to power"?

Will to power, according to Nietzsche, encompasses your ability to create and to live in the world on your own terms. This first requires that you embrace, rather than turn away from, those aspects of your life that make you human—those life-affirming experiences which include pain and suffering as well as joy and laughter. You need to know who and what you are before you can begin to distinguish yourself from the beasts. You need to know the dangers and seductions of human existence if you wish to avoid falling prey to sheep-like behaviour—to following others blindly. Will to power simultaneously warns you of the pitfalls of attempting to impose your beliefs and ideals on others. In other words, will to power is not synonymous with will to truth. This is an important distinction. Will to power does not involve sheep suddenly becoming shepherds. That is, it does not encourage individuals who have taken control over their own lives to then go on and impose their values and beliefs on others. Will to power is not the will to control or dominate or manipulate others but, rather, it is the will to live according to one's own beliefs—to control one's self.

Viewed from this perspective, the self cannot be regarded as a stable entity to be discovered; instead, it must be considered a dynamic force capable of change, always open to re-creation and re-invention. Your biology does not make you who you are any more than does your environment. These factors are the materials or media with which you can work to create, or to write, the story of your life.

This is a scary prospect. Think of all the possibilities. Each day you have the opportunity to make your life either into a uniquely beautiful canvas or, alternatively, into a copy of a Disney poster. Each day it is your choice. Your choice. The possibilities are so attractive yet so horrifying that most would rather turn away and pretend that the self is a stable, static entity out there waiting to be uncovered or discovered. The comforts of certainty and stability do lead most people to forget that the self is a creative force. Indeed, if the self were a static, determined entity, no one would be accountable for his or her actions. You could take comfort in the belief that you are the product of your mind, your unconscious, your genes or your environment, or some combination of these factors. You would be seen as merely a product, a victim even, of the world in which you find yourself. And, as such, you, your self, could not be held responsible for your actions. The self—each self—would be a helpless entity produced by some collection of forces that are both internal and external. Could there ever be anything more comforting, more safe, yet, ultimately, more false?

Nietzsche's view of the self is not for the faint of heart, for the unimaginative or for the uncourageous. It requires you to take risks and to accept the consequences. There is no safety net to catch the tightrope walker if he or she falls. What it does offer, however, is an account of the self that seems to fit with much of lived experience. This approach captures the uncertainties and insecurities that so often figure in daily life. As well, it emphasizes that, far from having your life determined for you, far from being the victim of some kind of biological or social fate, you are the creator of your own destiny. And thus it holds you accountable for your own life. It makes you think hard about the choices you make about the kind of person you wish to become.

However daring and appealing Nietzsche's view of the self may be, it too has its limitations. Are you really as free to create and invent your life as Nietzsche suggests? You have to get up in the morning, you have to make money in order to survive, you have to be careful what you say so that you don't offend others and you have to watch your more eccentric actions lest they be interpreted as perverse, insane or criminal. Even if you do have the ability to escape the herd, do you really want to? Humans need each other; they need the sense of safety and community offered to them by the group. They cannot simply strike out on their own without suffering consequences. And, lastly, it seems hard to imagine a time when you could have your own values and beliefs and not try to impose them on others. Given everyday experience, it is hard to imagine becoming something so different that you would not need to be either the leader or a follower.

It may seem that this short history of theories of the self has not really got us very far. What is the self? We still don't have a clear definition. Indeed, if anything, we might be more confused about the answer to this question than before we began. It is true that none of the thinkers discussed here arrived at a completely convincing account of the self. Many of them recognized this inadequacy themselves. Freud, for example, determined at the end of his career that he really did not understand human beings (particularly women) very well at all. Like others who have tried to explain

Edvard Munch's *The Scream* (1893)

the self, he found that his works were incomplete and full of inconsistencies. However, we should not be too quick to conclude that the works of Freud and the other thinkers discussed in this article were written in vain.

Indeed, this discussion has made clear that the self is an evolving concept. Far from being a stable and persistent entity, it is an idea. It is the product of history, politics and science. But the self is not just the outcome or end result of these factors; it also plays a role in shaping them. The self is an organizing principle—it helps set the agenda of issues to be investigated and developed by government officials, business executives and scientists.

This short history of sometimes competing theories of identity should serve as a cautionary tale, especially at the beginning of the 21st century. It is impossible to know how our present theories of the self will evolve. But they will evolve and with this evolution will come new challenges and insights. Not only will this change our perception of ourselves, but also of the world around us and of our relationship to it. If we change who we think we are, it has implications for our work, for our notions of justice and for our relationship to nature. The consequences of a changing view of ourselves are enormous, as we are the point from which we view all things. The words of the ancient Greek philosopher Socrates still serve as an apt warning and an appropriate conclusion: "Know thyself."

My Brain and I Are One

Richard Restak

I once attended the wedding of a thirty-five-year-old patient who five years earlier had come to me after seeing in broad daylight the ghost of her dead first husband.

At our first meeting she told me about the ghostly visitor, but only after I had asked a simple question: "Has anything strange . . . you know . . . out of the ordinary ever happened to you?"

"Like what?" she responded, fixing upon me a pair of now fully dilated eyes.

She then revealed that on occasion she experienced a wave of fear accompanied by "strange sensations," such as a metallic taste in her mouth or a smell in the environment like that of burning rubber. On other occasions while in her home she felt as if everything had been "somehow altered." Sometimes the alteration involved her own sense of herself as somehow split into two people: an observer who commented on her actions, and an actor who carried them out. ("Yet both of them are me," she said.)

When I asked for further details, she said: "It's as if I'm a character in a science fiction novel who inhabits one dimension of reality while the rest of the world lives in another."

The electroencephalogram, which measures the brain's electrical activity, provided me with proof of what I already suspected. Karen's disturbed sense of herself originated from an epileptic discharge deep within the left temporal lobe of her brain.

The temporal lobe is responsible for our sense of connectedness, our personal identity, the feeling of belonging we get from familiar surroundings. When it functions normally, we have no apprehensions about who we are, our situation, or the nature of things. But when the temporal lobe is diseased, strange things can occur. A seizure originating in the temporal lobe can produce disorientation, feelings of having previously experienced events happening at the moment (*déjà vu*), or equally troubling feelings that familiar objects and people are new and vaguely threatening (*jamais vu*).

Another temporal lobe epileptic I once treated spent long hours in the middle of the night writing philosophy. He filled notebook after notebook with philosophical ramblings that in broad daylight he was able to recognize as not likely to be of much interest to anybody but himself. A serious man, he made me think of prophets and seers. At times his **ruminations** on the nature of the spiritual world became ecstatic, almost sexual. **Dostoevsky**, a temporal lobe epileptic, described the process in *The Idiot*:

ruminations
reflections

Dostoevsky, Fyodor
Russian novelist

> *There was always one instant just before the epileptic fit... when suddenly in the midst of sadness, spiritual darkness and oppression, his brain seemed momentarily to catch fire, and in an extraordinary rush, all his vital forces were at their highest tension. The sense of life, the consciousness of self, were multiplied almost ten times at these moments which lasted no longer than a flash of lightning. His mind and his heart were flooded with extraordinary light; all his uneasiness, all his doubts, all his anxieties were relieved at once; they were all resolved into a lofty calm, full of serene, harmonious joy and hope, full of reason and ultimate meaning. But these moments, these flashes, were only a premonition of that final second (it was never more than a second) with which the fit began. That second was, of course, unendurable. Thinking of that moment later, when he was well again, he often said to himself that all these gleams and flashes of supreme sensation and consciousness of self, and, therefore, also of the highest form of being, were nothing but disease, the violation of the normal state; and if so, it was not at all the highest form of being, but on the contrary must be reckoned the lowest. Yet he came at last to an extremely paradoxical conclusion. "What if it is disease?" he decided at last. "What does it matter that it is an abnormal intensity, if the result, if the instant of sensation, remembered and analyzed afterwards in health, turns out to be the acme of harmony and beauty, and gives a feeling, unknown and undivined till then, of completeness, of proportion, of reconciliation, and of startled prayerful merging with the highest synthesis of life?"*

An encounter with a person suffering from temporal lobe epilepsy raises a question philosophers have argued about for centuries: What is the relationship of mind to brain? How can a disturbance within a fairly circumscribed area of the brain produce such **transcendental** experiences? Most experts have taken refuge from such questions in a vague and untidy dualism that, until fairly recently, was supported by our experiences with physics and machines.

transcendental
heightened beyond all expectations

Dualism, the metaphysical conception that body is separated from mind, originated with the seventeenth-century philosopher René Descartes. Descartes proposed that the body, especially the brain, is a machine with functions that can be explained by the mathematical laws of physics. But over the past sixty years physics has changed greatly. According to the principles of **quantum physics** the observer cannot be meaningfully separated from the experiment that he or she is

quantum physics
the study of the dynamic structure and motion of atoms and molecules that constitute all physical objects in the universe

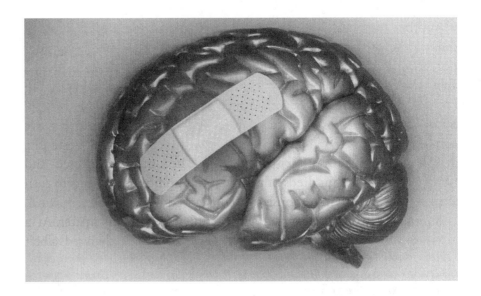

conducting. Indeed, the viewpoint of the observer often determines what is recorded by the experiment. . . .

The observer effect holds true for brain/mind dualism. . . . When I listen to my patients tell me about a frightening vision or hallucination—something far removed from everyday experience—I'm encountering the world of mind. But if I record my patient's brain waves during a hallucination and detect an epileptic seizure within the temporal lobe, I've shifted my focus . . . from one aspect of reality to another.

Marcus Raichle, head of the brain study group at the Washington University School of Medicine in St. Louis, suggests another way of thinking about such a **paradox**: "Because the brain is a physical structure, it exists in space; but the mind operates in time alone."

The brain as I stare at it depicted on a CAT scan or set out upon an autopsy table is very much an object. It takes up space; I can see it or its representation; I can pick up the autopsy specimen. We're talking about spatial matters here.

Mind, in contrast, can be captured only in the temporal dimension. My thoughts require time before I can communicate them to you in the form of words. Without motion or some form of behavior, mind cannot be inferred. Indeed, if I don't move or speak, can you really be sure I'm thinking at all?

The closer we look, the more difficult it is to maintain any neat division between mind and brain. Suppose I shout the word *fire* in a crowded theater. That word, *fire*, is conveyed by means of sound waves that stimulate the tympanic membranes in the ears of the listeners. Within milliseconds electrochemical events occur in the auditory

paradox
puzzling contradiction

nerve. They then traverse the labyrinthine pathway within the brain from auditory cortex to auditory association area to limbic system. There the word *fire* is loaded with fears traceable to the first caveman who burned his fingers before a campfire. Sound waves stimulate tympanic membranes, and physical alterations take place in the brain. Milliseconds later, thanks to the limbic involvement, the hypothalamus and sympathetic nervous system are drawn into the fray: heart rate increases, blood pressure rises, breathing becomes constricted and labored. The result: hundreds of people jump up from their seats to rush toward the exit—all in response to a concept conveyed by a mere word. Shouting the word *fire* exerted a powerful influence on matter. At a minimum the physical structure of the brain has been changed, albeit momentarily.

Other words and phrases of a different sort (*You're a failure; I want a divorce; I love you*) exert more permanent modifications within the brain. The PET scan of a schizophrenic or a manic-depressive shows a distinct variation from what, for lack of a better term, we call a normal brain. On the whole it's likely that these distinctions represent differences in the organization and function of the brains of those unfortunates who suffer from these illnesses. Alter the brain and you alter thoughts, feelings, and personal identity. And if you change an attitude or modify your own or someone else's behavior, you've worked a miracle, performed a successful experiment in **psychokinesis**: you've used the intangible mind to transform something in the physical world.

psychokinesis
moving objects with the mind alone

Mind can affect brain; brain can affect mind. But can either be separated from the other? Not any more than the other side of this paper can be separated from the side that you are now reading.

My experience with temporal lobe epileptics has raised a haunting personal question: How many of my own habits and propensities are determined for me by my brain? To what extent am I anything other than my brain? Is there any way of separating the brain from the person who just asked that question? My way of coping has been to fashion a simple mantra I repeat silently from time to time: "My brain and I are one. My brain and I are one." But even as I think and speak these words—my brain changing all the while as I do so—I still find it difficult to believe that this three-pound mass of protoplasm with the consistency of an overripe avocado is the seat of who I am, of who we all are.

The Skin We're In

Tim Adams

What does each of us think of when we think of our body? Do we see it as our friend or our enemy? The home of our pleasure or the source of our pain? Do we want to indulge and pamper it or starve and dominate it? What makes us desire to paint it and pierce it, abuse it and poison it? Are we imprisoned by it or liberated in it? And why is it that the more we think about it—its appetites and its urges, its faults and its perfections, all that stuff that goes on inside, all the time—the stranger it seems to us? One thing we do know for certain is that the body is the place where each of us lives, and the place where each of us will die: our body will always, in the end, betray us.

Another thing we know is that, given the choice, hardly any of us would select exactly the body that we inhabit. The desire to improve on our bodies, to mould and change them, seems to be coded somewhere deep within them.

Perhaps we are obsessed with the way our own bodies look and behave because we know how instinctively judgmental we are of the bodies we look at. One recent psychological survey proved that we make decisions about the attractiveness of people we meet in the space of 150 milliseconds, and that this instant perception of their beauty (or otherwise) hardly alters after longer examination.

This superficial appraisal has profound implications. In Dr. Nancy Etcoff's book *Survival of the Prettiest* she shows how this "lookism" shapes our world: those we consider most beautiful not only find sexual partners more readily but also get better jobs and more lenient treatment in court. We are, in the main, more willing to trust them, help them, lend money to them and love them.

You might say, therefore, in wanting to change our bodies, to improve on our birth-given beauty, we are simply exercising our human rights: indulging in a little redistribution of wealth from the imbalances of the genetic lottery.

Earlier this year I talked about some of this with James Watson, the man who, 50 years ago, first understood the structure of DNA. He foresaw a world where we could design our babies to look the way we wished we had looked. He was unashamedly excited about this possibility. "People say it would be terrible if we made all girls pretty," he suggested. "I say it would be great."

But would it really? In Margaret Atwood's novel *Oryx and Crake* the future is populated by genetically screened, physically perfected humans. And it feels like a nightmare (or at least like California). Our dreams of bodily perfection distance us further and further from the flesh we inhabit; and they undermine the notion, also ingrained, that it is our imperfections that make us fully human.

These fears are rooted in the complicated understanding of the relationship between our bodies and our essential selves. When we stop to think about it, which most of us do surprisingly rarely, it is impossible for us to define where our body ends and what we consider to be our self begins. We know our limbs, say, are part of us, but are they really us? Would most of us even recognize our elbows or our backs if we were asked to pick them out of a line-up?

This kind of dislocation between our thinking and our bodily selves has many implications. As Roy Porter explains in his wonderful, posthumously published book *Flesh in the Age of Reason*, it was the legacy of Enlightenment philosophers that a fit and healthy body, and a clear and open face, were the visible expressions of human virtue.

This perception still runs very deep in our culture. It underpins the stubborn prejudice against the overweight and the ageing; and it challenges us to make our outward selves representative of the traits our culture aspires to: the qualities of youth and sexuality. Because of this, the overriding theme of our times, we might contend, is that of self-transformation.

If psychoanalysis has, for nearly a century, offered us the possibility of transforming our interior lives, so the habits of gyming and slimming, as well as the techniques of plastic surgery and the personal branding of body art, offer us the chance to remake our outward selves also. We might think of this process as a desire to make ourselves feel at home in our skin: to make our "envelope" reflect more fully the message we feel within.

At its extreme this involves altering what nature considers unalterable. Since a landmark case in 1999, transsexuals are now able to demand to have their sex change operations on the National Health. When Jan (formerly James) Morris wrote her book *Conundrum* in 1974 about the sex change operation she had undergone in Casablanca she spoke of how she saw it "not just as a sexual enigma, but as a quest for unity."

This alignment of outward appearance with inward perception takes on many forms and is subject to the whim of fashion and class. We have always wanted our bodies to reflect our times. When, for example, cosmetic breast surgery first became a possibility in the early twentieth century, the women who could afford it used it almost exclusively for reduction, large breasts being associated with the lower classes. These days, middle-class girls (of a certain kind) are being given silicone as an eighteenth birthday present.

The body, in this sense, has become just another consumer purchase (plastic surgeons offer packages of treatment—buy one implant, as it were, and get one free). We can, in the spirit of our age, go shopping for bodily transformation. There have long been snake-oil salesmen willing to sell us wrinkle-free vitality: in the 1890s the injection of canine semen under the skin was seen as a way of enhancing the body's glow; now Botox offers hundreds of thousands of people smoothness in a lunch hour, and threatens to alter the way we smile for ever.

Whereas once such vanity was piqued by street corner hucksters, now it is fuelled by global advertising campaigns and a magazine culture that reflects an increasingly narrow palette of beauty. Naomi Wolf argued a decade ago in *The Beauty Myth* that this conjunction of international capitalism and personal insecurity produces almost unbearable pressure on women in particular to conform to norms of appearance (and to feel further undermined when, inevitably, they fall short).

"As each woman responds to the pressure," Wolf predicted, "it will grow so intense that it will become obligatory, until no self-respecting woman will venture outdoors with a surgically unaltered face."

Ten years ago this seemed a little hysterical. Now it feels less unlikely. Some New York plastic surgeons are currently recommending an annual "MOT" for the skin, in which the advance of lines from the eyes is checked and sags from the neck tightened on a regular and preventive basis; they want you to visit your surgeon like you would visit your dentist. "The industry takes out ads," wrote Wolf, "and gets coverage; women get cut open."

This paranoia of self-actualisation (or this liberating perfectionism) is also migrating south. If we want our face to sell our sense of self, so, in our overtly sexualised culture, we may well want our genitals to say something important about us, too.

There is growing demand for operations which tighten the vagina in the hope of increasing sensation during intercourse; and no male inbox is complete without at least one offer to add "three inches to your length."

You might say such marketing was aimed at increasing the sum of human happiness and personal fulfillment, and what on earth could be wrong with that? Feminists increasingly make the argument that cosmetic surgery is a statement of empowerment, allowing women to stress the strength of their sexuality and enhance their idea of self.

There is a sense, too, however, even as you put in the time on the treadmill at the gym, watching the statements of impossible physical perfection on MTV and Sky Sports, that the project of eternal youth is doomed, and at least in part an expression of desperation. Our bodies have always been our biography, tracing the "thousand natural shocks that flesh is heir to." There is a wonderful short story by Raymond Carver concerning a couple selling a secondhand car with a doctored mileometer out of desperation to keep a roof over their heads. The story ends with the couple in bed, the woman asleep, and the man running his fingertips gently over the route map of stretch marks on her hips and thighs. He has one thought in his head, which is also the story's title: "Are these actual miles?"

However much we desire to wipe the slate clean, to give ourselves a new skin, to make ourselves "like a virgin" once again, our bodies will eventually tell us otherwise; we cannot be innocent twice. One result of this, you could argue, is that we increasingly desire to be out of our bodies and to find our innocence elsewhere. We fetishise the supremacy of our spirit over our flesh, even as we fail to enforce it. The extreme of this urge for prolonged or recaptured innocence is one manifestation of the epidemic of eating disorders. This newspaper recently reported on the scores of pro-anorexia websites available on the Internet in which young girls across the world share the secret strategies of their addiction. "Nothing tastes as good as thin feels," said one. "That which nourishes me destroys me," announced another.

Saturated with the messages of a culture that invites us to indulge our appetites, the anorexic seems to want above all to destroy the messages her senses are giving her. It is a supreme irony that the models of beauty in our consumer culture are paradigms of arrested development, triumphs of defeated hunger.

Nancy Etcoff reports a study in which the facial proportions of cover girls from *Vogue* and *Cosmopolitan* were fed into a computer and analysed; the computer programme "guestimated" them as children between six and seven years of age. In this sense, we increasingly seem to want to use our body as a strategy of denial, as a way of mastering some of the trauma our psychology presents us with. In Don DeLillo's twenty-first century fable *The Body Artist*, his heroine, to obliterate the grief of her husband's death, punishes her body with "prayerful spans of systematic breathing"; she contorts herself with yoga, and shaves and

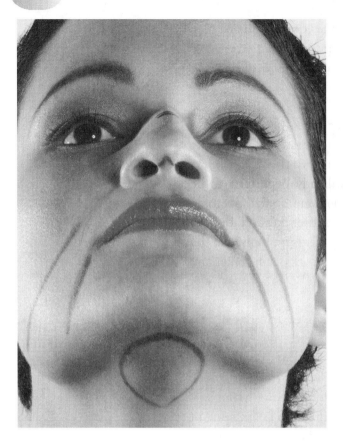

exfoliates with "clippers and creams that activated the verbs of abridgement and excision." She dreams of removing all evidence of herself from her body: "This was her work, to disappear from her former venues of aspect and bearing and to become a blankness, a body slate erased of every past resemblance." In the mirror, she has the desire to be someone "classically unseen, the person you are trained to look through, bled of familiar effect, a spook in the night static of every public toilet." Like the anorexic, she wants somehow to disappear.

Much as we may like to, however, the one thing we can never escape in life is our flesh. And increasingly we are coming to realise this flesh is also our fate. Coded within our genes (and uncoded in the Human Genome Project, the so-called Book of Life) is much of the information that will set the bounds of our life and predict our death, just as surely as a novelist dictates the lives of his characters. Undoubtedly, when it becomes properly understood, some of this information will also become our economic reality, too.

The use of genetic tests to assess risk for life premiums and critical illness insurance could, for example, become a reality within the next three years. The implications for those at genetic risk of contracting common illnesses such as breast cancer and Alzheimer's might be severe. There are even fears of a "genetic underclass" being created, people excluded from insurance and screened out of employment. (Britain has refused to join 31 other European countries, including France, Spain and Italy, who have signed the European convention on human rights and biomedicine, which prohibits genetic discrimination).

James Watson, who led the mapping of the Genome Project, was spurred on in his quest by the fact that his own son was a victim of what he calls "genetic injustice" and born with a severe form of autism. What he knows for certain about the new genetic universe is that the decisions we will have to make for our bodies are only going to get more complicated, and that increasingly they will be taken by individuals rather than governments. "If the technology becomes available," he says, "who are we to tell a mother she should not want a child that is prone to hereditary disease?"

Watson is an atheist: "If scientists are not going to play God, who is?" He is, too, a supreme optimist about the possibilities of our bodies. "I am sure that the capacity to love is inscribed in our DNA," he suggested to me. "And if some day those particular genes, too, could be enhanced by our science, to defeat hatreds and violence, in what sense would our humanity be diminished?"

The implications of such a technology are already beginning to be felt. Our bodies have for nearly a century become something of a battleground in our quest for self-fulfilment and self-expression. But the choices we will have to make about them are about to multiply, and the battles are only just beginning.

Am I Free or Determined?

Melanie Chaparian

Each of the theories of self discussed earlier in Unit 1 takes a stand on the philosophical debate between determinism and libertarianism. On one side of the debate, determinism is the position that all human actions are determined, or caused, by natural and/or environmental forces beyond human control. According to this theory, people do not have any free will. Behaviourism, as discussed in "From Biography to Biology: A Brief History of the Self," for example, views human beings as malleable creatures who can only behave in the ways that they have been conditioned by the rewards and punishments they encounter in their social and natural environments.

On the other side of the debate, libertarianism is the view that at least some human actions are free. Although many actions may be determined, there are some situations in which people can exercise their free will. Unlike computers, human beings seem to be capable of making real choices between alternative courses of action. Nietzsche's theory of the self, for example, takes the position that people have free will.

An Argument for Determinism

Determinism may be defended on the basis of the following rather simple argument: Every event in the world occurs because of cause and effect. Like every other event, human actions must be determined by cause and effect as well. If all of our actions are caused, we cannot possess free will because the same action cannot be both caused and free at the same time. Therefore, all human actions are determined, and no human actions are free.

Let's look at this argument in more detail. Few people today question the universality of cause and effect in the natural world. Traditional science teaches us that every natural phenomenon is the effect of a cause or set of causes. Indeed, most science assumes a deterministic model of the world. It is the very nature of science to look for the causes of the phenomena it studies. The nature of causality is such that there is an *inevitable* connection between a cause and its effect: if the cause occurs, the effect *must* also occur. For example, if heating water to a temperature of 100°C *determines* the water to turn into steam, then

"Am I Free or Determined?" is by Melanie Chaparian of the Humber College Institute of Technology and Advanced Learning. Used by permission.

every time water is heated to that temperature it *must* turn into steam. Heating water to 100°C is the *cause* and the water turning into steam is the *effect*. We never entertain the possibility that boiling water, or any other natural phenomenon, occurs because of pure chance. Scientists always try to discover the causes of the phenomena they study. Indeed, when they are unable to identify the cause of a particular phenomenon, such as the memory loss suffered by people affected by Alzheimer's disease, they do not conclude that no cause exists but rather that it simply has not *yet* been discovered.

But the deterministic view is not limited to the natural sciences such as physics, chemistry, biology and medicine. Determinism is also frequently assumed by the social sciences, such as psychology and sociology, which usually attempt to study and *discover the causes of human behaviour*. A determinist would agree that, although we may believe ourselves to be unique creatures, human beings are just as subject to the world of cause and effect as boiling water and Alzheimer's disease.

The determinist argues that our distinctive nature only means that the causes that determine our actions are more complex, and therefore harder to discover, than those that cause other events. The *kinds* of causes determining human behaviour depend on the determinist's particular view of human nature. Some point to *nature*, such as hereditary or instinctual forces, as the primary cause of a person's actions. Other determinists argue that a person's behaviour is fundamentally determined by *nurture*, that is, by environmental factors. Many, if not most, determinists, however, acknowledge that a *combination* of nature and nurture determines a person's actions. A Freudian psychologist, for example, believes that an individual's behaviour is caused by the way the *ego* moderates between drives of the *id*, which are determined by instinct or heredity, and the moral demands of the *superego*, which are determined by early childhood environment. Regardless of the kinds of causes they point to, all determinists agree that all human actions are determined or caused.

No matter how long and hard we may deliberate between different courses of action, the "choice" we finally make has already been decided for us by hereditary and/or environmental causes over which we have no control. This applies to all of our actions, from the most trivial to the most significant.

According to the determinist, an analysis of the motivations of different people reveals the various causes that result in the difference in their behaviour. The determinist is quick to point out that you do not freely choose what interests you. Your interests are determined by your nature, your environment or, most likely, by a combination of both. For example, you probably wish to pursue academic success. Why is this important to you? Maybe you have been gifted with a naturally intellectual mind. This is not an attribute that you freely chose to acquire. Or perhaps your family has always encouraged good grades. Again, the determinist points out that you have no control over the values your family has conditioned into you. You may be aware that good grades are essential for the new graduate to secure a decent position in today's highly competitive job market. Once again, the determinist points out that you have no control over the increasingly high academic requirements demanded by employers. *Your* actual motivations for persevering through your homework probably include some of those discussed here as well as a number of others. But whatever they may be, the determinist argues, they reveal that you do not freely choose to study hard.

At this point, you may be convinced that *your* actions are caused by forces outside your control. But how does the determinist explain the actions of other students in your class who socialize at the expense of studying and consequently earn low marks? After all, most of them also come from families that stress academic success, and all of them want good jobs after they graduate. It *seems* that these negligent students are making a free, although foolish, choice.

Things are not always as they first appear. According to the determinist's theory, if your negligent classmates are subject to exactly the same causal forces that determine your behaviour, they would of necessity be studying as hard as you are. The very fact that they sacrifice study time to socialize indicates that their personal histories are very different from yours. Perhaps their families have not so much *encouraged* academic success as relentlessly *pressured* them to do well in school. If so, they may have been determined to rebel by going to all the college parties instead of studying. Just as you have no control over the encouragement you receive, the rebellious students have no control over the pressure they suffer. Other students who neglect their homework may simply not have the maturity required for self-discipline. Having fun may be as important to them, or even more so, as earning good marks or preparing for their future. If so, the determinist points out that a person cannot simply decide to become mature. This is a developmental process that is determined by an individual's nature and upbringing. There is a host of other causes that may determine some students to neglect their studies. Whatever these causes may be in any actual case, the determinist argues that negligent students do not freely choose to ignore their homework. Although they may feel guilty that they are not studying, they simply cannot choose to do so. Therefore, neither the diligent student nor the negligent student really makes a genuine choice between studying or not studying. The course of action each takes is determined by causes over which neither has any control.

Nor do we have the freedom to make genuine choices concerning even the most important aspects of our lives. Nature or nurture, or both, determine such things as which profession we pursue, who we fall in love with, and how many children we have. According to the theory of determinism, *all* human actions are the effect of causes over which we have no control; consequently, free will is merely an illusion.

Because we usually pride ourselves on our freedom, we may feel reluctant to accept the determinist's conclusion. But this in itself is not a good reason to reject determinism. It would be hard to deny that the deterministic model has helped to advance our knowledge of the natural world in general and the human world in particular. Discovering the cause of an event not only increases our understanding of that phenomenon but also allows us to *predict* and sometimes *control* its future occurrence. If, for example, we know that a virus causes an illness in the human body, we can predict that a person will become ill when infected by that virus, and, moreover, we can control that illness by finding ways to prevent the virus from infecting more people. Or, if we know that a moderate amount of parental pressure causes a student to succeed in school, we can predict that a student subjected to that amount of guidance will earn good grades, and we can control such successes by teaching parents how to provide the proper dose of encouragement. The deterministic model also helps us to make sense of our personal lives. We are often remarkably successful, for instance, in predicting the actions of our close relatives and friends. If such predictions are not merely lucky guesses, the determinist argues, they must be based on our relatively extensive knowledge of the hereditary and environmental causes that determine the behaviour of those relatives and friends. The fact that we may not *like* the theory of determinism does not negate the wealth of evidence for its accuracy.

James's Critique of Determinism

In his famous lecture entitled "The Dilemma of Determinism," William James, an American philosopher and psychologist who lived from 1842 to 1910, defends libertarianism, the theory that human beings have free will. Before he actually begins his argument for this theory, however, James shows that determinism—its appeal to science notwithstanding—cannot be scientifically demonstrated.

William James

Science cannot really tell us, for example, if the negligent student's background is causing him to rebel. The fact that he does consistently neglect his assigned readings is not in itself conclusive proof that the student is determined to take this course of action. Moreover, *before the fact*—that is, before the student entered college—no one, not even the most learned determinist, could ascertain whether the student's background would lead him to socialize or to study. For instance, it would not have seemed inconceivable to suppose that excessive family pressure would prompt the student to study harder than any other student. Nor would it have been unreasonable to surmise that this pressure would compel him to overcome his immaturity and set his priorities in a more beneficial way. *Before the fact*, this series of events seems as likely to occur as the events that actually came to pass; thus, James argues, *after the fact*, there is no way to prove that the student was determined to neglect his studies. The same argument applies to all human actions. James therefore concludes that the determinist cannot prove that all actions are the inevitable effects of prior causes. While this in itself does *not* disprove determinism, it certainly dispels the myth that determinism has the weight of science on its side, and, furthermore, suggests that libertarianism should at least be reconsidered.

James's Argument for Free Will

Libertarians disagree among themselves about how far human freedom extends. On one extreme, existentialists such as Nietzsche claim that all human actions are potentially free. On the other extreme, some libertarians only argue that actions performed in the face of moral demands are free. In this discussion, we will focus on the views of William James, who defends a relatively moderate version of libertarianism. According to James, we are free whenever we have a genuine choice between at least two possible and desirable courses of action. This does not mean, of course, that we are free to perform any conceivable action whatsoever. Nor does this even mean that we are free to do anything we may desire, for the action that we find most tempting may not be included within the choice before us. All that is required to render an action free is the existence of one other alternative action that it is possible for us to perform.

Essential to James's definition of free will is the existence of *possible actions*: that is, actions that a person is not inevitably determined to do but may perform nonetheless. If an action is the result of free will, then it is, before the fact, merely one of two or more genuinely *possible* alternative actions that the person can *freely choose* to perform; and, after the fact, it is correct to say that the individual *could have acted otherwise* by choosing another alternative. For instance, the negligent student may have freely chosen to spend his time socializing instead of at the library; and even though he made this choice, he could have chosen to study instead. It is the idea of possible actions that puts James in stark opposition to determinism, which states that every action is the *inevitable* effect of a cause.

We have already discussed James's argument that determinism cannot be scientifically demonstrated. He does not attempt, however, to disprove this theory nor to prove libertarianism true. This is because he believes determinism and libertarianism to be two alternative theories of reality, neither of which can be objectively proven true or false. Thus, he claims that the best we can do is to examine both theories to see which one offers us the most rational explanation of human behaviour. According to James, a "rational" theory should not only explain objective reality but must account for subjective human experience as well. James's defence of libertarianism consists in the argument that the free will position is more rational in this sense than determinism.

A significant fact of human life is the *feeling of freedom* that we often experience. James argues that any theory of human behaviour must adequately explain this feeling. Unlike determinism, libertarianism conforms to our ordinary experience: we often feel free to choose between alternative courses of action. Of course, the determinist argues that this feeling is merely an illusion because our course of action has already been decided for us by causes beyond our control. But the "illusion" persists in our inner, subjective experience nonetheless. For example, the good student probably feels that he or she could have chosen to go to more parties while the negligent student likely feels that he or she could have decided to study harder. In his or her practical affairs, even the most staunch determinist probably feels free to choose between alternative courses of action. No matter how solidly convinced we may be that determinism offers us a rational account of all natural phenomena and perhaps most human behaviour, we still find it difficult—if not impossible—to believe subjectively that we are never free. Thus, determinism requires us to reject as illusory a universal human experience. Libertarianism, on the other hand, acknowledges the feeling of freedom as a natural part of the experience of exerting our free will. According to James, this is a good reason to adopt the free will thesis. While he concedes that determinism is a rational theory of reality from an objective standpoint, James argues that libertarianism is an

TO STUDY OR TO PARTY

Free Will Reconsidered

Suppose you have an examination tomorrow and a friend asks you to forgo studying and spend the evening at a party. Your friend does not urge or threaten or coerce you. You consider the alternatives, and after a moment's thought, decide to give up studying for the night and go to the party. We would ordinarily say that you are responsible for your decision. We think of such cases as actions in which you are free to decide one way or the other.

Contrast this to a situation in which a headache leads you to lie down and fall asleep on your bed instead of continuing to study. In this case it would not make sense to say that you are free to decide one way or the other about studying. The dispute between advocates of free will and advocates of determinism is basically a dispute whether incidents like the two so cited, which feel so different, are really radically and essentially different when viewed objectively.

Whereas the advocate of free will would perceive these two sorts of acts as essentially different, the determinist would not. The determinist might argue that although you may believe that your decision to stay home to study for the exam was an expression of free choice, nevertheless closer scrutiny would reveal that your behaviour was not really free after all. What you thought was a free choice was really a choice dictated by your desires, which in turn spring from your character, which in its turn is fashioned by the forces of heredity and environment, which are clearly beyond your control.

The central affirmation of determinism is that every event has a cause. By an analysis of the causes of any one of your actions, the determinist would cause your so-called freedom to vanish in a chain of causes that stretches back into the remote recesses of your heredity and environment. Nature and nurture, genes and society—those are the factors that made you what you are and cause you to act the way you do. The notion that you are free is really a misapprehension, an illusion.

Adapted from *An Introduction to Modern Philosophy* by Donald M. Borchert.

even more rational position because it can account for our inner, subjective experience of freedom.

Another important fact of human experience that James believes a rational theory must explain are *judgements of regret*. Our dissatisfaction with the world, especially with human behaviour, leads us to regret, that is, to "wish that something might be otherwise." After receiving a poor mark in the course, for instance, the negligent student may *regret* that he chose to spend all his time socializing. And because we regret the actions of others as well as our own, you may also *regret* that he had not studied. The most significant regrets concern the moral sphere. We do not accept as inevitable the senseless murders, rapes and cases of child abuse we read about in the newspaper; instead, we judge such acts to be bad or immoral to the highest degree and regret that they are part of our world.

A regret implies that something is bad, and "calling a thing bad means that the thing ought not to be, that something else ought to be in its stead." When we label someone's action immoral, we imply that it should not have been done and that the person should have acted otherwise. For instance, when we proclaim that a murderer is guilty of the highest moral offence, we mean that he should not have committed homicide and should have instead treated his victim in a peaceful, humane manner. Regrets obviously assume the existence of free will. For this reason, libertarianism offers us a better explanation of our regrets than does determinism.

The source of our deepest regrets is the recognition that the world is fraught with immorality. According to determinism, even the most heinous crimes are as much the result of cause and effect as the routine activities we do every day. Knowing the causes of immoral actions does not eliminate our regret that they occur, but it does make our regret merely futile hope. Libertarianism, on the other hand, recognizes immoral actions as the result of free will and, as such, acknowledges that other actions could have been performed instead. Since this applies to future as well as past actions, there exists the possibility that the world—although certainly imperfect—may be made a better and more moral place through free human action. Thus, from the libertarian viewpoint, regrets may virtually be taken at face value—as expressions of our belief that immoral actions *can* be avoided and *should not* take place. This, according to James, renders libertarianism a more rational theory of human existence.

James admits from the outset that his defence consists of the argument that libertarianism is more rational than determinism because it offers a better account of our feelings of freedom and judgements of regret. This is not a claim that can be proven objectively, but one that can only be "verified" by consulting our inner, subjective sense. Although James argues that determinism is also incapable of objective demonstration, he acknowledges that determinism appeals to a different kind of rationality, perhaps what we might call a scientific rationality. Even though James finds libertarianism to be more rational than determinism, it remains for each of us to study both theories to see which of the two *we* find to be the most rational.

Can Science Help?

B. F. Skinner

The Misuse of Science

By the middle of the seventeenth century it had come to be understood that the world was enclosed in a sea of air, much as the greater part of it was covered by water. A scientist of the period, Francesco Lana, contended that a lighter-than-air ship could float upon this sea, and he suggested how such a ship might be built. He was unable to put his invention to a practical test, but he saw only one reason why it might not work:

> . . . that God will never suffer this Invention to take effect, because of the many consequencies which may disturb the Civil Government of men. For who sees not, that no City can be secure against attack, since our Ship may at any time be placed directly over it, and descending down may discharge Souldiers; the same would happen to private Houses, and Ships on the Sea: for our Ship descending out of the Air to the sails of Sea-Ships, it may cut their Ropes, yea without descending by casting Grapples it may over-set them, kill their men, burn their Ships by artificial Fire works and Fire-balls. And this they may do not only to Ships but to great Buildings, Castles, Cities, with such security that they which cast these things down from a height out of Gun-shot, cannot on the other side be offended by those below.

Lana's reservation was groundless. He had predicted modern air warfare in surprisingly accurate detail—with its paratroopers and its strafing and bombing. Contrary to his expectation, God has suffered his invention to take effect.

And so has Man. The story emphasizes the irresponsibility with which science and the products of science have been used. Man's power appears to have increased out of all proportion to his wisdom. He has never been in a better position to build a healthy, happy, and productive world; yet things have perhaps never seemed so black. Two exhausting world wars in a single half century have given no assurance of a lasting peace. Dreams of progress toward a higher civilization have been shattered by the spectacle of the murder of millions of innocent people. The worst may be still to come. Scientists may not set off a chain reaction to blow the world into eternity, but some of the more plausible prospects are scarcely less disconcerting.

B. F. Skinner Foundation

In the face of this apparently unnecessary condition men of good will find themselves helpless or afraid to act. Some are the prey of a profound pessimism. Others strike out blindly in counter-aggression, much of which is directed toward science itself. Torn from its position of prestige, science is decried as a dangerous toy in the hands of children who do not understand it. The conspicuous feature of any period is likely to be blamed for its troubles, and in the twentieth century science must play the scapegoat. But the attack is not entirely without justification. Science has developed unevenly. By seizing upon the easier problems first, it has extended our control of inanimate nature without preparing for the serious social problems which follow. The technologies based upon science are disturbing. Isolated groups of relatively stable people are brought into contact with each other and lose their equilibrium. Industries spring up for which the life of a community may be unprepared, while others vanish leaving millions unfit for productive work. The application of science prevents famines and plagues, and lowers death rates—only to populate the earth beyond the reach of established systems of cultural or governmental control. Science has made war more terrible and more destructive. Much of this has not been done deliberately, but it has been done. And since scientists are necessarily men of some intelligence, they might have been expected to be alert to these consequences.

It is not surprising to encounter the proposal that science should be abandoned, at least for the time being. This solution appeals especially to those who are fitted by temperament to other ways of life. Some relief might be obtained if we could divert mankind into a revival of the arts or religion or even of that petty quarreling which we now look back upon as a life of peace. Such a program resembles the decision of the citizens of Samuel Butler's *Erewhon*, where the instruments and products of science were put into museums—as vestiges of a stage in the evolution of human culture which did not survive. But not everyone is willing to defend a position of stubborn "not knowing." There is no virtue in ignorance for its own sake. Unfortunately we cannot stand still: to bring scientific research to an end now would mean a return to famine and pestilence and the exhausting labors of a slave culture.

Science as a Corrective

Another solution is more appealing to the modern mind. It may not be science which is wrong but only its application. The methods of science have been enormously successful wherever they have been tried. Let us then apply them to human affairs. We need not retreat in those sectors where science has already advanced. It is necessary only to bring our understanding of human nature up to the same point. Indeed, this may well be our only hope. If we can observe human behavior carefully from an objective point of view and come to understand it for what it is, we may be able to adopt a more sensible course of action. The need for establishing some such balance is now widely felt, and those who are able to control the direction of science are acting accordingly. It is understood that there is no point in furthering a science of nature unless it includes a sizable science of human nature, because only in that case will the results be wisely used. It is possible that science has come to the rescue and that order will eventually be achieved in the field of human affairs.

The Threat to Freedom

There is one difficulty, however. The application of science to human behavior is not so simple as it seems. Most of those who advocate it are simply looking for "the facts." To them science is little more than careful observation. They want to evaluate human behavior as it really is rather than as it appears to be through ignorance or prejudice, and then to make effective decisions and move on rapidly to a happier world. But the way in which science has been applied in other fields shows that something more is involved. Science is not concerned just with "getting the facts," after which one may act with greater wisdom in an unscientific fashion. Science supplies its own wisdom. It leads to a new conception of a subject matter, a new way of thinking about that part of the world to which it has addressed itself. If we are to enjoy the advantages of science in the field of human affairs, we must be prepared to adopt the working model of behavior to which a science will inevitably lead. But very few of those who advocate the application of scientific method to current problems are willing to go that far.

Science is more than the mere description of events as they occur. It is an attempt to discover order, to show that certain events stand in lawful relations to other events. No practical technology can be based upon science until such relations have been discovered. But order is not only a possible end product; it is a working assumption which must be adopted at the very start. We cannot apply the methods of science to a subject matter which is assumed to move about capriciously. Science not only describes, it predicts. It deals not only with the past but with the future. Nor is prediction the last word: to the extent that relevant conditions can be altered, or otherwise controlled, the future can be controlled. If we are to use the methods of science in the field of human affairs, we must assume that behavior is lawful and determined. We must expect to discover that what a man does is the result of specifiable conditions and that once these conditions have been discovered, we can anticipate and to some extent determine his actions.

This possibility is offensive to many people. It is opposed to a tradition of long standing which regards man as a free agent, whose behavior is the product, not of specifiable antecedent conditions, but of spontaneous inner changes of course. Prevailing philosophies of human nature recognize an internal "will" which has the power of interfering with causal relationships and which makes the prediction and control of behavior impossible. To suggest that we abandon this view is to threaten many cherished beliefs—to undermine what appears to be a stimulating and productive conception of human nature. The alternative point of view insists upon recognizing coercive forces in human conduct which we may prefer to disregard. It challenges our aspirations, either worldly or otherworldly. Regardless of how much we stand to gain from supposing that human behavior is the proper subject matter of a science, no one who is a product of Western civilization can do so without a struggle. We simply do not want such a science.

Conflicts of this sort are not unknown in the history of science. When Aesop's lion was shown a painting in which a man was depicted killing a lion, he commented contemptuously, "The artist was obviously a man." Primitive beliefs about man and his place in nature are usually flattering. It has been the unfortunate responsibility of science to paint more realistic pictures. The Copernican theory of the solar system displaced man from his pre-eminent position at the center of things. Today we accept this theory without emotion, but originally it met with enormous resistance. Darwin challenged a practice of segregation in which man set himself firmly apart from the animals, and the bitter struggle which arose is not yet ended. But though Darwin put man in his biological place, he did not deny him a possible position as master. Special faculties or a special capacity for spontaneous, creative action might have emerged in the process of evolution. When that distinction is now questioned, a new threat arises.

There are many ways of hedging on the theoretical issue. It may be insisted that a science of human behavior is impossible, that behavior has certain essential features which forever keep it beyond the pale of science. But although this argument may dissuade many people from further inquiry, it is not likely to have any effect upon those who are willing to try and see. Another objection frequently offered is that science is appropriate up to a certain point, but that there must always remain an area in which one can act only on faith or with respect to a "value judgment": science may tell us *how* to deal with human behavior, but just *what* is to be done must be decided in an essentially nonscientific way. Or it may be argued that there is another kind of science which is compatible with doctrines of personal freedom. For example, the social sciences are sometimes said to be fundamentally different from the natural sciences and not concerned with the same kinds of lawfulness. Prediction and control may be forsworn in favor of "interpretation" or some other species of understanding. But the kinds of intellectual activities exemplified by value judgments or by intuition or interpretation have never been set forth clearly, nor have they yet shown any capacity to work a change in our present predicament.

The Practical Issue

Our current practices do not represent any well-defined theoretical position. They are, in fact, thoroughly confused. At times we appear to regard a man's behavior as spontaneous and responsible. At other times we recognize that inner determination is at least not complete, that the individual is not always to be held to account. We have not been able to reject the slowly accumulating evidence that circumstances beyond the individual are relevant. We sometimes exonerate a man by pointing to "extenuating circumstances." We no longer blame the uneducated for their ignorance or call the unemployed lazy. We no longer hold children wholly accountable for their delinquencies. "Ignorance of the law" is no longer wholly inexcusable: "Father, forgive them; for they know not what they do." The insane have long since been cleared of responsibility for their condition, and the kinds of neurotic or psychotic behavior to which we now apply this extenuation are multiplying.

But we have not gone all the way. We regard the common man as the product of his environment; yet we reserve the right to give personal credit to great men for their achievements. (At the same time we take a certain delight in proving that part of the output of even such men is due to the "influence" of other men or to some trivial circumstance in their personal history.) We want to believe that right-minded men are moved by valid principles even though we are willing to regard wrong-minded men as victims of erroneous propaganda. Backward peoples may be the fault of a poor culture, but we want to regard the elite as something more than the product of a good culture. Though we observe that Moslem children in general become Moslems while Christian children in general become Christians, we are not willing to accept an accident of birth as a basis for belief. We dismiss those who disagree with us as victims of ignorance, but we regard the promotion of our own religious beliefs as something more than the arrangement of a particular environment.

All of this suggests that we are in transition. We have not wholly abandoned the traditional philosophy of human nature; at the same time we are far from adopting a scientific point of view without reservation. We have accepted the assumption of determinism in part; yet we allow our sympathies, our first allegiances, and our personal aspirations to rise to the defense of the traditional view. We are currently engaged in a sort of patchwork in which new facts and methods are assembled in accordance with traditional theories.

If this were a theoretical issue only, we would have no cause for alarm; but theories affect practices. A scientific conception of human behavior dictates one practice, a philosophy of personal freedom another. Confusion in theory means confusion in practice. The present unhappy condition of the world may in large measure be traced to our vacillation. The principal issues in dispute between nations, both in peaceful assembly and on the battlefield, are intimately concerned with the problem of human freedom and control. Totalitarianism or democracy, the state or the individual, planned society or laissez-faire, the impression of_cultures upon alien peoples, economic determinism, individual initiative, propaganda, education, ideological warfare—all concern the fundamental nature of human behavior. We shall almost certainly remain ineffective in solving these problems until we adopt a consistent point of view.

We cannot really evaluate the issue until we understand the alternatives. The traditional view of human nature in Western culture is well known. The conception of a free, responsible individual is embedded in our language and pervades our practices, codes, and beliefs. Given an example of human behavior, most people can describe it immediately in terms of such a conception. The practice is so natural that it is seldom examined. A scientific formulation, on the other hand, is new and strange. Very few people have any notion of the extent to which a science of human behavior is indeed possible. In what way can the behavior of the individual or of groups of individuals be predicted and controlled? What are laws of behavior like? What over-all conception of the human organism as a behaving system emerges? It is only when we have answered these questions, at least in a preliminary fashion, that we may consider the implications of a science of human behavior with respect to either a theory of human nature or the management of human affairs.

UNIT 2

Change and the Social World

We make history ourselves, but, in the first place, under very definite antecedents and conditions. Among these the economic ones are ultimately decisive. But the political ones, etc., and indeed even the traditions which haunt human minds also play a part, although not the decisive one. . . .

Frederick Engels

Though women do not complain of the power of husbands, each complains of her own husband, or the husbands of her friends. It is the same in all other cases of servitude; at least in the commencement of the emancipatory movement. The serfs did not at first complain of the power of the lords, but only of their tyranny.

J.S. Mill

It is understood that in a developed society *needs* are not only quantitative: the need for consumer goods; but also qualitative: the need for a free and many-sided development of human facilities, the need for information, for communication, the need to be free not only from exploitation but from oppression and alienation in work and leisure.

A. Gorz

Introduction

The first unit of *The Human Project* focused on the struggle of individuals to know themselves, and, through this knowledge, to acquire the potential to live as free and as self-determined a life as possible. While Unit 1 acknowledged the significance of the social world (think of the nurture side of the nature versus nurture debate), the emphasis centred on the impact on the self. In Unit 2, the focus shifts to the community of *selves*. We will still pay attention to how it feels for individuals to live with the consequences of living in groups, but our shift in perspective now takes place in a much larger frame.

The great American sociologist C. Wright Mills spoke of the link between personal troubles and public issues. If a man goes to work one morning and is told that he "is no longer needed," he clearly faces a personal crisis. If he returns home to find a note from his wife saying that she has decided to leave him, he is having a disastrously bad day. On the personal level, his experience is crushing and tragic and we can all imagine how he must feel. Yet, if we re-examine his situation from the broader perspective of the larger society in which he works and lives, we see that many people lost their jobs that day. This fact doesn't diminish the suffering experienced by the individual, but it does place it in a larger context in a potentially useful way. Indeed, his job loss may be the result of the "creative destruction" that—as explained by George Bragues in "The Economics of Social Change"—spurs economic development in a capitalist society but, in the process, also rewrites the rules for economic success. If we discover that the laid-off man has been working for a high-tech dot.com company, for instance, we will see that major shifts have occurred throughout the entire industry: as stock markets have re-evaluated potential profitability, share prices have dropped, and, consequently, what may have been a thriving company yesterday is now reeling and struggling to survive. This knowledge is useful, if we can get it early enough, because it can help us to take action to soften the blow—sell our stock or, in the case of the man employed in the field, look for new work long before being "shown the door." If, alternatively, we find out that this individual has been working in a factory instead of a high-tech company, we may understand his job loss as a consequence of the global repositioning of manufacturing jobs to places where labour costs are lower. Once again, this need not be a surprise and the individuals in the field could make plans that anticipate the eventual closure of their workplace.

In a similar fashion, the marriage breakup, which occurs in about 50 percent of all marriages, can be viewed as just another example of social upheaval. Once again, there is little consolation in this fact for the man whose wife has left him. Yet, there is a useful message for the rest of us, and, indeed, for people who have experienced divorce. Although the cause of a specific divorce might be identified as an extramarital affair, for example, there also exist larger social forces that have the potential to undermine all marriages. As Michael Ignatieff explains in "Rights, Intimacy, and Family Life," there are some broader pressures on the institution of marriage that we need to acknowledge, such as unrealistic expectations around money, parenting or intimacy. In her provocative piece, "Marriage Is Made in Hell," Laura Kipnis goes so far as to enlist some of these observations to support her wholesale attack on the institution of marriage altogether. Determining the link between the crises in individual marriages and marriage in general can be tough; deciding what to do with that knowledge, moreover, can be even tougher. Nevertheless, a deeper understanding of the institution can't help but be useful for individuals because, as much as it might be a pleasant fantasy, we know that we cannot build a fence around our private lives that will successfully exclude larger social pressures.

These social pressures can even intrude upon and manage our most personal feelings and emotions. As Arlie Russell Hochschild explains in "Exploring the Managed Heart," employees, especially in the service sector, are hired to perform emotional labour that requires them to display feelings—confidence, happiness, friendliness, for example—as demanded by their employers and expected by their customers. This commercially inspired cheerfulness becomes a mask that employees must wear to work even at the cost of emotional authenticity. While this may not seem too high a price to pay for a job, it is important to recognize that the pressures emanating from the larger society may go so far as to undermine our personal goals.

The larger society is, nonetheless, the field upon which we try to execute strategies to maximize our happiness, but the size and quality of the field are constantly changing, as, too, are the social rules that help individuals navigate this field. To achieve our goals, we must acquire the power to manage at least some of the conditions on this field. Power doesn't necessarily imply power over others, but can simply mean power to influence the outcome of certain specific events: how to get things done at work, for example, or how to redecorate your home or how to spend the evening with friends. Yet power is also a complex business, as there are many competing voices arguing for their share.

Those who at any particular moment have their hands on the reins are loath to give them up: it just feels so "right" to watch events unfold as they think they should. So those in power at this moment wish to project their power into the future and resist the transfer of power to others. Yet, despite this resistance, change happens all the time. How does this struggle between the new and the old, between continuity and change, happen?

As pointed out by Neil Postman in "The Judgment of Thamus," this change is often due to the unforeseen consequences of our inventions. Take the birth control pill, for instance. It was intended to provide reliable control over reproduction, and, as a result, it was easy to predict that families would use this new technology to have fewer children. Soon after the pill was introduced in the early 1960s, however, it became apparent that women were also *delaying* having children in order to further their education. So, within a very short period of time, women were graduating with degrees and diplomas in record new numbers and, of course, they wanted to put their new skills into practice in the workforce. But these highly educated women encountered very unequal treatment on the job. Even when they had the same qualifications and were doing the same jobs as men, for example, women were almost always paid less than men. This injustice, among others, spurred the political lobbying that gave rise to various pay equity bills.

Yet these ambitious women still planned to begin families. They merely wanted the opportunity to take a break from work to have children—without being forced to give up their hard-fought-for jobs. Paid maternity leave was the government's response. After returning to work once the period of leave was up, furthermore, women needed reliable people to take care of their children. This need spawned the creation of professional daycare facilities staffed by educators trained to look after young children. This example illustrates what Postman means by the "ecological" change that can be created by the introduction of new technology: from specific technology meant to control reproduction, we ended up with the unforeseen consequences of pay equity legislation, maternity leave and an entirely new profession, all of which have significantly transformed expectations of, and for, women and men today both at home and on the job.

Because the pill so effectively reduced family size in Canada and elsewhere in the West, moreover, it became imperative for governments to encourage immigration to increase the workforce and thereby maintain healthy economic growth. Immigration has long been recognized as a spur to social change, as the ideas and values of "new" cultures meet and sometimes clash with the host culture. Perhaps more than any other country, Canada has encouraged immigration, as reflected in the welcoming official policy of multiculturalism that seeks to reassure immigrants that they don't have to abandon the ideas and values of their home countries. Canada, at least in the metropolitan centres of Montreal, Toronto and Vancouver, can in fact be distinguished by the intensely pluralistic nature of its society.

While immigration has proven to be a tremendous resource, it can also present difficult challenges as we try to accommodate many competing and fundamentally different world views. In "Can We All Just Get Along?" Greg Narbey turns to the philosopher John Rawls for help in determining a fair process by which we can negotiate some of the conflicts that naturally arise in a pluralistic society. In "Diversity versus Solidarity," Bhikhu Parekh advises that such societies need a common sense of community in order to ease this process of accommodation. The bonds of the community may be elastic and evolving, but they need to be there in order to build a sense of confidence in the survivability and mutuality of our community.

The Judgment of Thamus

Neil Postman

You will find in Plato's *Phaedrus* a story about Thamus, the king of a great city of Upper Egypt. For people such as ourselves, who are inclined (in Thoreau's phrase) to be tools of our tools, few legends are more instructive than his. The story, as Socrates tells it to his friend Phaedrus, unfolds in the following way: Thamus once entertained the god Theuth, who was the inventor of many things, including number, calculation, geometry, astronomy, and writing. Theuth exhibited his inventions to King Thamus, claiming that they should be made widely known and available to Egyptians. Socrates continues:

> Thamus inquired into the use of each of them, and as Theuth went through them expressed approval or disapproval, according as he judged Theuth's claims to be well or ill founded. It would take too long to go through all that Thamus is reported to have said for and against each of Theuth's inventions. But when it came to writing, Theuth declared, "Here is an accomplishment, my lord the King, which will improve both the wisdom and the memory of the Egyptians. I have discovered a sure receipt for memory and wisdom." To this, Thamus replied, "Theuth, my paragon of inventors, the discoverer of an art is not the best judge of the good or harm which will accrue to those who practise it. So it is in this; you, who are the father of writing, have out of fondness for your off-spring attributed to it quite the opposite of its real function. Those who acquire it will cease to exercise their memory and become forgetful; they will rely on writing to bring things to their remembrance by external signs instead of by their own internal resources. What you have discov-ered is a receipt for recollection, not for memory. And as for wisdom, your pupils will have the reputation for it without the reality: they will receive a quantity of information without proper instruction, and in consequence be thought very knowledgeable when they are for the most part quite ignorant. And because they are filled with the conceit of wisdom instead of real wisdom they will be a burden to society.

I begin my book with this legend because in Thamus' response there are several sound principles from which we may begin to learn how to think with wise circumspection about a technological society. In fact, there is even one error in the judgment of Thamus, from which we may also learn something of importance. The error is not in his claim that writing will damage memory and create false wisdom. It is demonstrable that writing has had such an effect. Thamus' error is in his believing that writing will be a burden to society and *nothing but a burden.* For all his wisdom, he fails to imagine what writing's benefits might be, which, as we know, have been considerable. We may learn from this that it is a mistake to suppose that any technological innovation has a one-sided effect. Every technology is both a burden and a blessing; not either-or, but this-and-that.

Nothing could be more obvious, of course, especially to those who have given more than two minutes of thought to the matter. Nonetheless, we are currently surrounded by throngs of zealous Theuths, one-eyed prophets who see only what new technologies can do and are incapable of imagining what they will *undo.* We might call such people Technophiles. They gaze on technology as a lover does on his beloved, seeing it as without blemish and entertaining no apprehension for the future. They are therefore dangerous and are to be approached cautiously. On the other hand, some one-eyed prophets, such as I (or so I am accused), are inclined to speak only of burdens (in the manner of Thamus) and are silent about the opportunities that new technologies make possible. The Technophiles must speak for themselves, and do so all over the place. My defense is that a dissenting voice is sometimes needed to moderate the din made by the enthusiastic multitudes. If one is to err, it is better to err on the side of Thamusian skepticism. But it is an error nonetheless. And I might note that, with the exception of his judgment on writing, Thamus does not repeat this error. You might notice on rereading the legend that he gives arguments *for* and *against* each of Theuth's inventions. For it is inescapable that every culture must negotiate with technology, whether it does so intelligently or not. A bargain is struck in which technology giveth and technology taketh away. The wise know this well, and are rarely impressed by dramatic technological changes, and never overjoyed. Here, for example, is Freud on the matter, from his doleful *Civilization and Its Discontents:*

> One would like to ask: is there, then, no positive gain in pleasure, no unequivocal increase in my feeling of happiness, if I can, as often as I please, hear the voice of a child of mine who is living hundreds of miles away or if I can learn in the shortest possible time after a friend has reached his destination that he has come through the long and difficult voyage unharmed? Does it mean nothing that medicine has succeeded in enormously reducing infant mortality and the danger of infection for women in child-birth, and, indeed, in considerably lengthening the average life of a civilized man?

Freud knew full well that technical and scientific advances are not to be taken lightly, which is why he begins this passage by acknowledging them. But he ends it by reminding us of what they have undone:

> If there had been no railway to conquer distances, my child would never have left his native town and I should need no telephone to hear his voice; if travelling across the ocean by ship had not been introduced, my friend would not have embarked on his sea-voyage and I should not need a cable to relieve my anxiety about him. What is the use of reducing infantile mortality when it is precisely that reduction which imposes the greatest restraint on us in the begetting of children, so that, taken all round, we nevertheless rear no more children than in the days before the reign of hygiene, while at the same time we have created difficult conditions for our sexual life in marriage ... And, finally, what good to us is a long life if it is difficult and barren of joys, and if it is so full of misery that we can only welcome death as a deliverer?

In tabulating the cost of technological progress, Freud takes a rather depressing line, that of a man who agrees with Thoreau's remark that our inventions are but improved means to an unimproved end. The Technophile would surely answer Freud by saying that life has always been barren of joys and full of misery but that the telephone, ocean liners, and especially the reign of hygiene have not only lengthened life but made it a more agreeable proposition. That is certainly an argument I would make (thus proving I am no one-eyed Technophobe), but it is not necessary at this point to pursue it. I have brought Freud into the conversation only to show that a wise man—even one of such a woeful countenance—must begin his critique of technology by acknowledging its successes. Had King Thamus been as wise as reputed, he would not have forgotten to include in his judgment a prophecy about the powers that writing would enlarge. There is a calculus of technological change that requires a measure of even-handedness.

So much for Thamus' error of omission. There is another omission worthy of note, but it is no error. Thamus simply takes for granted—and therefore does not feel it necessary to say—that writing is not a neutral technology whose good or harm depends on the uses made of it. He knows that the uses made of any technology are largely determined by the structure of the technology itself—that is, that its functions follow from its form. This is why Thamus is concerned not with *what* people will write; he is concerned *that* people will write. It is absurd to imagine Thamus advising, in the manner of today's standard-brand Technophiles, that, if only writing would be used for the production of certain kinds of texts and not others (let us say, for dramatic literature but not for history or philosophy), its disruptions could be minimized. He would regard such counsel as extreme naïveté. He would allow, I imagine, that a technology may be barred entry to a culture. But we may learn from Thamus the following: once a technology is admitted, it plays out its hand; it does what it is designed to do. Our task is to understand what that design is—that is to say, when we admit a new technology to the culture, we must do so with our eyes wide open.

All of this we may infer from Thamus' silence. But we may learn even more from what he does say than from what he doesn't. He points out, for example, that writing will change what is meant by the words "memory" and "wisdom." He fears that memory will be confused with what he disdainfully calls "recollection," and worries that wisdom will become indistinguishable from mere knowledge. This judgment we must take to heart, for it is a certainty that radical technologies create new definitions of old terms, and that this process takes place without our being fully conscious of it. Thus, it is insidious and dangerous, quite different from the process whereby new technologies introduce new terms to the language. In our own time, we have consciously added to our language thousands of new words and phrases having to do with new technologies—"VCR," "binary digit," "software," "front-wheel drive," "window of opportunity," "Walkman," etc. We are not taken by surprise at this. New things require new words. But new things also modify old words, words that have deep-rooted meanings. The telegraph and the penny press changed what we once meant by "information." Television changes what we once meant by the terms "political debate," "news," and "public opinion." The computer changes "information" once again. Writing changed what we once meant by "truth" and "law"; printing changed them again, and now television and the computer change them once more. Such changes occur quickly, surely, and, in a sense, silently. **Lexicographers** hold no plebiscites on the matter. No manuals are written to explain what is happening, and the schools are oblivious to it. The old words still look the same, are still used in the same kinds of sentences. But they do not have the same meanings; in some cases, they have opposite meanings. And this is what Thamus wishes to teach us—that technology imperiously commandeers our most important terminology. It defines "freedom," "truth," "intelligence," "fact," "wisdom," "memory," "history"—all the words we live by. And it does not pause to tell us. And we do not pause to ask. . . .

Here, there are several more principles to be mined from the judgment of Thamus that require mentioning because they presage all I will

lexicographers
writers of dictionaries

write about. For instance, Thamus warns that the pupils of Theuth will develop an undeserved reputation for wisdom. He means to say that those who cultivate competence in the use of a new technology become an elite group that is granted undeserved authority and prestige by those who have no such competence. There are different ways of expressing the interesting implications of this fact. Harold Innis, the father of modern communication studies, repeatedly spoke of the "knowledge monopolies" created by important technologies. He meant precisely what Thamus had in mind: those who have control over the workings of a particular technology accumulate power and inevitably form a kind of conspiracy against those who have no access to the specialized knowledge made available by the technology. In his book *The Bias of Communication,* Innis provides many historical examples of how a new technology "busted up" a traditional knowledge monopoly and created a new one presided over by a different group. Another way of saying this is that the benefits and deficits of a new technology are not distributed equally. There are, as it were, winners and losers. It is both puzzling and poignant that on many occasions the losers, out of ignorance, have actually cheered the winners, and some still do.

Let us take as an example the case of television. In the United States, where television has taken hold more deeply than anywhere else, many people find it a blessing, not least those who have achieved high-paying, gratifying careers in television as executives, technicians, newscasters, and entertainers. It should surprise no one that such people, forming as they do a new knowledge monopoly, should cheer themselves and defend and promote television technology. On the other hand and in the long run, television may bring a gradual end to the careers of schoolteachers, since school was an invention of the printing press and must stand or fall on the issue of how much importance the printed word has. For 400 years, schoolteachers have been part of the knowledge monopoly created by printing, and they are now witnessing the breakup of that monopoly. It appears as if they can do little to prevent that breakup, but surely there is something perverse about schoolteachers' being enthusiastic about what is happening. Such enthusiasm always calls to my mind an image of some turn-of-the-century blacksmith who not only sings the praises of the automobile but also believes that his business will be enhanced by it. We know now that his business was not enhanced by it; it was rendered obsolete by it, as perhaps the clearheaded blacksmiths knew. What could they have done? Weep, if nothing else.

We have a similar situation in the development and spread of computer technology, for here too there are winners and losers. There can be no disputing that the computer has increased the power of large-scale organizations like the armed forces, or airline companies or banks or tax-collecting agencies. And it is equally clear that the computer is now indispensable to high-level researchers in physics and other natural sciences. But to what extent has computer technology been an advantage to the masses of people? To steelworkers, vegetable-store owners, teachers, garage mechanics, musicians, bricklayers, dentists, and most of the rest into whose lives the computer now intrudes? Their private matters have been made more accessible to powerful institutions. They are more easily tracked and controlled; are subjected to more examinations; are increasingly mystified by the decisions made about them; are often reduced to mere numerical objects. They are inundated by junk mail. They are easy targets for advertising agencies and political organizations. The schools teach their children to operate computerized systems instead of teaching things that are more valuable to children. In a word, almost nothing that they need happens to the losers. Which is why they are losers.

It is to be expected that the winners will encourage the losers to be enthusiastic about computer technology. That is the way of winners, and so they sometimes tell the losers that with personal computers the average person can balance a checkbook more neatly, keep better track of recipes, and make more logical shopping lists. They also tell them that their lives will be conducted more efficiently. But discreetly they neglect to say from whose point of view the efficiency is warranted or what might be its costs. Should the losers grow skeptical, the winners dazzle them with the wondrous feats of computers, almost all of which have only marginal relevance to the quality of the losers' lives but which are nonetheless impressive. Eventually, the losers succumb, in part because they believe, as Thamus prophesied, that the specialized knowledge of the masters of a new technology is a form of wisdom. The masters come to believe this as well, as Thamus also prophesied. The result is that certain questions do not arise. For example, to whom will the technology give greater power and freedom? And whose power and freedom will be reduced by it?

I have perhaps made all of this sound like a well-planned conspiracy, as if the winners know all too well what is being won and what lost. But this is not quite how it happens. For one thing, in cultures that have a democratic ethos, relatively weak traditions, and a high receptivity to new technologies, everyone is inclined to be enthusiastic about technological change, believing that its benefits will eventually spread evenly among the entire population. Especially in the United States, where the lust for what is new has no bounds, do we find this childlike conviction most widely held. Indeed, in America, social change of any kind is rarely seen as resulting in winners and losers, a condition that stems in part from Americans' much-documented optimism. As for change brought on by technology, this native optimism is exploited by entrepreneurs, who work hard to infuse the population with a unity of improbable hope, for they know that it is economically unwise to reveal the price to be paid for technological change. One might say, then, that, if there is a conspiracy of any kind, it is that of a culture conspiring against itself.

In addition to this, and more important, it is not always clear, at least in the early stages of a technology's intrusion into a culture, who will gain most by it and who will lose most. This is because the changes wrought by technology are subtle if not downright mysterious, one might even say wildly unpredictable. Among the most unpredictable are those that might be labeled ideological. This is the sort of change Thamus had in mind when he warned that writers will come to rely on external signs instead of their own internal resources, and that they will receive quantities of information without proper instruction. He meant that new technologies change what we mean by "knowing" and "truth"; they alter those deeply embedded habits of thought which give to a culture its sense of what the world is like—a sense of what is the natural order of things, of what is reasonable, of what is necessary, of what is inevitable, of what is real. Since such changes are expressed in changed meanings of old words, I will hold off until later discussing the massive ideological transformation now occurring in the United States. Here, I should like to give only one example of how technology creates new conceptions of what is real and, in the process, undermines older conceptions. I refer to the seemingly harmless practice of assigning marks or grades to the answers students give on examinations. This procedure seems so natural to most of us that we are hardly aware of its significance. We may even find it difficult to imagine that the number or letter is a tool or, if you will, a technology; still less that, when we use such a technology to judge someone's behavior, we have done something peculiar. In point of fact, the first instance of grading students' papers occurred at Cambridge University in 1792 at the suggestion of a tutor named William Farish. No one knows much about William Farish; not more than a handful have ever heard of him. And yet his idea that a quantitative value should be assigned to human thought was a major step toward constructing a mathematical concept of reality. If a number can be given to the quality of a thought, then a number can be given to the qualities of mercy, love, hate, beauty, creativity, intelligence, even sanity itself. When Galileo said that the language of nature is written in mathematics, he did not mean to include human feeling or accomplishment or insight. But most of us are now inclined to make these inclusions. Our psychologists, sociologists, and educators find it quite impossible to do their work without numbers. They believe that without numbers they cannot acquire or express authentic knowledge.

I shall not argue here that this is a stupid or dangerous idea, only that it is peculiar. What is even more peculiar is that so many of us do not find the idea peculiar. To say that someone should be doing better work because he has an IQ of 134, or that someone is a 7.2 on a sensitivity scale, or that this man's essay on the rise of capitalism is an A– and that man's is a C+ would have sounded like gibberish to Galileo or Shakespeare or Thomas Jefferson. If it makes sense to us, that is because our minds have been conditioned by the technology of numbers so that we see the world differently than they did. Our understanding of what is real is different. Which is another way of saying that embedded in every tool is an ideological bias, a predisposition to construct the world as one thing rather than another, to value one thing over another, to amplify one sense or skill or attitude more loudly than another.

This is what Marshall McLuhan meant by his famous **aphorism** "The medium is the message." This is what Marx meant when he said, "Technology discloses man's mode of dealing with nature" and creates the "conditions of intercourse" by which we relate to each other. It is what Wittgenstein meant when, in referring to our most fundamental technology, he said that language is not merely a vehicle of thought but also the driver. And it is what Thamus wished the inventor Theuth to see. This is, in short, an ancient and persistent piece of wisdom, perhaps most simply expressed in the old adage that, to a man with a hammer, everything looks like a nail. Without being too literal, we may extend the truism: To a man with a pencil, everything looks like an image. To a man with a computer, everything looks like data. And to a man with a grade sheet, everything looks like a number.

But such prejudices are not always apparent at the start of a technology's journey, which is why no one can safely conspire to be a winner in technological change. Who would have imagined, for example, whose interests and what world-view would be ultimately advanced by the invention of the mechanical clock? The clock had its origin in the Benedictine monasteries of the 12th and 13th centuries. The impetus behind the invention was to provide a more or less precise regularity to the routines of the monasteries, which required, among other things, seven periods of devotion during the course of the day. The bells of the monastery were to be rung to signal the canonical hours; the mechan-

aphorism
brief statement

ical clock was the technology that could provide precision to these rituals of devotion. And indeed it did. But what the monks did not foresee was that the clock is a means not merely of keeping track of the hours but also of synchronizing and controlling the actions of men. And thus, by the middle of the 14th century, the clock had moved outside the walls of the monastery, and brought a new and precise regularity to the life of the workman and the merchant. "The mechanical clock," as Lewis Mumford wrote, "made possible the idea of regular production, regular working hours and a standardized product." In short, without the clock, capitalism would have been quite impossible. The paradox, the surprise, and the wonder are that the clock was invented by men who wanted to devote themselves more rigorously to God; it ended as the technology of greatest use to men who wished to devote themselves to the accumulation of money. In the eternal struggle between God and Mammon, the clock quite unpredictably favored the latter.

Unforeseen consequences stand in the way of all those who think they see clearly the direction in which a new technology will take us. Not even those who invent a technology can be assumed to be reliable prophets, as Thamus warned. Gutenberg, for example, was by all accounts a devout Catholic who would have been horrified to hear that accursed heretic Luther describe printing as "God's highest act of grace, whereby the business of the Gospel is driven forward." Luther understood, as Gutenberg did not, that the mass-produced book, by placing the Word of God on every kitchen table, makes each Christian his own theologian—one might even say his own priest, or better, from Luther's point of view, his own pope. In the struggle between unity and diversity of religious belief, the press favored the latter, and we can assume that this possibility never occurred to Gutenberg.

Thamus understood well the limitations of inventors in grasping the social and psychological—that is, ideological—bias of their own inventions. We can imagine him addressing Gutenberg in the following way: "Gutenberg, my paragon of inventors, the discoverer of an art is not the best judge of the good or harm which will accrue to those who practise it. So it is in this; you, who are the father of printing, have out of fondness for your off-spring come to believe it will advance the cause of the Holy Roman See, whereas in fact it will sow discord among believers; it will damage the authenticity of your beloved Church and destroy its monopoly."

We can imagine that Thamus would also have pointed out to Gutenberg, as he did to Theuth, that the new invention would create a vast population of readers who "will receive a quantity of information without proper instruction . . . [who will be] filled with the conceit of wisdom instead of real wisdom"; that reading, in other words, will compete with older forms of learning. This is yet another principle of technological change we may infer from the judgment of Thamus: new technologies compete with old ones—for time, for attention, for money, for prestige, but mostly for dominance of their world-view. This competition is implicit once we acknowledge that a medium contains an ideological bias. And it is a fierce competition, as only ideological competitions can be. It is not merely a matter of tool against tool—the alphabet attacking ideographic writing, the printing press attacking the illuminated manuscript, the photograph attacking the art of painting, television attacking the printed word. When media make war against each other, it is a case of world-views in collision.

In the United States, we can see such collisions everywhere—in politics, in religion, in commerce—but we see them most clearly in the schools, where two great technologies confront each other in uncompromising aspect for the control of students' minds. On the one hand, there is the world of the printed word with its emphasis on logic, sequence, history, exposition, objectivity, detachment, and discipline. On the other, there is the world of television with its emphasis on imagery, narrative, presentness, simultaneity, intimacy, immediate gratification, and quick emotional response. Children come to school having been deeply conditioned by the biases of television. There, they encounter the world of the printed word. A sort of psychic battle takes place, and there are many casualties—children who can't learn to read or won't, children who cannot organize their thought into logical structure even in a simple paragraph, children who cannot attend to lectures or oral explanations for more than a few minutes at a time. They are failures, but not because they are stupid. They are failures because there is a media war going on, and they are on the wrong side—at least for the moment. Who knows what schools will be like 25 years from now? Or 50? In time, the type of student who is currently a failure may be considered a success. The type who is now successful may be regarded as a handicapped learner—slow to respond, far too detached, lacking in emotion, inadequate in creating mental pictures of reality. Consider: what Thamus called the "conceit of wisdom"—the unreal knowledge acquired through the written word—eventually became the pre-eminent form of knowledge valued by the schools. There is no reason to suppose that such a form of knowledge must always remain so highly valued.

To take another example: In introducing the personal computer to the classroom, we shall be breaking a 400-year-old truce between the gregariousness and openness fostered by orality and the introspection and isolation fostered by the printed word. Orality stresses group learning, cooperation, and a sense of social responsibility, which is the context within which Thamus believed proper instruction and real knowledge must be communicated. Print stresses individualized learning, competition, and personal autonomy. Over four centuries, teachers, while emphasizing print, have allowed orality its place in the classroom, and have therefore achieved a kind of pedagogical peace between these two forms of learning, so that what is valuable in each can be maximized. Now comes the computer, carrying anew the banner of private learning and individual problem-solving. Will the widespread use of computers in the classroom defeat once and for all the claims of communal speech? Will the computer raise egocentrism to the status of a virtue?

These are the kinds of questions that technological change brings to mind when one grasps, as Thamus did, that technological competition ignites total war, which means it is not possible to contain the effects of a new technology to a limited sphere of human activity. If this metaphor puts the matter too brutally, we may try a gentler, kinder one: Technological change is neither additive nor subtractive. It is ecological. I mean "ecological" in the same sense as the word is used by environmental scientists. One significant change generates total change. If you remove the caterpillars from a given habitat, you are not left with the same environment minus caterpillars: you have a new environment, and you have reconstituted the conditions of survival; the same is true if you add caterpillars to an environment that has had none. This is how the ecology of media works as well. A new technology does not add or subtract something. It changes everything. In the year 1500, 50 years after the printing press was invented, we did not have old Europe plus the printing press. We had a different Europe. After television, the United States was not America plus television; television gave a new coloration to every political campaign, to every home, to every school, to every church, to every industry. And that is why the competition among media is so fierce. Surrounding every technology are institutions whose organization—not to mention their reason for being—reflects the world-view promoted by the technology. Therefore, when an old technology is assaulted by a new one, institutions are threatened. When institutions are threatened, a culture finds itself in crisis. This is serious business, which is why we learn nothing when educators ask, Will students learn mathematics better by computers than by textbooks? Or when businessmen ask, Through which medium can we sell more products? Or when preachers ask, Can we reach more people through television than through radio? Or when politicians ask, How effective are messages sent through different media? Such questions have an immediate, practical value to those who ask them, but they are diversionary.

They direct our attention away from the serious social, intellectual, and institutional crises that new media foster.

Perhaps an analogy here will help to underline the point. In speaking of the meaning of a poem, T.S. Eliot remarked that the chief use of the overt content of poetry is "to satisfy one habit of the reader, to keep his mind diverted and quiet, while the poem does its work upon him: much as the imaginary burglar is always provided with a bit of nice meat for the house-dog." In other words, in asking their practical questions, educators, entrepreneurs, preachers, and politicians are like the house-dog munching peacefully on the meat while the house is looted. Perhaps some of them know this and do not especially care. After all, a nice piece of meat, offered graciously, does take care of the problem of where the next meal will come from. But for the rest of us, it cannot be acceptable to have the house invaded without protest or at least awareness.

What we need to consider about the computer has nothing to do with its efficiency as a teaching tool. We need to know in what ways it is altering our conception of learning, and how, in conjunction with television, it undermines the old idea of school. Who cares how many boxes of cereal can be sold via television? We need to know if television changes our conception of reality, the relationship of the rich to the poor, the idea of happiness itself. A preacher who confines himself to considering how a medium can increase his audience will miss the significant question: In what sense do new media alter what is meant by religion, by church, even by God? And if the politician cannot think beyond the next election, then *we* must wonder about what new media do to the idea of political organization and to the conception of citizenship.

To help us do this, we have the judgment of Thamus, who, in the way of legends, teaches us what Harold Innis, in his way, tried to. New technologies alter the structure of our interests: the things we think *about*. They alter the character of our symbols: the things we think *with*. And they alter the nature of community: the arena in which thoughts develop.

As Thamus spoke to Innis across the centuries, it is essential that we listen to their conversation, join in it, revitalize it. For something has happened in America that is strange and dangerous, and there is only a dull and even stupid awareness of what it is—in part because it has no name. I call it Technopoly.

The Economics of Social Change

George Bragues

Think of all the products and technologies that have mushroomed in just the past thirty years: cell phones, personal computers, email, the Internet, video games, compact disc players, camcorders, digital cameras, microwave ovens, test-tube babies, Prozac and Viagra. It would take a mountain of books—indeed, such a mountain already exists—to explain the dramatic changes these inventions have wrought in the way we work, study, eat, play, relax, date, reproduce and socialize.

Think, too, of how much our practices and norms have altered. Take the issues of sexuality, gender and family. Thirty years ago, despite the fact that homosexuality had recently been legalized, gays and lesbians were still widely scorned as deviants and sinners. Today, they are on the verge of achieving national recognition of their right to marry. Women now work outside the home in far greater numbers and make up the majority of students in Canada's universities and colleges. Meanwhile, the nuclear family has gone from being the norm to just one of several legitimate options available to organize our households.

The pace of this change is all the more striking when we contrast it to how societies functioned in the past. In the 16th century, the average individual lived pretty much the same life as his or her counterpart in the seventh century. They both gained their livelihood from working the land using rudimentary implements and domesticated animals; they both lived in villages within extended families; and they both were subservient to a landowning elite class. A helpful way to gauge how rapid social change has become in modern times is to look at world population figures throughout history. Major shifts in population indicate that societies have somehow changed significantly in their capacity to sustain human life within the constraints posed by the natural environment.

As you can see from the graph on the next page, world population grew rather gradually from 400 BCE (the height of ancient Greek civilization) to 1750. Notice the dramatic increase in the numbers since then. In 2004, the world population was about 6.4 billion, which means that in the last 250 or so years, global population increased by a multiple of 10, whereas before that it took just over 2,000 years to merely quadruple.

"The Economics of Social Change" is by George Bragues of the Humber College Institute of Technology and Advanced Learning. Used by permission.

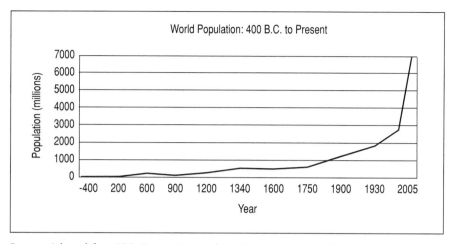

Sources: Adapted from U.S. Census Bureau (http://www.census.gov/ipc/www/worldhis.html) and the United Nations Population Division (http://www.esa.un.org/unpp/). Both sites accessed March 1/2004.

Why has social change accelerated? One cannot answer this question without first understanding how social change happens in the first place. To this end, we'll outline a model, with several illustrations, that explains social change as a result of economic forces. Change has become so rapid, as it turns out, due to the inner workings of the capitalist system motoring the economies of the industrialized world.

A Materialist-Individualist Model of Social Change

Philosophers, poets and historians have long speculated on the nature of social change as far back as ancient Greece. In the 19th century, however, this enquiry gained a special prominence as philosophers came to believe that such matters as God, truth, morality, the soul and the good life could finally be resolved by deciphering the processes of social evolution. Out of this effort, two German thinkers emerged with the most compelling alternative accounts of social change, both of which continue to frame the debate to this day. Georg W. F. Hegel (1770–1831) argued that ideas—how people think about religion, art, nature, society and justice—bring about change. We can call this an *idealist model of social change*. Karl Marx (1818–1883), on the other hand, argued that economics—how people make a living, satisfy their natural requirements and pursue comfort and security—is the decisive factor. This is a *materialist model of social change*. Marx is often described as turning the ideas of Hegel upside down by insisting that the way people think is dictated by how they earn their bread, rather than the other way around.

To illustrate the difference between the two models, consider how they might explain unemployment insurance. Britain was the first nation to introduce a government-run scheme of unemployment insurance in 1911. Canada didn't establish such a scheme until 1940. Before then, people who lost their jobs were left to rely on their own resources and the support of their families. Why did things change? A proponent of the idealist model would say that a new philosophy of government, developed and spread by intellectuals, took hold of people's minds. In other words, the 19th-century view that the government should stay out of people's economic concerns was replaced by the notion that the government should give people a helping hand when the economy slumps. By contrast, a proponent of the materialist model would say that workers, adversely affected by economic downturns, sought financial security by influencing politicians to institute unemployment insurance. In other words, economic motives instigated the change.

It is true that social change is often preceded by a debate pitting those in favour of the change against those opposing it. Such a debate presumes that it very much matters which set of ideas ends up winning people's minds. Before women obtained the right to pursue a career, for example, the case had to be successfully made that they are not naturally destined to specialize in child rearing and household tasks, but that their capacities allow them to flourish in business, politics and the professions as well.

Still, the idea that women are equal to men was advanced over two millennia ago by Plato, the ancient Greek philosopher, in one of the most influential books of all time, *The Republic*. Yet ancient Greek women did not experience a feminist revolution. That even the most logical ideas don't automatically propel social change suggests that something else is necessary—perhaps that the economic circumstances must be right. Adopting the economic point of view, however, does not mean we have to entirely accept Marx's framework. Contemporary economics, arguably the most successful of the social sciences, rejects Marx's view of the economy as a class struggle between capitalists and workers. Economists today see events as being driven by the acts of individuals, not classes.

Here, then, is a *materialist-individualist model of social change*. To begin with, think of society as the product of individuals interacting with each other and making decisions in pursuit of their goals. Now divide society into three parts:

a) *The economic sphere*—This is where individuals deal with resource scarcity to produce and consume goods and services; if the resulting distribution of incomes is unequal, we get social classes—that is, a number of hierarchically arranged groupings within which individuals are readily able to identify with each other because of similar levels of wealth and prestige.

b) *The political sphere*—This is where individuals manage their communal affairs via government.

c) *The cultural sphere*—This is where individuals associate with each other in families, social classes, friendships, sexual relationships, leisure activities, schools and religious and ethnic communities; it also refers to the way individuals think—how their beliefs, values, preferences and norms are expressed in religion, art, music, literature, philosophy, science and the media.

The fundamental contention of the materialist-individualist model is that changes generated within the economic sphere carry over into the other two spheres, and, in the process, alter society as a whole.

To understand exactly how this takes place, we need to clarify what motivates individual decisions. Individuals make decisions with a view to securing *benefits*. These benefits include some personally unique weighting of security, wealth, comfort, status, companionship, sex, love, knowledge and meaning in one's life. But, of course, individuals aren't free to obtain benefits in any way they please. They are constrained by the amount of time and resources available to them, as well as the social institutions and norms that they're expected to follow. You may want to go away for two months every winter to party in Acapulco, for example, but you cannot go because you can't afford it. Or you may want to be a movie star, but first you have to go to hundreds of auditions before you may win even a minor role because our social institutions happen to put the decision of who is cast in films in the hands of a relatively small group of movie directors. Put another way, any benefit that an individual may seek involves some *cost*. This being the case, we arrive at this principle of human behaviour: *individuals strive to achieve benefits that they figure are worth the cost.*

Grasping this principle, which is central to contemporary economics, is the key to understanding how social change occurs. According to this principle, once people have decided on a certain course of action, they won't change it unless the costs and benefits they face in pursuing their goals change. From time to time, economic forces alter these costs and benefits in such a way that lots and lots of people start making different decisions in the political and cultural spheres of society: this is essentially what the materialist-individualist model of social change says.

To briefly illustrate, consider how we went from a society in which it was frowned upon for individuals to have sex before marriage to the present-day situation where it is generally considered acceptable. What happened? Our model would observe that economic forces produced more effective contraceptives. This lowered the "cost" of having sex, inasmuch as individuals didn't have to worry as much about an unwanted pregnancy. Since people view sex as a benefit, they naturally responded to this turn of events by having more sex, including before marriage. Community norms about premarital sex shifted accordingly and thus did society change.

The Economic Sphere: Capitalism, Social Class and Creative Destruction

Let's move now to a more detailed explanation of the materialist-individualist model. Since this model proposes that change originates from the economic sphere, let's start by explaining how that part of society operates. In the industrialized nations of North America, Western Europe, Australia and Japan, economic decisions about what, how, when and where to produce goods and services are made within a framework known as *capitalism*. Over the last two decades, particularly since the fall of communism, capitalist institutions have also been introduced in Eastern Europe, Latin America, India and China. Capitalist economies have the following features:

- *Private property*—Individuals, both by themselves and in cooperation with others in companies, possess the right to control the use of productive resources such as land, buildings, machinery and money in addition to their own labour.

- *Specialization of productive tasks*—Instead of satisfying their desires by producing the bulk of their supplies on their own, individuals focus their time and energy on producing a specific good or service. For example, some are accountants or teachers, others are janitors or salespersons, and so on.

- *Trade and exchange*—Since each person only produces a specific good or service, people engage in trade and exchange to satisfy the full range of their desires. Thus, most people sell their labour for wages and then take the money they earn to buy things like food, clothes, entertainment, etc. Others invest their capital in businesses of their own and try to make a profit by selling goods and services to consumers. People are continually buying and selling. This is why capitalism is often referred to as a market economy.

- *Competition*—Individuals and companies pursue their interests by competing against others to offer the best deal in the market. Hence, workers compete for jobs, landlords compete for renters, investors compete for business opportunities and companies compete for customers.

- *Limited government*—The government does not involve itself in every nook and cranny of the economy, but generally confines itself to enforcing property rights and contracts. It does, however, intervene in the economy to protect the public interest by, for example, regulating monopolies and dangerous products and actively trying to stabilize economic cycles by adjusting spending, taxes and interest rates. Government also provides a social safety net and uses the tax system to redistribute incomes from the rich to the poor. Some governments are more active in economic affairs than others, with Sweden and Norway being especially interventionist and the United States endorsing a freer market. Canada is somewhere in the middle.

Politicians and intellectuals often complain that capitalism generates greed, alienation, inequality, fabricated desires and environmental harm. Whatever the merits of these charges, one thing cannot be legitimately doubted: capitalism produces enormous wealth. The established capitalist nations are the richest in the world. Nations, such as India and China, which have recently adopted capitalist practices, have seen their economies grow dramatically. Numerous studies quantitatively demonstrate a strong relationship between free markets and growth.[1] Even the greatest enemy of capitalism, Karl Marx, was forced to acknowledge this point in noting how capitalism, "during its rule of scarce one hundred years, has created more massive and colossal productive forces than have all preceding generations together."[2]

The critics of capitalism are right in observing that the wealth that capitalism creates isn't distributed equally. Still, viewed from a larger historical perspective, prevailing levels of inequality aren't particularly glaring. Before capitalism emerged in the 17th and 18th centuries, when most of the world's population lived in agricultural societies, a tiny landowning elite controlled the bulk of social wealth and systematically exploited a large peasant underclass, who were viewed as subhuman. As capitalism evolved, a large middle class emerged, a class that now makes up anywhere from 40 to 70 percent of Canada's population.[3] Even today, the established capitalist societies of the world tend to have much smaller classes of poor people than do non-capitalist societies. None of this should blind us to the fact that a class structure definitely exists in capitalism and that those on the top do disproportionately well. In 2002, according to Statistics Canada, the top 20 percent of families earned $11.70 of market income for every $1 that the bottom 20 percent of families made.[4]

Unequally as the pie may be divided, the question nevertheless remains: how does capitalism create so much wealth and make the pie bigger? Basically, it's because the competition for profit among individuals and companies motivates them to come up with ways to make goods more cheaply, improve product quality and satisfy new desires. More and better goods thus get produced for every hour people work and every dollar of capital invested in businesses. In other words, productivity rises. People become wealthier, in turn, because their work effort enables them to afford an ever greater menu of items. In 1780, for instance, it took 1,800 hours of work a year for a household to feed itself; today, thanks to the rise in productivity, it takes just 260 hours, leaving a lot of money to buy other things.[5]

Capitalism's wealth-creating process isn't necessarily pretty. It's actually a merciless Darwinian process in which those not efficient or inventive enough to meet consumer demand get displaced by those ushering in superior modes of production and new products. Industries continually rise and fall. At one point or another in the past two centuries, the latest thing went from being railroads to autos, then to radio and subsequently to airplanes. Now, the most vibrant industries are those involving computers and biotechnology. But people do get hurt along the path of capitalist evolution, as one might expect, with the unlucky workers in fallen industries having to find jobs elsewhere, often by acquiring new skills. Sadly, a few, especially the older ones, can't make the adjustment. Nor is it just individuals who suffer; entire communities that are reliant on a dying industry can become depressed.

Joseph Schumpeter, one of the great 20th-century economists, famously referred to this two-sided aspect of capitalism as *creative destruction*: "creative" insofar as it enhances productivity and wealth for society as a whole and "destructive" insofar as long-standing institutions are eliminated and some people suffer. This is how Schumpeter put it:

The fundamental impulse that sets and keeps the capitalist engine in motion comes from the new consumer goods, the new methods of production or transportation, the new markets, the new forms of industrial organization that capitalist enterprise creates . . . [there is a] process of industrial mutation—if I may use the biological term—that incessantly revolutionizes the economic structure *from within*, incessantly destroying the old one, incessantly creating a new one. This process of Creative Destruction is the essential fact about capitalism.[6]

In short, change is intrinsic to the nature of capitalism.

From Economics to Politics and Culture: Clarifying Some Questions

Combine this insight about the evolutionary character of capitalism with a model of social change that sees change flowing from the economy to the rest of society, and it becomes easier to understand why we live in groundbreaking times. Recall that our materialist-individualist model holds that an economic shift causes change elsewhere by altering the structure of costs and benefits that individuals face in their pursuit of happiness. Things that previously were unfeasible suddenly become practicable. When enough individuals vary their lives and beliefs, society becomes a different place. Let's illustrate this by clarifying five questions related to social change:

Why is the political system of our society democratic? This may seem a strange question to ask, because our government in Canada has been democratic for as long as anyone alive today remembers. But this question is still worth considering because the vast majority of societies throughout history (including our own in the past) have not been democratic. Also, the democratization of the political sphere is the foundation of subsequent, numerous changes in society. To make a very long story short, during the 19th and 20th centuries, democracies fully developed only after capitalist economies spread society's wealth more evenly, thereby fostering a large middle class. These individuals now had the resources to successfully fight for a system of popular voting more likely to promote their interests. Critical, too, was the increasing urbanization spawned by capitalism. As agriculture became more productive, fewer hands were required on farms. People increasingly moved to cities to work in factories. Living closer together, workers could more easily organize themselves and exercise influence in the political arena to protect themselves from the exploitive practices of their factory bosses. It's very important to note that the consolidation of democracy ended up instilling the idea that human beings are equal. That idea was a compelling force in the great social reform movements of the 20th century, including the civil rights, feminist and gay liberation movements. We'll see how the belief in equality helps explain several social changes discussed below.

Why are more and more people entering post-secondary studies? Fifty years ago, few people attended post-secondary institutions. The numbers have since grown sharply. Just in the last twenty years, the percentage of Canada's population that has attended college or university in some form went from 33 percent to about 50 percent.[7] Earlier, we observed that a society's wealth depends on its level of productivity. The same applies to individuals. An individual's productivity tends to rise with the level of his or her skills and knowledge, both of which are enhanced by more education. Hence, people are increasingly pursuing post-secondary education to improve their chance of earning a higher income. Making education an even better investment in the individual's future is that governments subsidize tuition fees—thanks to the pressure that parents and students are able to exert on democratically elected politicians, the calculation by policy-makers that a better-educated populace improves economic growth and the belief that a commitment to equality demands that everyone be given educational opportunities. An additional factor is the growing gap between the incomes of high-skilled and low-skilled workers. Part of the explanation for this is globalization, which mostly involves the spread of capitalist free trade between nations. Free trade puts the wages of low-skilled jobs under pressure because it allows for imports manufactured by low-paid workers in less developed countries. A low-skilled job that a high-school education would bring just doesn't look all that attractive any more.

Why is Canada multicultural? Except for members of the First Nations, everyone in Canada was either born, or has an ancestor who was born, in a foreign country. This is a country of immigrants. Up until quite recently, however, most of the population originated from Northern Europe, specifically Britain and France. In 1951, the descendants of these two nations represented 79 percent of Canada's inhabitants.[8] The Canadian government continued accepting immigrants in the post–World War II years, doing so principally on the economic calculation that each new person represented an additional source of productivity. Further pressure to increase immigration emerged in the mid-1980s as the birth rate fell well below levels reached during the post–World War II baby boom. But as Northern Europeans now had little economic reason to leave their homelands, immigrants started coming here from less prosperous regions of the world, such as

Southern Europe, Asia, the Middle East, Latin America and Africa. In the past, immigrants were expected to assimilate into the dominant Anglo-Saxon culture. As the recently arrived ethnic groups had become so numerous, however, they were able to convince politicians to let them retain and nurture their traditional cultures. Helping this along was the notion that equality required that no culture be suppressed. The policy of multiculturalism, one of Canada's most endearing and unique features, was born.

What explains the advances made by women? Not so long ago, social institutions and norms mandated that women tend to the household and take care of children, rather than pursue careers outside the home. While the barriers to women's advancement in the workplace haven't been entirely eliminated, they have been lessened. A key factor behind this, assisted by increasing economic prosperity, was a dramatic fall in the infant mortality rate. When this rate was high, women had more children to raise the odds that some would survive. A lower rate meant they had to get pregnant less often to reach their target. This allowed women to delay marriage, attain post-secondary education in the meantime and then enter the work force. Once married with fewer children, women had more freedom to work outside the home to add to their household income, a prospect that their husbands could find agreeable. Indeed, in cases where women could contribute more than men to household income, stay-at-home dads appeared. The growth in physically light employment tasks provided an additional incentive for women to enter the work force. So did the development of appliances like stoves, refrigerators, microwave ovens, dishwashers, washers and dryers, all of which served to reduce the time needed to stay at home to perform household tasks. Improvements in contraceptive technologies, especially the emergence of the birth control pill in the 1960s, also played a decisive role. Unwanted pregnancies apt to interrupt women's careers could now be better avoided. Legal access to abortion, won by an economically empowered feminist movement, ensured that unwanted pregnancies didn't have to result in children. In short, children made women dependent on men for support; once women could better control the incidence and number of children they bore, their freedom increased.[9]

Why are children treated more humanely? In the 19th century, child labour was prevalent in the most economically advanced countries of the time. The right of adults to strike children under their authority was once virtually unquestioned. Child labour has all but disappeared in the industrialized world, and many now challenge the legitimacy of corpo-

ral punishment of children. Indeed, Canada's Supreme Court recently prohibited the striking of children under the age of two and over 12.[10] Child sex abuse, once cloaked in silence, has become a matter of intense, vocal concern. Growing prosperity explains the end of child labour: parents could afford to forego the income their children might contribute to the household and, instead, invest in their children's future by putting them through school.[11] The decline in the birth rate, caused by women's greater opportunities in the workplace (as discussed above), moreover, means that families have gone from a "quantity" strategy in raising their children to a "quality" one.[12] More concern and resources are devoted to each child. Parents become far more sensitive to any abuse that they themselves, or others, might visit upon their children. Nor should we forget how the belief in equality has rendered people more sensitive to the plight of the vulnerable.

Looking Ahead?

Usually, those who advance a model of social change issue predictions. Marx, for example, forecast the overthrow of capitalism and the eventual installation of a communist utopia. More recently, Francis Fukuyama, adopting Hegel's idealist model of social change, declared the end of history.[13] By that, Fukuyama meant the victory of liberal democratic capitalism as the final form of government. But social and political predictions have a sorry track record. Capitalism has flourished despite Marx's prophecy. Fukuyama's take on Hegel has been cast into doubt by the September 11, 2001 terrorist attacks. The safer course is to predict nothing—except, that is, to say that society will continue to change at a dizzying rate, so long as capitalism remains in operation.

Notes

1. These studies are reviewed by Niclas Berggren in "The Benefits of Economic Freedom: A Survey," *The Independent Review* (Fall 2003), 193–211.

2. Karl Marx, "Manifesto of the Communist Party," *The Marx-Engels Reader*, 2nd ed., Robert Tucker ed. (New York: W.W. Norton, 1978), 477.

3. The estimated range is so wide because it depends on how the income and occupational data are interpreted.

4. *Statistics Canada*, "The Daily," May 20, 2004. Available at www.statcan.ca/Daily/English/040520/d040520b.html [Accessed May 25, 2004.] It should be noted, however, that the government's tax and spending policies significantly reduce this disparity. In 2002, after factoring in taxes and transfers, the top 20 percent of families ends up keeping $5.20 for every $1 received by the bottom 20 percent of families. This shows how government intervention in the economy redistributes income from the rich to the poor.

5. Charles Wheelan, *Naked Economics* (New York: W.W. Norton, 2003), 206.

6. Joseph Schumpeter, *Capitalism, Socialism, and Democracy* (New York: Harper Torchbooks, 1975), 83.

7. Data for 1981 and 2001, respectively, obtained from Statistics Canada. Available at www.statcan.ca/english/Pgdb/educ45.htm [Accessed February 15, 2004.]

8. "Ethnic Composition of Canada's Population." Available at www.cric.ca/en_html/opinion/opv2n23.html#facts

9. This account is based on the economic theory of sex proposed by Richard Posner in *Sex and Reason* (Cambridge, Mass: Harvard University Press, 1992), especially 173–180.

10. *Canadian Foundation for Children, Youth and the Law v. Canada* (Attorney General) [2004] SCC 4. Available at www.lexum.umontreal.ca/csc-scc/en/rec/html/2004scc004.wpd.html

11. See Eric V. Edmonds, "Does Child Labour Decline with Improving Economic Status?" *National Bureau of Economic Research Working Paper No. 10134* (December 2003). Available at www.nber.org/papers/w10134. This paper is cited from "Sickness or Symptom?" in *The Economist*, February 7, 2004, 73.

12. Wheelan, 111.

13. Francis Fukuyama, *The End of History and the Last Man* (New York: Free Press, 1992).

Exploring the Managed Heart

Arlie Russell Hochschild

The one area of her occupational life in which she might be "free to act," the area of her own personality, must now also be managed, must become the alert yet obsequious instrument by which goods are distributed.

C. Wright Mills, *White Collar*, p. 184

In a section in *Das Kapital* entitled "The Working Day," Karl Marx examines depositions submitted in 1863 to the Children's Employment Commission in England. One deposition was given by the mother of a child laborer in a wallpaper factory: "When he was seven years old I used to carry him [to work] on my back to and fro through the snow, and he used to work 16 hours a day.... I have often knelt down to feed him, as he stood by the machine, for he could not leave it or stop." Fed meals as he worked, as a steam engine is fed coal and water, this child was "an instrument of labor."[1] Marx questioned how many hours a day it was fair to use a human being as an instrument, and how much pay for being an instrument was fair, considering the profits that factory owners made. But he was also concerned with something he thought more fundamental: the human cost of becoming an "instrument of labor" at all.

On another continent 117 years later, a twenty-year-old flight attendant trainee sat with 122 others listening to a pilot speak in the auditorium of the Delta Airlines Stewardess Training Center. Even by modern American standards, and certainly by standards for women's work, she had landed an excellent job.[2] The 1980 pay scale began at $850 a month for the first six months and would increase within seven years to about $20,000 a year. Health and accident insurance is provided, and the hours are good.

The young trainee sitting next to me wrote on her notepad, "Important to smile. Don't forget smile." The admonition came from the speaker in the front of the room, a crew-cut pilot in his early fifties, speaking in a Southern drawl: "Now girls, I want you to go out there and really *smile*. Your smile is your biggest *asset*. I want you to go out there and use it. Smile. *Really* smile. Really *lay it on*."

The pilot spoke of the smile as the *flight attendant's* asset. But as novices like the one next to me move through training, the value of a personal smile is groomed to reflect the company's disposition—its confidence that its planes will not crash, its reassurance that departures and arrivals will be on time, its welcome and its invitation to return. Trainers take it as their job to attach to the trainee's smile an attitude, a viewpoint, a rhythm of feeling that is, as they often say, "professional." This deeper extension of the professional smile is not always easy to retract at the end of the workday, as one worker in her first year at World Airways noted: "Sometimes I come off a long trip in a state of utter exhaustion, but I find I can't relax. I giggle a lot, I chatter, I call friends. It's as if I can't release myself from an artificially created elation that kept me 'up' on the trip. I hope to be able to come down from it better as I get better at the job."

As the PSA jingle says, "Our smiles are not just painted on." Our flight attendants' smiles, the company emphasizes, will be more human than the phony smiles you're resigned to seeing on people who are paid to smile. There is a smile-like strip of paint on the nose of each PSA plane. Indeed, the plane and the flight attendant advertise each other. The radio advertisement goes on to promise not just smiles and service but a travel experience of real happiness and calm. Seen in one way, this is no more than delivering a service. Seen in another, it estranges workers from their own smiles and convinces customers that on-the-job behavior is calculated. Now that advertisements, training, notions of professionalism, and dollar bills have intervened between the smiler and the smiled upon, it takes an extra effort to imagine that spontaneous warmth can exist in uniform—because companies now advertise spontaneous warmth, too.

At first glance, it might seem that the circumstances of the nineteenth-century factory child and the twentieth-century flight attendant could not be more different. To the boy's mother, to Marx, to the members of the Children's Employment Commission, perhaps to the manager of the wallpaper factory, and almost certainly to the contemporary reader, the boy was a victim, even a symbol, of the brutalizing conditions of his time. We might imagine that he had an emotional half-life, conscious of little more than fatigue, hunger, and boredom. On the other hand, the flight attendant enjoys the upper-class freedom to travel, and she participates in the glamour she creates for others. She is the envy of clerks in duller, less well-paid jobs.

But a close examination of the differences between the two can lead us to some unexpected common ground. On the surface there is a difference in how we know what labor actually produces. How could the worker in the wallpaper factory tell when his job was done? Count the rolls of wallpaper; a good has been produced. How can the flight attendant tell when her job is done? A service has been produced; the customer seems content. In the case of the flight attendant, the *emotional style of offering the service is part of the service itself*, in a way that loving or hating wallpaper is not a part of producing wallpaper. Seeming to "love the job" becomes part of the job; and actually trying to love it, and to enjoy the customers, helps the worker in this effort.

In processing people, the product is a state of mind. Like firms in other industries, airline companies are ranked according to the quality of service their personnel offer. Egon Ronay's yearly *Lucas Guide* offers such a ranking; besides being sold in airports and drugstores and reported in newspapers, it is cited in management memoranda and passed down to those who train and supervise flight attendants. Because it influences consumers, airline companies use it in setting their criteria for successful job performance by a flight attendant. In 1980 the *Lucas Guide* ranked Delta Airlines first in service out of fourteen airlines that fly regularly between the United States and both Canada and the British Isles. Its report on Delta included passages like this:

> [Drinks were served] not only with a smile but with concerned enquiry such as, "Anything else I can get you, madam?" The atmosphere was that of a civilized party—with the passengers, in response, behaving like civilized guests. . . . Once or twice our inspectors tested stewardesses by being deliberately exacting, but they were never roused, and at the end of the flight they lined up to say farewell with undiminished brightness. . . .

> [Passengers are] quick to detect strained or forced smiles, and they come aboard wanting to *enjoy* the flight. One of us looked forward to his next trip on Delta "because it's fun." Surely that is how passengers ought to feel.[3]

The work done by the boy in the wallpaper factory called for a coordination of mind and arm, mind and finger, and mind and shoulder. We refer to it simply as physical labor. The flight attendant does physical labor when she pushes heavy meal carts through the aisles, and she does mental work when she prepares for and actually organizes emergency landings and evacuations. But in the course of doing this physical and mental labor, she is also doing something more, something I define as *emotional labor*.[4] This labor requires one to induce or suppress feeling in order to sustain the outward countenance that produces the proper state of mind in others—in this case, the sense of being cared for in a convivial and safe place. This kind of labor calls for a coordination of mind and feeling, and it sometimes draws on a source of self that we honor as deep and integral to our individuality.

Beneath the difference between physical and emotional labor there lies a similarity in the possible cost of doing the work: the worker can become estranged or alienated from an aspect of self—either the body or the margins of the soul—that is *used* to do the work. The factory boy's arm functioned like a piece of machinery used to produce wallpaper. His employer, regarding that arm as an instrument, claimed control over its speed and motions. In this situation, what was the relation between the boy's arm and his mind? Was his arm in any meaningful sense his *own*?[5]

This is an old issue, but as the comparison with airline attendants suggests, it is still very much alive. If we can become alienated from goods in a goods-producing society, we can become alienated from service in a service-producing society. This is what C. Wright Mills, one of our keenest social observers, meant when he wrote in 1956, "We need to characterize American society of the mid-twentieth century in more psychological terms, for now the problems that concern us most border on the psychiatric."[6]

When she came off the job, what relation had the flight attendant to the "artificial elation" she had induced on the job? In what sense was it her *own* elation on the job? The company lays claim not simply to her physical motions—how she handles food trays—but to her emotional actions and the way they show in the ease of a smile. The workers I talked to often spoke of their smiles as being *on* them but not *of* them. They were seen as an extension of the make-up, the uniform, the recorded music, the soothing pastel colors of the airplane decor, and the daytime drinks, which taken together orchestrate the mood of the passengers. The final commodity is not a certain number of smiles to be counted like rolls of wallpaper. For the flight attendant, the smiles are a *part of her work*, a part that requires her to coordinate self and feeling so that the work seems to be effortless. To show that the enjoyment takes effort is to do the job poorly. Similarly, part of the job is to disguise fatigue and irritation, for otherwise the labor would show in an unseemly way, and the product—passenger contentment—would be damaged.[7] Because it is easier to disguise fatigue and irritation if they can be banished altogether, at least for brief periods, this feat calls for emotional labor.

The reason for comparing these dissimilar jobs is that the modern assembly-line worker has for some time been an outmoded symbol of modern industrial labor; fewer than 6 percent of workers now work on assembly lines. Another kind of labor has now come into symbolic prominence—the voice-to-voice or face-to-face delivery of service—and the flight attendant is an appropriate model for it. There have always been public-service jobs, of course; what is new is that they are now socially engineered and thoroughly organized from the top. Though the flight attendant's job is no worse and in many ways better than other service jobs, it makes the worker more vulnerable to the social engineering of her emotional labor and reduces her control over the labor. Her problems, therefore, may be a sign of what is to come in other such jobs.

Emotional labor is potentially good. No customer wants to deal with a surly waitress, a crabby bank clerk, or a flight attendant who avoids eye contact in order to avoid getting a request. Lapses in courtesy by those paid to be courteous are very real and fairly common. What they show us is how fragile public civility really is. We are brought back to the question of what the social carpet actually consists of and what it requires of those who are supposed to keep it beautiful. The laggards and sluff-offs of emotional labor return us to the basic questions. What is emotional labor? What do we do when we manage emotion? What, in fact, is emotion? What are the costs and benefits of managing emotion, in private life and at work?

The Private and Public Faces of an Emotional System

Our search for answers to these questions leads to three separate but equally relevant discourses: one concerning labor, one concerning display, and one concerning emotion.

Those who discuss labor often comment that nowadays most jobs call for a capacity to deal with people rather than with things, for more interpersonal skills and fewer mechanical skills. In *The Coming of Post-Industrial Society* (1973), Daniel Bell argues that the growth of the service sector means that "communication" and "encounter"—"the response of ego to alter and back"—is the central work relationship today.[8] As he puts it, "The fact that individuals now talk to other individuals, rather than interact with a machine, is the fundamental fact about work in the post-industrial society." Critics of labor studies, such as Harry Braverman in *Labor and Monopoly Capital* (1974), point out a continual subdivision of work in many branches of the economy. Complex tasks in which a craftsman used to take pride are divided into simpler, more repetitive segments, each more boring and less well paid than the original job. Work is deskilled and the worker belittled. But celebrants and critics alike have not inspected at close hand or with a social-psychological eye what it is that "people jobs" *actually require* of workers. They have not inquired into the actual nature of this labor. Some do not know exactly what, in the case of emotional labor, becomes deskilled.

A second discourse, closer to the person and more remote from the overall organization of work, concerns the display of feeling. The works of Erving Goffman introduce us to the many minor traffic rules of face-to-face interaction, as they emerge at a card game, in an elevator, on the street, or at the dining table of an insane asylum. He prevents us from dismissing the small as trivial by showing how small rules, transgressions, and punishments add up to form the longer strips of experience we call "work." At the same time, it is hard to use Goffman's focus to explain why companies train flight attendants in smiling, or how emotional tone is supervised, or what profit is ultimately tied to emotional labor. It is hard, in other words, to draw on this discourse alone and see how "display work" fits into the larger scheme of things.

The third discourse takes place in a quiet side street of American social science; it deals with the timeless issues of what an emotion is and how we can manage it. . . .

To uncover the heart of emotional labor, to understand what it takes to do it and what it does to people, I have drawn on elements from all three discourses. Certain events in economic history cannot be fully understood unless we pay attention to the filigreed patterns of feeling and their management because the details of these patterns are an important part of what many men and women do for a living.

Because such different traditions are joined here, my inquiry will have a different relevance for different readers. Perhaps it will be most relevant for those who do the work it describes—the flight attendants. But most of us have jobs that require some handling of other people's feelings and our own, and in this sense we are all partly flight attendants. The secretary who creates a cheerful office that announces her company as "friendly and dependable" and her boss as "up-and-coming," the waitress or waiter who creates an "atmosphere of pleasant dining," the tour guide or hotel receptionist who makes us feel welcome, the social worker whose look of solicitous concern makes the client feel cared for, the salesman who creates the sense of a "hot commodity," the bill collector who inspires fear, the funeral parlor director who makes the bereaved feel understood, the minister who creates a sense of protective outreach but even-handed warmth—all of them must confront in some way or another the requirements of *emotional labor*.

Emotional labor does not observe conventional distinctions between types of jobs. By my estimate, roughly one-third of American workers today have jobs that subject them to substantial demands for emotional labor. Moreover, of all *women* working, roughly one-half have jobs that call for emotional labor. . . . Thus this inquiry has special relevance for women, and it probably also describes more of their experience. As traditionally more accomplished managers of feeling in private life, women more than men have put emotional labor on the market, and they know more about its personal costs.

This inquiry might at first seem relevant only to workers living under capitalism, but the engineering of a managed heart is not unknown to socialism; the enthusiastic "hero of labor" bears the emotional standard for the socialist state as much as the Flight Attendant of the Year does for the capitalist airline industry. Any functioning society makes effective use of its members' emotional labor. We do not think twice about the use of feeling in the theater, or in psychotherapy, or in forms of group life that we admire. It is when we come to speak of the *exploitation* of the bottom by the top in any society that we become morally concerned. In any system, exploitation depends on the actual distribution of many kinds of profits—money, authority, status, honor, well-being. It is not emotional labor itself, therefore, but the underlying system of recompense that raises the question of what the cost of it is.

Sources and Method

In describing the private and public face of an *emotional system*, and showing how it works, I have drawn on empirical samples from various distinct parts of it. I could have sampled more parts of it—by studying nurses or lawyers or salespeople, for example—as I hope very much someone will do. Or I could have gone much deeper into the material at hand. But for this project, the wide-sample approach seemed to make the most sense. For before the more usual sort of research can begin, we must confront the prior task of thinking about something that has been the object of surprisingly little previous thought. Given this early stage of inquiry, it seems to me that the most promising way to use materials is to point, to illustrate, and to comment, and that is what I have tried to do.

Illustrations for the ideas found in this book come mainly from three sources. The first was an inquiry into the question of how people of different sexes and social classes experience emotion and manage it. I gave out questionnaires to 261 students in two classes at the University of California, Berkeley, in 1974.[9] A good number of my illustrations . . .

are drawn from their responses to two requests: "Describe a real situation that was important to you in which you experienced a deep emotion," and "Describe as fully and concretely as possible a real situation that was important to you in which you either changed the situation to fit your feelings or changed your feelings to fit the situation." With two research assistants I analyzed the responses for awareness of emotion work.[10] Like a fisherman, I cast out these requests to see what I would find, but I had an eye out for a certain kind of catch—in this case, indications of *will* in how people talked about feelings. My respondents often spoke of acts *upon* feeling: of *trying* to fall in love or *putting a damper on* love, of *trying to feel* grateful, of *trying not* to feel depressed, of *checking* their anger, of *letting* themselves feel sad. In short, they spoke of managed feelings. The concept of emotion work . . . grew out of this initial project.

To manage private loves and hates is to participate in an intricate private emotional system. When elements of that system are taken into the marketplace and sold as human labor, they become stretched into standardized social forms. In these forms, a person's contribution of feeling is thinner, less freighted with consequence; but at the same time it is seen as coming less *from* the self and being less directed *to* the other. For that reason it is more susceptible to estrangement.

I followed emotion work into the job market via two routes. First I entered the world of the flight attendant. As a point of entry, I chose Delta Airlines for several reasons: it puts a higher premium on service than other airlines do; its in-flight training program is perhaps the best in the industry; its service has been ranked very high; and it is headquartered in the South and has no union for flight attendants. For all these reasons, Delta's company demands are higher and its worker demands lower than in other companies. Thus Delta exaggerates the demands put on all flight attendants. It gives sharper point to the general case about emotion work in public life.

The reason for exaggerating the case is to show just how far demands for emotional labor can go. Having done that, we may develop a benchmark for measuring other job demands. Even within the airline industry, emotional labor is much less evident now than it was in the mid-1950s when airplanes were smaller, the clientele more exclusive, and the ratio of flight attendants to passengers smaller. My point is that when emotional labor is put into the public marketplace, it behaves like a commodity: the demand for it waxes and wanes depending upon the competition within the industry. By focusing on a Southern nonunion company with the best training school, we can approximate a phase of high demand for a "commodity"—the trained management of feeling.

I gathered information at Delta in various ways. First, I watched. The head of the Delta Training Center in Atlanta, a gentle woman in her fifties, allowed me to attend classes there. I watched recruits learning passenger handling and meal service in the mock cabin. I got to know the trainers, who patiently explained their work to me. They were generous with their time, on duty and off; one trainer invited me home to dinner, and several repeatedly invited me to lunch. Over countless other breakfasts, lunches, and dinners, and in the airport bus, I talked with students doing Initial Training and with experienced flight attendants attending the mandatory Recurrent Training sessions.

I interviewed twenty Delta officials, from the executive vice-president through managers in personnel, recruitment, training, sales, and billing. I held a group interview with seven supervisors. I interviewed four advertising agents employed by the firm commissioned to promote Delta and its flight attendants, and I looked through microfilms of thirty years of Delta advertising. Finally, I also interviewed the two public relations officials who were in charge of "handling" me.

To supplement the Delta study, I observed the recruiting of flight attendants by Pan American Airways at its San Francisco base. (Delta politely declined my request to observe recruiting procedures.) I observed both group and individual interviews with job applicants, and I sat in as recruiters discussed candidates. I also conducted open-ended interviews lasting three to five hours each with thirty flight attendants in the San Francisco Bay Area; twenty-five were women and five were men. The airlines they worked for included Pan American, TWA, World Airways, United, American, and Delta. The average age was thirty-five, and 40 percent were married. One was in her first year on the job, and one was in his twenty-second. They averaged eleven years of experience.[11]

The choice to study flight attendants was also good from the point of view of understanding the relation of gender to jobs . . . for three reasons. First, it is not an elite occupation. We have many fine studies of professional women—doctors, lawyers, and academicians—but surprisingly few studies of secretaries and waitresses and factory workers. The flight attendant falls roughly between these two categories. Second, it is difficult to find jobs that allow us to compare the experience of men and women doing "the same" work. To study secretaries is to study almost only women; to study pilots is to study almost only men. Male and female doctors and lawyers tend to have different specialties and different clienteles. The male flight attendant, however, does the same work in the same place as the female flight attendant so that any differences in work experience are more likely due to gender. Third, in many studies, the problems of women as workers are confounded with the problems of being in a minority in a given occupation. In this work at least, the shoe is on the other foot: males comprise only 15 percent of flight attendants. They are the minority; and although being part of a minority usually works against the individual, this does not appear to be true in the case of male flight attendants.

I interviewed certain people with special angles of vision on flight attending, such as five union officials who were trying to persuade a reluctant local membership to accept the contract they had just proposed to American Airlines, and a sex therapist who in her ten years of practice had seen some fifty flight attendants as clients. I observed an assertiveness training course for flight attendants in which encounters with "problem" passengers were enacted. I might also mention stray conversations (with a Clipper Club receptionist at Pan American and with two pilots readying their plane for Hong Kong), a guided tour through a Pan Am plane, and a two-hour visit in the galley of a Delta plane where a flight attendant in blue jeans unloaded dirty trays and talked of escaping to law school.

I followed emotion work into the job market via another route as well. Whereas flight attendants do emotion work to enhance the status of the customer and entice further sales by their friendliness, there is another side of the corporate show, represented by the bill collectors who sometimes deliberately deflate the status of the customer with distrust and anger. As a miniproject, I interviewed five bill collectors, starting with the head of the Delta billing department, a man whose office overlooked nearly an acre of women sorting billing forms.

The flight attendant and the bill collector, the toe and the heel of capitalism, illustrate two extremes of occupational demand on feeling. I have drawn most of my illustrations from the world of the flight attendants. I did not make a full-scale study of the bill collectors, but my interviews with them do suggest that the same principles of emotional labor apply to very different jobs and very different feelings.

From these three pools of data, then, I have drawn three samplings of an emotional system. The first, taken from private accounts of students, reveals the private face of the emotion system. The second, drawn from the world of flight attendants, tells of its public front. The third, drawn from the world of bill collectors, tells of its public back. This . . . is not intended as an empirical report, or not simply as that. It provides what would have to *underlie* such a report—a set of illustrated ideas about how society uses feeling. Its purpose is to point in a certain direction and to offer the reader a fresh angle of vision. With the exception of illustrations from published prose or fiction (which are cited in the notes), all the quotations I offer are from real people.

Private and Commercial Uses of Feeling

A nineteenth-century child working in a brutalizing English wallpaper factory and a well-paid twentieth-century American flight attendant have something in common: in order to survive in their jobs, they must mentally detach themselves—the factory worker from his own body and physical labor, and the flight attendant from her own feelings and emotional labor. Marx and many others have told us the factory workers' story. I am interested in telling the flight attendant's story in order to promote a fuller appreciation of the costs of what she does. And I want to base this appreciation on a prior demonstration of what can happen to any of us when we become estranged from our feelings and the management of them.

We feel. But what is a feeling? I would define feeling, like emotion, as a sense, like the sense of hearing or sight. In a general way, we experience it when bodily sensations are joined with what we see or imagine.[12] Like the sense of hearing, emotion communicates information. It has, as Freud said of anxiety, a "signal function." From feeling we discover our own viewpoint on the world.

We often say that we *try* to feel. But how can we do this? Feelings, I suggest, are not stored "inside" us, and they are not independent of acts of management. Both the act of "getting in touch with" feeling and the act of "trying to" feel may become part of the process that makes the thing we get in touch with, or the thing we manage, *into* a feeling or emotion. In managing feeling, we contribute to the creation of it.

If this is so, what we think of as intrinsic to feeling or emotion may have always been shaped to social form and put to civic use. Consider what happens when young men roused to anger go willingly to war, or when followers rally enthusiastically around their king, or mullah, or football team. Private social life may always have called for the management of feeling. The party guest summons up a gaiety owed to the host, the mourner summons up a proper sadness for a funeral. Each offers up feeling as a momentary contribution to the collective good. . . .

What gives social pattern to our acts of emotion management? I believe that when we try to feel, we apply latent feeling rules. . . . We say, "I shouldn't feel so angry at what she did," or "given our agreement, I have no right to feel jealous." Acts of emotion management are not simply private acts; they are used in exchanges under the guidance of feeling rules. Feeling rules are standards used in emotional conversation to determine what is rightly owed and owing in the currency of feeling. Through them, we tell what is "due" in each relation, each role. We pay tribute to each other in the currency of the managing act. In interaction we pay, overpay, underpay, play with paying, acknowledge our dues, pretend to pay, or acknowledge what is emotionally due another person. In these ways . . . we make our try at sincere civility.

Because the distribution of power and authority is unequal in some of the relations of private life, the managing acts can also be unequal. The myriad momentary acts of management compose part of what we summarize in the terms *relation* and *role*. Like the tiny dots of a Seurat painting, the microacts of emotion management compose, through repetition and change over time, a movement of form. Some forms express inequality, others equality.

Now what happens when the managing of emotion comes to be sold as labor? What happens when feeling rules, like rules of behavioral display, are established not through private negotiation but by company manuals? What happens when social exchanges are not, as they are in private life, subject to change or termination but ritually sealed and almost inescapable?

What happens when the emotional display that one person owes another reflects a certain inherent inequality? The airline passenger may choose not to smile, but the flight attendant is obliged not only to smile but to try to work up some warmth behind it. What happens, in other words, when there is a *transmutation* of the private ways we use feeling?

One sometimes needs a grand word to point out a coherent pattern between occurrences that would otherwise seem totally unconnected. My word is "transmutation." When I speak of the transmutation of an emotional system, I mean to point out a link between a private act, such as attempting to enjoy a party, and a public act, such as summoning up good feeling for a customer. I mean to expose the relation between the private act of trying to dampen liking for a person—which overcommitted lovers sometimes attempt—and the public act of a bill collector who suppresses empathy for a debtor. By the grand phrase "transmutation of an emotional system" I mean to convey what it is that we do privately, often unconsciously, to feelings that nowadays often fall under the sway of large organizations, social engineering, and the profit motive.

Trying to feel what one wants, expects, or thinks one ought to feel is probably no newer than emotion itself. Conforming to or deviating from feeling rules is also hardly new. In organized society, rules have probably never been applied only to observable behavior. "Crimes of the heart" have long been recognized because proscriptions have long guarded the "preactions" of the heart; the Bible says not to covet your neighbor's wife, not simply to avoid acting on that feeling. What is new in our time is an increasingly prevalent *instrumental stance* toward our native capacity to play, wittingly and actively, upon a range of feelings for a private purpose and the way in which that stance is engineered and administered by large organizations.

This transmutation of the private use of feeling affects the two sexes and the various social classes in distinctly different ways. . . . As a matter of tradition, emotion management has been better understood and more often used by women as one of the offerings they trade for economic support. Especially among dependent women of the middle and upper classes, women have the job (or think they ought to) of creating the emotional tone of social encounters: expressing joy at the Christmas presents others open, creating the sense of surprise at birthdays, or displaying alarm at the mouse in the kitchen. Gender is not the only determinant of skill in such managed expression and in the emotion work needed to do it well. But men who do this work well have slightly less in common with other men than women who do it well have with other women. When the "womanly" art of living up to *private* emotional conventions goes public, it attaches itself to a different profit-and-loss statement.

Similarly, emotional labor affects the various social classes differently. If it is women, members of the less advantaged gender, who specialize in emotional labor, it is the middle and upper reaches of the class system that seem to call most for it. And parents who do emotional labor on the job will convey the importance of emotion management to their children and will prepare them to learn the skills they will probably need for the jobs they will probably get.

In general, lower-class and working-class people tend to work more with things, and middle-class and upper-class people tend to work more with people. More working women than men deal with people as a job. Thus, there are both gender patterns and class patterns to the civic and commercial use of human feeling. That is the social point.

But there is a personal point, too. There is a cost to emotion work: it affects the degree to which we listen to feeling and sometimes our very capacity to feel. Managing feeling is an art fundamental to civilized living, and I assume that in broad terms the cost is usually worth the fundamental benefit. Freud, in *Civilization and Its Discontents*, argued analogously about the sexual instinct: enjoyable as that instinct is, we are wise in the long run to give up some gratification of it. But when the transmutation of the private use of feeling is successfully accomplished—when we succeed in lending our feelings to the organizational engineers of worker-customer relations—we may pay a cost in how we hear our feelings and a cost in what, for better or worse, they tell us about ourselves. When a speed-up of the human assembly line makes "genuine" personal service harder to deliver, the worker may withdraw emotional labor and offer instead a thin crust of display. Then the cost shifts: the penalty becomes a sense of being phony or insincere. In short, when the transmutation works, the worker risks losing the signal function of feeling. When it does not work, the risk is losing the signal function of display.

Certain social conditions have increased the cost of feeling management. One is an overall unpredictability about our social world. Ordinary people nowadays move through many social worlds and get the gist of dozens of social roles. Compare this with the life of the fourteenth-century baker's apprentice described in Peter Laslett's *The World We Have Lost* (1968): it is a life that begins and ends in one locale, in one occupation, in one household, within one world view, and according to one set of rules.[13] It has become much less common that given circumstances seem to dictate the proper interpretation of them or that they indicate in a plainly visible way what feeling is owed to whom, and when, and how. As a result, we moderns spend more mental time on the question "What, in this situation, should I be feeling?" Oddly enough, a second condition more appropriate to Laslett's baker's apprentice has survived into more modern and fluid times. We still, it seems, ask of ourselves, "Who am I?" as if the question permitted a single neat answer. We still search for a solid, predictable core of self even though the conditions for the existence of such a self have long since vanished.

In the face of these two conditions, people turn to feelings in order to locate themselves or at least to see what their own reactions are to a given event. That is, in the absence of unquestioned external guidelines, the signal function of emotion becomes more important, and the commercial distortion of the managed heart becomes all the more important as a human cost.

We may well be seeing a response to all this in the rising approval of the unmanaged heart, the greater virtue now attached to what is "natural" or spontaneous. Ironically, the person like Rousseau's Noble Savage, who only smiles "naturally," without ulterior purpose, is a poor prospect for the job of waiter, hotel manager, or flight attendant. The high regard for "natural feeling," then, may coincide with the culturally imposed need to develop the precise opposite—an instrumental stance toward feeling. We treat spontaneous feeling, for this reason, as if it were scarce and precious; we raise it up as a virtue. It may not be too much to suggest that we are witnessing a call for the conservation of "inner resources," a call to save another wilderness from corporate use and keep it "forever wild."

With the growing celebration of spontaneity have come the robot jokes. Robot humor plays with the tension between being human—that is to say, having feeling—and being a cog in a socioeconomic machine. The charm of the little robot R2–D2, in the film *Star Wars*, is that he seems so human. Films like this bring us the familiar in reverse: every day, outside the movie house, we see human beings whose show of feeling has a robot quality. The ambiguities are funny now.

Both the growing celebration of spontaneity and the jokes we tell about being robots suggest that in the realm of feeling, Orwell's 1984 came in disguise several years ago, leaving behind a laugh and perhaps the idea of a private way out.

Notes

1   Marx, *Capital* (1977), pp. 356–357, 358.

2   For stylistic convenience, I shall use the pronoun "she" when referring to a flight attendant, except when a specific male flight attendant is being discussed. Otherwise I shall try to avoid verbally excluding either gender.

3   *Lucas Guide* 1980, pp. 66, 76. Fourteen aspects of air travel at the stages of departure, arrival, and the flight itself are ranked. Each aspect is given one of sixteen differently weighted marks. For example, "The friendliness or efficiency of the staff is more important than the quality of the pilot's flight announcement or the selection of newspapers and magazines offered."

[4] I use the term *emotional labor* to mean the management of feeling to create a publicly observable facial and bodily display; emotional labor is sold for a wage and therefore has *exchange value*. I use the synonymous terms *emotion work* or *emotion management* to refer to these same acts done in a private context where they have *use value*.

[5] Marx, in his *Economic and Philosophic Manuscripts* (Tucker 1972), may have provided the last really basic idea on alienation. Among the recent useful works on the subject are Blauner (1964), Etzioni (1968), Kohn (1976), and Seeman (1967).

[6] Mills (1956), p. xx.

[7] Like a commodity, service that calls for emotional labor is subject to the laws of supply and demand. Recently the demand for this labor has increased and the supply of it drastically decreased. The airline industry speed-up since the 1970s has been followed by a worker slow-down. The slowdown reveals how much emotional labor the job required all along. It suggests what costs even happy workers under normal conditions pay for this labor without a name. The speed-up has sharpened the ambivalence many workers feel about how much of oneself to give over to the role and how much of oneself to protect from it.

[8] Jobs that Bell includes in the service sector are those in transportation and utilities, distribution and trade, finance and insurance, professional and business services, jobs deriving from demands for leisure activities (recreation and travel), and jobs that deal with communal services (health, education, and government). Only some of these service-sector jobs call for much emotion management.

[9] The purpose of this analysis was to explore, in the course of answering more general questions about feeling, the question of who showed an awareness of emotion work, how much, and in what context. Using this coding, we found that 32 percent of females and 18 percent of males spontaneously mentioned emotion management in the course of their descriptions. Although our indicators for social class were poor (father's occupation only), more middle-class than working-class respondents mentioned emotion work; the sex difference remained when class was controlled.

[10] Initially, I took responses to these questions to indicate self-portraits of coping styles. The responses fell into four types. One group (the instrumentalists) portrayed themselves as changing the world, not themselves. They spoke of feelings as something that had been acted upon, as an assumed basis for action. They did not describe feelings as crumbling in the face of situational obstacles or as something to be "worked on" or managed. The second group (the accommodators) portrayed themselves as changing an attitude or behaviour, though not an underlying feeling or orientation. They spoke of the world as immutable, a place requiring certain superficial alterations of self. The accommodators spoke of not following their "true" feelings which remained "true" or unchanged. In contrast, the third group (the adapters) melted in the face of a demanding world. They spoke of the self as fluid and malleable and of the world as correspondingly rigid. Their feelings were not experienced as a solid basis for action; they indicated that feelings change not by effort but naturally, as a matter of course. The fourth type, which I later labeled the "emotion workers," took an active stance toward feeling. They said, "I psyched myself up," "I suppressed my anger," "I made myself have a good time." They adapted, but in an active rather than a passive way.

[11] Although this exploratory study was not designed to be representative, the respondents were not far removed from the general profile of the 5,075 flight attendants employed by Pan American: the average age of the respondents was 32.7, 34 percent were married, and their average seniority was five years. Roughly a quarter of my interviewees had working-class fathers, a quarter had lower-middle-class fathers, and half had fathers with roughly upper-middle-class jobs. The mothers of half were housewives and the mothers of the other half were clerical or service workers; none had professional mothers. The average annual salary of the flight attendants was $16,250.

[12] In general the term *feeling* connotes fewer or milder physical sensations—flushing, perspiring, trembling—than the term *emotion* does. Feeling, in this sense, is a milder emotion. For the purposes of this inquiry, the two terms are interchangeable....

[13] Laslett (1968); Stone (1965); Swidler (1979).

Rights, Intimacy, and Family Life

Michael Ignatieff

During the past forty years, the rights revolution has penetrated the most intimate spheres of private life. As rights talk moved from the public sphere to the family dinner table and then into the bedroom, it overturned sex roles, the family division of labour, and sexual identity itself. The rights revolution has become a sexual revolution, and in the process, it has transformed all our most important social relationships: between men and women, between parents and children, and between heterosexuals and homosexuals.

All liberal democracies have gone through the same social transformation. The only distinctive aspect of the Canadian pattern has been the speed with which courts and legislatures have responded to demands for children's rights, easier divorce, abortion rights, the equation of marriage and co-habitation, and the full entrenchment of rights to sexual difference. The fact that these rights were conceded speedily does not mean that they were conceded without a struggle, however. Nor does it mean that the struggle is over. Women still do not earn equal pay for equal work and the burdens of unpaid child care still fall disproportionately upon them. Homosexuals still do not enjoy the same rights to marry, to adopt, or to inherit pensions and other assets from their spouses.[1] Yet even though the rights revolution in private life remains unfinished, it is hard to imagine that it will not run its full course. The reason is simply that the rights revolution appeals to an idea of equality and against this idea there is no remaining court of appeal.

The demand for equal rights in intimate life is also a demand for recognition. I've said a lot about rights and very little about recognition. It's time to define the term. Recognition is a very Canadian idea, since it was a Canadian philosopher, Charles Taylor, who first put it into common parlance among political philosophers.[2] To recognize someone in common speech is to put a name to a face, to single him or her out from a crowd. To be recognized is to emerge from anonymity, to be seen and acknowledged for what you are. When you are recognized, you cease to be a nobody and you become a somebody in someone else's eyes. Groups are fighting for a similar kind of recognition. They want the majority to recognize them, to see them anew, to acknowledge that they are equal, not only in law, but also in moral consideration. Equality of rights is the precondition for recognition, but it is not sufficient to ensure it. When individuals and groups seek recognition, they want their equality recognized, but they want their differences acknowledged as well. Beyond legal equality, groups seek acknowledgment of the value of their culture, heritage, and distinctive point of view. Struggles for recognition typically require a group of people to recognize themselves first, to overcome their own shame or lack of self-worth and then project an image of themselves as they wish to be seen by the watching world. Once this process occurs, the struggle turns into a demand that the watching world change its view of the group, engage with its own clichéd or stereotyped views and reach out to its members both as equals and as people whose differences from the mainstream are to be acknowledged and welcomed.

The whole difficulty about recognition turns on the question of whether it means acquiescence, acceptance, or approval.[3] When a majority grants a minority rights, is it required to acquiesce to, accept, or actively approve the practices of this group? Certainly gay groups, for example, are asking not just for toleration, but for approval. And approval seems to follow from the idea of equality. But does equality of rights necessarily require equality of approval? The majority has conceded equality of rights to homosexuals, but this seems not to imply approval, merely reluctant tolerance.

In the era of the rights revolution, demands for equal rights have also become demands for approval. Indeed, it might even be claimed that anything less than full approval denies the excluded individual (or group) recognition of his or her status as an equal. But there is a problem here—and it is colloquially called political correctness. One fundamental critique of the rights revolution is that it engenders a coercive culture of ritualized, insincere approval. When every excluded group is demanding both equal rights and recognition, the majority can feel that it is being compelled to accord moral approval to practices that, at best, it only tolerates. So political correctness becomes a code word for a new form of moral tyranny: the tyranny of the minority over the majority. You can't speak of sexual promiscuity among gay people, lest you appear to be demeaning gays in general. You can't speak against affirmative-action programs that favour women, lest you seem to be denying women full recognition and respect. And so on.

Whether these constraints on public speech are actually a form of tyranny is another matter. Anyone with a memory knows that coarse, offensive, and demeaning remarks about women and gays were commonplace in the male culture of recent times. Creating a culture where groups are freed from the dismal drizzle of these remarks cannot be regarded as a serious constraint on the free speech of those attached to these stereotypes. So on balance, the idea that the rights revolution ends in coercive political correctness seems obviously misconceived. Yet closing down a culture of casual and ill-considered abuse is quite different from moving a culture towards full-hearted approval of same-sex activity and positive discrimination in favour of women. Rights equality changes moral culture because groups demand recognition. As they do so, they force sexual majorities beyond toleration towards acceptance and approval. So long as this process is negotiated, so long as it is not presented as a unilateral demand for surrender, rights equality can be followed successfully by full recognition. But if the majority feels coerced into according approval, rather than just toleration, the result is likely to be a backlash. Once the relationship between rights and moral change is understood as a protracted process of intercultural negotiation between majority and minority, it becomes clear that rights are a necessary precondition for recognition, but not a sufficient one. Even if they secure equal rights, same-sex couples may still have to await their fellow citizens' recognition of them as moral equals. The process will take some time and properly should do. But again, it seems hard to imagine that this respect will not follow eventually.

In this lecture, I am examining the intertwined process by which a rights revolution became a sexual revolution, which in turn became a moral revolution driven by a demand for equal recognition. But even this doesn't begin to describe the magnitude of the change that has overtaken private life since I came to manhood in the 1960s. The rights revolution surfed on top of a much bigger wave, which brought with it improved access to higher education for women, the entry of married women into the workforce, the arrival of the birth control pill, and the development of social security systems that cushioned the impact of family breakup.

The American social theorist Francis Fukuyama has called this converging set of moral, technological, demographic, and legal changes "the great disruption."[4] All advanced societies were affected by it, but as Fukuyama argues, Western societies were more disrupted than any other. In a society like Japan, the great disruption did not sweep away traditional marriages or increase the rate of divorce. This fact helps us to see that rights talk in the West did more than ratify social changes that were already under way. It actually helped trigger the social changes themselves. What raised divorce rates in Western society, but not in Japan, was the Western endorsement of values of individual autonomy, which in turn eroded the fabric of female self-sacrifice upon which the family depended as an institution.

Forty years after these changes, we are still trying to take account of their effects. The ledger has many double entries. There is more sexual freedom and more divorce. There are more varieties of sexual identity and more confusion about what kind of sexual beings we actually are. Abortion rights have increased the freedom of women, while at the same time raising bitter and contentious debate about our right to terminate the life of the unborn.[5] There are more types of families— same-sex, single-mother, single-father—and yet more anxiety about whether family intimacy and stability can endure.

In this lecture, I want to tell the story of this double revolution in rights and sexual conduct and ask whether rights talk is weakening or strengthening our capacity to sustain intimate life. We all need intimacy, children especially, but intimacy requires permanence. Is the rights revolution threatening permanence? Is there too much talk of rights in intimate life and not enough talk of responsibility?

Questions like these are not new. Indeed, they are the hardy perennials of modern self-doubt. By modern, I mean any society based on markets and individual rights. In North America and Western Europe, we have been living in such societies at least since 1700 and ever since then social critics have contended that market life endangers stabilizing institutions such as the family. As the great Harvard economist Joseph Schumpeter argued, capitalism depends upon values such as trust and mutual confidence; without these, no one would feel safe enough to enter into contracts and exchanges.[6] Now, the source of such values is the family. But the "creative destruction" of the capitalist investment process recurrently overturns stable ways of life and work based on existing technologies. These convulsions make it difficult for families to maintain continuities of care. If wage pressure and time pressure deplete the emotional reserves of family life, children are less likely to learn the values on which the larger society depends. Children who do not learn how to trust and how to love turn into selfish and aggressive adults. The result, if family breakdown becomes general, is a brutal and uncaring social order. This chain of reasoning is very familiar. There is no more enduring fear in capitalist life than that the system erodes the very values it needs to maintain order.

Capitalism's chronic instability used to be chiefly blamed for harming family life. But newer critiques emphasize the destabilizing effects of abundance. Abundance changes the moral economy of a society by favouring values of consumption over saving, self-assertion over self-restraint, present-mindedness over future-orientation. Abundance has other moral effects as well. Societies of scarcity are obsessed with distribution and therefore with equality; societies of abundance care less about distribution once poverty ceases to manifest itself as absolute deprivation. Paradoxically, abundant societies that could actually solve the problem of poverty seem to care less about doing so than societies of scarcity that can't. This paradox may help to explain why the rights revolution of the past forty years has made inequalities of gender, race, and sexual orientation visible, while the older inequalities of class and income have dropped out of the registers of indignation. Abundance has awakened us to denials of self while blinding us to poverty. We idly suppose that the poor have disappeared. They haven't. They've merely become invisible.

There is little doubt that the rights revolution of the 1960s is the product of the most sustained period of affluence in the history of the developed world. The old virtues, the old limits, lost their legitimacy. The new virtues—self-cultivation, self-indulgence, self-development—acquired the force of moral imperatives. This is the context that explains why the old moral economy of self-denial began to lose not only its economic rationale but its moral dignity as well.

In societies of abundance, the old argument—that capitalism consumes the basis of its own legitimacy—takes on a new twist in the claim that the rights demanded in an era of abundance erode the family structures on which social stability depends.[7] The rights sought in eras of abundance are in fact demands to throw off the order of restraint and repression that prevailed in eras of scarcity. Can family life survive this revolutionary demand for freedom? Is it possible that rights are destroying the very institution that teaches us moral virtue?

A good place to begin the story of the impact of modern rights on intimate life is with divorce. All modern societies liberalized their marriage laws in the 1960s as part of a wave of social legislation, which also included welfare reform and the decriminalization of consensual same-sex activity between adults. In Canada, the Divorce Act of 1968, the first national divorce law in our history, permitted termination of marriage on grounds of adultery and cruelty or if couples had already lived apart three years. When the act was amended in 1985, this waiting period was reduced to one year.[8] This provision effectively introduced no-fault divorce into Canadian life and the impact was felt immediately. By the 1990s, one marriage in three in Canada was ending in divorce. The results, for children, have been dramatic. It is estimated that half of the children currently growing up in developed nations will see their parents divorce by the time they are eighteen.[9] Most troubling is the possibility that rising divorce rates are correlated with rising levels of child abuse. This would be the case if children turned out to be more at risk of abuse from step-parents than from their natural kin. It is not clear whether child abuse is actually increasing, but if there were a correlation between such an increase and rising divorce rates, then the rights revolution would be having disturbing effects indeed.

As divorce rates have risen, so have rates of cohabitation, couples living together outside of marriage.[10] The rise of cohabitation reveals the new rights that have been asserted in intimate life since the 1960s: the right to found and dissolve intimate partnerships at will and to do so without the intervention of church, state, or family. Cohabitation was a declaration of sovereignty by the couple, an assertion that they, rather than the state, would define the terms of their relationship. In fact, of course, as these relationships foundered, cohabiting couples, like married ones, found themselves returning to the state (i.e., to the courts) to seek the rights to maintenance, child support, and family property provided by formal marriage. Indeed, as the incidence of cohabitation has increased, the pressure has grown to accord cohabiting couples the same rights as married ones. So the course of the rights revolution has had an ironic outcome. Couples might have wanted to keep the state out of their relationships at the point of getting together, but they discovered that they needed to get the state back in as an adjudicator when these relationships fell apart.

Forty years into the rights revolution, we are no longer sure what role courts and legislatures should play in family life. Should the law be promoting a certain standard of family life, or should it just be serving **in loco parentis** for children at risk from family violence and breakdown? This issue has turned many people's politics upside down. Feminists who once insisted that the state had no business in their bedrooms now clamour for state intervention to protect women against family violence. Conservatives who once denounced the nanny state now plead for government to enforce frayed moral standards. As for liberals, many secretly wonder whether their revolution has gone too far.

in loco parentis
in the place of a parent

The controversy over whether there should be laws against corporal punishment in families brings out all our perplexities about the relationship between state and family life. Some people believe that a state ban on corporal punishment would align the force of the law on the side of a crucial moral principle. Others maintain that punishing parents who use physical correction against children would be an invasion of family life. An Ontario court judge recently ruled against outlawing physical correction of children on the grounds that it infringed on the family's essential margin of autonomy.[11] It seems clear that the right of the child that needs defending is the same one accorded adults: the right to live free of fear. Children should respect their parents but never fear them, for fear always casts a shadow of mistrust over love and care. Children will never trust the love of someone who has made them frightened. So we do not want to strike children unless there is simply no other way to stop them from doing harm to themselves or others. But as soon as we concede that some forms of mild and non-harmful physical punishment may occasionally be necessary, it becomes difficult to enforce a distinction between legitimate and illegitimate correction. Do we need to? There are already sufficient laws to protect children against physical abuse, and these allow the state to take children into care. So their rights already have protection. Additional legislation may only multiply the number of wrongful prosecutions of parents, which would weaken rather than strengthen family life.

What this story illustrates best, I think, is that the state has only a limited capacity to protect children. We already have a vast apparatus for child protection—social workers, welfare officers, family physicians, court-appointed guardians, and so on—but despite the (mostly) conscientious efforts of those who work in this area, our society continues to be disgraced and shamed by the unheard screams of children. Sometimes these cries are very close by: through the party wall, across the garden fence, in the next aisle of the supermarket. What this says to me is that rights are not enough. The welfare state is not enough. Indeed, sometimes we enact rights in the statute books and the result only weakens our responsibilities. This might be the case with children in danger of abuse. The child-protection bureaucracy, necessary as it is, sometimes confiscates responsibilities that properly lie in society itself, with neighbours, friends, and good-hearted strangers. Ultimately, child protection is not up to the state; it is up to us. If we see a child being beaten, we must raise the alarm. A rights revolution is meaningless unless it calls forth our civic courage to intervene when we know we should.

Inevitably, the rights revolution—and the sexual revolution that went with it—produced backlash. Since the mid-1970s, conservative politicians and social analysts have been arraigning the liberal reforms of the 1960s and condemning their consequences. The backlash has reversed the usual conservative position on rights. Conservatives used to be strong exponents of individual rights, since rights define the limits of state intervention and conservatives were anxious to set limits on the power of the post-war state. Liberals, on the other hand, used to be more hostile to individual rights talk, because some rights, especially property and privacy rights, were invoked by conservatives to resist crucial liberal objectives, such as the establishment of graduated income tax and the creation of a welfare state. The revolution in family life has turned this alignment upside down. Now conservatives say that rights have gone too far, while liberals are trying to stay the course of a rights agenda.

The problem with liberal rights talk, conservatives argue, is that it individualizes people. Once people begin speaking about their rights, they start counting the costs of all relationships with other human beings that involve sacrifice. And family life is based on sacrifice: parents devoting years to the care of children when they might prefer to be furthering their own interests, and husbands and wives devoting themselves to each other when other persons and possibilities beckon.

This argument has something to say for it, but not much. Conservatives are wrong to suppose that rights talk invalidates sacrifice itself. Even we heartless liberals need intimacy and we know that we cannot have intimacy without sacrifice. These sacrifices, both moral and material, are worth bearing when they are borne mutually, when both partners share the load, and when the result of equal sacrifice is renewed affection. Much of the complaint about family life focuses not on sacrifice per se, but on inequality of sacrifice. This inequality is not imagined: it is painfully real. In Canada, statistics show that even now, after a generation of feminist progress, 70 percent of the burden of caring for children, the aged, the disabled, and the sick falls on women, most of whom receive no pay for these essential tasks.[12] These enduring facts help us to see that the revolt against family life in the 1960s was a revolt not against sacrifice but against inequality of sacrifice. And to judge from the statistics, the revolution remains unfinished.

But feminism was much more than a revolt against inequalities of sacrifice. It was also a revolt against certain kinds of sacrifice, notably the sacrifice of female identity. Young women coming of age in the 1960s looked back on the lives of their own mothers, women who had come of age in the Depression and the Second World War, and felt that they had thrown away their lives for the sake of their husbands and children. The sacrifice that had been made was of their very selves. This was the cardinal wrong that had to be righted. When daughters raised this issue, the results were often painful. What daughters accusingly called sacrifice, some mothers poignantly felt as fulfillment, at least of a kind. But sometimes the confrontation between generations ended with both feeling the same sense of injustice.

As a man who came of age in the late 1960s, I was deeply affected by feminist rights talk, and by this reckoning between mothers and daughters. Like many men, I was soon to go through my own version of *Fathers and Sons*. The central idea I absorbed then—chiefly, if not exclusively, from feminism—was that each of us has a right to choose the life we lead and that we must fight to exercise this right against all comers. This could be called the ideal of authenticity.[13] In the name of this ideal, we all went off to find ourselves. This meant getting away from family, career, and society, and going in search of the self's authentic impulses. Sometimes the results were laughable: the 1960s cult of authenticity produced dull conformity in no time. We all went in search of ourselves and ended up in graduate school. Even those who dropped out tended to end up conforming to a non-conformist lifestyle.

For many of us, even those for whom the 1960s were either an episode or just a memory, the ideal of authenticity exerted a powerful influence on our very idea of what it was to have a life and a career. Authenticity taught us that we had a duty to ourselves and not just to others, and that in the face of a conflict between these two duties, we would sometimes have to choose for ourselves—against children, families, lovers, and friends.

So to summarize the argument so far, two moral ideas were the heart of the rights revolution in private life: first, that family sacrifice is unjust unless it is equal; and second, that each of us owes a duty to ourselves, and this is equal to the duty we owe to others. Let's admit immediately that these were highly contentious values. Conservative social critics would argue that these ideals are just fancy ways to justify selfishness. What I have been calling the rights revolution, conservatives would dismiss as the permissive revolution. The cardinal vice of permissiveness is wanting rights without responsibilities: wanting sex without love, wanting intimacy without commitment, and worst of all, wanting children without being willing to care for them. Liberalism, so the argument goes, has made a devil's bargain with permissiveness. In the name of an ethics of authenticity, rights talk is actually undermining the very possibility of moral behaviour, since it appears to authenticate every selfish impulse: to quit marriages when they don't work, to abandon children when work calls, to flee responsibility when pleasure beckons. To make matters worse, conservative critics say, the state colludes in this selfishness by providing welfare benefits for unmarried mothers, so that the costs of irresponsibility are paid not by the guilty, but by the hard-pressed taxpayer.

When divorce is the norm, conservatives argue, children grow up in a moral world in which all trust is conditional, because betrayal is always possible.[14] According to the conservative critique, we risk producing a future generation of children who trust so few people that they no longer start families themselves.

And even when families survived the permissive revolution, conservatives argue, they were damaged by it. The mistake was believing that the family could be run as a community of rights-bearing equals. Children are not the equals of their parents; they need limits and rules. Permissive parenting, on a rights-equality model, so it is argued, has produced a generation of young adults who came of age in the 1990s, never having learned the meaning of self-discipline.

Let us grant what we can to the conservative counterattack. Let us grant that freedom is not a licence to do whatever you please. Let us insist that fathers and mothers must know how to say the word no; that moral life for children begins with the understanding of limits; that any person who embarks upon the adventure of marriage must judge the result not by happiness alone, but by other, more arduous standards, such as staying the course. None of this is alien to the liberal temperament or inconsistent with a commitment to rights equality between men and women. Indeed, it is impossible to envisage marriage surviving at all unless both partners strive towards equality.

The conservative critique of permissiveness has its points, but it is reactionary in the strict meaning of the term. It wants to turn the clock back, and to do so by means of coercive legislation—such as making divorce more difficult and penalizing single parents—which would violate conservatism's own commitments to the freedom of the individual. A liberal position is simply more consistent with that commitment. Moreover, a liberal rights culture does not obliterate responsibilities: it presumes them. To father a child is to shoulder responsibility for its upbringing. If a father abandons his family and fails to pay maintenance, he should be pursued and, if he still fails to pay up, punished. If pregnant mothers so abuse themselves with drugs and alcohol that they damage their children, they should feel the penalties of the law.[15] A state whose child-protection agencies fail to pin responsibility on defaulting parents, and whose welfare institutions then mutely step in to cope with the consequences, is undermining the link between rights and responsibilities that makes a rights culture consistent with public order. On this issue, a liberal and a conservative will see eye to eye.

But on others, the divide is unbridgeable. What conservatives see as the collapse of the family, liberals view as its mutation into new forms. Nowadays, there are many types of good parents and many types of good families: nuclear, extended, single-parent, same-sex. The fact that there are many types of families does not mean that there are no longer any fixed standards about what a good family is. The test of goodness is loose but evident: it's a community where each member receives and displays lifelong moral concern for the well-being of everyone else. The key is not love necessarily, or hugs, or sentimental Disney eyewash, but an enduring moral commitment. A child needs to feel that her development matters intensely to another person, and that this person will stay the course with her to ensure that she develops as best she can. What a liberal insists upon is the idea that it is possible to reconcile a commitment to absolute standards of care and responsibility in family life with a faith that these standards can be met by a wide variety of persons and a wide variety of possible family forms.

So-called family values, as propagated in the rhetoric of North American popular entertainment, pulpit sermonizing, and political homily, are a downright tyranny. They make people feel inadequate, ashamed, or guilty about their inability to conform to what is in fact a recent, post-war suburban norm of family domesticity.

We need family values all right, but the ones we actually need must be pluralistic. We need to understand that the essential moral needs of any child can be met by family arrangements that run the gamut from arranged marriages right through to same-sex parenting. Nature and natural instinct are poor guides in these matters. If good parenting were a matter of instinct, families wouldn't be the destructive institutions they so often are. It is frequently the case that perfect strangers turn out to be better parents or step-parents than natural ones. This is not always the case, of course, as the incidence of abuse by step-parents attests.

The point is not to invalidate one type of parent. Instead, it is to insist that ideology will not help us here: if we insist that one category or type of parent will always do a better job than any other, we are certain to be wrong. Same-sex parents have taught us that there is no necessary relationship between heterosexuality and good parenting. The question to be asked in every case is not what kind of sexual creatures these parents are, or even what kind of biological or other relationship they have to these children, but what kind of parents they are. The test of goodness here is the capacity for sustained moral concern and to be willing to make reasonable sacrifices for the sake of children's interests. A family is not a bus station: children will not develop well when there is no continuity of care and concern. Continuity implies sacrifice but reasonable sacrifice doesn't necessarily mean putting children's interests first. No model of family life will work if it is based on unequal and unlimited sacrifice. As a moral training ground, families ought to teach the lesson that no one's interests should automatically come first and certainly not the children's.

Getting any of this to work is not easy. None of us is always capable of unconditional moral concern for another human being, but some surprising people routinely do it better than we do. Opening our eyes to the different ways other families work is more useful than despising those who do things differently. Pluralism does not mean relativism. It means humility.

But, conservatives say, even if one admits the viability of same-sex, single-parent, or divorced families, the problem is that these new family forms do not endure. They are eaten from within by the liberal ideology that family life should be satisfying, and that if it isn't, each member should exercise their right of secession.

Let us acknowledge that fathers—and mothers—are deserting their families in the name of "finding themselves," and that children are paying a high price for the inability of adults to reconcile duty and desire, freedom and responsibility. As a father, I find it hard not to be pained by the statistics about modern fatherhood and divorce in Canada: mothers get custody of children in 86 percent of cases, and more than 40 percent of children in Canada's divorced families see their fathers only once a month. Even when both parents remain present in their children's lives, research in England shows that, in families where both spouses work, mothers spend ninety minutes a day with their children and fathers only fifteen minutes. The same pattern must be broadly true among Canadian working families. Here the ideal of authenticity—of both parents seeking lives that fully express their capacities—risks being purchased at our children's expense. But let's stop lamenting these trends as if we were powerless to do anything about them, as if they were some malign kind of fate. We've made the rights revolution, and we need to fix it. And that is precisely what working families are trying to do. There isn't a responsible working couple I know who aren't conscious of this conflict between what they owe themselves and what they owe their children. Many of them have tried to have it all and discovered that they need one item more than any other: time with each other.

Many families do break up under the strain of these competing claims. Some parents simply abscond altogether. The disappearing dad—who neither pays child support nor visits his children—is a fact that cannot be denied, and his absence from his children's lives can have painful effects.[16] These effects do not just harm children, of course. They also harm women. Divorce has become a multiplier of inequality in Canada: deprivation is heavily concentrated among single mothers with children.[17]

Yet this crisis is too complex to be blithely blamed on "deadbeat dads" alone. In hearings before a parliamentary committee in Canada in 1998, groups of fathers bitterly complained that they were bearing the brunt of public blame for what has happened to the family. In fact, they claimed that they were discriminated against. Courts were favouring mothers over fathers in custody disputes, and the divorce process was being abused by lawyers despoiling working men of their assets. These groups demanded that the "custody and access" regime created by the Divorce Act of 1985 be replaced with a "shared parenting" regime in which both parents are given equal rights to bring up their children.[18] These are sensible and overdue suggestions, and the fact that they're being made shows that men and women are struggling to correct the rights revolution, so that equality works for everyone.

In facing up to these issues, liberals also need to face up to their responsibilities. Let us acknowledge that the rights revolution must shoulder some share of the blame for family breakup and its consequences in our society. Even if a lot of other factors also come into play—the pressure of work in capitalist society, the mobility that market success requires of many families—it has to be true that we divorce more frequently than our grandparents because of the kinds of freedom we take for granted, and hence the kind of persons we have become. We do believe we have a right to happiness; we do believe we want to live our lives instead of silently enduring them; we are much more explicit than our grandparents about wanting sexual happiness and a wide variety of sexual experience.

But the conservative critique, which denigrates these desires as selfishness, gets us nowhere. People can and do repent of selfishness and they can turn their back on appetite. But the rights revolution has been propelled by something stronger than appetites: it's propelled by the values of authenticity that shape our ideas of what a good life should be. The divorce rates tell us that men and women are no longer willing to suffer and be still. Our rights culture endorses complaint and it dignifies discontent. It offers moral legitimacy to departure.

There is a deeper conflict than our parents' generation imagined between being faithful to others and being faithful to ourselves. It is entirely possible to be true to others—your spouse and your children, for example—and betray yourself. By betrayal, I mean giving yourself to others in ways that sacrifice your talents, your special gifts, your unique ability to contribute. If you betray yourself in this way, you then render yourself useless to others, incapable of carrying out your duties and responsibilities with conviction and self-respect. It is this moral insight—more than just sexual temptation or appetite—that drives so many modern marriages onto the rocks. Marriages can survive sexual temptation. They can even survive betrayal. What they cannot survive is either partner believing they have betrayed something essential about themselves. We ought to be candid enough to admit that when a marriage forces a couple to betray themselves, it deserves to fail.

Even if we should accord respect to divorce, let no one suppose that there can ever be such a thing as a painless one. Even those who make a happy escape can be burdened for the rest of their lives by a real sense of sadness and failure. And the harm done to children is real, though this harm must be evaluated against what might be called the contra-factual harm: what would have happened had the parents stayed together. Indeed, all one can ever say about divorce is that it can teach children something sad but true about life: that love is not eternal, that trust can be lost as well as won, that betrayal is a fact of life. Some believe that children should always be sheltered from these facts. But I don't see why innocence should enjoy these moral prerogatives, because I don't see why concealing the truth helps children. And besides, children know more than we think. Anybody who breaks up a marriage certainly learns one thing: if you cannot justify divorce to your children, you cannot justify it to yourself. And justify it you must. But this truth is underpinned by another: that a modern family is a realm of moral equals, each with claims and each with rights, one of which is a right to justification.

We owe children truth; we owe them reasons for our conduct. Sustained moral concern implies helping them to understand us as the imperfect but struggling agents we are. Divorce takes everyone off the pedestal. But why did we put ourselves on the pedestal in the first place? Parents needn't be heroes—moral or otherwise. Nor should they be friends. They should be parents.[19]

Children do have rights. They have the right not just to be sheltered and cared for and protected from abuse, but also to be treated as moral agents in their own right, with intentions, purposes, and visions of the world that we should not presume are identical to our own. A liberal ideal of parenting puts empathy at the heart of modern family life—that is, no longer taking children for granted, no longer assuming that they should be the silent and obedient witnesses to the godlike dramas played out above their heads, but acknowledging that they are incipient adults whose minds must be read, whose hearts must be understood, and whose love must be earned.

Will a society of children raised in divorced families be a society in which individuals no longer know how to trust one another? This will happen only if we lie to them, only if we pretend to be happy when we're not, only if we fail to treat their emotions with the respect they deserve. Only if we fail to give them what we know we need ourselves: the continuous light and warmth of sustained moral concern.

Only a complacent person could possibly be happy with the state of modern married life and the family. The conservative blames the rights agenda for creating discontentments with family life that didn't exist before. But this is false. The unhappiness was there; the rights revolution simply enabled men and women to act on the unhappiness they once felt powerless to change. What rights have done is to enlarge people's sense of themselves as agents: empowering them to think of their urgent needs as entitlements and giving dignity to their complaints about the unfairness and injustice of family life. But this injustice exists. It cannot be conjured away by greater acts of will and self-repression and it cannot be dispersed by the law.

Nor can we go back on what we have already done. The changes in family life are not a transient effect of 1960s fashion; they are not the consequence of some blind descent into moral selfishness. They are here to stay and we need to make the promise of moral equality in intimate life real for all of our citizens. Families that divorce need help so that parenting responsibilities can be genuinely shared, not reluctantly conceded in rigid custody-and-access schemes that end up dividing children from their parents. We need to create new cheap and efficient institutions that mediate family conflict instead of impoverishing families with exorbitant legal costs. Instead of abandoning the equality agenda that began in the 1960s, we need to complete it. Same-sex couples should be entitled to the same rights of marriage, adoption, and parenthood as other-sex couples and they should be held to exactly the same standards of responsibility and accountability.

Families that work need help to survive—help that includes decent public education, publicly funded daycare, universal health care free at point of need, and accident and unemployment insurance. Families also need respite from the devouring impact of work and stress on intimate life. We need to change the employment laws so that family life is not

squeezed between the millstones of two
precarious incomes. The key goal of our
social policy should be to give families the
time they need to be together.

In the new century, most families that
survive do so not by jettisoning the values of
their parents, but by reinventing them and
rebalancing the division of labour. They
balance rights against responsibilities, seek to
equalize sacrifice, and manage to impose
rational limits on children's behaviour. But
no vision of family values has a chance of
commanding genuine assent—and that is
the test of an ethic's legitimacy—unless it
accords respect for the individual's needs
against the devouring claims of family life.

Much as deficit-reducing conservatives
may lament the fact, the test of serious moral
commitment to the family is a willingness to
spend public money. Effective child protection, universal access to health care, afford-
able child care, first-rate primary and
secondary education—these are the building
blocks of the protective arch that society
must raise over its families. This institutional
arch doesn't come cheap, but those exponents of family values who won't stump up
for it are just engaging in cheap talk.

The rights revolution has not launched us on a slippery slope towards
nihilism and social collapse. We are simply trying, with as much success
as failure, to live by the twin ideals of equality and authenticity, to fashion lives that reflect our choices and do not depend on thwarting the
lives of others. There is wreckage at our feet, but the new forms of
family and intimate life that are emerging do what these institutions
have always done: sustain us with a shared experience of moral concern.
There is much that we could do better, and we had better acknowledge,
sooner rather than later, that we cannot have it all. If we want happy
children and happy spouses, we had better fight back the claims of
work; if we want to be treated equally, we will have to treat others
equally; if we want our children to respect us, we will have to respect
their need for rules and order. What I think cannot be changed is our

sense of ourselves as free agents: the idea that all family members have rights; that we have duties to ourselves, as well as to others; that no one is there to serve, honour, obey, and suffer in silence; that we are committed to perceiving each other not as equals—since parents and children cannot be equals—but as moral entities entitled to reasons, the best ones we can devise. The liberal proposition is that children deserve reasons as much as love, and that reasons are a form of love.

It is often said that we should beware of what we want, because we are likely to get it. We need to see our anguish and disarray about the family as a struggle to face up to the consequences of having got what we wanted. We wanted freedom and we should stop apologizing for it. We must simply pay its price. As Isaiah Berlin once said, freedom is a chilly virtue: it is not justice, equality, or a quiet life; it is merely freedom.[20] Almost everybody is frightened of it. And almost everybody would restrict somebody else's freedom if he could get away with it. Freedom is not the only moral virtue, not the only moral priority, but it happens to be the precondition of all the others. An agent who is not free cannot be a responsible one at all. If we value responsibility, then we need to have the courage to embrace our freedom. It is the very condition of responsibility, not to mention self-respect, and hence the very basis of an authentic life. The rights revolution has been in the service of freedom and we need to have the courage to continue with it until we can genuinely say that everyone shares its benefits and not just its costs.

Notes

[1] Mary McCarthy and Joanna Radbord, "Family Law for Same-Sex Couples: Chart(er)ing the Course," *Canadian Journal of Family Law* 15, no. 101 (1998).

[2] Taylor, "The Politics of Recognition," in *Multiculturalism*, ed. Gutmann.

[3] Michael Walzer, *On Toleration* (New Haven, Conn.: Yale University Press, 1997).

[4] Francis Fukuyama, *The Great Disruption: Human Nature and the Reconstitution of Social Order* (New York: The Free Press, 1999). See also Roderick Phillips, *Putting Asunder: A History of Divorce in Western Society* (Cambridge: Cambridge University Press, 1988).

[5] George Grant, *English-Speaking Justice* (Toronto: Anansi, 1974, 1985), 69–90.

[6] Joseph Schumpeter, *Capitalism, Socialism, and Democracy* (New York: Harper & Brothers, 1942).

[7] Christopher Lasch, *Haven in a Heartless World* (New York: Basic Books, 1977); see also Fukuyama, *The Great Disruption*.

[8] Nicholas Bala, "A Report from Canada's Gender War Zone: Reforming the Child-Related Provisions of the Divorce Act," *Canadian Journal of Family Law* 16, no. 2 (1999): 163–227.

[9] Fukuyama, *The Great Disruption*, 41–42, 82, 115.

[10] Winifred Holland, "Intimate Relationships in the New Millenium: The Assimilation of Marriage and Cohabitation," *Canadian Journal of Family Law* 17, no. 1 (2000): 114–68.

[11] "Judge Refuses to Ban Spanking of Children," *Globe and Mail*, 6 July 2000.

[12] Statistics Canada, *Household Unpaid Work* (Ottawa, 1995).

[13] Lionel Trilling, *Sincerity and Authenticity* (Cambridge, Mass.: Harvard University Press, 1972); see also Marshall Berman, *The Politics of Authenticity* (New York: Atheneum, 1970).

[14] Fukuyama, *The Great Disruption* (New York: The Free Press, 1999).

[15] Teresa Foley, "Dobson v. Dobson: Tort Liability for Expectant Mothers," *Saskatchewan Law Review* (1998): 61, 177; see also Sandra Rogers, "Case Comment and Note: Winnipeg Child and Family Services v. D.F.G.: Juridical Interference with Pregnant Women in the Alleged Interest of the Fetus," *Alberta Law Reveiw* 36, no. 711 (1998).

[16] Statistics Canada, *Divorces 1995* (Ottawa, 1995), table 8 at 20. See also Bala, "Canada's Gender War Zone," note 1.

[17] Bala, note 1.

[18] Bala, note 1.

[19] I first made these arguments in a lecture titled "Liberal Values, a Defence: The Keith Davey Lecture," delivered at Victoria College, University of Toronto, 1996.

[20] Isaiah Berlin, *Four Essays on Liberty* (New York: Oxford University Press, 1969), 167–72.

Marriage Is Made in Hell

Laura Kipnis

Marriage: The new blue-light case of the week. Everyone is terribly worried about its condition: can it be cured? Or has the time arrived for drastic measures—just putting it out of its misery? Euthanasia is a dirty word but, frankly, the prognosis is not so great for this particular patient: a stalwart social institution is now scabby and infirm, gasping for each tortured breath. Many who had once so optimistically pledged to uphold its vows are fleeing its purported satisfactions. In the US, a well-publicised 50 per cent failure rate hardly makes for optimism; in Britain, too, the Office for National Statistics reports that divorce has reached a record high at around 15 per cent. But this lower figure goes with a drop in the number of weddings—at their lowest level since the reign of Queen Victoria; this should mean fewer divorces, since not getting married in the first place seems the best way—these days—of avoiding this sorry (often expensive, usually ego-damaging) **denouement**.

denouement

conclusion

Certainly, there are happy marriages. No one disputes that and all those who are happily married can stop reading here. Additionally, there is always serial monogamy for those who can't face up to the bad news—yes, keep on trying until you get it right, because the problem couldn't be the institution itself or its impossible expectations. For these optimists, the problem is that they have somehow either failed to find the "right person," or have been remiss in some other respect. If only they'd put those socks in the laundry basket instead of leaving them on the floor, everything would have worked out. If only they'd cooked more (or less) often. If only they'd been more this, less that, it would have been fine.

And what of the growing segment of the population to whom the term "happily married" does not precisely apply, yet who nonetheless valiantly struggle to uphold the tenets of the marital enterprise, mostly because there seems to be no viable option? A 1999 Rutgers University study reported that a mere 38 per cent of Americans who are married describe themselves as actually happy in that state. This is rather shocking: so many pledging to live out their lives here on earth in varying degrees of discontent or emotional stagnation because that is what's expected from us, or "for the sake of the children," or because wanting more than that makes you selfish and irresponsible. So goes the endless moralizing and fingerpointing this subject tends to invite.

Let us contemplate the everyday living conditions of this rather large percentage of the population, this self-reportedly unhappily married majority: all those households submersed in low-level misery and soul-deadening tedium, early graves in all respects but the most forensic. Regard those couples—we all know them, perhaps we are them—the bickering; the reek of unsatisfied desires and unmet needs; a populace downing anti-depressants, along with whatever other forms of creative self-medication are most easily at hand, from triple martinis to serial adultery.

Yes, we all know that domesticity has its advantages: companionship, shared housing costs, childrearing convenience, reassuring predictability, occasional sex, and many other benefits too varied to list. But there are numerous disadvantages as well—though it is considered unseemly to enumerate them—most of which are so structured into the expecta-tions of contemporary coupledom that they have come to seem utterly natural and inevitable. But are they?

Consider, for instance, the endless regulations and interdictions that provide the texture of domestic coupledom. Is there any area of married life that is not crisscrossed by rules and strictures about every-thing from how you load the dishwasher, to what you can say at dinner parties, to what you do on your day off, to how you drive—along with what you eat, drink, wear, make jokes about, spend your discretionary income on?

What is it about marriage that turns nice-enough people into petty dictators and household tyrants, for whom criticising another person's habits or foibles becomes a conversational staple, the default setting of domestic communication? Or whose favourite marital recreational activity is mate behaviour modification? Anyone can play—and every-one does. What is it about modern coupledom that makes policing another person's behaviour a synonym for intimacy? (Or is it something about the conditions of modern life itself: is domesticity a venue for control because most of us have so little of it elsewhere?)

Then there's the fundamental premise of monogamous marriage: that mutual desire can and will last throughout a lifetime. And if it doesn't? Well apparently you're just supposed to give up on sex, since waning desire for your mate is never an adequate defence for "looking else-where." At the same time, let's not forget how many booming busi-nesses and new technologies have arisen to prop up sagging marital desire. Consider all the investment opportunities afforded: Viagra, couples pornography, therapy. If upholding monogamy in the absence of desire weren't a social dictate, how many enterprises would immediately fail? (Could dead marriages be good for the economy?)

And then there's the American mantra of the failing relationship: "Good marriages take work!" When exactly did the rhetoric of the factory become the default language of coupledom? Is there really anyone to whom this is an attractive proposition, who, after spending all day on the job, wants to come home and work some more? Here's an interesting question: what's the gain to a society in promoting more work to an overworked population as a supposed solution to the travails of marital discontent?

What if luring people into conditions of emotional stagnation and deadened desires were actually functional for society? Consider the norms of modern marriage: here is a social institution devoted to maximising submission and minimising freedom, habituating a populace to endless compliance with an infinite number of petty rules and interdictions, in exchange for love and companionship.

Perhaps a citizenry schooled in renouncing desire—and whatever quantities of imagination and independence it comes partnered with— would be, in many respects, socially advantageous. Note that the conditions of marital **stasis** are remarkably convergent with those of a **cowed** workforce and a docile electorate. And wouldn't the most elegant forms of social control be those that come packaged in the guise of individual needs and satisfactions, so wedded to the individual psyche that any contrary impulse registers as the anxiety of unlovability? Who needs a policeman on every corner when we're all so willing to police ourselves and those we love, and call it upholding our vows?

In this respect, perhaps rising divorce rates are not such bad news after all. The Office for National Statistics blames couples' high expectations for the upswing in divorce. But are high expectations really such a bad thing? What if we all worked less and expected more—not only from our marriages or in private life, but in all senses—from our jobs, our politicians, our governments? What if wanting happiness and satisfaction—and changing the things that needed changing to attain it— wasn't regarded as "selfish" or "unrealistic" (and do we expect so much from our mates these days because we get so little back everywhere else?). What if the real political questions were what should we be able to expect from society and its institutions? And, if other social contracts and vows beside marriage were also up for re-examination, what other **ossified** social institutions might be next on the hit list?

stasis
lifeless inertia

cowed
frightened

ossified
rigid decay

Can We All Just Get Along?

Greg Narbey

In Los Angeles in 1992, rioting occurred as a response to the acquittal of four LAPD officers who had been videotaped beating Rodney King. Startled by the violence and scope of the rioting, Mr. King responded to a television interview by asking: "Can we all just get along?" Indeed, "getting along" has always been one of the most pressing problems in any society and, therefore, one of the greatest political challenges. In modern society, this challenge is to find some way to balance the requirements of social cohesion (unity) on the one hand and diversity (pluralism) on the other. The uneven distribution of power between majority groups and minority groups has always made this challenge difficult to meet.

Traditionally, minority groups were usually simply ignored or repressed by force by the majority. As the ancient Greek historian Thucydides once observed, "The strong do what they can while the weak suffer what they must." Often the Ottoman Empire is presented as an early forerunner of today's multicultural society. It is important to recognize, however, that the empire offered toleration but not real equality for minority religious groups: the predominantly Muslim society tolerated Christian and Jewish minorities provided they did not try to spread their religion, but the minorities were never accorded equal rights to political participation. Even this degree of toleration was imperfect, however, with periodic pogroms launched against minority religious groups.*

The Challenge of Pluralism

The permanent disenfranchisement or marginalization of minority groups cannot be justified in today's modern, multicultural and democratic societies. Modern democracy is premised on the principle, commonly held since at least the 18th century, that governmental legitimacy rests on the consent of the governed. As John Stuart Mill (1806–1873) recognized, moreover, a democracy that denied equality

---

"Can We All Just Get Along?" is by Greg Narbey of the Humber College Institute of Technology and Advanced Learning. Used by permission.

*Editors' note: Indeed, in 1915 the leaders of the Ottoman Empire launched a genocidal campaign against their Armenian subjects in an attempt to resolve "the Armenian question" once and for all.

to minority groups would not be sustainable in the long run. As more of the countries of the world move toward some democratic form of government (about 120 countries out of the 191 nations that comprise the membership of the UN), the challenge of political pluralism has become the most critical political issue to be confronted in the 21st century.

Pluralism is the human condition. It results from the fact that people who do not share the same moral values, cultural practices, religious observations or languages must inhabit a common and finite planet. All human civilizations have been to a greater or lesser extent pluralist. However, the revolution in global transportation, communications and trade has made almost every country pluralist to a degree never before imagined. There are around 8,000 distinctive cultural groups living in the 191 nations that comprise the United Nations.[1] Because the earth and its territory are finite, but culture and religion are dynamic and constantly changing, it is inconceivable that each distinctive cultural group could be granted its own territory (even if that were desirable). As the ability to travel, communicate and trade becomes cheaper and easier, greater interaction among different religious, moral and cultural outlooks becomes inevitable, and, in turn, the issue of whether we can all get along becomes even more pressing. To put the problem another way, the challenge for modern pluralist societies is to find a balance between diversity and social unity. How that balance should be struck cannot be settled in advance.

The challenge of "getting along" in an increasingly pluralized world is heightened by the very arbitrary nature of national boundaries. The boundaries of identifiable countries are human creations (they are not rooted in nature). Because no nation on earth is entirely *autarchic* (completely self-sufficient), because every nation on earth contains minority groups and because every nation is, in principle, divisible, the long-term success of a nation will largely be determined by how well the many different interests within the borders of that nation can be satisfied. Two examples should serve to illustrate this point.

Sri Lanka is a country that has been torn apart for decades by a ferocious civil war fought between the Tamil minority and the Singhalese majority. In 1956 the Singhalese majority made Singhala the only official language of Sri Lanka (at that time called Ceylon). The Tamil minority claimed that nothing short of political independence from the Singhalese majority could secure their long-term rights, language and culture. Currently, however, peace negotiations are underway to try to devise a political constitution that will preserve a single Sri Lanka, but will offer sufficient protection for the minority Tamil culture.

Similarly, during the latter part of the 20th century, Canadians were preoccupied by the demands of some Québécois for political independence from Canada. Only in a sovereign Québec, the separatists argued, would the Québécois truly be able to defend their language and distinct culture. Two referendums (in 1980 and 1995) on separating from Canada were fought over this issue in Québec. There were also a number of attempts to institute constitutional change to satisfy Québec's demands for greater autonomy within a unified Canada. During the last Québec referendum in 1995, moreover, both the Cree in northern Québec and English speakers in Montréal pointed out that if Canada was divisible so was Québec. In an independent Québec, they would be minorities. In short, if the majority of Québécois voted to separate from the rest of Canada, the Cree and anglophone Montréal threatened to hold their own referendums to separate from Québec and remain a part of Canada. In any event, the success of an independent Québec would still depend on whether the majority francophone population could convince non-francophone minorities that their rights would be respected in an independent Québec. Obviously the future success of Canada will depend on our ability to reconcile minority and majority rights and interests.

In the simplest possible terms the challenge of pluralism is this: How much accommodation or acceptance must majorities extend to minority groups, and when is accommodation or acceptance unreasonable? Furthermore, do minority groups deserve more than just accommodation or tolerance, i.e., how can their values and norms be reflected in the laws and customs of the larger nation? Before you say no to the question of whether accommodation or acceptance should be offered, think twice. As Mill recognized, in a democracy all of us are at one time or another part of a minority group. Perhaps you were opposed to Canada's participation in the NATO-led military intervention in Kosovo and the bombing of Serbia in 1999. If so, you would have represented a minority viewpoint in Canadian society. Cultural differences within a nation also have an impact upon whether your opinions and cultural, religious and linguistic practices place you in the majority or a minority position. If you support the right of gays and lesbians to be legally married, you will be in a minority in Alberta, but part of a small majority in Ontario, and part of a larger majority in Toronto.

So the ability to accommodate and accept minority groups within a society is critical to all of us. Moreover, the development of permanent minority groups cut off from power and influence in a society is a recipe for the failure of democracy. Why is this so?

Three Principles of Democratic Society

The development and spread of democratic governments over the past three centuries was premised on a number of assumptions about human rights. Political thinkers such as Hobbes and Locke argued that human beings were *equal*; there was no natural, or divinely established, hierarchy; and, as such, governments had to justify their right to rule. This meant that a government had to pass laws that treated all citizens equally, at a minimum, in order to be able to claim legitimacy as a government. Furthermore, thinkers as diverse as Locke, Rousseau, Voltaire, Marx and Mill argued that *liberty* was a primary human good, and, thus, any legitimate government had to maximize human liberty. As you will learn from the article "Politics in the Life of the Individual" in the next unit, there is considerable disagreement on how equality and liberty are to be maximized and how they are to be balanced. However, since the 18th century it has largely been accepted that governments that establish two tiers of citizenship, and dramatically restrict the liberty of their citizens, are illegitimate.

There was one other fundamental assumption about government that accompanied the democratic revolutions of the 18th and 19th centuries. It was assumed that government must be neutral in its treatment of citizens, i.e., that a legitimate government cannot offer advantages (or disadvantages) to one group of citizens that it does not offer to others. It was the assumption of *government neutrality* that led most modern democracies to insist on the separation of religion and state. Many of the earliest democracies in Europe had learned through bitter experience that when government and religion were connected, religious disagreement had the potential to become civil war as different religious faiths fought for control of the government. This doctrine of state neutrality with respect to religion gradually broadened to include state neutrality with respect to moral issues. Governments could legitimately make laws governing the behaviour of individuals and groups where the safety and well-being of others was concerned, but otherwise they had to respect the decisions made by individuals that did not directly harm the interests of other citizens. This is an idea formalized by Mill in his famous "harm principle."

Justice and Fairness: Formal and Substantive Equality

The neutrality of the government with respect to religious or moral conduct, the equal treatment of all citizens and the maximization of liberty are three of the essential rights on which most modern democracies rest. These basic human rights can also serve as a guide to help us negotiate the challenges raised by the increasingly pluralistic world we live in today. One of the 20th century's greatest political thinkers, John Rawls, recognized that the most critical issue facing democracy was how the conflicts generated by pluralism could be negotiated. His starting point was the issue of *fairness*. Everyone wants to be treated fairly, but often conflict arises when we try to determine what it means to be fair. Indeed, when we try to figure out what is fair we often reason in ways that reinforce our particular advantage. Rawls proposed a way of thinking about issues of fairness that would encourage us to look past our own particular advantage or disadvantage. He invited us to participate in a thought experiment. Imagine you are behind a "veil of ignorance"—imagine you have no knowledge about your particular characteristics. You do not know whether you were born to a wealthy family or a poor family. You do not know your sex or sexual orientation. Furthermore, you do not know your race or ethnicity or country of birth. Lastly, you do not know what your particular abilities or disabilities may be. When we think about questions of what is fair, Rawls argues, this is the position from which we should start. He called this imaginary situation "the original position."

   How can this process of reasoning help us with pluralistic conflict? Take the example of whether gays and lesbians should be able to legally marry. Since all of us take it for granted that we should be treated fairly, what is a fair law on this issue? Without knowledge of our personal characteristics, most of us would probably acknowledge that forming a permanent, stable, loving relationship that is legally recognized is something that many adults desire. Marriage is both a legal institution and a cultural way of regulating and acknowledging this type of relationship. So, given that in the original position, I, for example, have no knowledge of my own particular sexual orientation, it is unlikely that I would think that it was fair to restrict marriage only to the heterosexual majority. In the same way, if I had no knowledge of my race, I would not consider it fair to establish some form of legally sanctioned racism (such as the apartheid system formerly practised in South Africa).

The thought experiment of the original position can help us think more clearly about what is fair. However, one feature of pluralistic societies is that not all conflicts can be resolved by reference to simple equality. It has long been recognized that treating everyone exactly the same way—*formal equality*—does not always produce fairness. In Canada during the 20th century, for example, the federal government established residential schools for the education of aboriginal children. Children were removed from their families and placed in boarding schools far from their communities of birth. These schools (sometimes severely) punished students who used their native language or engaged in non-Christian forms of worship. The native children were to be educated in either French or English, just like any other Canadian child. One could argue that the native students were simply being given education equal to that of any other student in Canada.

However, what this analysis overlooks is that by failing to educate the native children in their own languages, the residential schools were stripping them of their language and, ultimately, their culture. Sometimes treating people fairly means that their differences have to be recognized and accommodated. Recognizing and accommodating people's differences where greater fairness will result is known as *substantive equality*. While an exclusive reliance on formal equality can result in unfairness, it is also important to realize that an exclusive reliance on substantive equality can have the same effect. A danger of substantive equality is that it can lead to oversimplifying the identity of the minority group by focusing on one element of their identity, resulting in stereotyping or pigeonholing them. One of the great challenges for modern democracies is deciding when formal equality or substantive equality should take precedence. In any particular case, this decision should be guided by the question: "What will produce the greatest fairness?"

In 2004 a debate gripped France that perfectly illustrates the difficulty of balancing social unity and diversity. The issue was the role of religious observance in public life. Specifically, the government passed legislation that prohibited the wearing of hijabs, yarmulkes, large crosses or turbans by students in the public education system. The president of France, Jacques Chirac, argued that, ever since the French revolution, France has been committed to being a secular society with respect to politics and public life. The assumption of the French legislature was that religious toleration can only really occur in a secular society. The legislation aimed at public religious observance was justified as a way to preserve the secular tradition of France. Predictably, the proposal was met with strong opposition. France is home to Europe's largest Muslim population (about 5 million). Many Muslims saw this proposal as an attempt to marginalize their role in French society and to assimilate them. This dispute is a classic illustration of deciding which version of equality will produce the greatest fairness. The French government (and a majority of French citizens) sees the legislation as *upholding* formal equality (the restriction on public religious observance applies to all French people). Muslim, Jewish, Christian and Sikh groups see this as a *denial* of equality. A secular culture is being enforced and those with religious values and norms are being told that their religion will be tolerated provided it is confined to private life. The perspective of the religious groups conforms to substantive equality: religious differences should be acknowledged and accommodated. There are good arguments to be made on both sides of this issue.

Once again, the original position may be a good place to start in helping us figure out what is reasonable and what will produce the greatest fairness. If we had no knowledge of our religious faith and the requirements of observing that faith, would we be willing to live in a society that made the public observance of our religion difficult or impossible? Furthermore, we might ask ourselves whether other members of society who do not share our faith are harmed if our religion requires a particular mode of dress. It is unlikely that from the perspective of the original position many would agree with the ban on public religious observance.

Competing Moral Doctrines: Reasonable Pluralism

This example also raises another difficulty faced by pluralist democracies—the distinction between public life and private life. Where no harm is done to other citizens, most democracies are willing to permit fairly broad latitude in terms of how people can worship and what they say and do in private. This distinction between public and private spheres can be a source of frustration for many minority groups in a pluralistic society. Often it appears that the larger majority will tolerate them provided they keep their views and activities private. In Canada, for example, some evangelical Christians claim that their form of Christianity is tolerated provided they do not try to publicly advocate for laws on the basis of their faith. This has been particularly true, they claim, with respect to the issues of same-sex marriage and abortion. Limited tolerance is also a problem that Rawls confronted as it relates to his overall concern for fairness.

It is important to recognize that democratic governments have to pass laws that apply to all, while, at the same time, there is broad disagreement about how we should live our lives. Ideally, democratic government should not favour one comprehensive moral, cultural or political perspective over another. As long as no harm is done to other citizens in the pursuit of a good life, the decisions about how we live our lives should be left to individuals and communities. Rawls called religious, moral and cultural world views *comprehensive doctrines*. They are comprehensive because the core assumptions that lie behind many religious and moral belief systems guide our behaviour in the day-to-day conduct of our lives. If there are many comprehensive doctrines in a society, how can a government hope to govern without simply enforcing the majority position? Over time wouldn't the society become destabilized by conflict between people with very different comprehensive doctrines?

Rawls argued that a reasonable pluralism was possible. Again, we return to the issue of fairness. I, for example, might think that society would be much better off if it was governed according to the comprehensive religious or moral doctrine I follow. In this case, suppose I follow the religious doctrines of Jehovah's Witnesses and I believe that society would be better off without drinking or smoking. If I could attract enough followers to my faith, I may gather together a majority of voters who, like me, would like to ban smoking and drinking. However, would it be reasonable, or desirable, to live in a society where majority comprehensive views could be imposed on the minority who don't share those comprehensive moral doctrines? Again, think about what you would agree to in the original position, not knowing what your religious or moral outlook is. If I wanted to ban alcohol and tobacco, I would have to present reasons for doing so that others who did not share my faith might find reasonable and acceptable. For example, I might point out the cost to the health-care system of permitting smoking, as well as the deaths and injuries that arise from drunk driving, as reasons for banning cigarettes and alcohol. If I simply went ahead and banned these things on the basis of my faith alone, I would be inviting a constant fight over political power between groups of different religious and moral doctrines that could in some extreme circumstances result in a civil war. Rawls called this form of political argument *public reason*. A commitment to public reason is simply a commitment to present political arguments in ways that do not require others to accept our comprehensive moral standards. Since almost all of us prefer political stability to political instability, it would make sense for us to make our arguments about government legislation in ways that those who do not share our comprehensive doctrines could find reasonable and acceptable.

For example, many religious groups oppose same-sex marriage because it violates their understanding of their scripture. As such, they may refer to scripture as the basis for prohibiting same-sex marriage. However, not everyone shares their faith or their interpretation of their faith. Subsequently, to use faith-based arguments as the foundation for governmental prohibition of same-sex marriage ultimately invites a competition between religious and non-religious comprehensive doctrines for political power that may ultimately fragment and destabilize our society. Instead, those who oppose same-sex marriage should phrase their argument in terms that those who do not share their faith might find reasonable. They may point to the traditional connection between marriage and child rearing, for example, and argue that governments have an obligation to protect the definition of the traditional marriage because it promotes traditional child rearing. This is a reason I, for one, don't find compelling, but it is something that I can respond to as part of a larger societal debate because it does not require me to accept the assumptions of those who are opposed to same-sex marriage for particular religious reasons. An argument rooted in faith is very hard to respond to for those who do not share that particular faith or interpretation of it.

The willingness to phrase our arguments about government policy in terms that others who do not share our comprehensive views can accept is what Rawls called an *overlapping consensus*. All citizens of pluralist democracies have an interest in explaining themselves to their fellow citizens in ways that those who do not share their comprehensive views can accept, or at least debate, and find reasonable. It may not be too great an exaggeration to say that the ability of the citizens of pluralist democracies to debate and resolve their differences in this way will decide whether we can all get along. Guided by a concern for fairness and using reason as the basis for debate will not make the conflicts and differences that characterize pluralist societies go away. They will, however, enable us to debate and create laws that, even when we are part of the minority group, we might be more willing to live with and accept.

Note

[1] Adeno Addis, "On Human Diversity and the Limits of Toleration," in *Ethnicity and Group Rights*, eds. I. Shapiro and W. Kymlicka.

Diversity versus Solidarity— the Progressive Dilemma of 21st-Century Politics

Bhikhu Parekh

We would all agree that diversity is a fact of modern life. It is, further, an unavoidable fact of life because not all differences can be rationally and conclusively resolved. It is also going to increase with the passage of time, for a variety of reasons. Globalization means that people are exposed to different cultural influences. Trade and commerce are never culturally neutral and, therefore, as we get integrated into a global economy, we are increasingly going to be a porous society, whose boundaries will not be able to resist cultural influences.

There are also other reasons why diversity is an inescapable and persistent fact of life, and bound to remain so. This has to do with the fact that people increasingly want to make their own choices. In our kind of society, people tend to define their dignity in terms of their capacity to make choices. They also define themselves in terms of self-fulfilment or self-expression. There is a "self" which they seek to express or articulate, and that self is unique to each individual.

Then, of course, there is the fact of immigration. Diversity has nothing to do with immigrants per se. In fact, many immigrants might be only too willing to assimilate into society. Even if immigration were to stop tomorrow, diversity would remain an inescapable and intractable fact of life.

I would go further and argue that diversity is not only a fact of life, but also an important source of moral, economic and social energy. It brings together different ways of looking at life and, therefore, enables us to learn from others and deepen our insights into human life. No culture is perfect. Each expresses one particular vision of life, stressing certain values and ignoring others. Cultural interaction is one way in which we can liberate ourselves from the limitations of our own culture and open up our consciousness to the impact of others.

Cultures also bring different forms of imagination and creativity. We can see this influence in our own country to a great extent post-1948, or in the US, which was built by immigrants. Immigrants also bring

---

This excerpt is reprinted from the *RSA Journal*, April 2003, pp. 47–48.

different sensibilities, values, forms of imagination, sources of energy and moral and cultural resources and engage the host society.

No society can be based on diversity alone. It needs a strong sense of community. Why? First, we can't hold a diverse society together unless there is a certain basic commitment or a common sense of belonging. Second, a society which is not confident in itself will not be able to live with its differences. Such confidence comes from the recognition that these differences are not going to tear the nation apart. And third, we need a sense of community so that we care for each other, and are prepared to both share our resources with others, and pay higher taxes for the benefit of the underprivileged.

We therefore need both diversity and a sense of community or a common sense of belonging. The loss of one doesn't automatically privilege the other. If we have a community where diversity is sacrificed, we would purchase the sense of community at the cost of liberty and individual self-expression. If, on the other hand, we had diversity alone, society would not be able to hold itself together. Since we need both, the question is: how can we reconcile their occasionally conflicting demands in such a way as to create a society with a strong sense of unity, as well as a great respect for and delight in its diversity?

I would suggest that there are several ways in which we can reconcile the demands of diversity and community. It is extremely important that people growing up in society should not only retain—if they so want—their own different cultural, religious and other identities, but also ascribe to an overarching common identity which they share as citizens. The only overarching identity is a political identity, which disciplines the demands of narrower religious, cultural, ethnic and other identities.

The second requirement would be to define our citizenship, our political identity, in such a way that it accommodates a large number of diversities. Thus we should define Britishness in order that all British citizens, whatever their religion, colour, and ethnicity, can identify with it without having to sacrifice their non-political identities. If political identity were to be so defined that it required abandonment of cultural, religious and other identities, then it would demand an unacceptably heavy price from its citizens and alienate a large group of them. A political community can be cohesive only if it respects legitimate differences.

It is sometimes said that such a multicultural society cannot deliver social justice, because the latter requires redistribution which people will accept only if they can identify with others and find them culturally similar. The argument is false. Switzerland and Canada are multicultural, but also based on a strong sense of social justice. By contrast, the US has a strong sense of national and cultural unity but a weak sense of social justice. Margaret Thatcher strove to create a culturally homogeneous society in Britain during her period of office, but it was also a period marked by an emphasis on self-interest and a weak sense of redistributive justice. In short, cultural homogeneity does not guarantee, and cultural diversity does not mitigate against, either social justice or a strong sense of community. It all depends on how members of a society relate to each other and whether or not they develop a sense of belonging. And these depend on their bonds of common interest, their sense of justice, and the policies of the government.

Finally, a multicultural society requires that its citizens share a broadly common body of basic values, and know enough about each other's background, history and culture to feel at ease in each other's company.

A multicultural education, therefore, has much to be said for it. When properly defined and designed, it develops understanding between cultures, respect for differences, and a shared sense of common belonging.

UNIT 3

The Individual and the Collective: Conflict and Cooperation

No man is an island entire of itself; every man is a piece of the continent, a part of the main. If a clod be washed away by the sea, Europe is the less, as well as if a promontory were, as well as if a manor of thy friend's or thine own were. Any man's death diminishes me, because I am involved in mankind, and therefore never send to know for whom the bell tolls; it tolls for thee.

John Donne

One always bakes the most delicate cakes
Two is the really superb masseur
Three sets your hair with exceptional flair
Four's brandy goes to the Emperor
Five knows each trick of advanced rhetoric
Six bred a beautiful brand-new rose
Seven can cook every dish in the book
And eight cuts you flawlessly elegant clothes
Do you think those eight would be happy
if each of them could climb so high
and no higher
before banging their heads on equality
if each could be only a small link
in a long and heavy chain
Do you still think it's possible
to unite mankind...

Marquis de Sade in the play Marat-Sade by Peter Weiss, adapted by Adrian Mitchell

Out of timber so crooked as that from which man is made nothing entirely straight can be built.

Immanuel Kant

Introduction

In this unit of *The Human Project,* we move from the societal to the political arena. We aren't leaving the study of social issues behind, however, so much as sharpening our focus more specifically on the way power is formally regulated in society. Just as our reflections on the self in Unit 1 led us to consider many of the social forces we later analyzed in Unit 2, our discussion of change in the social world led us to anticipate some of the political issues we will encounter in Unit 3. Any thoughtful inquiry into the social changes wrought by women's rights within the context of the family, for example, inevitably leads to a consideration of politics. Every political theory, moreover, presupposes a specific interpretation of the nature of society as well as the individual. In short, our analysis of politics in this unit builds upon our previous inquiries into self and society.

Conflict

While you may fully expect to encounter the topic of conflict in a unit on politics, you may have been surprised that it has figured so prominently in our discussion of self and society as well. Conflict in the political realm, however, is merely a reflection of the conflict that is so prevalent in every aspect of human life.

What is all this conflict about? Postman leads us to the idea that, at least in part, it may be due to the struggle between the "winners" and "losers" created by the "ecological" change new technology brings. Or, as Bragues suggests, conflict may result from the "creative destruction" that drives economic development in a capitalist system insofar as it has, paradoxically, facilitated a belief in equality even as it has created relative inequality of wealth. On the cultural front, moreover, Narbey points out that conflict is to some extent inevitable in the highly pluralistic societies, such as Canada's, that exist today in the West. In the private sphere, Ignatieff proposes that conflict has been exacerbated in family life due to the "rights revolution." And Freud, you will recall, attributes conflict to the incompatibility between our primitive instincts for pleasure and aggression on the one hand and our drive to conform to internalized social rules on the other. Alternatively, Nietzsche sees conflict as the result of the urge to break free from the herd and exercise will to power.

Power

Indeed, the struggle for *power* does seem to be key to understanding all these explanations of conflict. After all, power can give us a measure of control that allows us the *freedom* to live life as we wish. And since "no [wo]man is an island"—since we are either blessed or cursed, depending on your perspective, to live among others within society—we usually measure our share of power in relation to that of others. But how much power do we need? Enough to give us the ability to live "the good life."

Ideology

Not everyone agrees, however, on what "the good life" entails. Usually, our view of the good life is influenced by one of the many competing *ideologies* advocated in the political arena. As George Bragues suggests in "The Game We Call Politics," these ideologies determine our understanding of what it is to win the "game" of politics: a liberal, for example, seeks political office with the intention of limiting the role of government in private life while at the same time enhancing governmental regulation of the economy; a conservative, on the other hand, seeks political office with the goal of limiting the role of government in the economy but simultaneously endorsing governmental initiatives that uphold traditional values. Important players in the "game" of politics as it is played in Canada are our different political parties—the Liberals, the Conservatives, the New Democrats, the Bloc Québécois—each of which generally represents a different ideology that endorses a distinct view of "the good life."

These ideologies, which significantly influence "real-world" politics in Canada and elsewhere today, reflect the thought of some of the great political philosophers discussed by Morton Ritts in "Politics in the Life of the Individual." In each case, the theorist's conception of good government is determined by his understanding of human nature and, on that basis, his view of "the good life"—that is, the best life possible given the human condition as it is. For Hobbes, this is a life in which personal security is guaranteed by a strong government with absolute power; for Locke, on the other hand, this is a life in which individual rights to life, liberty and property are protected by a strong government with limited power. For Marx, the good life can be lived only within a communist society in which material needs are readily satisfied and, therefore, the pursuit of "truly human" needs becomes possible; for

Mill, however, the good life is already attainable within existing society as long as government protects individual rights to political participation and free speech. It is not really that hard to see how these ideas are reflected in political life today. The security measures taken in Canada after the September 11, 2001 terrorist attacks on the U.S., for example, tend to reflect a Hobbesian perspective; the backlash to some of these extreme measures, on the other hand, seems to emanate from a Lockean point of view.

Ends and Means

Each conception of "the good life" has its allure. Further complicating the political arena, moreover, is the fact that an ideology can come up short when put into practice. It is hard to find fault with the Locke-inspired founding principles of the American Republic, for example, but in that same country slavery became a long-standing institution and, even after its abolition, African-Americans suffered so much discrimination that the civil rights movement was necessary 100 years after the Civil War. While African-Americans overwhelmingly agreed with the goal of the civil rights movement—to insure that they enjoyed the same rights to "life, liberty and the pursuit of happiness" as their compatriots—there was less agreement on the best means for obtaining this end. As Ritts explains in "Soul Force versus Physical Force," Martin Luther King insisted on following the principles of non-violent civil disobedience that he learned from Gandhi, while Malcolm X argued that the violence suffered by African-Americans justified their rebellion by "whatever means necessary."

The impact of ideology extends beyond national boundaries, moreover, into the international realm as well. The theories of Hobbes, Locke, Marx and Mill all stem from Western civilization, the contemporary manifestation of which is significantly determined by the development of capitalism. Yet the "creative destruction" that capitalism brings is not limited to the West. As Benjamin Barber explains in "Jihad vs. McWorld," the globalizing imperatives of transnational capitalism threaten to render obsolete the unique practices, traditions, beliefs, languages and very ways of life that have historically distinguished different cultures from one another. Yet this economically driven homogenization of the world has been met by resistance from peoples all over the globe who are not ready to trade their traditional cuisine for the Big Mac. Such resistance has taken the form of independence movements, demands for autonomy, civil wars and even terrorism. Indeed, some see terrorist acts against Western societies, such as the toppling of the World Trade Centre in New York City, the bombing of the railway in Madrid, and the devastation of the resort island of Bali (a magnet for Australian tourists) as a cold attempt to use violence to resist the assault of Western culture.

Clearly, then, ideology does matter. This is even more important to keep in mind when we consider ideologies that dehumanize and, thereby, render expendable entire groups of people. The "good life," according to such views, whether touted by anti-Tutsi nationalists in Rwanda, anti-Semitic Nazis in Germany, anti-Black white supremacists in the U.S. or anti-Armenian Turks in the Ottoman Empire, requires that the "other" be eliminated—through expulsion or ethnic cleansing or even genocide.

Apathy versus Awareness

As Mitchell Lerner explains in "On Inhumanity," the utter brutality of genocide—the "intent to destroy, in whole or in part, a national, ethnic, racial or religious group"—is so incomprehensible that we may be tempted to disbelieve that ordinary people could ever carry out genocidal acts. Hard as it is to face, however, genocide occurs precisely because large numbers of ordinary people choose to follow orders instead of their conscience. The best safeguard against resurgence of this "banality of evil," moreover, is a public that acknowledges genocide as an ugly yet real phenomenon that has, regrettably, occurred throughout history but which, fortunately, can be prevented if people speak out against prejudice, hatred and ignorance.

Conversely, apathy—disinterest in social and political issues— preserves the power of those who wield it. In circumstances like the Ottoman Empire or Nazi Germany, this can, indeed, have devastating consequences. But in a tolerant liberal democracy such as that of modern-day Canada, the dangers of an uninformed public are less obvious.

Nonetheless, in "Righting the Ship of Democracy," Bruce Ackerman and James Fishkin argue that a politically aware public is important enough to justify the institution of "Deliberation Day"—a national holiday strategically scheduled just weeks before a federal election and devoted to discussion of the major issues central to the election. Since this exercise would encourage citizens to cast their votes based not on 30-second political advertisements but on a more reflective consideration of the issues, voters would make choices that are more "public-spirited." In "Smooth Sailing," by contrast, Richard Posner argues that

"Deliberation Day" would merely encourage voters to take unrealistic, extreme positions and, therefore, would be a waste of time.

If Posner is correct, maybe we should skip this entire unit of *The Human Project*. Perhaps, moreover, the whole book should be shelved permanently. After all, you have other textbooks to read for other courses, courses that are more directly related to your career goals. Or perhaps *The Human Project* should only be read by those students studying to become "rulers," who Posner boldly describes as "officials . . . drawn from . . . a governing class consisting of ambitious, determined, and charismatic seekers of power." By implication, the rest of us should attend to more everyday matters such as making a living wage, taking care of our homes, enjoying our leisure time, and voting when the urge hits us. At first sight, this may seem to be a tempting proposition (especially if you have a full schedule of courses!). Before adopting this position too readily, however, it is important to recognize that this kind of willed disinterest amounts to nothing less than a *choice* to be power*less*, to relinquish *your* political power to the ruling politicians, to *trust* them to use this power in a way that is best for you and society at large. If you find this to be a reasonable position, you might as well skip this unit. If, however, you have any doubts about trusting politicians and the political process in this way, read on.

The Game We Call Politics: A Primer

George Bragues

Hard as it may be to believe, politics once was held in high esteem—at least that was the case 2500 years ago in ancient Greece when government was first systematically studied. Aristotle (384–322 BCE), the Greek philosopher who founded political science, believed that politics is the most important human activity because it is the arena in which our happiness and fulfillment are decided. He even thought politicians are uniquely positioned to display god-like moral qualities by serving the common good.

For most people today, the idea that politics could make us happy and that a politician could be god-like is laughable. Whenever politics comes up in conversation these days, it isn't too long before someone calls politicians a bunch of lying, sweet-talking, promise-breaking, power-lusting scoundrels looking out only for themselves and whoever else is willing to put money in their pockets to finance their election campaigns. Voter turnout during elections, both in Canada and the United States, has been steadily declining over the last 40 years, perhaps because people see the political process as hopelessly dominated by special interests and, therefore, unresponsive to the concerns of ordinary individuals. Simply put, many people feel increasingly alienated from government, and young people, who exhibit the lowest voting turn-outs, appear to be especially apathetic and cynical.

Is politics really this bad? To help you better explore that question, this article surveys the core elements and driving forces operating in the realm of politics and government. As such, we'll be pursuing a different approach to the study of politics than that implicit in Morton Ritts's article, "Politics in the Life of the Individual." While he focuses on the "*normative*" approach taken by some of the great philosophers and political activists of the past who thought about how government *should* work, here we take a "*positive*" approach by considering how government *really does* work. A particularly fruitful way to understand the machinery of government is to see politics as a kind of game, albeit one with very high stakes.

"The Game We Call Politics: A Primer" is by George Bragues of the Humber College Institute of Technology and Advanced Learning. Used by permission.

The Players

Like any game, politics has its players, each trying to steer the government in the direction that best furthers their interests and causes. The list of players is as follows:

- *Politicians*—These are the most active players, the people who immediately come to mind whenever we think about government and politics. Their chief concern is to secure political office—whether it be city councillor, mayor, Member of Parliament, Prime Minister, Senator, Chancellor, or President—from which they can influence the laws and policies executed by government.

- *Parties*—These represent a coalition of various individuals and groups with common values and goals who provide institutional and financial support for specific people vying for political office. Parties typically aim to control the machinery of government. In Canada, for example, the major political parties include the Liberal Party, Conservative Party, New Democratic Party (NDP) and Bloc Québécois. Except for the Bloc, they all put candidates forward during elections in the hopes of capturing a majority of seats in Parliament and forming the government. In the United States, there are two major parties, the Democrats and the Republicans.

- *Interest Groups*—Like parties, these are coalitions with shared values and goals but, unlike parties, they only seek to influence the government, not control it. Interest groups also tend to focus on more specific objectives, while political parties typically pursue broader platforms. Interest groups come in two varieties: some pursue their own economic interests, while others seek to advance a moral or social agenda. The Canadian Marketing Association, which lobbies governments to enact policies friendly to advertisers and marketers, is an example of the first kind. Amnesty International, which pressures governments worldwide to respect human rights, is an example of the second kind.

- *Civil Servants*—Sometimes also known as bureaucrats, these individuals work within government agencies, like the Departments of Justice and Finance, and are responsible for administering laws and policies on a day-to-day basis. They are the people you would deal with if, say, your tax return were audited. Key concerns for civil servants include maintaining the standing and budgets of their departments as well as progressing in their careers individually. Though operating behind the scenes, bureaucrats often exercise substantial influence by giving politicians advice, interpreting the laws that the government enacts and, sometimes, even hindering the implementation of government policies that they do not approve. This was illustrated in a 1980s British television comedy, "Yes Minister," which showed Sir Humphrey Appleby, a top bureaucrat, often getting the better of his political master Jim Hacker.

- *The Media*—This group gathers, interprets and communicates information about matters related to government. It includes those who produce political content for newspapers, magazines, radio, television and the Internet. Because journalists can enhance their reputations and careers by uncovering corruption and scandal in government, the media are widely seen as watchdogs. Nothing better exemplifies this function than the efforts of Carl Bernstein and Bob Woodward who, as reporters for *The Washington Post,* exposed the Watergate scandal that led to U.S. President Nixon's resignation in 1974. The media also serve as venues for journalists, intellectuals, activists, businesspeople and politicians to express their opinions and further their agendas.

- *The Public*—In a democratic society, like Canada, the public plays a crucial role in the political game by exercising its right to vote. This role is obviously more limited in non-democratic nations, though even in such countries the government must assure its authority and legitimacy by not outraging the populace to the point of inviting an uprising. After all, in every political society, the people being ruled far outnumber those doing the ruling. It's worth recalling that East Germany's communist regime suddenly fell in 1989, and with it the Berlin Wall that symbolized the Cold War between Western nations and the Soviet Union, after only two months of mass protests.

Inside the Heads of the Players: Political Ideologies

Influencing the moves players make in the political game is *ideology*. Simply put, an ideology is a belief system that gives its adherents a picture of how human beings and societies function, and, as well, sets forth guiding principles about what needs to be done in the political realm. As you are about to see, the leading political ideologies of our time contain ideas similar to those expounded by the great philosophers you will read about later in this unit of the book.

Liberalism goes back to the 17th and 18th centuries when modern democracies first emerged. This ideology holds that the government ought not to be involved in promoting a specific way of life. Rather, the government should give people the freedom to pursue their own conceptions of happiness in association with others so long as everyone is treated equally and no one is allowed to harm others (think of John Stuart Mill here). Liberals thus support *limited government*, one that ensures a *zone of privacy* in which individuals can hold and pursue property (think of Locke here) and exercise their rights to practise the culture and religion of their choice as well as to freely express themselves. When it comes to the economy, liberals insist that the government must play an active role by regulating business, smoothing economic cycles, providing social programs, redistributing wealth and ensuring equal opportunities in education and employment. Adherents of liberalism include Canada's Liberal Party, *The Toronto Star* newspaper and the Democratic Party in the U.S.

Conservatism originally emerged as a reaction to the French revolution in the 18th century. One thing that distinguishes conservatives from liberals is their willingness to enlist the government in promoting specific values and lifestyles. More often than liberals, conservatives oppose efforts to decriminalize marijuana as well as advocate policies for advancing conventional family values and traditional sexual morality. Unlike liberals, too, conservatives are more likely to favour *laissez-faire* economic policies, which involve minimizing the level of government intervention in the economy by deregulating business, cutting taxes and reducing government expenditures. An up-and-coming ideology that combines elements of conservatism and liberalism is *libertarianism*. Proponents of that view argue that the government should generally stay out of our personal and economic lives, that is, both out of our homes (and, especially, our bedrooms) and our wallets. The Conservative Party in Canada and the Republican Party in the U.S. both adhere to conservative ideology. *The National Post* newspaper presents a mixture of conservative and libertarian thinking.

Advocates of *social democracy* sympathize with Karl Marx's critique of the modern capitalist economy. To social democrats, capitalism inherently favours employers and big corporations at the expense of workers, making the rich richer and the poor poorer. Social democrats *don't* agree with Marx, however, that a revolution is necessary to bring about economic justice. Instead, they recommend working within the capitalist system, promoting the role of unions and demanding that the government influence more of the economy so that the people can decide their economic fate through the democratic process. The New Democratic Party embodies this social democratic perspective.

In political discussions, you'll often hear people and policies being described as left-wing or right-wing, which refers to the *ideological spectrum* (see Figure 1 below). Conservatism and libertarianism are considered to be on the right of that spectrum, and hence are known as right-wing ideologies, whereas liberalism and social democracy are considered to be on the opposite end of the spectrum, and are thus called left-wing ideologies.

The Democratic Rules of the Game

Games have rules that the players are supposed to obey, and politics is no exception. In any particular game of politics, the most basic rules are set by the established form of government. In Western industrialized nations, such as Canada, the United States and those in Western Europe, the reigning form of government is *liberal democracy*. In this kind of political system, the people, rather than one individual or a small group, ultimately decide what laws and policies the government implements. This is not to say that the populace can dictate anything it wishes, as

Figure 1: The Ideological Spectrum

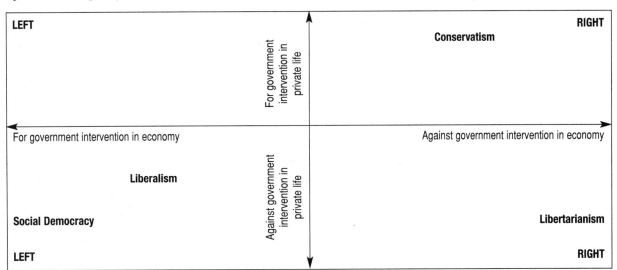

Source: Mark O. Dickerson and Thomas Flanagan, *An Introduction to Government and Politics: A Conceptual Approach*, 6th edition (Scarborough, Ontario: Nelson Thomson Learning, 2002), p. 137.

would be the case in a *pure democracy*. Liberal democracies impose legal constraints on the people's authority, restricting them from doing things like oppressing minorities, violating private property and invading our personal lives. In other words, liberal democracy is characterized by the *rule of law*.

Further limiting the people's influence in most liberal democracies is the fact that they generally cannot vote on specific legislative and policy proposals. Such opportunity only exists in a *direct democracy*. Instead, the public chooses someone to represent their interests and values and decide political issues for them. As such, most liberal democracies adopt a system of *representative democracy*.

This system generally comes in two forms: *parliamentary* and *presidential*.[1] In both, a *legislative* branch, composed of those who *make* the laws, is distinguished from an *executive* branch, made up of those who *enforce* the laws. In both, too, each branch has to give its approval to any law. The key difference is that the legislative and executive branches are not as strictly separated in a parliamentary system as they are in a presidential system. In the parliamentary system, for instance, the executive essentially consists of the Prime Minister and the Cabinet, who table legislation in the House of Commons. Since members of the ruling party want to stay in the Prime Minister's good graces, either to obtain or to keep a Cabinet position, legislation proposed by the executive is, more often than not, successfully passed. The table on the next page describes these two forms of government, using Canada and the United States as examples.

Notice that in Canada, which inherited the parliamentary system from Britain, the Prime Minister has more power to pass whatever laws he or she may desire than the U.S. President does. It is for this reason that Jeffrey Simpson, political columnist for *The Globe and Mail*, has argued that the Prime Minister's authority produces a "friendly dictatorship."[2] On a more positive note, having a powerful leader does have its benefits: things can get done quickly and decisively.

Whoever gets chosen to represent the people must pay heed to their wishes, if only because he or she will have to seek their vote again at some point in the future to continue in power. This does not mean, however, that elected officials always perfectly reflect the preferences of their constituents. Indeed, due to their generally greater education and higher socioeconomic status, politicians tend to embrace different values from those held by ordinary people. Add to this the fact that people may not have the time to monitor every vote their representative makes. Even if voters become aware of a particular difference in opinion, they may think it worth tolerating if the rest of their views are amenable and alternative candidates hold more disagreeable positions overall.

Table 1 Parliamentary versus Presidential System—Canada and the U.S.

System	Nation	Legislative Branch	Executive Branch	Passage of Laws
Parliamentary	Canada	**Parliament:** 1) *House of Commons* —elected, usually every 3–5 years 2) *Senate* —appointed	**Prime Minister:** —member of House of Commons —leads party with most seats in the House **Cabinet:** —members of House of Commons —appointed by Prime Minister to head government ministries **Governor General:** —representative of the monarchy —mostly plays a ceremonial function	**Legislation:** —tabled by executive —must be supported by majority in the House **Prime Ministerial Power:** high
Presidential	U.S.	**Congress:** 1) *House of Representatives* —elected every two years 2) *Senate* —elected every six years	**President:** —elected every four years —not a member of Congress **Cabinet:** —appointed by President to head government departments —must be confirmed by Senate	**Legislation:** —President must form majority coalition among members of Congress to pass laws **Presidential Power:** limited

A prime instance where the beliefs of the public and elected officials diverge is capital punishment. This was abolished in 1976 by Parliament and rejected again when its reinstitution came up for a vote in 1987—even though opinion polls consistently show that a majority of the public supports capital punishment. By thus permitting government to be imperfectly reflective of voter preferences, representative democracy provides significant leeway to those who play the game of politics as a profession—chiefly, politicians, but also those who interact regularly with them, such as civil servants, parties and special interest groups.

Concern that the professional political classes too easily ignore the people's wishes has recently generated calls for more direct democracy. One widely touted proposal is the *recall vote* mechanism, which allows voters to remove elected politicians before their allotted term ends. In California, this mechanism was recently used to remove Governor Gray Davis, who had won an election just a year earlier, and to elect instead movie star Arnold Schwarzenegger. Other popular methods of direct democracy include *initiatives* and *referendums*. Both entail giving the people the opportunity to vote on a specific issue, with the only difference being that initiatives are launched by the public, whereas referendums are tabled by elected officials. Initiatives and referendums are common in the United States, but rare in Canada. Only three referendums have ever been held here, the most recent concerning the 1992 Charlottetown Accord, a set of proposed amendments to our constitution. Ten years earlier, when our constitution was patriated from Britain and significantly amended, the matter was never actually put to a vote before the people.

The original democracies of ancient Greece were direct democracies. Citizens would go to the local assembly, take part in debates, decide issues and elect individuals to execute the laws. Making this possible was the fact that the citizens were a relatively small group, limited to non-slave males, who lived in small city-states. As such, it was easy for people to congregate. In modern democracies, this is not so easy because territories and voting populations are so much larger—a key reason why we've stuck with representative democracy. Another reason stems from the belief that the public does not have the same resources to adequately inform themselves of complex policy issues that professional politicians do. The Internet holds out the promise of transcending these barriers, however, by potentially allowing everyone to readily gather political information, debate with others on chat lines, seek out supporters, and vote on matters like marijuana legalization and human cloning with a click of the mouse. Some Internet enthusiasts are even calling for an electronic direct democracy along these lines. In the days ahead, as online technology continues to advance, that call is likely to become louder and more debated.

Refereeing the Game: the Judiciary

We've neglected one thing thus far in our comparison of politics to a game. Who acts as the referee? Who signals and sanctions rule violations by the political players? In principle, at least, that job belongs to the judges, who together make up the third branch of government, the judiciary. The most important judges are those who sit on the highest court of the land, the Supreme Court. In both Canada and the United States, the Supreme Court consists of nine appointed individuals, whose chief task is to interpret the Constitution, the country's highest law. In doing so, Supreme Court judges exercise *judicial review* in being able to nullify laws passed by elected officials.

For much of Canada's history, the Supreme Court has been marginal, mostly deciding turf wars between the provinces and Ottawa. That all changed in 1982 with the introduction of *The Charter of Rights and Freedoms*, which enshrined freedoms of speech, conscience and association in addition to individual rights to life, liberty, equality, personal

Prime Minister Paul Martin

security and due process in criminal proceedings. Mirroring a pattern seen in the United States, Canada's Supreme Court has used the Charter to strike down a wide array of laws. In this way, for example, refugees were granted the right to a hearing of their case before they could be deported. So, too, abortion was legalized, capital punishment was effectively precluded from being revived by Parliament and gays and lesbians were granted equal standing under the law, leading the way to the legalization of gay marriage. Critics of the Supreme Court argue that judges have overstepped their proper role as referees and, instead, have become players in the political game by imposing their own values on the community. Defenders of the court, on the other hand, insist that it is simply checking majority tyranny (recall John Stuart Mill) by ensuring that the public no longer discriminates against traditionally oppressed groups, like foreigners, women, criminals and homosexuals.

How the Liberal Democratic Game Stacks Up

What sort of results does the liberal democratic game of politics tend to produce? On issues of general interest—such as the economy, crime, foreign policy, health care and education—liberal democratic regimes usually end up with policies that generally reflect the preferences of middle-of-the-road voters. In a democracy, after all, politicians must compete against other politicians for power by attracting the most votes. Voters tend to be concentrated in the centre of the ideological spectrum, holding a mix of conservative and liberal opinions. Each of the main political parties, then, has an obvious incentive to advance "centrist" platforms, leaving the public with a choice between very similar alternatives. True, one side will typically have a more left-wing tinge to its agenda, while the other will be slightly more right-wing, but it will still very much be a contest pitting tweedle-dum against tweedle-dee. Unable to readily tell the difference between the parties, voters get swayed by scandals, the thirst for change, the personality of the candidates and the state of the economy. In the end, power flows to those politicians and parties that do the best job of following the shifting opinions of the median voter.[3] The dominance of Canada's Liberal Party, ruling 72 out of the last 103 years, is largely owing to its mastery of this task.

On issues that chiefly appeal only to special interests, liberal democracy produces more disturbing results. Imagine a country with one million taxpaying citizens, several hundred of which are chess enthusiasts. They'd love nothing more than to spend all their waking hours playing the game but are prevented from doing so since they, like everyone else, must hold down regular jobs to pay their bills. One day, a couple of the chess players successfully propose that they all form the "Chess Advancement Society," an organization that will lobby the government to build facilities for chess and fund licensed players (they'd have to pass a rigorous chess test) with an annual stipend of $30,000 so that they can focus on perfecting their game. They ask for $1 million, justifying the request by insisting that chess promotes rational thinking. Ridiculous as it may sound, politicians would have an incentive to grant the chess players the money. They would secure the chess players' votes in the next election and perhaps even a campaign donation as well. At the same time, politicians need not worry about losing votes from the non-chess-playing citizens footing the bill because the cost would be spread among all of the one million taxpayers amounting to a mere dollar each. That's not enough to anger taxpayers, assuming they even find out about the Chess Advancement Society. Whether it be a corporation getting a tax break or a local industry obtaining protection from cheap imports, this story illustrates why special interests flourish in our democracies: an organized minority can transfer wealth and privileges to itself by simply passing on the costs in small individual chunks to the majority. As more and more people do the same thing, of course, the costs add up.

Still, after tallying the positives against the negatives, the liberal democratic political game does a reasonably good job of furnishing what most people want: economic prosperity. The fact that politicians can be removed in a democracy makes them more likely to adopt sound economic policies, and, as well, inhibits them from engaging in corruption and looting the nation's wealth. Not only that, the rule of law and private property, both essential elements of liberal democracy, generate economic growth by providing legal assurance to people that they'll be able to keep the fruits of their investments and work. Winston Churchill put it best: "Democracy is the worst form of government, except for all those other forms that have been tried from time to time."

Notes

[1] Some nations, like France and Portugal, combine both systems.

[2] Jeffrey Simpson, *The Friendly Dictatorship* (Toronto: McClelland and Stewart, 2001).

[3] This is more formally known as the median voter theorem. See Harold Hotelling, "Stability in Competition," *Economic Journal*, 39: 41–57, 1929; and Anthony Downs, *An Economic Theory of Democracy* (New York: Harper and Row, 1957).

Politics in the Life of the Individual

Morton Ritts

Politics

As we saw in the previous unit, we live in a time of unprecedented change. Technology, demographics and the clash between old and new values are just some of the things that cause change. But so is something we haven't paid much attention to yet—politics. Whether we care or not, politics matters. Political decisions affect jobs, taxes, social policy, immigration and other current issues. Politics helps to define our society's notions of freedom, law and justice.

Politics isn't something that happens only at election time. Politics occurs when students protest higher tuition fees, business groups lobby for free trade, unions go on strike, women and minorities fight for employment equity, and governments act—or don't act.

In its broadest sense, politics refers to the complex relations among various members and groups in society. There is politics between you and your boss, you and your parents, you and your teachers, you and your boy- or girlfriend. Politics is about power—competing for it, sharing it, imposing it. We want power not simply because we want things our own way. We want power because it gives us the feeling that we have some control over our lives, that we are free.

Obviously certain individuals and groups in society are more powerful than others. What is the basis of this power? Does "might make right"? Does sex, race, wealth, intelligence, status or tradition? Or moral or religious authority? Or a commitment to ethical principles? In some way, these are all factors in determining how much or how little power people have.

Government

Simply put, government is the mechanism that regulates power relations and the rights and duties of citizens and their rulers. According to the Greek philosopher Aristotle, there are basically three kinds of

---

"Politics in the Life of the Individual" is by Morton Ritts of the Humber College Institute of Technology and Advanced Learning. Used by permission.

government: government by one person; government by the few; and government by the many. Every government is an example of one of these three basic forms.

Whatever the case may be, some individuals and groups have more rights than others. And this in turn, as we've already suggested, depends to a large extent on a society's notions of freedom, law and justice. Later we'll examine how political thinkers like Thomas Hobbes, John Locke, John Stuart Mill and Karl Marx thought about these issues.

Whatever our political philosophy, however, we must acknowledge the role that government plays in our daily lives. Consider a government's monetary and fiscal policies, which affect everything from inflation to interest rates—in other words, everything from your ability to find a job to your ability to borrow money to start a business, or to buy a house or car.

At the same time, consider the degree to which a government is involved in economic and social matters. Those who argue for more state intervention claim that government investment in areas such as education, health care and transportation is vital for the national interest. They argue that government regulation is also necessary to ensure that businesses don't pollute the environment, treat employees unfairly or take advantage of consumers.

On the other hand, those who adopt a "laissez-faire" or hands-off approach believe that government involvement in social and economic matters should be minimal and that it is best to allow the "market" to regulate itself.

Another important question about government is constitutional. How should power be divided among central, regional and local governments? Over the past 30 years in Canada, an extraordinary amount of energy has been devoted to the question of federal-provincial relations. Compared to other countries, Canada is already very decentralized, and many people who objected to the Meech Lake and Charlottetown agreements did so because they feared that these agreements would further weaken the federal government's power.

Of all forms of government, democracy (in theory at least) encourages the greatest redistribution of power and the greatest amount of change. In Canada and the United States, women, visible minorities, the disabled, aboriginals, environmentalists, gays and lesbians have been in the forefront of such controversial political issues as employment equity, human rights, land claims and same-sex benefits.

Of course, this kind of freedom to challenge the status quo and to fight for political change doesn't exist in every society. Freedom of speech and individual rights are values that we associate with liberal democracy. You don't have to look beyond the nearest headline or newscast to see that most of the time most governments around the world suppress human rights, crush dissent and persecute minorities.

When governments act this way, we often aren't surprised. Because many of us, consciously or otherwise, seem to accept self-interest as the norm in politics, we tend not to have a very high opinion of those who practise it. And too often their actions fail to shock us: patronage, corruption, dirty tricks, broken promises, slush funds, sex scandals—the dirty laundry list of unsavoury political practices, even in a liberal democracy, can turn us off any interest in politics at all.

Apathy and Activism

apathy
lack of interest or concern

Many political theorists argue that such **apathy** is dangerous, however. Whether we vote or not, politics affects us in large and small ways. It determines the programs we watch on TV and the music we hear on the radio—because decisions about Canadian content are political decisions. It determines whether there is room for us at college or a job when we're finished—because education and employment policy decisions are political. So are decisions about how much money comes off our paycheques, what social programs our taxes will fund and which regions of the country will get them.

But apathy is only one response to the frustration that we may feel about how we are governed. Another, and opposite, reaction is to become politically engaged. Such activism may even take the form of new political parties, like the new Conservative Party or the Bloc Québécois, which capitalize on public discontent.

Of course, political activity isn't always legal or peaceful. The Los Angeles riots in the aftermath of the first Rodney King verdict were a spontaneous and violent expression of rage against the L.A. police and state authorities. In Quebec, the tense stand-off at Oka was the result of years of frustration by the Mohawks against all levels of Canadian government.

The ultimate reaction to an insensitive or unjust government is revolution. This occurs when governments lose touch with people and efforts at legal and peaceful reform have failed to produce a satisfactory redistribution of power. The consensus that has bound people together breaks down, and a new political structure is needed. The violent overthrow of the existing order is seen as the only way to make this happen.

The Social Contract

Many of you may be familiar with the film *The Road Warrior* or the novel *Lord of the Flies*. In these and similar works, we're presented with a vision of the world in which law and order, morality and peace have broken down. In such apocalyptic, or end-of-the-world, visions, life is ruled by naked power—by selfishness, fear, superstition, mistrust, brute force. Without the guiding authority of tradition, laws and institutions, without consensus, society may descend into anarchy.

For this reason, no political philosopher would argue that we should trade society for the raw state of nature—not even the great French social philosopher Jean Jacques Rousseau (1712–1778), whose writings contrast the natural goodness of people with the largely destructive impact of social institutions. But while Rousseau denounced his own artificial, class-ridden society with the famous words, "Man was born free, and everywhere he is in chains," he nevertheless understood that we are first and foremost social beings. We are united, he argued, by the arrangement that we make with each other to surrender at least some of our desires in exchange for the satisfaction of at least some of our needs. Rousseau, Thomas Hobbes and John Locke called this arrangement "the social contract."

For them, the effectiveness of the social contract depends on our ability to obtain a satisfactory balance between what we want and what we're prepared to give up to get it. The social contract breaks down when people believe they're surrendering too much or not getting enough in return. Or when they lose the trust that binds them to others and to a government that may be incompetent, unfair or tyrannical.

In the absence of effective government, then, the social contract crumbles and no one has any security. Freedom, laws, justice and human rights are ignored, replaced by the social chaos of Bosnia and Rwanda. We need government to maintain the social contract, and we need the social contract if we want to survive.

What Kind of Government Is Most Desirable?

The answer to this question depends on a number of things, but mainly what people believe to be the purpose of government. Is it to maintain peace and stability at any price? To promote a particular set of religious beliefs? To promote the interests of an elite, land-owning class? To preserve the rule of a king or queen? Or to guarantee freedom, rights, law and justice, which we have said are the underlying principles of liberal democracy?

Our definition of the most desirable form of government may depend on more than what we believe to be government's purpose. It may depend on some of the most fundamental questions that we ask about human nature. Are people good or bad? Are they ruled by reason or emotion? Which people are best suited to make decisions? How much freedom should ordinary people have? Are we motivated by self-interest or a desire to help others?

By the time we reach college, we have no doubt asked at least some of these questions to try to determine what kind of relationship ought to exist between ourselves and others in society, what we are willing to give up to fulfill our part of the social contract and what we expect in return.

Political philosophers since the time of Plato have tried to describe which arrangements they believe will make society function most effectively. And they often begin by trying to identify what motivates the social contract in the first place. Thomas Hobbes (1588–1679), for example, argued that it was primarily fear.

The Fear Motive

Thomas Hobbes

Hobbes lived through a tumultuous period in English history when civil war had torn his country apart, and when law, order and security had broken down. The war reinforced Hobbes's view that people are naturally aggressive, violent and competitive, dominated by their emotions and instincts, or by what Freud would later call "the id."

Because this is human nature, Hobbes argued, people have the natural right to secure whatever they want by any means within their power. And, since we have unlimited desires and not enough resources, this leads us to inevitable conflict with others. Thus people live in a constant state of fear, and therefore their first impulse is to overpower others before being overpowered themselves. Hobbes described this state of nature before the social contract as a situation in which "every man is enemy to every man" and life is "solitary, poor, nasty, brutish and short."

Imagine that all laws in your city have been suspended for 24 hours and that the police are on strike. In effect, this would be a one-day "state of nature." Is this the time to fly off for a holiday? Or would you stay home with a shotgun and make sure that no one tried to grab your property? According to Hobbes, fear would keep you at home. What's more, he argued, you may decide to take this opportunity to relieve any defenceless neighbours of their property.

In other words, Hobbes said that we are indeed creatures of greed and passion who are driven by a desire to dominate and control. Hobbes painted a picture of human beings who are nothing more than pleasure-seeking machines. As such, they constantly seek to maximize pleasure and minimize pain.

But we're also reasonable creatures who realize that our interests are better served within a framework of law, morality, peace and security than in a state of violence and anarchy. Fear motivates us to agree to the social contract and to accept the power of government to enforce it. And the job of government, or what Hobbes called "the sovereign," is to make sure that the social contract doesn't become unstuck.

How much power should the sovereign, or governing authority, have over us? Hobbes believed that whether the sovereign is in the hands of one person, a few people, or all the people, it should have absolute power to do its job well. That means giving up not only some of our desires but also most of our rights—such as freedom of speech, the right to assembly and anything else that could threaten political and social stability. But, like Freud, Hobbes believed that such stability came at a price, although unlike Freud he thought the price was rarely too high.

Hobbes personally favoured autocracy as the most desirable form of government, believing that a single ruler could act far more efficiently than any government requiring the support of a fickle electorate and the unpredictable mechanics of democracy.

The Property Motive

Like Hobbes, John Locke (1632–1704) lived in a time of great social and political upheaval when the belief in an absolute monarch who ruled by divine right was being challenged and power was being transferred from the king to the people in the form of parliamentary democracy. Locke fully supported these radical changes.

John Locke

Locke believed that all people are born free, equal, rational and moral. He also believed that we have certain God-given natural rights of life, liberty and property, which form the basis of the social contract and which it is the chief purpose of government to protect. To do so, it must be given the power to resolve conflicts and restrain violent and criminal acts. If the government fails to do its job properly, the people have the right to overthrow it—violently if necessary. To avoid this possibility, Locke advocated a system of checks and balances in which the branches of representative government are separate and distinct.

Locke's ideas on natural rights had an influence that extended well beyond the development of liberal democracy in England. They also helped to shape the thinking of the leaders of the American Revolution in their fight for independence. Indeed, Locke's theory that natural rights form the basis of the social contract is the ideology of liberal democracies everywhere, particularly in the United States where individual rights are paramount. The core of these rights, Locke argued, is private property.

But what exactly is private property? And why is it the defining feature of that economic system we call capitalism? Private property is more than the piece of land we own or the house we live in. It is, Locke said, whatever "we mix with our labour." It includes "the labour of [our] body and the work of [our] hands." It is also the fruits of our labour—the products we make and the goods we buy. They belong to us because we've earned them.

For Locke, private property is important because it defines the boundaries of individual freedom. Within the boundaries of their property, the individual has the right to do as he or she wishes and the state has no right to intrude. This principle may seem obvious to us, to the point where we take it for granted. But it wasn't always the case, certainly not before Locke's time, when land defined wealth and most of the land was owned by a relatively small aristocratic elite or the sovereign.

Locke believed in extending the right of private ownership beyond the privileged few. In doing so, he also endorsed the right to privacy itself, a mainstay of a free and open society. In 1968, Prime Minister Pierre Trudeau echoed Locke's view when he proclaimed, "The state has no business in the bedrooms of the nation." In the privacy of our own homes, Trudeau meant, the state has no business defining what is acceptable or unacceptable sexual behaviour between consenting adults. (Locke, of course, could never have anticipated how the rapid growth of technology over the past two decades has made us more vulnerable than ever to invasions of privacy. The "information highway" allows governments, corporations and individuals to gain access to our bank accounts, medical records, political affiliations and other forms of highly personal information. Despite the warnings of the federally appointed Privacy Commissioner, we are becoming an increasingly closely monitored society.)

As industrial capitalism in Western Europe and North America developed, Locke's notion of ownership and private property was expanded to include the tools, machines, factories, transportation systems, capital and human resources that made further accumulation of property possible. But clearly not everyone benefitted under such a system, and the freedom, rights, laws and justice that protected the privileged minority class did not extend to the masses.

So where Locke saw private property as the basis of freedom, socialist thinkers like Karl Marx saw it as the basis of exploitation. And where Locke argued that property was the basis of liberty, Marx replied that it was the basis of inhumanity. According to Marx, private ownership created an intolerable conflict between the "haves" and "have-nots," and, therefore, the only way to eliminate this conflict was to eliminate private property.

The Class Motive

Born in Germany and living much of his life in exile, Karl Marx (1818–1883) analyzed the great divide in terms of wealth and power between the owner/capitalist class and the workers or proletariat. Rejecting Locke's view of the sanctity of individual ownership, Marx called for a revolution to redistribute social, economic and political power. According to Marx, history showed that it was not natural rights that defined the nature of our relationship to society. It was class status—rich and poor, haves and have-nots, the powerful and the powerless. To resolve the conflict between the classes and re-organize the social order in a way that guaranteed true freedom, rights and justice, it was necessary to abolish private property.

Karl Marx

Marx disagreed with those historians and political philosophers who contend that our innate human nature predisposes us to one kind of society or another. According to Marx, it is the other way round: the kind of society we live in determines our consciousness, or how we act and think. If people are selfish and greedy, the reason has little to do with human nature and much to do with social conditions.

As proof, Marx turned to capitalism. Throughout industrialized Europe, Marx saw men, women and children working long hours in unsafe mines and factories for wages that were a fraction of what their labour entitled them to. They had no pensions, health insurance or safety protection. They had no collective agreements, job security or social safety net. Capitalism, Marx argued, really offers only two possibilities: be a loser or a winner, exploit others or be exploited yourself.

Marx believed that this "survival of the fittest" mentality is the very essence of industrial capitalism. The division of labour and alienation that turns workers into products, into property belonging to someone else, destroys the human spirit and causes untold suffering. If life is a Hobbesian war of all against all, it is not, according to Marx, human nature that causes this war but a society based on class conflict.

Marx did not look to government or the church to change this situation. In his view, government, religion, media, the education system—all the institutions of capitalist society—serve the interests of the owners who control them and keep the workers in their place. Marx was especially critical of the role played by organized religion ("the opiate of the people"), which, he said, makes people passive and accepting of their misery in this life by promising them rewards in the next.

But there is no afterlife, Marx argued, only this one. And he looked to the proletariat to lead the revolution that would destroy class conflict, eradicate scarcity and alter the course of world history: "Workers of the world unite!" he wrote in *The Communist Manifesto*, adding, "You have nothing to lose but your chains!"

Marx's view of history led him to reason that just as slavery had given way to feudalism, and feudalism to capitalism, so too capitalism would inevitably lead to socialism. Under socialism, ownership of the means of production would be collective, not private. The welfare of people would come before profit, and everyone would share in society's resources and wealth—"from each according to his abilities, to each according to his needs." Beyond socialism lay the "classless society" of communism, the promised land where, according to Marx, the state itself would "wither away."

Marx's influence on the twentieth century is undeniable. Until the collapse of the Soviet Union, over a third of the world's population claimed to be living under some form of communism. But whether Marx would have been happy with those who have practised what he preached is highly unlikely. Communist revolutions in Europe, Asia, Latin America and Africa have resulted in nothing like the free, classless and just societies that Marx envisioned.

Nevertheless, Marx's socialist ideals have had a profound impact on capitalism itself. Today free schooling to age 16, government student loans and scholarships, universal health care and progressive taxation policies are characteristic of many capitalist societies. And so is the belief in a mixed economy of public and private ownership. Ironically, Marx's legacy may have been to help renew the very capitalist system that he was so certain was doomed.

The Happiness Motive

For John Stuart Mill (1806–1879), yet another English political theorist, the purpose of life is the pursuit of happiness. And this, not natural rights or class conflict, is the guiding principle of human action. According to Mill's "utilitarian" philosophy (derived from Jeremy Bentham [1748–1832]), actions are good if they promote the greatest happiness for the greatest number of people. But this position doesn't include just any kind of happiness. Mill argued that some types of happiness are better than others; as he said, "it is better to be a human being dissatisfied than a pig satisfied." In other words, it is better to aspire to intellectual and aesthetic pleasures than to simply satisfy physical desire. Mill believed that a society that values rights, laws and justice is the best guarantee of both individual and collective happiness.

John Stuart Mill

In what kind of society can happiness best be achieved? A society, Mill argued, liberal enough to allow individuals maximum freedom to do whatever they want, as long as their actions don't harm others. Because he believed that people are basically decent and by nature are rational, cooperative and sensitive to the needs of others, Mill trusted people's ability to choose what is best for themselves. And what is "best," of course, is whatever makes people happy.

Mill argued that the primary job of government is to preserve individual rights and freedoms. He rejected the libertarian notion that government should simply stand back and let people fend for themselves. He advocated instead the idea of government intervention—not to tell people what to do or to curtail their liberty—but rather to provide the means for them to make choices through enlightened education, progressive laws and a fair justice system.

As we have already suggested, Mill believed that once government has made the advantages of liberal democracy available to all, it should restrain an individual's actions *only* when they significantly harm or interfere with the actions, interests or liberty of others. But some of us may have problems with the "harm principle." For example, how can we be sure when you smoke that I, a non-smoker, am not harmed? You can argue that you'll take responsibility if you get lung cancer. But your second-hand smoke can give me lung cancer too. So where does your right to smoke end and my right to clean air begin?

You might also argue that the government has no right to enforce measures of individual choice such as whether you wear a seat-belt. You may say you'll take your chances in your own car, thank you very much. But if you go through the windshield, whose tax dollars will help to pay for your rehabilitation—assuming you survive?

And then, of course, there's the issue of freedom of speech. Does free speech mean that you have the right to say things that could threaten the interests, rights and even physical well-being of certain racial, religious or other groups?

Mill's "harm principle" does not deal fully with problems resulting from the impact that an individual's actions may have on others (abortion is an even more troubling example). However, Mill did anticipate objections to his utilitarian principle of "the greatest happiness for the greatest number."

You may recall that in Unit 2 we noted how the ideas, customs, laws, privileges and opportunities that bring happiness to the greatest number in society can sometimes bring misery to minorities. Mill acknowledged the potential dangers of this "tyranny of the majority." He believed, therefore, that a democratic society should not only be liberal (i.e., promote individual rights), but should also be representative and pluralistic (i.e., safeguard minority rights).

Unlike Marx, Mill did not call for the demise of capitalism. Nor did he view history as a class conflict between owners and workers, haves and have-nots. The issue for Mill was the conflict between individual freedom and government control. Mill believed strongly that in this struggle the balance of power should rest with the individual because the purpose of government is to serve the people, not the other way round.

THOMAS HOBBES

Whatsoever therefore is consequent to a time of war, where every man is enemy to every man; the same is consequent to the time, wherein men live without other security, than what their own strength and their own invention shall furnish them withal. In such condition there is no place for industry; because the fruit thereof is uncertain: and consequently no culture of the earth; no navigation, nor use of the commodities that may be imported by sea; no commodious building; no instruments of moving, and removing, such things as require much force; no knowledge of the face of the earth; no account of time; no arts; no letters; no society; and which is worst of all, continual fear, and danger of violent death; and the life of man, solitary, poor, nasty, brutish, and short.

Thomas Hobbes, *Leviathan*

JOHN LOCKE

The great and chief end, therefore, of men's uniting into commonwealths and putting themselves under government is the preservation of their property. To which in the state of nature there are many things wanting:

First, There wants an established, settled, known law, received and allowed by common consent to be the standard of right and wrong and the common measure to decide all controversies between them. . . .

Secondly, In the state of nature there wants a known and indifferent judge with authority to determine all differences according to the established law. . . .

Thirdly, In the state of nature, there often wants power to back and support the sentence when right, and to give it due execution. . . .

Men . . . enter into society . . . the better to preserve himself, his liberty and property . . . the power of the society, or legislative constituted by them, can never be supposed to extend farther than the common good. . . . And so whoever has the legislative or supreme power of any commonwealth is bound to govern by established standing laws, promulgated and known to the people, and not by extemporary decrees. . . .

John Locke, *Second Treatise on Government*

KARL MARX

The State, therefore, has not existed from all eternity. There have been societies which managed without it, which had no conception of the State and State power. At a certain stage of economic development, which was necessarily bound up with the cleavage of society into classes, the State became a necessity owing to this cleavage.

As the State arose out of the need to hold class antagonisms in check, but as it, at the same time, arose in the midst of the conflict of these classes, it is, as a rule, the State of the most powerful, economically dominant class, which by virtue thereof becomes also the dominant class politically, and thus acquires new means of holding down and exploiting the oppressed class. Thus the ancient State was above all the slaveowners' State for holding down the slaves, as a feudal State was the organ of the nobles for holding down the peasantry, bondmen and serfs and the modern representative State is the instrument of the exploitation of wage-labour by capital.

Karl Marx, *The German Ideology*

JOHN STUART MILL

The object of this Essay is to assert one very simple principle, as entitled to govern absolutely the dealings of society with the individual in the way of compulsion and control, whether the means used be physical force in the form of legal penalties, or the moral coercion of public opinion. *That principle is, that the sole end for which mankind are warranted, individually or collectively, in interfering with the liberty of action of any of their number, is self-protection.*[1] That the only purpose for which power can be rightfully exercised over any member of a civilized community, against his will, is to prevent harm to others. His own good, either physical or moral, is not a sufficient warrant. He cannot rightfully be compelled to do or forbear because it will be better for him to do so, because it will make him happier, because, in the opinion of others, to do so would be wise, or even right. These are good reasons for remonstrating with him or reasoning with him, or persuading him, or entreating him, but not compelling him, or visiting him with any evil, in case he do otherwise. To justify that, the conduct from which it is desired to deter him, must be calculated to produce evil to someone else. The only part of the conduct of anyone, for which he is amenable to society, is that which concerns others. In the part which merely concerns himself, his independence is, of right, absolute. Over himself, over his own body and mind, the individual is sovereign.

$$\star\star\star\star\star$$

The worth of a State, in the long run, is the worth of the individuals composing it; and a State which postpones the interests of *their* mental expansion and elevation to a little more of administrative skill, or of that semblance of it which practice gives, in the details of business; a State which dwarfs its men, in order that they may be more docile instruments in its hands even for beneficial purposes—will find that with small men no great thing can really be accomplished; and that the perfection of machinery to which it has sacrificed everything will in the end avail it nothing, for want of the vital power which, in order that the machine might work more smoothly, it has preferred to banish.

John Stuart Mill, *On Liberty*

Note

[1] Italics added.

Soul Force versus Physical Force

Morton Ritts

Marx argued that social change could only come about as a result of revolutionary economic change. Mill, on the other hand, believed that social change was the result of enlightened political reform. Like Mill, Mahatma Gandhi (1869–1948) was also a reformer. But he believed that social change was the result of spiritual change—a transformation of the soul that would be the basis of a new and truly just social order.

This revolutionary idea was embodied in Gandhi's criticism of the Hindu caste system, which separated people into various classes from Brahmin at the upper end to the Untouchables at the lower. Rejecting his own high-caste background, Gandhi sought to eliminate the enormous social divisions created by such a hierarchy and replace them with a classless society (similar to Marx's) that affirmed the brotherhood and sisterhood of all.

Gandhi had a very benign view of human nature, believing that people are good, the world is ultimately just and that peaceful political change is eminently possible. According to Gandhi, real and lasting change was achieved not through violence but through the Hindu principle of *ahimsa*, or non-violence. Gandhi believed that *ahimsa* was a universal spiritual force within all humans that could be awakened by example.

The way to awaken the conscience of one's oppressor was through non-violent acts of civil disobedience that Gandhi called *satyagraha*— "soul force" as opposed to "body force." This turning of the other cheek wasn't some masochistic invitation to be beaten by the police or army during strikes, mass demonstrations or marches. Instead, satyagraha was a way to change an enemy's hatred to love, his or her resistance to acceptance.

Despite his charismatic leadership, Gandhi was assassinated just a few months before India gained its independence from Britain in 1948. While his non-violent politics of liberation had an enormous global influence, it nonetheless had its critics. Theorists who side with Darwin, Freud or Hobbes think Gandhi's views of human nature and political change are naïve and simplistic. Moreover, they argue that while non-violence may have been successful in the struggle against British colonialism, it would have been useless against the radical evil

"Soul Force versus Physical Force" is by Morton Ritts of the Humber College Institute of Technology and Advanced Learning. Used by permission.

of Nazi Germany. Gandhi's harshest critics believed him to be an impractical and even dangerous idealist.

"We Are All Created Equal"

But Gandhi has had his supporters—social reformers inspired by his spirituality and the philosophy of satyagraha. One man who was strongly influenced by Gandhi was the American civil rights leader Martin Luther King Jr. (1929–1968). Like Gandhi, King believed in the innate goodness of human nature, that "we are all God's children," and that the universe is a moral and just place.

One of the great public speakers in American history, King was a Baptist minister from the American South steeped in the prophetic tradition of the Bible, which he saw as a narrative of liberation and deliverance. King's Jesus was a social activist who championed the rights of the poor and downtrodden. It wasn't difficult for King to identify with Gandhi's struggle against the bondage of colonialism. After all, the United States was a country that claimed to be a beacon of freedom and equality, but a hundred years after the Civil War, black Americans had a long way to go before they could enjoy the "liberty, equality and freedom" that the Constitution promised everyone.

Like Marx, King saw the struggle between haves and have-nots as the defining feature of history. But unlike Marx, for whom religion was an oppressive institution, King saw religion as a liberating force that led to social and political change. He believed that white America was ultimately a just society but, like Gandhi, disagreed with Marx's ideology of violent revolution. Violence, he argued, led only to more violence. It could never form the basis of a viable social contract.

King believed it was possible to achieve his goal of an integrated society by changing people's hearts and minds. Reform the spirit, he preached, and you will reform the attitudes and laws that bar blacks from being part of the American Dream. Few leaders in the world today dare to talk about issues like rights and freedom in a spiritual context. King did, and succeeded in raising the debate over justice to a level of moral significance not seen in American political culture since the time of Lincoln.

In his famous "Letter" from Birmingham Jail, where he was briefly imprisoned for breaking a local ordinance against political demonstrations, King pointed out that there were two kinds of laws: just and unjust. Just laws were those that uplifted the human spirit. People have a legal and moral obligation to obey them. Unjust laws, on the other hand, were those that degraded the human spirit—laws that prohibited blacks from using "whites only" wash-rooms and restaurants, or denied them the same opportunities as whites for employment, housing and educa-tion. According to King, we have a moral responsibility to actively disobey unjust laws.

His argument has profound implica-tions for human behaviour. For exam-ple, if more people had acted like Oscar Schindler and resisted the laws and official directives that sent millions to the Nazi death camps in World War II, they could have changed the course of history. King's moral universe of civil disobedience based on princi-ple exists in direct contrast to the usual political motives of expedience and self-interest.

Martin Luther King
Washington, DC, 28 August 1963

But for King, as we've said, civil disobedience had to be non-violent. Like Gandhi, he had no doubt that soul force was stronger than physical force, and that loving one's enemy was the only way to truly humanize and change him. Throughout the late 1950s and 1960s, King helped to organize countless voter registration drives, freedom rides, sit-ins, marches and rallies involving thousands of black and white Americans who were often harassed, threatened, beaten, arrested and killed for their efforts.

In the end, the civil rights movement stirred the conscience of America and the world. Landmark civil rights legislation was introduced in 1965 and King won the Nobel Peace Prize. But he paid dearly. He was assassinated in 1968. Like Moses, he led his long-suffering people to the Promised Land, and, like Moses, he didn't live to enter.

"By Any Means Necessary"

Martin Luther King promoted non-violence as the means to reform an unjust society because, like Gandhi, he believed in the fundamental decency of human nature and in a world where, in the end, good triumphs over evil. But just as Gandhi had his critics, so did King. And since his death some of their voices seem to speak more loudly to black Americans than his.

In the United States today, for example, the Nation of Islam has a powerful following among those African-Americans who argue that racial integration can't work, that the separation of black and white races is both desirable and necessary, and that blacks must reconnect with their African roots. If such views sound surprising in light of King's reputation, it is important to remember that even at the height of the civil rights movement, King was only one of several major African-American leaders who didn't always agree on ideology or strategy. One of King's major rivals for the loyalty of black Americans was Malcolm X (1925–1965).

Malcolm X's critical analysis of white American society and his prescription for change differed radically from King's. Malcolm X came into contact with the ideas of the Nation of Islam while in prison. Subsequently, he changed his surname from "Little" to "X" to indicate that, as the descendant of slaves, he'd been stripped of his ancestral identity.

Once out of prison, he soon became chief spokesman for the Nation of Islam and its founder, Elijah Muhammad. In brilliant speeches that were inflammatory and confrontational, Malcolm X condemned white people as "blue-eyed devils" who could never be trusted. He rejected Christianity as a racist, oppressive "white man's religion" that didn't speak to the true black identity, which was African. King and other black Christians had "sold out," Malcolm X said.

The philosophy of the Nation of Islam stressed the need for black pride, independence, discipline and power. These could be achieved if African-Americans challenged whites on their own terms by developing their own banks and businesses, their own churches and schools, their own social and cultural support systems. Only through "black power" would African-Americans gain the freedom, justice and equality that was their right.

For the Nation of Islam, black power meant separation, not integration. Black Muslims also disagreed with King's philosophy of non-violence. Self-preservation "by any means necessary" was justified, Malcolm X said. This meant fighting back, not turning the other cheek.

In 1964, Malcolm X went to Mecca in Saudi Arabia, the spiritual capital of Islam. There he met Muslims of all races and nations worshipping together in peace, equality and dignity. The experience moved him to reject racial hatred as a liberation strategy. He began to view the struggle against oppression in universal terms, not exclusively African-American.

After returning to the United States, he broke with Elijah Muhammad and the Nation of Islam, becoming an orthodox Sunni Muslim who believed that the social order should embrace all peoples. It was while preaching this new message of hope and solidarity that he was gunned down on February 21, 1965. He was 40 years old. Malcolm X, Martin Luther King and Mahatma Gandhi may have shared similar violent ends, but their words and actions continue to haunt and shape contemporary politics.

By Any Means Necessary

Malcolm X

You make my point, that as long as a white man does it, it's all right. A Black man is supposed to have no feelings. So when a Black man strikes back, he's an extremist. He's supposed to sit passively and have no feelings, be nonviolent, and love his enemy. No matter what kind of attack, be it verbal or otherwise, he's supposed to take it. But if he stands up and in any way tries to defend himself, then he's an extremist.

No, I think that the speaker who preceded me is getting exactly what he asked for. My reason for believing in extremism—intelligently directed extremism, extremism in defence of liberty, extremism in quest of justice—is because I firmly believe in my heart that the day that the Black man takes an uncompromising step and realizes that he's within his rights, when his own freedom is being jeopardized, to use any means necessary to bring about his freedom or put a halt to that injustice, I don't think he'll be by himself.

I live in America, where there are only 22 million Blacks against probably 160 million whites. One of the reasons that I'm in no way reluctant or hesitant to do whatever is necessary to see that Black people do something to protect themselves [is that] I honestly believe that the day that they do, many whites will have more respect for them. And there will be more whites on their side than are now on their side with this little wishy-washy "love-thy-enemy" approach that they've been using up to now.

And if I'm wrong, then you are racialists.

As I said earlier, in my conclusion, I'm a Muslim. I believe in the religion of Islam, I believe in Allah, I believe in Muhammad, I believe in all of the prophets. I believe in fasting, prayer, charity, and that which is incumbent upon a Muslim to fulfill in order to be a Muslim. In April I was fortunate to make the **hajj** to Mecca, and went back again in September to try and carry out my religious functions and requirements.

> hajj
> pilgrimage to Mecca

But at the same time that I believe in that religion, I have to point out I'm also an American Negro, and I live in a society whose social system is based upon the castration of the Black man, whose political system is based on castration of the Black man, and whose economy is based upon the castration of the Black man. A society which, in 1964, has more subtle, deceptive, deceitful methods to make the rest of the world think that it's cleaning up its house, while at the same time the same things are happening to us in 1964 that happened in 1954, 1924, and in 1894.

They came up with what they call a civil rights bill in 1964, supposedly to solve our problem, and were murdered in cold blood. And the FBI head, [J. Edgar] Hoover, admits that they know who did it. They've known ever since it happened, and they've done nothing about it. Civil rights bill down the drain. No matter how many bills pass, Black people in that country where I'm from—still, our lives are not worth two cents. And the government has shown its inability, or its unwillingness, to do whatever is necessary to protect life and property where the Black American is concerned.

So my contention is that whenever a people come to the conclusion that the government which they have supported proves itself unwilling or proves itself unable to protect our lives and protect our property because we have the wrong colour skin, we are not human beings unless we ourselves band together and do whatever, however, whenever is necessary to see that our lives and our property is protected. And I doubt that any person in here would refuse to do the same thing, were he in the same position. Or I should say, were he in the same condition.

Just one step farther to see, am I justified in this stand? And I say, I'm speaking as a Black man from America, which is a racist society. No matter how much you hear it talk about democracy, it's as racist as South Africa or as racist as Portugal, or as racist as any other racialist society on this earth. The only difference between it and South Africa: South Africa preaches separation and practises separation; America preaches integration and practises segregation. This is the only difference. They don't practise what they preach, whereas South Africa preaches and practises the same thing. I have more respect for a man who lets me know where he stands, even if he's wrong, than one who comes up like an angel and is nothing but a devil.

The system of government that America has consists of committees. There are sixteen senatorial committees that govern the country and twenty congressional committees. Ten of the sixteen senatorial committees are in the hands of southern racialists, senators who are racialists. ...Thirteen of the twenty congressional committees were in the hands of southern congressmen who are racialists. Which means out of the thirty-six committees that govern the foreign and domestic direction of that government, twenty-three are in the hands of southern racialists— men who in no way believe in the equality of man, and men who would do anything within their power to see that the Black man never gets to the same seat or to the same level that they are on.

The reason that these men from that area have that type of power is because America has a seniority system. And these who have that seniority have been there longer than anyone else because the Black people in the areas where they live can't vote. And it is only because the Black man is deprived of his vote that puts these men in positions of power, that gives them such influence in the government beyond their actual intellectual or political ability, or even beyond the number of people from the areas that they represent.

So we can see in that country that no matter what the federal government professes to be doing, the power of the federal government lies in these committees. And any time any kind of legislation is proposed to benefit the Black man or give the Black man his just due, we find it is locked up in these committees right here. And when they let something through the committee, usually it is so chopped up and fixed up that by the time it becomes law, it's a law that can't be enforced.

Another example is the Supreme Court desegregation decision that was handed down in 1954. This is a law, and they have not been able to implement this law in New York City, or in Boston, or in Cleveland, or Chicago, or the northern cities. And my contention is that any time you have a country, supposedly a democracy, supposedly the land of the free and the home of the brave, and it can't enforce laws—even in the northernmost, cosmopolitan, and progressive part of it—that will benefit a Black man, if those laws can't be enforced, how much heart do you think we will get when they pass some civil rights legislation which only involves more laws? If they can't enforce this law, they will never enforce those laws.

So my contention is that we are faced with a racialistic society, a society in which they are deceitful, deceptive, and the only way we can bring about a change is to talk the kind of language—speak the language that they understand. The racialists never understand a peaceful language. The racialist never understands the nonviolent language. The racialist we have, he's spoken his language to us for 400 years.

We have been the victim of his brutality. We are the ones who face his dogs that tear the flesh from our limbs, only because we want to enforce the Supreme Court decision. We are the ones who have our skulls crushed, not by the Ku Klux Klan but by policemen, only because we want to enforce what they call the Supreme Court decision. We are the ones upon whom water hoses are turned, with pressure so hard that it rips the clothes from our backs—not men, but the clothes from the backs of women and children. You've seen it yourselves. Only because we want to enforce what they call the law.

Malcolm X

Well, any time you live in a society supposedly based upon law, and it doesn't enforce its own law because the colour of a man's skin happens to be wrong, then I say those people are justified to resort to any means necessary to bring about justice where the government can't give them justice.

I don't believe in any form of unjustified extremism. But I believe that when a man is exercising extremism, a human being is exercising extremism in defence of liberty for human beings, it's no vice. And when one is moderate in the pursuit of justice for human beings, I say he's a sinner.

And I might add, in my conclusion—in fact, America is one of the best examples, when you read its history, about extremism. Old Patrick Henry said, "Liberty or death!" That's extreme, very extreme.

I read once, passingly, about a man named Shakespeare. I only read about him passingly, but I remember one thing he wrote that kind of moved me. He put it in the mouth of Hamlet, I think it was, who said, "To be or not to be"—he was in doubt about something. "Whether it was nobler in the mind of man to suffer the slings and arrows of outrageous fortune"—moderation—"or take up arms against a sea of troubles and by opposing end them."

And I go for that. If you take up arms, you'll end it. But if you sit around and wait for the one who's in power to make up his mind that he should end it, you'll be waiting a long time.

And in my opinion the young generation of whites, blacks, browns, whatever else there is—you're living at a time of extremism, a time of revolution, a time when there's got to be a change. People in power have misused it, and now there has to be a change and a better world has to be built, and the only way it's going to be built is with extreme methods. And I for one will join in with anyone. I don't care what colour you are, as long as you want to change this miserable condition that exists on this earth.

Non-Violent Resistance

Mohandas K. (Mahatma) Gandhi

Means and Ends

Reader: Why should we not obtain our goal, which is good, by any means whatsoever, even by using violence? Shall I think of the means when I have to deal with a thief in the house? My duty is to drive him out anyhow. You seem to admit that we have received nothing, and that we shall receive nothing by petitioning. Why, then, may we not do so by using brute force? And, to retain what we may receive we shall keep up the fear by using the same force to the extent that it may be necessary. You will not find fault with a continuance of force to prevent a child from thrusting its foot into fire? Somehow or other we have to gain our end.

Gandhi: Your reasoning is plausible. It has deluded many. I have used similar arguments before now. But I think I know better now, and I shall endeavour to undeceive you. Let us first take the argument that we are justified in gaining our end by using brute force because the English gained theirs by using similar means. It is perfectly true that they use brute force and that it is possible for us to do likewise, but by using similar means we can get only the same thing that they got. You will admit that we do not want that. Your belief that there is no connection between the means and the end is a great mistake. Through that mistake even men who have been considered religious have committed grievous crimes. Your reasoning is the same as saying that we can get a rose through planting a noxious weed. If I want to cross the ocean, I can do so only by means of a vessel; if I were to use a cart for that purpose, both the cart and I would soon find the bottom. "As is the God, so is the **votary**," is a maxim worth considering. Its meaning has been distorted and men have gone astray. The means may be likened to a seed, the end to a tree; and there is just the same inviolable connection between the means and the end as there is between the seed and the tree. I am not likely to obtain the result flowing from the worship of God by laying myself prostrate before Satan. If, therefore, any one were to say: "I want to worship God; it does not matter that I do so by means of Satan," it would be set down as ignorant folly. We reap exactly as we

Gandhi

votary
a person bound by vows to live a
life of religious worship

"Non-Violent Resistance" is reprinted by permission of the Navajivan Trust and the
Mahatma Gandhi Estate.

sow. The English in 1833 obtained greater voting power by violence. Did they by using brute force better appreciate their duty? They wanted the right of voting, which they obtained by using physical force. But real rights are a result of performance of duty; these rights they have not obtained. We, therefore, have before us in England the force of everybody wanting and insisting on his rights, nobody thinking of his duty. And where everybody wants rights, who shall give them to whom? I do not wish to imply that they do no duties. They don't perform the duties corresponding to those rights; and as they do not perform that particular duty, namely, acquire fitness, their rights have proved a burden to them. In other words, what they have obtained is an exact result of the means they adopted. They used the means corresponding to the end. If I want to deprive you of your watch, I shall certainly have to fight for it; if I want to buy your watch, I shall have to pay for it; and if I want a gift, I shall have to plead for it; and, according to the means I employ, the watch is stolen property, my own property, or a donation. Thus we see three different results from three different means. Will you still say that means do not matter?

Now we shall take the example given by you of the thief to be driven out. I do not agree with you that the thief may be driven out by any means. If it is my father who has come to steal I shall use one kind of means. If it is an acquaintance I shall use another; and in the case of a perfect stranger I shall use a third. If it is a white man, you will perhaps say you will use means different from those you will adopt with an Indian thief. If it is a weakling, the means will be different from those to be adopted for dealing with an equal in physical strength; and if the thief is armed from top to toe, I shall simply remain quiet. Thus we have a variety of means between the father and the armed man. Again, I fancy that I should pretend to be sleeping whether the thief was my father or that strong armed man. The reason for this is that my father would also be armed and I should succumb to the strength possessed by either and allow my things to be stolen. The strength of my father would make me weep with pity; the strength of the armed man would rouse in me anger and we should become enemies. Such is the curious situation. From these examples we may not be able to agree as to the means to be adopted in each case. I myself seem clearly to see what should be done in all these cases, but the remedy may frighten you. I therefore hesitate to place it before you. For the time being I will leave you to guess it, and if you cannot, it is clear you will have to adopt different means in each case. You will also have seen that any means will not avail to drive away the thief. You will have to adopt means to fit each case. Hence it follows that your duty is not to drive away the thief by any means you like.

Let us proceed a little further. That well-armed man has stolen your property; you have harboured the thought of his act; you are filled with anger; you argue that you want to punish that rogue, not for your own sake, but for the good of your neighbours; you have collected a number of armed men, you want to take his house by assault; he is duly informed of it, he runs away: he too is incensed. He collects his brother robbers, and sends you a defiant message that he will commit robbery in broad daylight. You are strong, you do not fear him, you are prepared to receive him. Meanwhile, the robber pesters your neighbours. They complain before you. You reply that you are doing all for their sake, you do not mind that your own goods have been stolen. Your neighbours reply that the robber never pestered them before, and that he commenced his depredations only after you declared hostilities against him. You are between Scylla and Charybdis. You are full of pity for the poor men. What they say is true. What are you to do? You will be disgraced if you now leave the robber alone. You, therefore, tell the poor men: "Never mind. Come, my wealth is yours, I will give you arms, I will teach you how to use them; you should belabour the rogue; don't you leave him alone." And so the battle grows: the robbers increase in numbers; your neighbours have deliberately put themselves to inconvenience. Thus the result of wanting to take revenge upon the robber is that you have disturbed your own peace; you are in perpetual fear of being robbed and assaulted; your courage has given place to cowardice. If you will patiently examine the argument, you will see that I have not overdrawn the picture. This is one of the means. Now let us examine the other. You set this armed robber down as an ignorant brother; you intend to reason with him at a suitable opportunity; you argue that he is, after all, a fellow man; you do not know what prompted him to steal. You, therefore, decide that, when you can, you will destroy the man's motive for stealing. Whilst you are thus reasoning with yourself, the man comes again to steal. Instead of being angry with him you take pity on him. You think that this stealing habit must be a disease with him. Henceforth, you, therefore, keep your doors and windows open, you change your sleeping-place, and you keep your things in a manner most accessible to him. The robber comes again and is confused as all this is new to him; nevertheless, he takes away your things. But his mind is agitated. He inquires about you in the village, he comes to learn about your broad and loving heart, he repents, he begs your pardon, returns you your things, and leaves off the stealing habit. He becomes your servant, and you will find for him honourable employment. This is the second method. Thus, you see, different means have brought about totally different results. I do not wish to deduce from this that robbers will act in the above manner or that all will have the same pity and love like you, but I only wish to show that fair means alone can produce fair results, and that, at least in the majority of cases, if not indeed in all, the force of love and pity is infinitely greater than the force of arms. There is harm in the exercise of brute force, never in that of pity.

Now we will take the question of petitioning. It is a fact beyond dispute that a petition, without the backing of force, is useless. However, the late Justice Ranade used to say that petitions served a useful purpose because they were a means of educating people. They give the latter an idea of their condition and warn the rulers. From this point of view, they are not altogether useless. A petition backed by force is a petition from an equal and, when he transmits his demand in the form of a petition, it testifies to his nobility. Two kinds of force can back petitions. "We shall hurt you if you do not give this," is one kind of force; it is the force of arms, whose evil results we have already examined. The second kind of force can thus be stated: "If you do not concede our demand, we shall be no longer your petitioners. You can govern us only so long as we remain the governed; we shall no longer have any dealings with you." The force implied in this may be described as love-force, soul-force, or, more popularly but less accurately, passive resistance. This force is indestructible. He who uses it perfectly understands his position. We have an ancient proverb which literally means: "One negative cures thirty-six diseases." The force of arms is powerless when matched against the force of love or the soul.

Now we shall take your last illustration, that of the child thrusting its foot into fire. It will not avail you. What do you really do to the child? Supposing that it can exert so much physical force that it renders you powerless and rushes into fire, then you cannot prevent it. There are only two remedies open to you—either you must kill it in order to prevent it from perishing in the flames, or you must give your own life because you do not wish to see it perish before your eyes. You will not kill it. If your heart is not quite full of pity, it is possible that you will not surrender yourself by preceding the child and going into the fire yourself. You, therefore, helplessly allow it to go to the flames. Thus, at any rate, you are not using physical force. I hope you will not consider that it is still physical force, though of a low order, when you would forcibly prevent the child from rushing toward the fire if you could. That force is of a different order and we have to understand what it is.

Remember that, in thus preventing the child, you are minding entirely its own interest, you are exercising authority for its sole bene-fit. Your example does not apply to the English. In using brute force against the English you consult entirely your own, that is the national, interest. There is no question here either of pity or of love. If you say that the actions of the English, being evil, represent fire, and that they proceed to their actions through ignorance, and that therefore they occupy the position of a child and that you want to protect such a child, then you will have to overtake every evil action of that kind by whom-soever committed and, as in the case of the evil child, you will have to sacrifice yourself. If you are capable of such immeasurable pity, I wish you well in its exercise.

Righting the Ship of Democracy

Bruce Ackerman and James Fishkin

Presenting Deliberation Day: A Radical Proposal to Help Voters Make Better Decisions

In our soon-to-be-released book, we offer a new way of thinking about democratic reform, proposing a new national holiday—Deliberation Day. It would replace Presidents' Day, which does no service to the memories of Washington and Lincoln, and would be held two weeks before major national elections.

Registered voters would be called together in neighborhood meeting places, in small groups of 15 and larger groups of 500, to discuss the central issues raised by the campaign. Each deliberator would be paid $150 for the day's work of citizenship. To allow the business of the world to carry on and as many as possible to participate, the holiday would be a two-day affair.

If Deliberation Day succeeded, everything else would change: the candidates, the media, the activists, the interest groups, the spin doctors, the advertisers, the pollsters, the fundraisers, the lobbyists, and the political parties. All would have no choice but to adapt to a more attentive and informed public. When the election arrived, the people would speak with a better chance of knowing what they wanted and which candidates were more likely to pursue the popular mandate.

Why can't people simply organize themselves without the assistance of a new civic holiday and its associated social engineering? After all, we don't live in a civic vacuum. Sustained conversations do take place in countless settings, from the breakfast table to the coffee break at the office to the meeting at the neighborhood church or union hall. And their intensity and frequency do increase during election campaigns. But the social context that motivates public deliberation is usually lacking, and the resulting levels of public information are disappointing.

If six decades of modern public opinion research have established anything, it is that the general public's political ignorance is appalling by

Bruce Ackerman and James Fishkin, "Righting the Ship of Democracy," from *legalaffairs*, www.legalaffairs.org/issues/January-February-2004/feature_ackerman_janfeb04.html. Accessed January 1, 2004. Reprinted by permission.

any standard. As one influential researcher concludes, "the political ignorance of the American voter is one of the best-documented features of contemporary politics." And another: "The verdict is stunningly, depressingly clear: most people know very little about politics, and the distribution behind that statement has changed very little if at all over the survey era."

George Bishop and his colleagues at the University of Cincinnati dramatized this point in their study of attitudes toward the "Public Affairs Act of 1975." Asked for their opinion of the act, large percentages of the public either supported or opposed it, even though no such act was ever passed. In 1995, *The Washington Post* celebrated the "twentieth unanniversary" of the nonexistent act by asking respondents about its "repeal." Half the respondents were told that President Clinton wanted to repeal the act; the other half were informed that the "Republican Congress" favored its repeal. The respondents apparently used these cues to guide their answers, without recognizing the fictional character of the entire endeavor.

Even opinions about actual issues are often highly unstable impressions based on sound bites and headlines. Some researchers argue that citizens can function effectively without the kinds of specific knowledge called for by most survey questions. What is really important, they claim, is for voters to place candidates or political parties in the broader framework of the basic liberal-conservative spectrum. Yet Robert Luskin, a political scientist at the University of Texas, has shown that the American public does a terrible job at this task as well. Once corrections for guessing and nonresponses are introduced, surveys show that the American public does slightly worse in classifying parties or policies as "liberal" or "conservative" than it would do if it proceeded by flipping a coin.

None of this is really controversial. Indeed, the past generation of political economists has gone to great lengths to explain why voter ignorance is only to be expected. Acquiring and analyzing information is a time-consuming business. Time spent on public affairs competes with time acquiring information on more personal matters, like the price and quality of cars or houses. In these areas, each of us suffers a direct cost for ignorant decisions—I may buy a lemon unless I am careful to analyze my options ahead of time. In contrast, nobody pays a price for voting ignorantly, since the outcome of a major election never hinges on a single ballot. As a consequence, it may well be "rational" for individual voters to remain ignorant about public matters. They can then reserve all their time for analyzing information on cars, houses, and other matters of personal consumption, where the sanction for ignorant decisions is felt directly.

This point doesn't depend on whether voters are public-spirited citizens. Even if they are deeply concerned about the nation's future, their individual votes still don't make a difference, and so there isn't an instrumental reason to make their choice a well-informed one.

The problem this raises is obvious: Why should politicians consider the interests of all citizens if most voters are uninformed and selfish?

Since the days of Madison, constitutional thought has struggled with this problem, and there is no reason to think it will ever be solved definitively. Nevertheless, the political world is constantly changing, and these changes alter the terms in which the problem is expressed and the institutional modes through which it may be ameliorated, if not resolved.

Madison famously focused on the capacities of political elites to filter out the most irrational and self-interested aspects of public opinion. One of the aims of *The Federalist Papers* was to defend a constitutional framework that subtly rewarded elites for filtering, rather than mirroring, these selfish impulses, thereby encouraging leaders to steer the republic in more enlightened directions. Our first task is to consider how the introduction of Deliberation Day might contribute to this filtering process.

Our argument proceeds by appealing to the "law of anticipated reaction": Politicians try to look ahead and adapt their behavior to new risks as they emerge on the horizon. Suppose that a groundswell of popular support finally pushes our proposal through Congress in the form of the Deliberation Day Act of 2012. Put yourself in the place of the man or woman who wins the presidential election that year. Other things being equal, how will the introduction of Deliberation Day modify your political calculus as president?

Consider a central aspect of modern politics: government by public-opinion poll. No sitting politician would think of taking an important step without hiring a pollster or two to test the waters, and modern White Houses are famous for their elaborate polling operations. Deliberation Day will require presidents to rethink their relation to this steady stream of polling data, and in ways that promise a more reflective relation to the public good.

Our new holiday need not attract a huge turnout to the nation's schools and community centers. The key question is not how many Americans use the holiday as a convenient excuse to catch up on their sleep, but whether the folks who do show up can swing the election. Call this a critical mass.

If a critical mass does show up, modern polling will suddenly seem old-fashioned, and present-day techniques will dramatically depreciate in political value. Today, what polls of citizens generally measure are raw, poorly formed preferences based on very weak information. But a politician has no reason to believe that her constituents' preferences will be much less raw on the distant day they go to the polls; the campaign mobilization may make some difference, but not a huge one. As a consequence, the politician can extrapolate existing polling data to the future—that is, Election Day—with a certain degree of confidence.

If Deliberation Day is established and a critical mass shows up to participate in the holiday, sophisticated politicians will no longer be so interested in monitoring the existing patterns of raw preferences. They will want to know about their constituents' refined preferences: what the voters will think after they have engaged in the discussion and reflection precipitated by Deliberation Day.

Deliberation Day is a new idea, but it builds on a host of smaller experiments involving ordinary citizens deliberating on public issues. In many different forums, in different cities and countries around the world, citizens have gathered together for experiments in serious and balanced public discussion. Many of these experiments have proved remarkably successful, but we will focus on one particular method of citizen consultation, the deliberative poll. Because the deliberative poll, or DP, is designed as a social science experiment, it provides the best evidence for the viability of our proposal. Since one of us, Jim Fishkin, has spent the past decade of his professional life designing and observing deliberative polls on a wide variety of issues, we can use these experiments with a solid understanding of their strengths and limitations.

A deliberative poll is a survey of a random sample of citizens before and after the group has had a chance to deliberate seriously on an issue. The process begins by selecting a representative sample from the population and asking each person a set of questions on the issue raised at the deliberative poll. This initial survey is the standard sort conducted by social scientists doing public-opinion research. The respondents are then invited to a specified place for a weekend of discussion. A small honorarium and travel expenses are paid to recruit a representative sample.

In preparation for the event, the participants receive briefing materials to lay the groundwork for the discussion. These materials are typically supervised for balance and accuracy by an advisory board of relevant experts and stakeholders. On arrival, the participants are randomly assigned to small groups with trained moderators. When they meet, they not only discuss the general issue but try to identify key questions that merit further exploration. They then bring these questions to balanced panels of competing experts or policymakers in larger

plenary
open to all

plenary sessions. The small groups and plenary sessions alternate throughout the weekend. At the end of the process, the respondents take the same questionnaire they were given on first contact.

What have we learned from our study of DPs that might be relevant to the viability of Deliberation Day?

First, deliberation makes a difference. When one compares the attitudes and opinions that respondents had at the end of the process with those they had on first contact, there are many large and statistically significant differences. As in the first deliberative poll on crime (broadcast on Britain's Channel Four in 1994), it is not unusual for deliberation to significantly change the balance of opinion on two-thirds of the policy questions. And more than half of the respondents typically change their positions on particular policy items after sustained conversation.

Carmel Meredith, a British participant in the DP on crime, put the point in human terms. Speaking on the TV broadcast, she said that "the questionnaire that I filled in four weeks ago, I might as well rip up now and put it in the bin. It was an absolute waste of time because I didn't know enough about it." After discussions, she had come to seriously re-evaluate the top-of-the-head views that she had given to the interviewer in the initial survey. In describing her experience, she was speaking for many other DP participants.

What is going on to produce this kind of change? Some of it occurs in anticipation of the event. During the British DP on crime, the spouse of one of the respondents came up to thank Jim Fishkin. In 30 years of marriage, her husband had never read a newspaper, but the DP invitation had prompted him to read "every newspaper every day" (and, as a result, he was going to be "much more interesting to live with in retirement"). This encapsulated our aspiration to create incentives to overcome rational ignorance and to motivate people to behave a bit more like ideal citizens.

The research that has come out of deliberative polls suggests not only that participants change their political attitudes but that these changes are driven by better information. It suggests not only that these changed attitudes generate different voting intentions but that these preferences become more public-spirited and collectively consistent. These changes occur throughout the population and aren't limited to the more educated. Finally, deliberation is intrinsically satisfying once people are given a serious chance to engage with one another in an appropriate setting.

These results contrast sharply with a growing literature in political science. On this view, citizens who became well informed wouldn't vote very differently than they do today. Advocates of this position suggest that poorly informed voters already use various simplifying devices to approximate the same conclusions that they would reach if they were well informed. If citizens know, for example, who is for a proposal or who is against it, they can use this cue to guide their voting behavior without taking the trouble to study the issue themselves.

Samuel Popkin, author of *The Reasoning Voter*, presents the example of President Gerald Ford choking on a tamale while campaigning against Ronald Reagan in the 1976 Republican primary in Texas. The president didn't know that he was supposed to shuck the tamale before eating it. Popkin claims that Mexican-American voters could reasonably infer from Ford's ignorance about their food that he knew little about them or their culture. As a consequence, they had good reason to prefer Reagan, without needing to know much about the detailed policy positions of the rival candidates. Popkin's example serves as a caution about the potential abuses of informational shortcuts: The unshucked tamale did not, in fact, serve as a very good indicator of the comparative positions of Ford and Reagan.

Apart from such anecdotes, the thesis, as the political scientist Arthur Lupia puts it, that "shortcuts" can produce the same voting behavior as "encyclopedic" knowledge rests primarily on statistical models developed from survey data. These models compare the preferences of uninformed voters with those who are better informed but are otherwise similar. But it is possible to construct equally plausible models from survey data that lead to a very different conclusion: that the public's ignorance makes a real difference in how elections come out. If people were better informed, they would vote differently, and these differences would be large enough to change election results. The deliberative polls provide convincing evidence to support this view. As we have seen in the cases of Australia and Britain, relatively ignorant voters do change their voting preferences substantially once they deliberate on the basis of better information.

Up until now we have delayed discussion of cost. Deliberation Day will, of course, be expensive. But there is more at stake than totaling up the dollars and cents. We must ask what the dollar signs mean. Is Deliberation Day like an enormously expensive Mercedes-Benz, which we are free to reject merely because other consumer goods better satisfy our desires? Or are the costs involved more akin to those spent on educating the young or defending the country?

We can't answer these questions with economic reasoning alone. To motivate the requisite political reflection, we focus on one of our "big-ticket" items: the proposal to pay each participating citizen a stipend of $150. Such payments are hardly unprecedented; similar (but smaller) stipends are paid every day to Americans serving as jurors in criminal and civil trials throughout the nation. But these $150 payments will add up to many billions each Deliberation Day, especially if our initiative is successful and tens of millions of Americans turn out to discuss the issues.

This big budgetary item will lead us to reflect on a curious asymmetry in modern public finance. National and local governments spend hundreds of billions of dollars a year on highways and healthcare and other goods and services. When the state is viewed as a machine for satisfying needs and wants, our budgetary imagination knows no bounds. But when it comes to citizenship development, we spend almost nothing. Is this disparity justified? Is the $150 stipend a mere luxury or an essential aspect of our initiative?

From the layman's point of view, it may also seem very costly to use countless school classrooms and governmental office buildings as sites for tens of millions of deliberators. But this may not be the case. It should be said here that we are not giving Americans a new day off for Deliberation Day; we are appropriating an already existing holiday, Presidents' Day, for a better civic purpose. Currently school buildings remain empty on Presidents' Day, when the government closes for business. Since the buildings are empty for a day anyway, there is no opportunity cost involved in using them for deliberative purposes, and we should not add billions of dollars to our cost estimates to reflect their "rental value." The same point applies to the economic production lost when half the working population takes at least one day off during our two-day holiday. Since many people currently take Presidents' Day off, the opportunity cost is greatly reduced along this dimension as well.

This hardly implies that Deliberation Day will be cheap. Lots of work will go into preparing for the holiday, organizing its operations, and cleaning up afterward. (And don't forget the free lunch served to tens of millions of deliberators in school cafeterias throughout the land!) While these real resource costs will range in the billions, the magnitudes will seem quite manageable once placed within a suitable political and economic framework. (For those who are interested, a more detailed cost analysis is located in our book.)

Americans may well reject our initiative, but they should not do so because of its economic costs. The question is whether ordinary people can convince themselves that popular sovereignty has a future in America and that it remains possible to take back control over politics by constructing a new place for face-to-face dialogue. If Americans retain their democratic faith, they will find the economic costs easy to accept; if they give it up, much more than Deliberation Day is at stake.

We hope the new national holiday, like the deliberative polls, will lift participants out of the routines of everyday life. There will be an air of anticipation as tens of millions prepare for the day's discussions. Participants won't want to make fools of themselves before their neighbors. Millions will start paying more attention to the news, and their dinner table conversations will begin to focus on Deliberation Day as it approaches. There will also be lots of hubbub during and after the holiday: exit polls, countless conversations, media commentary. The overall level of popular engagement will far exceed that of any DP in the past or future. And Deliberation Day will retain the features that have made DPs such a powerful tool for reflective decision making: Each deliberator is one voice in 15 in a small group and one voice in a few hundred at the plenary sessions. We may be old-fashioned, but we continue to believe that substance counts for more than media hype. Deliberation Day will provide tens of millions with the opportunity to take the great phantom of "public opinion" away from pollsters and political advertisers and make it a creation of popular deliberation. We should never underestimate the power of simple ideas to inspire genuine commitment.

Smooth Sailing

Richard Posner

> Democracy doesn't need Deliberation Day. If spending a day talking about the issues were a worthwhile activity, you wouldn't have to pay voters to do it.

The proposal by Professors Ackerman and Fishkin for a Deliberation Day, on which citizens lured by federal financial incentives would engage in collective deliberation over issues and candidates in the forthcoming national election, seems to me to misunderstand what modern political democracy is and should be.

The remote inspiration for Deliberation Day is Athenian democracy, in which the citizenry as a whole was both the legislature and the principal court, and the appointment of most executive officials by lot prevented a distinct governing class from emerging (or at least impeded its emergence). It was a genuine and in many respects progressive and attractive system of self-rule, but one utterly irrelevant to a vast and complex modern polity such as the United States or, for that matter, a small and complex polity such as Belgium.

Modern democracy, for reasons of efficiency and feasibility, is representative democracy, which involves a division between rulers and ruled. The rulers are officials who are drawn from—to be realistic—a governing class consisting of ambitious, determined, and charismatic seekers of power, and the role of the citizenry is to vote candidates for officialdom in and out of office on the basis of their perceived leadership qualities and policy preferences. The system exploits the division of labor and resembles the economic market, in which sellers and consumers constitute distinct classes. In the marketplace, the slogan "consumer sovereignty" signifies that the essentially negative power of the consumer—the power not to buy a particular product, a power to choose though not to create—constrains the behavior of sellers despite the vast gulf of knowledge and incentives that separates sellers and consumers. The same relationship exists between politicians and voters.

There is no Deliberation Day on which consumers engage in collective deliberation over competing brands of toasters or about whether to use microwave ovens instead. Consumers economize on their time by

Richard Posner, "Smooth Sailing," from *legalaffairs*, www.legalaffairs.org/issues/January-February-2004/feature_posner_janfeb04.html. Accessed January 30, 2004. Reprinted by permission.

responding to alternative sales pitches and using their experience of particular sellers and products to guide their evaluation of the pitches. It is the same in the political marketplace. Voters are guided by their reactions to the presentation of issues and candidates in political campaigns and by their experience of living under particular officials and particular policies.

As we recently learned in the California recall election, the wrath of a disappointed electorate can be mighty. And so can the power of an alienated, "turned-off" electorate. The fact that only about half of all eligible voters (and often even fewer) actually bother to vote in most political elections is commonly taken as a failure of democracy. Not at all. The decision not to vote may reflect equal satisfaction with the candidates, equal dissatisfaction, or rational indifference between them. It is as important that citizens not be forced to vote as it is that the barriers to new parties and to insurgents like Arnold Schwarzenegger be kept low so that our two-party system does not degenerate into **duopoly**.

duopoly
a two-party system that does not allow for the emergence of new parties

Under democracy, presidents and other political big shots have to listen to their underlings, who might otherwise rally public opinion against them. Some of the greatest errors and atrocities of nondemocratic regimes are committed because no one dares to stand up against the tyrant, who becomes progressively isolated from the criticism and feedback that would enable him to correct his course.

Despite the undoubted mediocrity of many of our politicians and the ignorance and apathy of many of our citizens, our system of representative democracy has served us well. Has there been, all things considered, a more successful nation in world history than the United States?

I am unclear about what collective deliberation would add to our political system, but I am pretty clear about what it would subtract. It would subtract from the time that people have for their other pursuits—personal, familial, and commercial. Most people work fewer than 250 days a year after the deduction of weekends, holidays, vacations, and sick leave. Adding another national holiday would represent a small but not trivial reduction in the amount of productive work.

Unlike Hannah Arendt, and perhaps Ackerman and Fishkin as well, I do not believe that private concerns are petty and that people are fully human only when they are deliberating about the "common good." I do not even think such deliberations are productive of much except sound and fury. Widespread deliberation by citizens at large on issues of politics would mainly just reduce the civility of our politics by raising the temperature of public debate, making our politics more ideological and therefore more divisive.

It is one of the glories of a two-party system that by focusing the parties' attention on the swing voter, the system tends to draw the parties together ideologically, since the swing voters are the least likely to be drawn to ideological extremes. Multiparty systems tend, in contrast, to spawn ideological parties, because in such systems a minority party organized around an ideology can achieve influence or even dominance. It seems to me that the last thing we need in order to solve the problems of our country is ideological strife.

I will be called cynical for doubting the value of political debate among ordinary citizens, for casting them in the role of passive onlookers of a struggle among ambitious politicians, and for questioning the possibility of meaningful reform of policy. I am merely being realistic. Reform does not well out of deliberation, but reflects passions and interests. Abolitionism, the suffrage movement, the civil rights movement, the opposition to the war in Vietnam, the rise of free-market ideology, welfare reform, and the gay-rights movement were not the product of discussion among voters debating on the model of the academic seminar (the implicit model, naturally, of academic reflection on the political process by the proponents of deliberative democracy, academics all). They were the product of moral and political entrepreneurs tapping into wells of discontent among minorities and eventually getting the attention of the politicians.

People are intelligent and engaged about issues that concern them directly and that do not require abstract analysis to understand. The more local and concrete the issue, the more meaningful deliberation by average citizens is; the more remote and abstract, the less meaningful such deliberation is. People know when they are hurting, and the knowledge motivates and engages them in political struggle. They have no interest in debate. That interest resides in the articulate class. Rights are seized; they are not bestowed by average citizens enticed into deliberative conclaves weeks before a national election.

I have difficulty suppressing the uncharitable thought that there may be an element of bad faith in the deliberative-democracy movement generally (I do not mean in Ackerman and Fishkin particularly). I think that what motivates many deliberative democrats is not a love of democracy or a faith in the people, but a desire to change specific political outcomes, which they believe they could do through argument, if only anyone could be persuaded to listen, because they are masters of argumentation. I infer this secret agenda from the fact that most proponents of deliberative democracy advocate aggressive judicial review, which removes many issues from democratic control; are coy about indicating what policies they dislike but would accept; and are uncommonly fond of subjecting U.S. citizens to control by international organizations of questionable, and often of no, democratic pedigree. I sense a power grab by the articulate class whose comparative advantage is—deliberation.

Jihad vs. McWorld

Benjamin Barber

Just beyond the horizon of current events lie two possible political futures—both bleak, neither democratic. The first is a retribalization of large swaths of humankind by war and bloodshed: a threatened **Lebanonization** of national states in which culture is pitted against culture, people against people, tribe against tribe—a Jihad in the name of a hundred narrowly conceived faiths against every kind of interdependence, every kind of artificial social cooperation and civic mutuality. The second is being borne in on us by the onrush of economic and ecological forces that demand integration and uniformity and that mesmerize the world with fast music, fast computers, and fast food—with MTV, Macintosh, and McDonald's, pressing nations into one commercially homogeneous global network: one McWorld tied together by technology, ecology, communications, and commerce. The planet is falling precipitantly apart and coming reluctantly together at the very same moment.

These two tendencies are sometimes visible in the same countries at the same instant: thus Yugoslavia, clamoring just recently to join the New Europe, is exploding into fragments; India is trying to live up to its reputation as the world's largest integral democracy while powerful new fundamentalist parties like the Hindu nationalist Bharatiya Janata Party, along with nationalist assassins, are imperiling its hard-won unity. States are breaking up or joining up: the Soviet Union has disappeared almost overnight, its parts forming new unions with one another or with likeminded nationalities in neighboring states. The old interwar national state based on territory and political sovereignty looks to be a mere transitional development.

The tendencies of what I am here calling the forces of Jihad and the forces of McWorld operate with equal strength in opposite directions, the one driven by **parochial** hatreds, the other by universalizing markets, the one re-creating ancient subnational and ethnic borders

Lebanonization
a reference to the disintegration of Lebanon as a result of civil war

parochial
local and limited

Benjamin R. Barber is Kekst Professor of Civil Society at the University of Maryland, Director, New York office, of The Democracy Collaborative and the author of many books including *Strong Democracy* (1984), *Jihad vs. McWorld* (Times Books, 1995), *A Place for Us* (Farrar, Strauss & Giroux, 1998), *A Passion for Democracy: American Essays* (Princeton University Press, 1998), *The Truth of Power: Intellectual Affairs in the Clinton White House* (W.W. Norton & Company, 2001), and *Fear's Empire: War, Terrorism and Democracy* (W.W. Norton & Company, 2003).

from within, the other making national borders porous from without. They have one thing in common: neither offers much hope to citizens looking for practical ways to govern themselves democratically. If the global future is to pit Jihad's **centrifugal** whirlwind against McWorld's **centripetal** black hole, the outcome is unlikely to be democratic—or so I will argue.

centrifugal
a decentralizing force
centripetal
a force pulling many different things toward itself and making them the same in the process

McWorld, or the Globalization of Politics

Four **imperatives** make up the dynamic of McWorld: a market imperative, a resource imperative, an information-technology imperative, and an ecological imperative. By shrinking the world and diminishing the **salience** of national borders, these imperatives have in combination achieved a considerable victory over factiousness and particularism, and not least of all over their most virulent traditional form—nationalism. It is the realists who are now Europeans, the utopians who dream nostalgically of a resurgent England or Germany, perhaps even a resurgent Wales or Saxony. Yesterday's wishful cry for one world has yielded to the reality of McWorld.

imperatives
essentials

salience
significance

The market imperative. Marxist and Leninist theories of imperialism assumed that the quest for ever-expanding markets would in time compel nation-based capitalist economies to push against national boundaries in search of an international economic **imperium**. Whatever else has happened to the scientistic predictions of Marxism, in this domain they have proved farsighted. All national economies are now vulnerable to the inroads of larger, transnational markets within which trade is free, currencies are convertible, access to banking is open, and contracts are enforceable under law. In Europe, Asia, Africa, the South Pacific, and the Americas such markets are eroding national sovereignty and giving rise to entities—international banks, trade associations, transnational lobbies like OPEC and Greenpeace, world news services like CNN and the BBC, and multinational corporations that increasingly lack a meaningful national identity—that neither reflect nor respect nationhood as an organizing or regulative principle.

imperium
power or rule

The market imperative has also reinforced the quest for international peace and stability, requisites of an efficient international economy. Markets are enemies of parochialism, isolation, fractiousness, war. Market psychology **attenuates** the psychology of ideological and religious cleavages and assumes a concord among producers and consumers—categories that ill fit narrowly conceived national or reli-

attenuates
undermines

gious cultures. Shopping has little tolerance for blue laws, whether dictated by pub-closing British paternalism, Sabbath-observing Jewish Orthodox fundamentalism, or no-Sunday-liquor-sales Massachusetts puritanism. In the context of common markets, international law ceases to be a vision of justice and becomes a workaday framework for getting things done—enforcing contracts, ensuring that governments abide by deals, regulating trade and currency relations, and so forth.

Common markets demand a common language, as well as a common currency, and they produce common behaviors of the kind bred by cosmopolitan city life everywhere. Commercial pilots, computer programmers, international bankers, media specialists, oil riggers, entertainment celebrities, ecology experts, demographers, accountants, professors, athletes—these compose a new breed of men and women for whom religion, culture, and nationality can seem only marginal elements in a working identity. Although sociologists of everyday life will no doubt continue to distinguish a Japanese from an American mode, shopping has a common signature throughout the world. Cynics might even say that some of the recent revolutions in Eastern Europe have had as their true goal not liberty and the right to vote but well-paying jobs and the right to shop (although the vote is proving easier to acquire than consumer goods). The market imperative is, then, plenty powerful; but, notwithstanding some of the claims made for "democratic capitalism," it is not identical with the democratic imperative.

The resource imperative. Democrats once dreamed of societies whose political autonomy rested firmly on economic independence. The Athenians idealized what they called **autarky**, and tried for a while to create a way of life simple and austere enough to make the **polis** genuinely self-sufficient. To be free meant to be independent of any other community or polis. Not even the Athenians were able to achieve autarky, however: human nature, it turns out, is dependency. By the time of **Pericles**, Athenian politics was inextricably bound up with a flowering empire held together by naval power and commerce—an empire that, even as it appeared to enhance Athenian might, ate away at Athenian independence and autarky. Master and slave, it turned out, were bound together by mutual insufficiency.

The dream of autarky briefly engrossed 19th-century America as well, for the underpopulated, endlessly bountiful land, the cornucopia of natural resources, and the natural barriers of a continent walled in by two great seas led many to believe that America could be a world unto itself. Given this past, it has been harder for Americans than for most to accept the inevitability of interdependence. But the rapid depletion of

autarky
self-sufficiency

polis
an ancient Greek city-state, such as Athens

Pericles (495–429 BCE)
Athenian statesman and general

resources even in a country like ours, where they once seemed inexhaustible, and the maldistribution of arable soil and mineral resources on the planet, leave even the wealthiest societies ever more resource-dependent and many other nations in permanently desperate straits.

Every nation, it turns out, needs something another nation has; some nations have almost nothing they need.

The information-technology imperative. Enlightenment science and the technologies derived from it are inherently universalizing. They entail a quest for descriptive principles of general application, a search for universal solutions to particular problems, and an unswerving embrace of objectivity and impartiality.

Scientific progress embodies and depends on open communication, a common discourse rooted in rationality, collaboration, and an easy and regular flow and exchange of information. Such ideals can be hypocritical covers for power-mongering by elites, and they may be shown to be wanting in many other ways, but they are entailed by the very idea of science and they make science and globalization practical allies.

Business, banking, and commerce all depend on information flow and are facilitated by new communication technologies. The hardware of these technologies tends to be systemic and integrated—computer, television, cable, satellite, laser, fiber-optic, and microchip technologies combining to create a vast interactive communications and information network that can potentially give every person on earth access to every other person, and make every datum, every byte, available to every set of eyes. If the automobile was, as George Ball once said (when he gave his blessing to a Fiat factory in the Soviet Union during the Cold War), "an ideology on four wheels," then electronic telecommunication and information systems are an ideology at 300 000 kilometers per second—which makes for a very small planet in a very big hurry. Individual cultures speak particular languages; commerce and science increasingly speak English; the whole world speaks logarithms and binary mathematics.

Moreover, the pursuit of science and technology asks for, even compels, open societies. Satellite footprints do not respect national borders; telephone wires penetrate the most closed societies. With photocopying and then fax machines having infiltrated Soviet universities and **samizdat** literary circles in the eighties, and computer modems having multiplied like rabbits in communism's bureaucratic warrens thereafter, **glasnost** could not be far behind. In their social requisites, secrecy and science are enemies.

The new technology's software is perhaps even more globalizing than its hardware. The information arm of international commerce's sprawling

samizdat
underground circulation of secret publications in the Soviet Union

glasnost
openness

body reaches out and touches distinct nations and parochial cultures, and gives them a common face chiseled in Hollywood, on Madison Avenue, and in Silicon Valley. Throughout the 1980s one of the most-watched television programs in South Africa was *The Cosby Show*. The demise of apartheid was already in production. Exhibitors at the 1991 Cannes film festival expressed growing anxiety over the "homogenization" and "Americanization" of the global film industry where for the third year running, American films dominated the awards ceremonies. America has dominated the world's popular culture for much longer, and more decisively. In November of 1991 Switzerland's once insular culture boasted best-seller lists featuring *Terminator 2* as the No. 1 movie, *Scarlett* as the No. 1 book, and Prince's *Diamonds and Pearls* as the No. 1 record album. No wonder the Japanese are buying Hollywood film studios even faster than Americans are buying Japanese television sets. This kind of software supremacy may in the long term be far more important than hardware superiority, because culture has become more potent than armaments. What is the power of the Pentagon compared with Disneyland's? Can the Sixth Fleet keep up with CNN? McDonald's in Moscow and Coke in China will do more to create a global culture than military colonization ever could. It is less the goods than the brand names that do the work, for they convey life-style images that alter perception and challenge behavior. They make up the seductive software of McWorld's common (at times much too common) soul.

Yet in all this high-tech commercial world there is nothing that looks particularly democratic. It lends itself to surveillance as well as liberty, to new forms of manipulation and covert control as well as new kinds of participation, to skewed, unjust market outcomes as well as greater productivity. The consumer society and the open society are not quite synonymous. Capitalism and democracy have a relationship, but it is something less than a marriage. An efficient free market after all requires that consumers be free to vote their dollars on competing goods, not that citizens be free to vote their values and beliefs on competing political candidates and programs. The free market flourished in **junta**-run Chile, in military-governed Taiwan and Korea, and, earlier, in a variety of autocratic European empires as well as their colonial possessions.

junta
a group of military officers who seize control of government

The ecological imperative. The impact of globalization on ecology is a cliché even to world leaders who ignore it. We know well enough that the German forests can be destroyed by Swiss and Italians driving gas-guzzlers fueled by leaded gas. We also know that the planet can be asphyxiated by greenhouse gases because Brazilian farmers want to be part of the 20th century and are burning down tropical rain forests to clear a little land to plow, and because Indonesians make a living out of converting their lush jungle into toothpicks for fastidious Japanese diners, upsetting the delicate oxygen balance and in effect puncturing our global lungs. Yet this ecological consciousness has meant not only greater awareness but also greater inequality, as modernized nations try to slam the door behind them, saying to developing nations, "The world cannot afford *your* modernization; ours has wrung it dry!"

Each of the four imperatives just cited is transnational, transideological, and transcultural. Each applies impartially to Catholics, Jews, Muslims, Hindus, and Buddhists; to democrats and totalitarians; to capitalists and socialists. The Enlightenment dream of a universal rational society has to a remarkable degree been realized—but in a form that is commercialized, homogenized, depoliticized, bureaucratized, and, of course, radically incomplete, for the movement toward McWorld is in competition with forces of global breakdown, national dissolution, and centrifugal corruption. These forces, working in the opposite direction, are the essence of what I call Jihad.

Jihad, or the Lebanonization of the World

OPEC, the World Bank, the United Nations, the International Red Cross, the multinational corporation . . . there are scores of institutions that reflect globalization. But they often appear as ineffective reactors to the world's real actors: national states and, to an ever greater degree, subnational factions in permanent rebellion against uniformity and integration—even the kind represented by universal law and justice. The headlines feature these players regularly: they are cultures, not countries; parts, not wholes; sects, not religions; rebellious factions and dissenting minorities at war not just with globalism but with the traditional nation-state. Kurds, Basques, Puerto Ricans, Ossetians, East Timoreans, Québécois, the Catholics of Northern Ireland, Abkhasians, Kurile Islander Japanese, the Zulus of Inkatha, Catalonians, Tamils, and, of course, Palestinians—people without countries, inhabiting nations not their own, seeking smaller worlds within borders that will seal them off from modernity.

A powerful irony is at work here. Nationalism was once a force of integration and unification, a movement aimed at bringing together disparate clans, tribes, and cultural fragments under new, assimilationist flags. But as Ortega y Gasset noted more than 60 years ago, having won its victories, nationalism changed its strategy. In the 1920s, and again today, it is more often a reactionary and divisive force, pulverizing the very nations it once helped cement together. The force that creates nations is "inclusive," Ortega wrote in *The Revolt of the Masses.* "In periods of consolidation, nationalism has a positive value, and is a lofty standard. But in Europe everything is more than consolidated, and nationalism is nothing but a mania."

This mania has left the post-Cold War world smoldering with hot war; the international scene is little more unified than it was at the end of the **Great War**, in Ortega's own time. There were more than 30 wars in progress last year, most of them ethnic, racial, tribal, or religious in character, and the list of unsafe regions doesn't seem to be getting any shorter. Some new world order!

The aim of many of these small-scale wars is to redraw boundaries, to implode states and resecure parochial identities: to escape McWorld's dully insistent imperatives. The mood is that of Jihad: war not as an instrument of policy but as an emblem of identity, an expression of community, an end in itself. Even where there is no shooting war, there is fractiousness, secession, and a quest for ever smaller communities. Add to the list of dangerous countries those at risk: In Switzerland and Spain, Jurassian and Basque separatists still argue the virtues of ancient identities, sometimes in the language of bombs. Hyperdistintegration in the former Soviet Union may well continue unabated—not just a Ukraine independent from the Soviet Union but a Bessarab Ukraine independent from the Ukrainian republic; not just Russia severed from the defunct union but Tatarsa severed from Russia. Yugoslavia makes even the **disured**, ex-Soviet, nonsocialist republics that were once the Soviet Union look integrated, its sectarian fatherland springing up within factional motherlands like weeds within weeds within weeds. Kurdish independence would threaten the territorial integrity of four Mid-Eastern nations. Well before the current cataclysm Soviet Georgia made a claim for autonomy from the Soviet Union, only to be faced with its Ossetians (164 000 in a republic of 5.5 million) demanding their own self-determination within Georgia. The Abkhasian minority of Georgia has followed suit. Even the good will established by Canada's

Great War
World War I (1914–1918)

disured
dissolution of legal ties between states

once promising Meech Lake protocols is in danger, with Francophone Quebec again threatening dissolution of the federation. In South Africa the emergence from apartheid was hardly achieved when friction between Inkatha's Zulus and the African National Congress's tribally identified members threatened to replace Europeans' racism with an indigenous tribal war. After 30 years of attempted integration using the colonial language (English) as a unifier, Nigeria is now playing with the idea of linguistic multiculturalism—which could mean the cultural breakup of the nation into hundreds of tribal fragments. Even Saddam Hussein has benefited from the threat of internal Jihad, having used renewed tribal and religious warfare to turn last season's mortal enemies into reluctant allies of an Iraqi nationhood that he nearly destroyed.

The passing of communism has torn away the thin veneer of internationalism (workers of the world unite!) to reveal ethnic prejudices that are not only ugly and deep-seated but increasingly murderous. Europe's old scourge, anti-Semitism, is back with a vengeance, but it is only one of many antagonisms. It appears all too easy to throw the historical gears into reverse and pass from a Communist dictatorship back into a tribal state.

Among the tribes, religion is also a battlefield. ("Jihad" is a rich word whose generic meaning is "struggle"—usually the struggle of the soul to avert evil. Strictly applied to religious war, it is used only in reference to battles where the faith is under assault, or battles against a government that denies the practice of Islam. My use here is rhetorical, but does follow both journalistic practice and history.) Remember the Thirty Years War? Whatever forms of Enlightenment universalism might once have come to grace such historically related forms of monotheism as Judaism, Christianity, and Islam, in many of their modern incarnations they are parochial rather than cosmopolitan, angry rather than loving, **proselytizing** rather than **ecumenical**, zealous rather than rationalist, sectarian rather then deistic, ethnocentric rather than universalizing. As a result, like the new forms of hypernationalism, the new expressions of religious fundamentalism are fractious and pulverizing, never integrating. This is religion as the Crusaders knew it: a battle to the death for souls that if not saved will be forever lost.

The atmospherics of Jihad have resulted in a breakdown of civility in the name of identity, of **comity** in the name of community. International relations have sometimes taken on the aspects of gang war—cultural turf battles featuring tribal factions that were supposed to be sublimated as integral parts of large national, economic, postcolonial, and constitutional entities.

proselytizing
attempting to convert to a narrow view

ecumenical
having worldwide value

comity
courtesy

The Darkening Future of Democracy

tableaux vivants
images that tell a story

These rather melodramatic *tableaux vivants* do not tell the whole story, however. For all their defects, Jihad and McWorld have their attractions. Yet, to repeat and insist, the attractions are unrelated to democracy. Neither McWorld nor Jihad is remotely democratic in impulse. Neither needs democracy; neither promotes democracy.

McWorld does manage to look pretty seductive in a world obsessed with Jihad. It delivers peace, prosperity, and relative unity—if at the cost of independence, community, and identity (which is generally based on difference). The primary political values required by the global market are order and tranquillity, and freedom—as in the phrases "free trade," "free press," and "free love." Human rights are needed to a degree, but not citizenship or participation—and no more social justice and equality than are necessary to promote efficient economic production and consumption. Multinational corporations sometimes seem to prefer doing business with local **oligarchs**, inasmuch as they can take confidence from dealing with the boss on all crucial matters. Despots who slaughter their own populations are no problem, as long as they leave markets in place and refrain from making war on their neighbors (Saddam Hussein's fatal mistake). In trading partners, predictability is of more value than justice.

oligarchs
members of an elite that hold power in a state

The Eastern European revolutions that seemed to arise out of concern for global democratic values quickly deteriorated into a stampede in the general direction of free markets and their **ubiquitous**, television-promoted shopping malls. East Germany's Neues Forum, that courageous gathering of intellectuals, students, and workers which overturned the Stalinist regime in Berlin in 1989, lasted only six months in Germany's mini-version of McWorld. Then it gave way to money and markets and monopolies from the West. By the time of the first all-German elections, it could scarcely manage to secure three per cent of the vote. Elsewhere there is growing evidence that *glasnost* will go and *perestroika*—defined as privatization and an opening of markets to Western bidders—will stay. So understandably anxious are the new rulers of Eastern Europe and whatever entities are forged from the residues of the Soviet Union to gain access to credit and markets and technology—McWorld's flourishing new currencies—that they have shown themselves willing to trade away democratic prospects in pursuit of them: not just old totalitarian ideologies and command-economy production models but some possible indigenous experiments with a third way between capitalism and socialism, such as economic cooper-

ubiquitous
occurring everywhere

perestroika
economic restructuring

atives and employee stock-ownership plans, both of which have their ardent supporters in the East.

Jihad delivers a different set of virtues: a vibrant local identity, a sense of community, solidarity among kinsmen, neighbors, and countrymen, narrowly conceived. But it also guarantees parochialism and is against outsiders. And solidarity often means obedience to a hierarchy in governance, fanaticism in beliefs, and the obliteration of individual selves in the name of the group. Deference to leaders and intolerance toward outsiders (and toward "enemies within") are hallmarks of tribalism—hardly the attitudes required for the cultivation of new democratic women and men capable of governing themselves. Where new democratic experiments have been conducted in retribalizing societies, in both Europe and the Third World, the result has often been anarchy, repression, persecution, and the coming of new, noncommunist forms of very old kinds of despotism. During the past year, Havel's velvet revolution in Czechoslovakia was imperiled by partisans of "Czechland" and of Slovakia as independent entities. India seemed little less rent by Sikh, Hindu, Muslim, and Tamil infighting than it was immediately after the British pulled out, more than 40 years ago.

To the extent that either McWorld or Jihad has a *natural* politics, it has turned out to be more of an antipolitics. For McWorld, it is the antipolitics of globalism: bureaucratic, technocratic, and meritocratic, focused (as Marx predicted it would be) on the administration of things—with people, however, among the chief things to be administered. In its politico-economic imperatives McWorld has been guided by ***laissez-faire*** market principles that privilege efficiency, productivity, and beneficence at the expense of civic liberty and self-government.

laissez-faire
a policy of non-intervention by government in the economy

For Jihad, the antipolitics of tribalization has been explicitly antidemocratic: one-party dictatorship, government by military junta, theocratic fundamentalism—often associated with a version of the ***Fuhrerprinzip*** that empowers an individual to rule on behalf of a people. Even the government of India, struggling for decades to model democracy for a people who will soon number a billion, longs for great leaders; and for every Mahatma Gandhi, Indira Gandhi, or Rajiv Gandhi taken from them by zealous assassins, the Indians appear to seek a replacement who will deliver them from the lengthy travail of their freedom.

Fuhrerprinzip
principle of authoritarian leadership

The Confederal Option

How can democracy be secured and spread in a world whose primary tendencies are at best indifferent to it (McWorld) and at worst deeply **antithetical** to it (Jihad)? My guess is that globalization will eventually

antithetical
directly opposed

ethos
spirit or character

prescient
possessing foreknowledge

remonstrate
quarrel

Maastricht
city in Belgium where the treaty
was signed to create the
European Union

vanquish retribalization. The **ethos** of material "civilization" has not yet encountered an obstacle it has been unable to thrust aside. Ortega may have grasped in the 1920s a clue to our own future in the coming millennium.

> Everyone sees the need of a new principle of life. But as always happens in similar crises—some people attempt to save the situation by an artificial intensification of the very principle which has led to decay. This is the meaning of the "nationalist" outburst of recent years . . . things have always gone that way. The last flare, the longest; the last sigh, the deepest. On the very eve of their disappearance there is an intensification of frontiers—military and economic.

Jihad may be a last deep sigh before the eternal yawn of McWorld. On the other hand, Ortega was not exactly **prescient**; his prophecy of peace and internalism came just before blitzkrieg, world war, and the Holocaust tore the old order to bits. Yet democracy is how we **remonstrate** with reality, the rebuke our aspirations offer to history. And if retribalization is inhospitable to democracy, there is nonetheless a form of democratic government that can accommodate parochialism and communitarianism, one that can even save them from their defects and make them more tolerant and participatory: decentralized participatory democracy. And if McWorld is indifferent to democracy, there is nonetheless a form of democratic government that suits global markets passably well—representative government in its federal or, better still, confederal variation.

With its concern for accountability, the protection of minorities, and the universal rule of law, a confederalized representative system would serve the political needs of McWorld as well as oligarchic bureaucratism or meritocratic elitism is currently doing. As we are already beginning to see, many nations may survive in the long term only as confederations that afford local regions smaller than "nations" extensive jurisdiction. Recommended reading for democrats of the 21st century is not the U.S. Constitution or the French Declaration of Rights of Man and Citizen but the Articles of Confederation, that suddenly pertinent document that stitched together the 13 American colonies into what then seemed a too loose confederation of independent states but now appears a new form of political realism, as veterans of Yeltsin's new Russia and the new Europe created at **Maastricht** will attest.

By the same token, the participatory and direct form of democracy that engages citizens in civic activity and civic judgment and goes well beyond just voting and accountability—the system I have called "strong democracy"—suits the political needs of decentralized communities as well as theocratic and nationalist party dictatorships have done. Local neighborhoods need not be democratic, but they can be. Real democracy has flourished in diminutive settings: the spirit of liberty, Tocqueville said, is local. Participatory democracy, if not naturally apposite to tribalism, has an undeniable attractiveness under conditions of parochialism.

Democracy in any of these variations will, however, continue to be obstructed by the undemocratic and antidemocratic trends toward uniformitarian globalism and intolerant retribalization which I have portrayed here. For democracy to persist in our brave new McWorld, we will have to commit acts of conscious political will—a possibility, but hardly a probability, under these conditions. Political will requires much more than the quick fix of the transfer of institutions. Like technology transfer, institution transfer rests on foolish assumptions about a uniform world of the kind that once fired the imagination of colonial administrators. Spread English justice to the colonies by exporting wigs. Let an East Indian trading company act as the vanguard to Britain's free parliamentary institutions. Today's well-intentioned quick-fixers in the National Endowment for Democracy and the Kennedy School of Government, in the unions and foundations and universities zealously nurturing contacts in Eastern Europe and the Third World, are hoping to democratize by long distance. Post Bulgaria a parliament by first-class mail. FedEx the Bill of Rights to Sri Lanka. Cable Cambodia some common law.

Yet Eastern Europe has already demonstrated that importing free political parties, parliaments, and presses cannot establish a democratic civil society; imposing a free market may even have the opposite effect. Democracy grows from the bottom up and cannot be imposed from the top down. Civil society has to be built from the inside out. The institutional superstructure comes last. Poland may become democratic, but then again it may heed the Pope, and prefer to found its politics on its Catholicism, with uncertain consequences for democracy. Bulgaria may become democratic, but it may prefer tribal war. The former Soviet Union may become a democratic confederation, or it may just grow into an anarchic and weak conglomeration of markets for other nations' goods and services.

Democrats need to seek out indigenous democratic impulses. There is always a desire for self-government, always some expression of participation, accountability, consent, and representation, even in traditional hierarchical societies. These need to be identified, tapped, modified, and incorporated into new democratic practices with an indigenous flavor.

The tortoises among the democratizers may ultimately outlive or outpace the hares, for they will have the time and patience to explore conditions along the way, and to adapt their gait to changing circumstances. Tragically, democracy in a hurry often looks something like France in 1794 or China in 1989.

It certainly seems possible that the most attractive democratic ideal in the face of the brutal realities of Jihad and the dull realities of McWorld will be a confederal union of semi-autonomous communities smaller than nation-states, tied together into regional economic associations and markets larger than nation-states—participatory and self-determining in local matters at the bottom, representative and accountable at the top. The nation-state would play a diminished role, and sovereignty would lose some of its political potency. The Green movement adage "Think globally, act locally" would actually come to describe the conduct of politics.

This vision reflects only an ideal, however—one that is not terribly likely to be realized. Freedom, Jean-Jacques Rousseau once wrote, is a food easy to eat but hard to digest. Still, democracy has always played itself out against the odds. And democracy remains both a form of coherence as binding as McWorld and a secular faith potentially as inspiring as Jihad.

On Inhumanity

Mitchell Lerner

> There is a universal tendency to avoid seeing, as well as remembering, the human capacity for evil. Adolf Hitler understood that well when, on August 22, 1939, he said to his military commanders regarding his plans for Poland: "Who, after all, speaks today of the annihilation of the Armenians?"
>
> Donald E. Miller and Lorna Touryan Miller, *Survivors*

The Problem

Ever since Cain raised his hand against his brother Abel, the Earth has witnessed inhumanity, brutality and indifference. Even as I write this essay, newspaper stories and photos convey painful images of the latest atrocity—the Rwandan civil war. In this fight between the Hutu and the Tutsi, the blood of hundreds of thousands of men, women and children has been spilled. More than a million refugees have fled to neighbouring areas, where many are dying of disease.

A million refugees here . . . ethnic cleansing there . . . the imagery of human tragedy marks both the present and the past. How do we as individuals make sense of distant suffering and death on a massive scale? How do we comprehend what is happening in Rwanda today, Bosnia yesterday, and other places 50 and 80 years ago? How do we think about the magnitude of human evil? Can thinking about what it means to be human ensure our survival?

In this essay, we address the very difficult concepts of genocide, dehumanization and the banality of evil.

> "Thinking is the . . . work of a species that bears responsibility for its own survival . . . to carry on thinking [is] the authority by which we survive in human form."
>
> Hannah Arendt, *Life of the Mind*

Genocide

The term "genocide" comes from the Greek word *genos*, meaning people, and the Latin word, *cide*, referring to killing. Raphael Lemkin coined the term in 1944 to describe the attempt to destroy a nation or an ethnic group either by killing them or by depriving them of the ability to live and procreate. In 1948, the United Nations resolved that genocide means an intent to destroy, in whole or in part, a national, ethnic, racial or religious group:

"On Inhumanity" is reprinted by permission of Mitchell Lerner.

a) by killing members of the group;

b) by causing serious bodily or mental harm to members of the group;

c) by deliberately inflicting on the group conditions of life calculated to bring about its physical destruction, in whole or in part;

d) by imposing measures intended to prevent births within the group;

e) by forcibly transferring children of the group to another group.

Over the years, genocide has come to mean a form of one-sided mass killing in which a state or another authority intends to destroy a group, as that group and membership in it are defined by the perpetrator.[1]

machinations
hostile manoeuvres

This definition is important in several ways. First, it acknowledges that there is no reciprocity in genocide: it is not a war, although it may and often does occur in the midst of war, hiding in the **machinations** of war.

Second, genocide means that all group members are targets, regardless of individual characteristics. Einstein and Freud were Jews and, as such, didn't have the right to exist in the Nazi universe. Not long ago, the Soviets and the Americans pointed weapons of mass destruction at each other, putting humanity at great risk. The enormous power of nuclear weapons makes possible the indiscriminate destruction of entire national groups and allows us to conceive of the enemy as an entire people.

Third, those who attempt genocide regard specific populations as dispensable. The notion that entire groups of people are disposable demeans the value of human life and negates all the spiritual, religious, and cultural aspirations of the species.

The indiscriminate destruction of an entire people is genocidal, and the genocidal illusion is that we can become more pure by eradicating those who are different from ourselves. Genocide is the worst outcome of labelling and stereotyping. Blinded by prejudice, we cannot see or hear others as they are. This, then, is the genocidal mentality—irrational, merciless, making no exceptions.

The 20th century's first instance of genocide occurred in 1915, when the ruling government of the Ottoman Empire, the Young Turks, attempted to create a new order for their state. Their ideology of Pan-Turanianism required that all of Turkey be of one religion: Muslim. The government of Enver and Talaat perceived the several million Armenians who lived in the eastern Ottoman Empire as a threat, and secretly declared them undesirable and expendable. The Turkish Armenians were a cultured, civilized, creative, educated people who had expected to receive some form of sovereignty within the Ottoman Empire.

Instead, hiding behind the smokescreen of World War I, the Turkish government implemented a bureaucratic system to destroy the Armenians. After allying with Germany, the Turkish military invaded Armenian population centres, conducted deportations, and brutally slaughtered approximately 1.5 million Armenians. To this day, the Turkish government denies the extent of the killings, and keeps many of its documents sealed to investigators. Armenians around the world and others continue to urge political leaders to acknowledge the genocide that prefigured and predated the Nazi Holocaust by some 20 years. They contend that the present Turkish government, by not acknowledging the destruction of a people, is attempting to dispense with historical fact the way its predecessors dispensed with Armenian souls.

Since 1945, at least 22 documented examples fit within the definition of genocide. The estimated number of deaths, between three and nine million people, does not include the 1.5 million Armenians or the six million Jews who died in the Nazi Holocaust.

"The most painful question of genocide," write authors Chalk and Jonassohn, "is, How is it possible for people to kill other people on such a massive scale? The answer seems to be that it is not possible. At least not as long as the potential victims are perceived as people. We have no evidence that genocide was ever performed on a group of equals. The victims must not only *not* be equals, but also be clearly defined as something less than fully human."[2]

Inmates in a Nazi concentration camp.

When European pioneers haphazardly slaughtered North American aboriginals, when the Khmer Rouge campaigned to slaughter the urban population of Cambodia, when white slave traders ripped apart black families on the Ivory Coast, when the Hutu macheted the Tutsi, what must these individuals have been thinking? What understanding of another human being must go on in the head of a person who is shredding, burning, stabbing or enslaving human beings?

Chalk and Jonassohn raise an important and essential point. It is *not* possible for genocide to occur unless the perpetrator regards all members of the target group as less than human. The victims must be dehumanized. Since dehumanization is a process that happens over time, it contains enough warnings that it can be stopped.

Dehumanization

Hitler's "Final Solution," the Nazi's clinical term for mass murder, involved the systematic slaughter of six million Jews. It was designed to eliminate an entire people by using the efficient mechanisms of an industrial culture. The Holocaust took place in the midst of a culture that was rich in art, music, philosophy and science. The term *Holocaust* is reserved for this particular tragedy of the 20th century, which was the ultimate ideological genocide. It refers to the period from January 1933, when Hitler seized power on a platform of racial purity and superiority, to May 1945, when the Nazi regime dissolved.

German statistics indicate that 5.8 million Jews were murdered. The recognized figure of non-Jewish civilians murdered is six million, including Gypsies, Serbs, Polish intelligentsia, resistance fighters, German opponents of Nazism, homosexuals, Jehovah's Witnesses, habitual criminals and the disabled.

European Jewish culture was destroyed, along with a host of other "less-than-humans." German technical specialists engineered mass-murder camps, known as concentration camps, and built special killing apparatus. In these devices, which included gas chambers, crematoria and burial pits, the destruction of a people transpired. Hundreds of thousands of Nazis actively participated in the ghettoizing, deportation and mass killings of the Jews, which went on for six years. Fathers, mothers, grandparents and 1.5 million children were sent up in flames.

Like all genocides, dehumanization was a necessary precondition of the Holocaust. Dehumanization involves fear of the other. Like the body's immune system, which attacks foreign elements, the mind seems to attack foreign ideas and ways before it can understand them. The process of dehumanization, of deconstructing another, is a way of asserting one's own identity. But being unlike the other does not empower you to deny those others their existence. The essence of civilization—the essence of a social contract—is the acknowledgement of shared basic rights. And none is more fundamental than the right to existence. Dehumanization, then, is the process by which we devalue the other and remove their right to exist.

Possessed of a long militaristic, patriotic, nationalistic history, the Germans felt humiliated by their loss in World War I and by the excessive demands of the post-war Treaty of Versailles. By **promulgating** theories that the Germans belonged to a "master race," the Nazis redefined dehumanization and made it into a high art. The fiercely proud and **narcissistic** tendencies in German culture were exploited to the hilt by the Nazi propaganda machine. The Germans scapegoated and stereotyped their targeted group, the Jews, as inferiors and a national threat, and instituted laws to curtail their rights. The long history of anti-Semitism in Europe simplified the process.

The Nazi illusion of grandeur and perfection threatens our understanding of civilization, as formulated from ancient times. Civilization does not mean that some are superior and some inferior, or that some are masters and others are slaves. Civilization demands that we accept others as part of a broader human community; that others are different from, not less than, ourselves; that others are strange, not threatening. Civilization, like marriage, requires compromise. But for Hitler, his thugs and the passive European population, there was no compromise.

promulgating
promoting

narcissistic
self-obsessed

The Banality of Evil

banality
trite predictability

We told them not to be afraid, we wouldn't do anything to them, they should just stand in front of the wall. But it was taken for granted among us that they should be killed. So when somebody said, 'Shoot,' I swung around and pulled the trigger, three times, on automatic fire. I remember the little girl with the red dress hiding behind her granny.

One sunny morning in June 1992, Borislav Herak and two other Serb nationalist soldiers gunned down a Muslim family found hiding in a basement. Later, from a jail cell, he described many crimes he had committed to a reporter from the *New York Times*. "[H]is account was offered in a matter-of-fact manner, and always with a keen attention to detail. As he shifted between one killing and another, and between rapes, the young Serb gave the names of many of his victims. He described where they were killed, what they were wearing, and what they said immediately before they died."

What does a soldier think of as he carries out the genocidal policies of his government? The soldier quoted above, like many others, seemed to be obeying orders and following the crowd, with the rules around him laid down by the circumstances of war. Where was his conscience? Why do so few people involved in genocide recognize their own ability to take a moral stand and oppose evil? The soldiers doing the hacking in

Rwanda, the rape in Bosnia, the slaughter of "non-desirables" anywhere, go against conscience by participating in thoughtlessness as much as they participate in genocide.

The philosopher Hannah Arendt, whose studies of totalitarianism remain central to all scholarship on this topic, has made a simple but startling observation: there is no great demon who acts as a mastermind behind evil. Evil comes out of the hearts of ordinary people who prefer to obey rather than think. This, then, is the banality of evil. Destruction arises not from some demonic vision but from ordinary thoughtlessness, indifference and silence. Some argue that historical precedents, economic conditions or cultural conflict cause people to be seduced by what appear to be passionate but simplistic solutions. And while it may be easier to get swept away by the crowd, we need courage to stand up against it.

Some Conclusions

Many follow the crowd, while a few say "No." Even in a world of horror there are some who act according to their conscience, such as the righteous people of Le Chambon-sur-Lignes, France, who saved 5000 Jewish lives during World War II.

For you and me, genocidal events may seem to defy ordinary language and cause us to disbelieve the truth. They may seem so irrational and incredible that we may prefer to ignore, doubt or deny the documented facts. The numbing effect of the incomprehensible may inhibit the thoughtfulness that we need in order to resist. As hard as it is to do, we should not let the experience of the unthinkable overwhelm our ability to fasten to the truth.

All the testimonies of survivors; all the elaborate words, ideas and structures of scholars attempting to frame the subject; all the memoirs written to recall the slain and condemn the injustice—all these are words in a vocabulary of responsibility to the human family. We owe it to the victims of genocide, to each other, and to our children to respond with thoughtfulness, conscience and spirit.

Notes

[1] Helen Fein, *Genocide Watch* (Ed. Yale, 1992).

[2] Frank Chalk and Kurt Jonassohn, *The History and Sociology of Genocide* (Yale, 1990).

UNIT 4

Science and the Natural World

It seems to me that those sciences are vain and full of error which do not spring from experiment, the source of all certainty.

Leonardo da Vinci

I cannot believe that God plays dice with the cosmos.

Albert Einstein

The opposite of a correct statement is an incorrect statement, but the opposite of a profound truth is another profound truth.

Neils Bohr

Science cannot solve the ultimate mystery of nature. And it is because in the last analysis we ourselves are part of the mystery we are trying to solve.

Max Planck

Introduction

In this unit of *The Human Project*, we will focus on science: its history as seen through the lens of cosmology; the criteria that render science a distinct way of knowing; the impact of science, especially evolutionary theory, on our understanding of what it means to be human; the ethical issues that science and technology raise; and the limits of what we can expect science to teach us. At first glance, this may seem to point us in a totally new direction, but it becomes clear upon reflection that we have been attending to science and technology—albeit somewhat subtly—throughout the first three units of this book. All of the thinkers discussed in Unit 1—including the geneticists and the behaviourists but also Descartes, Freud, and even to some extent Nietzsche—were careful to construct their models of self in such a way as to take into account the relevant medical and/or psychological (i.e., scientific) findings of their day. The social issues surveyed in Unit 2, from the changing dynamics of the family to the changing composition of society, cannot really be fully understood without considering Postman's account of the "ecological" impact of new technology. And each of the theorists discussed in Unit 3—including those prescribing how best to construct good government as well as those advocating how most effectively to fight against bad government—assumed a certain view of human nature that reflected prevailing theories of their time in the fields of psychology and political science. In short, science has informed all our discussions in *The Human Project* thus far. This should come as no surprise if we recognize that psychology, sociology, economics and political science are, indeed, social *sciences*.

Natural Science and Social Science

In Unit 4, we will set our sights more specifically on the *natural* or *physical* sciences, in particular cosmology, genetics, evolutionary biology and medicine. This does not mean that we will abandon the social sciences, however. Indeed, we will see that the findings of the natural sciences frequently lead us to reconsider our views in these fields. If you adopted a Lockean view of human nature and good government in Unit 3, for example, you might reconsider your position after reading Edward O. Wilson's "Is Humanity Suicidal?" In this article, Wilson summarizes a disturbing view of human nature put forward by evolutionary theory: "people are programmed by their genetic heritage to be so selfish that a sense of global responsibility will come too late. Individuals place themselves first, family second, tribe third, and the rest of the world a distant fourth." Serious reflection on this statement may lead you to reluctantly reconsider Freud's view of human nature, Hobbes's theory of good government and Barber's account of international relations.

Science and Self-Understanding

Even scientists' account of the nature of the cosmos—a field far removed from everyday concerns—has a tremendous effect on how we understand ourselves. In "Making Sense of the Universe," Suzanne Senay traces the development of cosmology from its beginnings in ancient Greece to the 21st century—from Aristotle's geocentric model of the universe to Galileo's heliocentric model, from Newton's account of universal gravitation to Einstein's theory of relativity. This fascinating history demonstrates how science develops through augmenting and/or re-evaluating the established "background knowledge" of the day as well as how science is influenced by and, in turn, influences prevailing metaphysical and religious views regarding our place in, and our (un)importance to, the cosmos. Indeed, as scientific knowledge has advanced, the importance of humankind seems to have diminished, as our home planet has been "displaced" from its stationary position at the centre of the universe and "relocated" to a revolving position around an ordinary star somewhere on the edge of the universe.

Evolutionary Theory and Religion

This mundane view of humankind has been bolstered by the development of evolutionary theory. In "The Tale of the Ancient Molecule," Paul Davies elegantly describes the process by which genetic mutation sometimes gives an organism an advantage in the struggle for survival and, thus, facilitates its selection in the evolutionary process. As he takes care to point out, there "is no cosmic musician scrutinizing the score of life and exercising quality control." In other words, God plays no role in this process: mutations do *not* occur by design, most of them *disad*-vantage the organisms that inherit them and those that are beneficial to the inheriting organisms occur purely through *chance*.

But not all scientists who accept evolutionary biology reject faith in God. In "Finding Darwin's God," Kenneth R. Miller argues that the theory of evolution does *not* eclipse religious faith but actually comple-ments it. "In biological terms," Miller states, "evolution is the only way a Creator could have made us the creatures we are—free beings in a world of authentic and meaningful moral and spiritual choices." In other words, evolution confirms the creative power of God insofar as this process gave rise to *free* beings who may *choose* to follow the right path in life instead of puppet-like beings who can only "choose" to follow the course *determined* for them.

Scientific Methodology

Thus, the findings of the natural sciences are important not just to scientists and science enthusiasts, but to all of us as we struggle to understand ourselves, our species and, yes, our natural world as well in order to make informed life choices. So, what precisely is science? In "Can We Know the Universe? Reflections on a Grain of Salt," Carl Sagan defines science as a "way of thinking" that seeks to discover regularities, that is, laws of nature or physical laws, that allow us to acquire knowledge of the incredibly vast and complex world in which we live. When this methodology is applied to human biology, great advances in medicine are gained. As Atul Gawande cautions us in "When Doctors Make Mistakes," however, we must always account for the possibility of human error, which, in the context of medicine, can, of course, have tragic consequences. However advanced our scientific knowledge becomes, then, we must not forget that human beings are always potentially fallible in its application.

Senay shows us, moreover, that what it means to "know" a phenomenon scientifically has changed throughout history—from Aristotle's view that its four causes must be known, to Newton's perspective that its cause-and-effect relationships need simply be measurable mathematically, to Hawking's view that causal explanations are in theory unknowable. These intriguing historical differences aside, Senay also shows that a theory, to be scientific, must, at least in principle, be grounded in sensory observation, i.e., empirical evidence; tested through experimentation; and potentially verifiable or falsifiable through the evidence gathered via experiment. In other words, "good" science—that is, science done properly—must satisfy these criteria. This is not to imply that ideas and theories that don't meet these standards aren't valuable but merely that they aren't scientific.

Science and Ethics

Some scientists argue, however, that this value-neutral way of evaluating scientific theories is not acceptable. In "Can Science Be Ethical?" Freeman Dyson introduces a distinction between "good" and "bad" science that is clearly grounded in a value judgment: "good" science strives to meet the basic needs of the world's poor while "bad" science aims either to sell "toys for the rich" or to advance knowledge far removed from everyday life. Dyson argues that ethics and religion should be enlisted to help direct research toward "good" science.

Science and the Environment

Wilson also expresses optimism that the "greening of religion" may serve as a force that helps humankind to become more environmentally conscious—a goal that, in his view, must be met to avoid environmental disaster. With this statement, he sides with *environmentalism*—the view that the welfare of humankind is fundamentally dependent on nature—and against *exceptionalism*—the view that humanity is smart enough and determined enough to always figure out a way to "fix" the ecological problems we create. Indeed, Wilson cautions us that it is urgent that we begin to take environmental problems seriously because we run the risk of waiting until it is too late.

In "The Truth about the Environment," Bjorn Lomborg takes issue with the "litany" of environmental concerns expressed by environmentalists, namely, that the unprecedented growth of the human population worldwide threatens to lead to the decimation of natural resources, the food supply, animal and plant species, and clean air and water. A statistician by profession, Lomborg analyzes the relevant available data to argue that the global environment is not nearly as imperiled as we are usually led to believe and, moreover, that the future generally looks encouraging. Since both Wilson and Lomborg consider the same environmental issues, this debate, like all scientific debates, ultimately must be settled by appeal to the empirical evidence.

Making Sense of the Universe

Suzanne Senay

Historians of science often claim that all scientific activity originated with simple human curiosity, our natural desire to know about our world. The ancient Greek philosopher Aristotle (384–322 BCE) wrote that curiosity leads to wonder, the awe we feel when we look at "the Moon and . . . the Sun and . . . the stars, and [think about] the genesis of the universe." Wonder urges us not just to witness but also to question and examine in order, ultimately, to understand, to know. Descartes also wrote of wonder, calling it "a sudden surprise of the soul which brings it to *consider with attention* the objects that seem to it unusual and extraordinary" (emphasis added). In this article, we will see how cosmology, the science of the order and structure of the universe, "considers with attention" the universe itself.

Most ancient cultures watched the heavens the way we might watch the weather, as an inescapable influence on daily life. Scientific cosmology grew out of this fascination, but gradually discarded the mythological meanings and interpretations given to the stars and planets. Aristotle was one of the first philosophers to attempt a full description of the emerging scientific perspective and his efforts earned him the title "first scientist." Our exploration of science begins with his approach and briefly sketches the development of cosmology to the present time. Along the way, we will try to answer some questions about science in general as a form of knowledge: What is a scientific theory? How is theory related to reality and truth? (Think of the expression, "It's *just* a theory.") How do scientific practices and concepts—such as observation, experiment, hypothesis, prediction and evidence—develop and change?

phenomenon/ phenomena (pl.)

an observable fact, object or event, e.g., the phases of the moon, a flower, a water molecule (seen through a microscope)

cause

1. produces an effect, is always and unconditionally followed by a certain phenomenon (modern definition)
2. a combination of matter, form, source of change and final purpose (Aristotle's definition)

Aristotle's Cosmology

Aristotle argued that a scientific explanation of a **phenomenon** must "grasp the 'why' of it" by identifying and understanding its **causes**. He believed that any cause has four aspects: matter or substratum; form or essence; source of change; and final purpose. A complete Aristotelian causal explanation is complex, but we can briefly illustrate how his concepts of matter and form help explain the ancient Greek belief that the Earth is a

---

"Making Sense of the Universe" is by Suzanne Senay of the Humber College Institute of Technology and Advanced Learning. Used by permission.

solid sphere sitting motionless at the centre of the (also spherical) universe. According to Aristotle, the Earth is composed of particles of a material substratum called "earth," the form of which is heaviness. Together, earth and heaviness serve as causes of the Earth's shape and position. Heavy particles occupy a natural position at the centre, or lowest point, of the universe. (The centre is lowest because it is farthest from every point on the circumference). Any heavy particle lying away from the centre has a natural inclination or motion back toward it. The particle does not come to rest until it is as close to the centre as possible. This is why heavy objects fall to the ground when dropped; they are exhibiting their natural motion back toward the centre. Heaviness is Aristotle's account of gravity. Because all the heavy particles naturally move toward the lowest point, they crowd together, forming a solid sphere, the Earth.

This explanation may seem strange to us, but it was accepted as true in the Western world from the time of Aristotle's death until Galileo challenged it in 1610. Our modern concept of cause generally focuses on an occurrence that invariably precedes the effect or phenomenon we are trying to explain, for example, the turning of the ignition that starts an engine, or the inhalation of bacteria that produces infection. By comparison, Aristotle's concept seems to involve too much subjective interpretation. Despite the weakness of his particular theory of cause, however, most modern scientists still agree with Aristotle that identifying the cause of a phenomenon is an essential part of understanding it scientifically.

Aristotle held that all knowledge begins with **sensory observation**. The activities of looking at, listening to or touching phenomena in the world give us accurate information about the way the natural world really is. For example, "Our eyes tell us that the heavens revolve in a circle," and, therefore, we conclude that the objects in the heavens—the Moon, planets, stars, even the Sun—all move. By contrast, our observations of the objects in our immediate environment seem to tell us that the Earth itself does not move. These two perceptions help to explain Aristotle's view, called *geocentrism*, that the Earth sits stationary at the centre of the universe while the heavens revolve around it.

Aristotle divided the universe into two realms, the *sublunary*, which extends from the centre of the Earth to just below the Moon, and the *heavenly*, which begins at the Moon and includes the Sun, planets and stars. Beyond the stars lies the Prime Mover, or God, the first cause of all existence. The concept of the Prime Mover is a **first principle**, something that is known but is not *demonstrable*, that is, not provable via evidence or argument. In Aristotelian science, first principles are causes

sensory observation
using faculties of sight, hearing, smell, taste or touch (which are often extended by technology, e.g., microscopes, telescopes) to detect phenomena in nature such as color, pitch, scent, sweetness or shape

first principle
a fundamental truth that needs no proof; e.g., every effect has a cause; something cannot simultaneously exist and not exist

that set supposedly rational requirements for the natural world. Aristotle argued that since the heavenly realm is closest to the Prime Mover, it must have divine qualities, including perfection and eternity. This means that the shape, motion and organization of the heavenly bodies must exhibit perfection and eternity. The Greeks believed that circles and spheres are perfect, eternal shapes, because they have neither beginning nor end. Therefore, all of the heavenly bodies must be spheres and move in circles. Eternity implies, moreover, the persistence of one, unchanging state, while change involves the ending of one state and the beginning of another. Thus, the heavenly realm cannot change.

The ideas of eternity and perfection also dictate the nature of the substance of the heavens. They are composed entirely of ether, sometimes called the "fifth element." Unlike substances in the sublunary realm, ether is neither heavy nor light. Its natural place in the universe is determined by its perfection, not by its weight. Its motion, obviously, must be perfect and, hence, circular. And because they cannot change, objects made of ether cannot speed up or slow down, but must move uniformly. Ether explains why the heavenly bodies stay in the heavens. It forms a set of nesting, transparent crystalline spheres, each one enclosing the next. One heavenly body is attached to each sphere, beginning with the Moon, followed by Mercury, Venus, the Sun, Mars, Jupiter, Saturn and the fixed stars or constellations. The whole universe is thus a set of transparent globes within globes, containing the Earth at the centre. The Prime Mover lies beyond the sphere of the stars and sets the entire universe in motion.

Unlike the heavenly realm, the sublunary realm is composed of four substances: earth, water, air and fire, listed in order from heaviest to lightest. Weight is an intrinsic feature or form of each substance and determines its *natural place* and *natural motion*. Earth's natural place is at the centre of the universe, water belongs above earth, air above water, and fire, the lightest, above air, closest to the Moon, in the form of comets and meteors. Of course, observation also tells us that the sublunar substances are not always found in their natural places. A volcano burns underground and spews stones into the air. Cirrus clouds carry heavy ice crystals high in the atmosphere. Meteorites cast burning rock to the ground. According to Aristotle, the fundamental reason behind all these phenomena is change. Everything in the sublunary realm changes because the four substances transform into one another. Each exhibits particular qualities: earth is dry and cold; water is wet and cold; air is moist and warm; and fire is dry and hot. When these qualities change, the whole substance changes. For example, a log is made primarily of earth, and is therefore heavy, dry and cold. But if heated, it begins to burn, becoming fire, which is dry and hot. Since a log is heavy, its natural place is on the ground. But as it becomes fire, the light flames move to the natural place of fire, i.e., into the air. As some particles of fire cool, they fall back to the ground as ash, a form of earth.

This brief summary illustrates one of the inconsistencies of Aristotelian science. Aristotle claimed that all knowledge must be based on observation. Yet, his cosmology also invokes supposedly rational, *un*observed first principles, including the concepts of the Prime Mover, perfection and eternity, which are not grounded in observation. He turned to first principles when observation did not provide a complete or satisfying causal explanation. Modern scientists reject Aristotle's concept of first principles and are much more careful about invoking so-called rational ideas in explanations. In addition, Aristotle's cosmology contains many scientific conclusions we now know to be false. For instance, there are more than four basic substances in nature; indeed, at this writing, there are 118 elements in the periodic table. Moreover, our Earth does not rest at the centre of the universe, but orbits the Sun. We no longer use ideas of perfection and eternity to divide the universe into two different parts comprised of distinct substances. In fact, we find many of the same elements on the Earth, in meteorites, on the Moon and now on Mars. Consequently, we have come to believe that the Earth and the heavens are part of the same universe, made of the same materials, governed by the same natural laws.

While Aristotle's cosmological views have not fared well, three features of his account of scientific thinking have nonetheless become foundations of modern scientific practice: 1) Sensory observation is essential to acquiring knowledge about the natural world. 2) Scientific explanation seeks to identify causes. 3) Science is systematic—it connects various phenomena with their causes to create a comprehensive account or **theory**.

Explaining Observations: Ptolemy

Aristotle's cosmology became the dominant theory of the universe after his death. But it was not able to explain certain important observations. The planets posed two particular problems. Astronomers who tracked the motions of the planets noticed that they do not revolve in unchanging, perfect circles around the Earth. We can see this for ourselves. Over several nights, anyone observing the clear sky from the same spot could see that the planets generally appear to move from west to east against the background of stars. But periodically, each planet appears to reverse

theory
system of interconnected generalizations and observations that explains phenomena, e.g., Newton's laws of motion explain the effects of gravity on physical objects on Earth as well as in "the heavens"

direction, moving from east to west. This backtracking was called *retrograde* motion. Because it involves change of direction, retrograde motion violates the Aristotelian principle that the heavenly bodies exhibit eternal or unchanging circular motion. The second problem involved Venus, Mars and Jupiter, all of which seem to be brighter at some times and dimmer at others. Again, we can observe this for ourselves. For Aristotelians, variation in brightness is a form of change and, therefore, theoretically impossible in the heavenly realm.

Conflict between theory and observation is a common occurrence in science, and can be addressed in various ways. At the extremes, a whole theory may be discarded, or particular observations simply denied. But most often, this tension drives the reworking of theory, the gathering and analysis of more observations and sometimes the emergence of radical new perspectives. Even if it is incomplete, a dominant theory serves as **background knowledge**, the generally accepted understanding of nature at a given time. Background knowledge is a takeoff point: it suggests what additional observations or explanations might be needed to get a clearer or more accurate picture of nature.

Aristotelian cosmology served as background knowledge for the Greek astronomer Ptolemy, who lived in Egypt around 125 CE. In his book the *Almagest*, he explained retrograde motion and variations in brightness while preserving, more or less, the principles of perfection and eternity. According to Aristotle, a planet traces the circumference of one circle around the Earth, appearing to go in the same direction all the time. Ptolemy suggested that a planet simultaneously follows the path of two distinct circles, a smaller one, the *epicycle*, rotating along the circumference of a larger one, the *orbit*. As the small circle rotates, the planet will appear to move backward and then forward again. By adding this feature to the theory, Ptolemy responded to and explained the generally accepted observations. His scheme was considered a success, and, until the time of Copernicus, was used to calculate the locations of the planets and stars in order to determine dates for important religious feasts. This illustrates a common approach to the problem created by observations that cannot be explained by an accepted theory. Details of a theory can be changed in order to incorporate the observations, while the general outline of the theory is preserved.

background knowledge

a spectrum of accepted beliefs against which new theories, hypotheses and experiments are formulated, e.g., Einstein's Theory of Special Relativity, because it is very well supported and generally accepted, forms part of our background knowledge about the universe and, therefore, is assumed when new hypotheses, like that of the Big Bang, are tested

The Influence of Christianity on Science

Historians have not yet determined what role the written works of Aristotle and Ptolemy played in Europe after the fall of the Roman Empire to barbarian invasions in the fifth century. But as Christianity spread, Greek culture's promotion of human curiosity lost favour. Interest in examination of the natural world was replaced by interest in how to get to the next world, the afterlife, and how to achieve salvation and avoid suffering there. The Church argued that all knowledge must be justified by appeal to God, revelation (the Bible) or the clergy, not the human senses. The observational and rational abilities of the individual had to be subordinated to these authorities.

During this period, the works of Aristotle and Ptolemy were apparently lost to the Christian world. But Muslim scholars in North Africa preserved them. When Islamic invaders came to Spain from North Africa in the eighth century, they brought Arabic translations of many of these works. In 1085, Christians retook Toledo and the Muslims fled, but among the books they left behind were the *Almagest* and Aristotle's scientific treatises. These texts catalyzed scientific curiosity in the Christian world. By the middle of the 13th century, leading universities in Paris and Oxford taught Aristotle's works. His ideas became so famous that he was often referred to simply as "the Philosopher."

Christian scholars were keen to show that ancient learning supported their religious beliefs. Although Aristotle was a pagan, they believed that he had accurately observed and explained the physical aspects of God's cosmic plan. They interpreted his ideas about the perfection of the heavens in Christian terms. Passages from the Bible were used to show that God and the Philosopher both held that the Earth sat motionless at the centre of the universe as the focus of creation: "Yea, the world is established, that it cannot be moved" (Psalm 93); God "fixed the Earth upon its foundation not to be moved forever" (Psalm 103). But while Christian philosophers accepted Aristotle's conclusions about the structure of the universe, they did not share his deep commitment to observation. They required that scientific theory accord absolutely with Church dogma. Observations had to be interpreted to support religious belief. Theories had to be vetted by Church authorities. Scientists had to hide or deny any work that conflicted with approved views.

Copernicus and Heliocentrism: The Importance of Hypothesis

Despite the widespread acceptance of Aristotle by religious authorities, some scientists were dissatisfied with his cosmology. Foremost among these was Polish astronomer Nicholas Copernicus (1473–1543). When he combined the views of Aristotle and Ptolemy in an effort to develop a single cosmology, two points particularly concerned him. First, if Ptolemy's epicycles are real (rather than merely apparent from our position on Earth), then planetary motion is a messy, almost wild business. Christian ideas favoured a stately procession of planets and stars over this mad dance. Second, some of Ptolemy's additions "fudged" the geometry of the circle, distorting the relationship between the centre point and the circumference. Copernicus viewed this as a "monstrous" deviation from divine perfection.

In order to dispense with the "monstrosity" of imperfection and to "simplify" the account of planetary motion, Copernicus challenged the most fundamental tenet of geocentrism. He proposed the **hypothesis**, called *heliocentrism*, that the Sun, not the Earth, occupies the centre of the universe. He deliberately treated heliocentrism as a hypothesis, which is an assumption or conjecture, around which he reorganized the theory of the heavens. Placing the Sun at the centre, he recalculated the orbits of the planets and located the Earth third in line from the Sun. Copernicus did not claim his hypothesis was true, however, but only that it "permitted him to ascertain whether explanations sounder than those of [his] predecessors could be found." The hypothesis gave him the "freedom to imagine any circles whatever for the purpose of explaining the heavenly phenomena." But it also had practical value. In his preface to *On the Revolutions of the Heavenly Spheres*, Copernicus indicated that official Church astronomers were having difficulty calculating the ecclesiastical calendar because motions of the Sun and Moon could not be accurately measured. His theory offered a solution to this problem.

Copernicus's heliocentrism is a good example of a pure hypothesis, in other words, an alternative theoretical explanation for already accepted observations. He developed his theory, not on the basis of new observations, but by inventing a new explanation. Thus, for example, while Aristotle and Ptolemy explained the apparent rising and setting of the Sun as real motion, Copernicus explained this same observation as an effect of the Earth's motion around the Sun. His theory of heliocentrism shows that hypothesis is a powerful explanatory tool; it enables us to re-imagine a physical system and explain known data from a new perspec-

hypothesis
an assumption or proposal put forward as a possibility that directs the course of further investigation

tive. It even provides a new background against which to measure and interpret data. Copernicus believed his hypothesis was superior to Ptolemy's because it restored the idea of perfect circular motion to cosmology. But the Church considered it heresy because it moved the Earth out of the centre of the universe. Ironically, this heretical work did indeed make it easier for Church astronomers to calculate the positions of stars and planets in order to set the religious calendar. Copernicus's astronomical tables were widely used for this purpose for almost two hundred years, even though his heliocentric theory was forbidden.

The New Science: Galileo and Bacon

Copernicus feared that his great treatise would be seen as a challenge to Christian doctrine and refused to publish it until shortly before his death. He never saw its effects on the scientific community. Some scientists immediately embraced it for its elegance and explanatory power. But in doing so, they risked their lives. In 1600, philosopher Giordano Bruno was burned at the stake by the Inquisition, charged in part with supporting Copernicanism.

Nonetheless, heliocentrism fuelled changes in scientific method. Foremost among its supporters was the Italian mathematician and professor Galileo Galilei (1564–1642). In 1610 he bought a telescope, lengthened its focal distance and turned it on the Moon. Because he taught Aristotelian science, Galileo knew that Aristotle believed the Moon to be a perfect sphere. But when he observed the Moon through his telescope, he saw mountains and craters, not a perfectly smooth surface. He concluded that the Moon is not made of ether but is, in fact, quite similar to Earth. He also discovered four small bodies revolving around Jupiter. Over a period of several days, he observed that one of them went behind Jupiter and emerged again on the other side. If Jupiter was attached to or embedded in a crystal shell, as Aristotle had said it was, it would not be possible for any object to circle it without breaking through the crystal. Galileo concluded that there were no crystalline spheres and that heavenly bodies could orbit each other, and not just the Earth. Aristotelian cosmology simply could not explain what Galileo had seen. These observations suggested that the Copernican system was at least possible. Then Galileo observed the phases of Venus, caused by its revolution around the Sun (just as the visible phases of the Moon are caused by its rotation around the Earth and the Sun). Now he had observational evidence, clear to anyone who looked through a telescope, confirming Copernicus' claim that the planets revolve around the Sun instead of the Earth.

In 1616, the Vatican's College of Research endorsed Galileo's specific observations but denied that they supported Copernicanism. They placed Copernicus's treatise on the *Index,* the list of publications banned by the Catholic Church, forbidding anyone to read it on penalty of excommunication. But that did not stop the popularization of Galileo's views. Pamphlets circulated, arguing that Copernicus and Galileo were right and the Vatican was wrong. As Galileo's fame grew, however, so did the danger he faced. In June of 1633, he was called before the Inquisition, which demanded he reject Copernicanism. Mindful of Giordano Bruno's fate, and perhaps hoping to pursue his research in secret, Galileo recanted and was sentenced to house arrest for the remainder of his life. But the persuasive power of his observations permanently shifted scientific method away from reliance on authorities such as the Church and Aristotle, and toward the search for evidence and use of new technologies. He was one of a wave of thinkers—which included René Descartes, discussed in Unit 1—who sought to establish the autonomy of the individual human intellect as a tool to gain knowledge. Galileo made the conflict between authority and evidence plain: do we believe tradition *or* do we believe our own eyes?

Galileo made a second important contribution to scientific method through his clarification of the role of mathematics and its bearing on the difference between **qualitative** and **quantitative** explanation. Aristotle defined natural causes qualitatively: earth, air, heat, cold, heaviness and lightness are *qualities* that explain, because they directly cause, physical effects. He defined gravity, for example, as the heaviness of some kinds of bodies: heaviness is a form or quality, not a measurable quantity. Since weight can be measured, we might think that Aristotle's definition is quantitative as well as qualitative. But, in his theory, heaviness is not just a different amount of substance from lightness: it is an intrinsically different *kind* of thing altogether. The difference is captured partly by the fact that the natural motion of heavy objects is down, while the natural motion of light ones is up. A simple numerical measurement does not reflect or describe this difference, which involves direction and not just amount. Since gravity is just heaviness, the speed of a falling body must be a direct manifestation of its heaviness. If two objects fall to Earth, the heavier one should fall faster and hit the ground first. Unlike Aristotle, Galileo believed that causes should be understood mathematically or quantitatively. He claimed that "the book of nature is written in the language of mathematics." Experiments

---

quality / qualitative(ly)
a nature, trait, characteristic, value / assessed in terms of characteristic features

quantity / quantitative(ly)
a measurable amount / assessable in terms of numerical values

showed, moreover, that the heavier body did *not* in fact hit the ground first. Galileo argued that the acceleration of a falling body is determined, not by intrinsic heaviness, but by distance and time. He expressed the general principle of acceleration in the famous law of falling bodies, which states that distance is proportional to the square of the time elapsed. This law ultimately helped overturn Aristotle's view that objects fall to Earth because they are heavy. It showed that the substance, earth, and its quality or form, heaviness, were not in fact the causes of the gravitational effect. It also showed the power of mathematical explanations of natural phenomena: Galileo's general mathematical law explained falling phenomena more accurately than Aristotelian qualities did.

While Galileo undermined Aristotelianism with observations, a second important figure of this period proposed an entirely new purpose for science. Englishman Francis Bacon (1561–1626) argued that the function of science is not to support religious doctrine, tradition or authority, but to improve the quality of human life by giving people greater control over nature. He embraced human curiosity even more vehemently than Aristotle had, claiming, "Knowledge is power." Bacon developed a method he called **induction** that encouraged experiment. He also conceived science as a social pursuit the progress of which requires scientists to work together, comparing and contrasting their findings.

According to Bacon, merely collecting observations does not yield genuine understanding. Scientists must not consider only those observations that support a favourite theory, while ignoring other, potentially contradictory ones. Nor may they be permitted to skew observations to fit a theory. Instead, a true induction must be made. This requires gathering as many relevant observations as possible, but also carefully analyzing them before drawing conclusions. While the details of Bacon's concept of induction differ from our modern one, his recognition of the importance of observing widely and analytically forms the foundation of the modern notion of experiment. Taken together, the works of Galileo and Bacon reveal the relationship between hypothesis and observation: Galileo showed that observational evidence must be used to evaluate a hypothesis; Bacon showed that in order to yield scientific knowledge, evidence for or against a hypothesis must be gathered inductively, through experiment.

The relationships between hypothesis, experiment and evidence become clearer when we consider how they work together in an example. Let's consider the conflict between hypotheses about the

induction

1. a form of reasoning by probability from past experience to predictions of future. 2. a method whereby a hypothesis generates a prediction that is then tested experimentally (an observation is made), e.g., Halley's hypothesis that the comet orbits elliptically predicted that the comet would be visible again in 1758, which was tested by observing the relevant position in the sky to see if the comet did in fact appear

shape of the Earth. Of course, this question was resolved well before Galileo and Bacon lived. But the example is useful because it involves simple observations that anyone can make. If we see a vast prairie, we might indeed interpret our observation as evidence that the Earth is flat. But an isolated piece of evidence does not tell the whole story. Christopher Columbus, among others, noticed that when he was standing on shore watching a ship sail away from him, the mast seemed to sink into the water. When the ship sailed toward him, on the other hand, the mast seemed to rise. If one accepts the hypothesis of a flat Earth, these observations will certainly discourage sailing! But as an experienced sailor himself, Columbus knew that the "sinking" and "rising" mast was merely an appearance, not reality. (When standing on deck, a sailor does not observe the mast sinking as the ship sails away from land.) He believed this optical illusion suggested a different hypothesis, namely, that the Earth is round. The mast appears to sink as the ship sails away because the surface of a sphere curves away from itself. The observations of the prairie and of the mast both describe how things appear to us under certain circumstances. There is nothing wrong with appearances, but they must not be taken at face value. In order to be accepted as observational evidence, they must be subjected to experiment, that is, a gathering, comparison and analysis of many observations. With ingenuity and luck, we may devise what Bacon called a **crucial experiment**, which provides evidence that tips the balance toward a particular hypothesis. That is exactly what Columbus did. His trip to the "New World," during which he did not fall off the edge of a flat Earth, was the crucial experiment that showed that his hypothesis of a round Earth is the accurate one.

crucial experiment
an experiment the outcome of which strongly confirms or refutes a hypothesis, e.g., Galileo's observation of the motions of the satellites of Jupiter strongly refuted Aristotle's hypothesis of the crystalline spheres attached to each planet

Newton

Copernicus, Galileo and Bacon challenged Aristotelian views, but not with the thoroughness or originality of the English mathematician and scientist Isaac Newton (1642–1727). He developed a cosmology that incorporated the heliocentrism of Copernicus, the observations of Galileo and the mathematical descriptions of planetary motion of the German mathematician and astronomer Johannes Kepler (1571–1630). Newton's work was so extraordinary that in his own lifetime the leading poet of the day Alexander Pope (1688–1744) prepared an epitaph for him:

> Nature and Nature's laws lay hid in night:
> God said, "Let Newton be!" and all was light.

Newton's laws of motion proposed an entirely new cosmology. To gain some understanding of his theory, let us consider where Galileo left things. His observations of the Moon, the satellites of Jupiter and the phases of Venus suggested that Copernicus's views gave a better account of the solar system than Aristotle's and Ptolemy's. But he was not able to explain why the heavenly bodies moved in their orbits. If the Aristotelian system is wrong, and there are no crystalline spheres holding the Moon, the planets and the stars in their orbits, then why does the Moon, for example, revolve around the Earth instead of flying off into space or (if it is made of a heavy substance) crashing into the Earth?

To answer this question, Newton looked to the concept of gravity. Galileo had already shown that observation did not support Aristotle's distinction between the sublunary and heavenly realms. Newton recognized that if the Moon and the Earth are not so different, then the same physical principles might apply to both. This meant that the concept of gravity might not be restricted to explaining the motions of objects close to Earth, but might explain the motion of the Moon as well.

Newton's laws of motion, introduced in 1687 in *The Mathematical Principles of Natural Philosophy*, implied a comprehensive new theory of gravity. Simply stated, Newton's laws are as follows: (1) The Law of Inertia: An object in motion tends to remain in motion in a straight line, while an object at rest tends to remain at rest unless a force acts upon it. (2) Force is equal to mass multiplied by acceleration. (3) To every action there is always opposed an equal and opposite reaction. While Aristotle explained the motions of bodies in terms of the nature of their substance and location in the universe, Newton explained them in terms of measurable quantities and mathematical laws. Even the title of his book captures the importance of mathematics as the key to understanding nature.

Newton's three laws give a unified explanation of the behaviour of heavenly bodies and physical objects on or near Earth. The first law does away with Aristotle's concepts of natural circular motion and natural place. According to the *law of inertia*, any object in motion, anywhere in the universe, will move continuously in a straight line unless a force diverts it. Therefore, the Moon moves because of inertia, not because it is made of ether. It revolves around the Earth because the force of the Earth's gravity pulls it into an elliptical orbit, not because perfection requires circular motion. The Moon stays in orbit because the force of gravity pulling it toward the Earth is opposed by an equal and opposite centrifugal force pulling it away from the Earth. There is no crystalline sphere holding it in place. Since the forces balance each other, the

Moon remains in orbit, neither flying off into space nor crashing into the Earth. These same laws of motion explain why apples hang down by their stems, why stones thrown into the air fall back to the ground, why Earth revolves around the Sun, why the tides rise and fall and a host of other natural phenomena.

Newton's breakthrough represents a modern kind of scientific explanation, appealing to quantity rather than essential qualities, uniformity throughout nature rather than separate realms, and mathematical laws rather than religious ideas. Newton's laws of motion form the basis of a comprehensive system explaining the cosmos. But while Aristotle's theory tells us exactly what gravity is, i.e., heaviness, Newton's does not. According to Newton's definition, gravity is an attractive force measured in mathematical terms. But that does not meet Aristotle's standard of explanation because it does not specify a cause for the force. Newton defended this feature of his work:

> It is enough that gravity really exists and acts according to the laws that we have set forth and is sufficient to explain all the motions of the heavenly bodies and of our sea.

It does not matter, in other words, that we do not know the ultimate cause or true nature of gravity. It is enough that we can measure it mathematically. This idea, that causal explanation has limits, is a hallmark of modern science. It reflects our willingness to give up notions of perfection, eternity, essence and purpose as guiding or limiting concepts in explanation. It means that science need not trace a chain of causes to a metaphysical "first cause," such as God, in order to explain phenomena. But it also means that we may never have complete understanding of our universe.

Newton's insight about gravity was a new hypothesis. One of the functions of a hypothesis is to generate *predictions* or observations that can be verified or checked. The English astronomer Edmund Halley (1656–1742) made one of the most famous predictions in science based on Newton's hypothesis about gravity. Comets had always been difficult phenomena to explain. Prior to Newton's time, people believed each sighting indicated a unique comet. In 1682, people all over Europe saw a particularly bright comet. Halley knew from astronomical records that twice before, in 1531 and 1607, a comet had appeared along the same path in the sky. He also knew Newton's new theory of gravity. He surmised that if a comet is affected by the force of gravity of some suitably large celestial body, such as the Sun, then it would have an elliptical orbit and circle that body continually along the same path. If this is so, then there were not three comets, but one. Based on his calculation of the number of years between previous sightings, i.e., 76, Halley predicted that, if the orbit was elliptical, the comet would reappear in 1758. Such a prediction is useful because it specifies exactly what must be observed in order to judge the hypothesis. In other words, the prediction tests the hypothesis: if it turns out to be correct, it is evidence **confirming** the hypothesis; if it turns out to be incorrect, it **falsifies** the hypothesis. Unfortunately, by 1758, Halley had already died, but that December the comet appeared just where he said it would, and it now bears his name. His prediction was accurate and it confirmed his hypothesis that the comet was indeed subject to gravity and orbited the Sun.

Theory and Truth

Newtonian mechanics is still used today to describe the behaviour of most physical objects under ordinary circumstances. Does that mean that Newton's views are "true"? The concept of **falsifiability** can help to answer this question. Originated by the Austrian-born philosopher Karl Popper (1902–1994), the concept of falsifiability implies that we can never prove a scientific theory true with absolute certainty. While evidence can demonstrate the falsehood of a given theory, a "good" theory, one considered to be a "fact," is a theory that we have not, despite our best efforts, been able to falsify. From Popper's perspective, Newton's theory isn't true; we simply have not proved that it is false. There is a problem with Popper's perspective, however: a wide variety of competing and contradictory theories and hypotheses can all be "not false" and Popper does not give any satisfactory grounds for choosing among the group of "not false" possibilities.

If science cannot discover reality or truth, are we left with the conclusion that scientific theories are "just theories"? The answer is no. Popper's principle of falsification does not mean that we cannot trust science. Nor does it mean that any "not false" theory is as good as any other. Good theories must survive more than the test of falsification; they must also be confirmed by evidence. A theory is confirmed when it generates predictions that are borne out. The more successful a theory is at making accurate predictions, the more useful is its explanation of our world. The social nature of scientific activity ensures that scientists continually test and refine their own and others' theories. As a consequence, generally accepted theories are usually the best available at the time, given the standards of scientific practice. The fact is, hypothesis, evidence, experiment and prediction function successfully in the context of actual scientific practice, without requiring a standard of

confirm
to strengthen or verify a hypothesis through supporting evidence

falsify
to weaken or refute a hypothesis through non-supporting evidence (from the principle that inductive statements cannot be proved, but only disproved)

falsifiability
principle stating that a scientific theory must set out the conditions under which it can be proven false

absolute certainty. From the perspective of most scientists, this practical standard of truth is enough.

Einstein and Beyond

While Newtonian mechanics suffices to explain most ordinary physical phenomena, 20th-century physicists discovered features of the universe that Newton never imagined and could not have explained. Their work calls into question Aristotle's idea that in order to explain a phenomenon, one must discover its cause. According to the modern concept, a cause explains its effect because they are connected by necessity. This means that there is an invariable relationship between them. If the effect has occurred, the cause *must* have occurred previously. If the cause occurs, the effect follows necessarily, without exception. This is the fundamental principle of determinism discussed in Unit 1. Its scientific usefulness is clear: discovering the necessary connection between cause and effect makes possible the reliable prediction of natural phenomena. Even the **Theory of Relativity** discovered by the German-born American physicist Albert Einstein (1879–1955) did not challenge this principle. Newton conceived time and space as absolutes, unaffected by what occurs within them. But Einstein argued that they are affected by the speed and mass of physical objects. Special Relativity shows the mathematical relationship among energy, mass and the speed of light in the equation $E = mc^2$. General Relativity shows that the gravitational mass of a physical body bends the shape of space itself. But, according to Einstein, even if basic phenomena are relative, the laws of nature are still deterministic. As he famously said, "God does not play dice with the Universe."

Despite his commitment to determinism, Einstein's own work on the light *quantum*—a fixed, indivisible elemental unit—contributed to Quantum Mechanics, a theory that undermines determinism. Quantum Mechanics explains the behaviour of physical systems at very short distances. In order to predict the future behaviour of a physical system, we must be able to observe its present state. But the German physicist Werner Heisenberg (1901–1976) showed that this is impossible at the quantum level. His view, now called the **Uncertainty Principle**, states that we can measure the speed *or* the position of a subatomic particle, but not both simultaneously. While Einstein argued that there is an actual or real value, a "**hidden variable**," for both speed and position that we simply cannot observe, other physicists, the English cosmologist Stephen Hawking (b. 1942) among them, have argued that there exists no such actual or real value. If we cannot accurately measure changes in speed or position, then we cannot accurately predict what their effects will be.

Theory of Relativity
Einstein's concept that space and time are not static, absolute containers or backgrounds for objects and events in the physical universe, but part of a continuum that changes with the gravitational effects of material bodies; a useful metaphor illustrates the Newtonian universe as the volume of an unbounded, regular solid and the Einsteinian universe as the flexible surface area of rubber balloon.

Uncertainty Principle
the impossibility of (or limit on) accurately measuring two phenomena simultaneously, e.g., the speed and position of a subatomic particle

hidden variable
an actual value that cannot be observed

If we do not know the cause-and-effect relationships among phenomena, we cannot devise laws to describe them.

If Hawking and his like-minded colleagues are correct, the implication for scientific method is that Aristotle's goal for explanation, the discovery of causes, cannot always be met. This is a different problem from that of the limits of explanation. Newton believed there is an explanation for gravity, but that not knowing it did not weaken his theory. Hawking's interpretation of the Uncertainty Principle, however, implies that sometimes there is no explanation, no actual cause, for certain phenomena. They happen, but no law of science can describe or predict them. If he is correct, then, at least at the quantum level of the universe, determinism does not hold.

We do not know yet whether Quantum Mechanics will change the nature of scientific explanation. The debate between Hawking and his opponents is still underway. In the meantime, scientific activity continues. Hypotheses are posed, experiments devised, observations predicted and made. Our daily lives make us aware that Bacon was correct—knowledge is power. Science has given us great benefits, like life-saving medicines, but also great challenges, like global warming. Most fundamentally, however, it changes the way we think about ourselves as knowers and about the world around us. When we look into the night sky, we see the same constellations as the ancient Greeks saw, but because of the activity of science, we also see a great deal more.

Can We Know the Universe? Reflections on a Grain of Salt

Carl Sagan

> Nothing is rich but the inexhaustible wealth of nature. She shows us only surfaces, but she is a million fathoms deep.
>
> – Ralph Waldo Emerson

Science is a way of thinking much more than it is a body of knowledge. Its goal is to find out how the world works, to seek what regularities there may be, to penetrate to the connections of things—from subnuclear particles, which may be the constituents of all matter, to living organisms, the human social community, and thence to the cosmos as a whole. Our intuition is by no means an infallible guide. Our perceptions may be distorted by training and prejudice or merely because of the limitations of our sense organs, which, of course, perceive directly but a small fraction of the phenomena of the world. Even so straightforward a question as whether in the absence of friction a pound of lead falls faster than a gram of fluff was answered incorrectly by Aristotle and almost everyone else before the time of Galileo. Science is based on experiment, on a willingness to challenge old dogma, on an openness to see the universe as it really is. Accordingly, science sometimes requires courage—at the very least the courage to question the conventional wisdom.

Beyond this the main trick of science is to *really* think of something: the shape of clouds and their occasional sharp bottom edges at the same altitude everywhere in the sky; the formation of a dewdrop on a leaf; the origin of a name or a word—Shakespeare, say, or "philanthropic"; the reason for human social customs—the incest taboo, for example; how it is that a lens in sunlight can make paper burn; how a "walking stick" got to look so much like a twig; why the Moon seems to follow us as we walk; what prevents us from digging a hole down to the center of the Earth; what the definition is of "down" on a spherical Earth; how it is possible for the body to convert yesterday's lunch into today's muscle and sinew; or how far is up—does the universe go on forever, or if it does not, is there any meaning to the question of what lies on the other side? Some of these questions are pretty easy. Others, especially the last, are mysteries to which no one even today knows the answer. They are natural questions to ask. Every culture has posed such questions in one way or another. Almost always the proposed answers are in the nature of "Just So Stories," attempted explanations divorced from experiment, or even from careful comparative observations.

But the scientific cast of mind examines the world critically as if many alternative worlds might exist, as if other things might be here which are not. Then we are forced to ask why what we see is present and not something else. Why are the Sun and the Moon and the planets spheres? Why not pyramids, or cubes, or **dodecahedra**? Why not irregular, jumbly shapes? Why so symmetrical, worlds? If you spend any time spinning hypotheses, checking to see whether they make sense, whether they conform to what else we know, thinking of tests you can pose to substantiate or deflate your hypotheses, you will find yourself doing science. And as you come to practice this habit of thought more and more you will get better and better at it. To penetrate into the heart of the thing—even a little thing, a blade of grass, as Walt Whitman said—is to experience a kind of exhilaration that, it may be, only human beings of all the beings on this planet can feel. We are an intelligent species and the use of our intelligence quite properly gives us pleasure. In this respect the brain is like a muscle. When we think well, we feel good. Understanding is a kind of ecstasy.

dodecahedra
shape with twelve sides

But to what extent can we *really* know the universe around us? Sometimes this question is posed by people who hope the answer will be in the negative, who are fearful of a universe in which everything might one day be known. And sometimes we hear pronouncements from scientists who confidently state that everything worth knowing will soon be known—or even is already known—and who paint pictures of a **Dionysian** or Polynesian age in which the zest for intellectual discovery has withered, to be replaced by a kind of subdued **languor**, the lotus eaters drinking fermented coconut milk or some other mild hallucinogen. In addition to maligning both the Polynesians, who were intrepid explorers (and whose brief respite in paradise is now sadly ending), as well as the inducements to intellectual discovery provided by some hallucinogens, this contention turns out to be trivially mistaken.

Dionysus
Greek god of pleasure
languor
weakness, pleasurable stillness

Let us approach a much more modest question: not whether we can know the universe or the Milky Way Galaxy or a star or a world. Can we know, ultimately and in detail, a grain of salt? Consider one microgram of table salt, a speck just barely large enough for someone with keen eyesight to make out without a microscope. In that grain of salt there are about 10^{16} sodium and chlorine atoms. This is a 1 followed by 16 zeros, 10 million billion atoms. If we wish to know a grain of salt, we must know at least the three-dimensional positions of each of these atoms. (In fact, there is much more to be known—for example, the nature of the forces between the atoms—but we are making only a modest calculation.) Now, is this number more or less than the number of things which the brain can know?

How much *can* the brain know? There are perhaps 10^{11} neurons in the brain, the circuit elements and switches that are responsible in their electrical and chemical activity for the functioning of our minds. A typical brain neuron has perhaps a thousand little wires, called dendrites, which connect it with its fellows. If, as seems likely, every bit of information in the brain corresponds to one of these connections, the total number of things knowable by the brain is no more than 10^{14}, one hundred trillion. But this number is only one percent of the number of atoms in our speck of salt.

So in this sense the universe is intractable, astonishingly immune to any human attempt at full knowledge. We cannot on this level understand a grain of salt, much less the universe.

But let us look a little more deeply at our microgram of salt. Salt happens to be a crystal in which, except for defects in the structure of the crystal lattice, the position of every sodium and chlorine atom is predetermined. If we could shrink ourselves into this crystalline world, we would see rank upon rank of atoms in an ordered array, a regularly alternating structure—sodium, chlorine, sodium, chlorine, specifying the sheet of atoms we are standing on and all the sheets above us and below us. An absolutely pure crystal of salt could have the position of every atom specified by something like 10 bits of information.

This would not strain the information-carrying capacity of the brain.

Chlorine is a deadly poison gas employed on European battlefields in World War I. Sodium is a corrosive metal which burns upon contact with water. Together they make a placid and unpoisonous material, table salt. Why each of these substances has the properties it does is a subject called chemistry, which requires more than 10 bits of information to understand.

If the universe had natural laws that governed its behavior to the same degree of regularity that determines a crystal of salt, then, of course, the universe would be knowable. Even if there were many such laws, each of considerable complexity, human beings might have the capability to understand them all. Even if such knowledge exceeded the information-carrying capacity of the brain, we might store the additional information outside our bodies—in books, for example, or in computer memories—and still, in some sense, know the universe.

Human beings are, understandably, highly motivated to find regularities, natural laws. The search for rules, the only possible way to understand such a vast and complex universe, is called science. The universe forces those who live in it to understand it. Those creatures who find everyday experience a muddled jumble of events with no predictability, no regularity, are in grave peril. The universe belongs to those who, at least to some degree, have figured it out.

It is an astonishing fact that there *are* laws of nature, rules that summarize conveniently—not just qualitatively but quantitatively—how the world works. We might imagine a universe in which there are no such laws, in which the 10^{80} elementary particles that make up a universe like our own behave with utter and uncompromising abandon. To understand such a universe we would need a brain at least as massive as the universe. It seems unlikely that such a universe could have life and intelligence, because beings and brains require some degree of internal stability and order. But even if in a much more random universe there were such beings with an intelligence much greater than our own, there could not be much knowledge, passion or joy.

Fortunately for us, we live in a universe that has at least important parts that are knowable. Our common-sense experience and our evolutionary history have prepared us to understand something of the workaday world. When we go into other realms, however, common sense and ordinary intuition turn out to be highly unreliable guides. It is stunning that as we go close to the speed of light our mass increases indefinitely, we shrink toward zero thickness in the direction of motion, and time for us comes as near to stopping as we would like. Many people think that this is silly, and every week or two I get a letter from someone who complains to me about it. But it is a virtually certain consequence not just of experiment but also of Albert Einstein's brilliant analysis of space and time called the Special Theory of Relativity. It does not matter that these effects seem unreasonable to us. We are not in the habit of traveling close to the speed of light. The testimony of our common sense is suspect at high velocities.

Or consider an isolated molecule composed of two atoms shaped something like a dumbbell—a molecule of salt, it might be. Such a molecule rotates about an axis through the line connecting the two atoms. But in the world of quantum mechanics, the realm of the very small, not all orientations of our dumbbell molecule are possible. It might be that the molecule could be oriented in a horizontal position, say, or in a vertical position, but not at many angles in between. Some rotational positions are forbidden. Forbidden by what? By the laws of nature. The universe is built in such a way as to limit, or quantize, rotation. We do not experience this directly in everyday life; we would find it startling as well as awkward in sitting-up exercises, to find arms outstretched from the sides or pointed up to the skies permitted but many intermediate positions forbidden. We do not live in the world of the small, on the scale of 10^{-13} centimeters, in the realm where there are twelve zeros between the decimal place and the one. Our common-sense intuitions do not count. What does count is experiment—in this case observations from the far infrared spectra of molecules. They show molecular rotation to be quantized.

The idea that the world places restrictions on what humans might do is frustrating. Why *shouldn't* we be able to have intermediate rotational positions? Why *can't* we travel faster than the speed of light? But so far as we can tell, this is the way the universe is constructed. Such prohibitions not only press us toward a little humility; they also make the world more knowable. Every restriction corresponds to a law of nature, a regularization of the universe. The more restrictions there are on what matter and energy can do, the more knowledge human beings can attain. Whether in some sense the universe is ultimately knowable depends not only on how many natural laws there are that encompass widely divergent phenomena, but also on whether we have the openness and the intellectual capacity to understand such laws. Our formulations of the regularities of nature are surely dependent on how the brain is built, but also, and to a significant degree, on how the universe is built.

For myself, I like a universe that includes much that is unknown and, at the same time, much that is knowable. A universe in which everything is known would be static and dull, as boring as the heaven of some weak-minded theologians. A universe that is unknowable is no fit place for a thinking being. The ideal universe for us is one very much like the universe we inhabit. And I would guess that this is not really much of a coincidence.

Can Science Be Ethical?

Freeman Dyson

One of my favorite monuments is a statue of Samuel Gompers not far from the Alamo in San Antonio, Texas. Under the statue is a quote from one of Gompers' speeches:

> What does labor want?
> We want more schoolhouses and less jails,
> More books and less guns,
> More learning and less vice,
> More leisure and less greed,
> More justice and less revenge,
> We want more opportunities to cultivate our better nature.

Samuel Gompers was the founder and first president of the American Federation of Labor. He established in America the tradition of practical bargaining between labour and management which led to an era of growth and prosperity for labour unions. Now, 70 years after Gompers' death, the unions have dwindled, while his dreams, more books and fewer guns, more leisure and less greed, more schoolhouses and fewer jails, have been **tacitly** abandoned. In a society without social justice and with a free-market ideology, guns, greed, and jails are bound to win.

tacitly
quietly

When I was a student of mathematics in England 50 years ago, one of my teachers was the great mathematician G.H. Hardy, who wrote a little book, *A Mathematician's Apology*, explaining to the general public what mathematicians do. Hardy proudly proclaimed that his life had been devoted to the creation of totally useless works of abstract art, without any possible practical application. He had strong views about technology, which he summarized in the statement "A science is said to be useful if its development tends to accentuate the existing inequalities in the distribution of wealth, or more directly promotes the destruction of human life." He wrote these words while war was raging around him.

Still, the Hardy view of technology has some merit even in peacetime. Many of the technologies that are now racing ahead most rapidly, replacing human workers in factories and offices with machines,

---

making stockholders richer and workers poorer, are indeed tending to accentuate the existing inequalities in the distribution of wealth. And the technologies of lethal force continue to be as profitable today as they were in Hardy's time. The marketplace judges technologies by their practical effectiveness, by whether they succeed or fail to do the job they are designed to do. But always, even for the most brilliantly successful technology, an ethical question lurks in the background: the question whether the job the technology is designed to do is actually worth doing.

The technologies that raise the fewest ethical problems are those that work on a human scale, brightening the lives of individual people. Lucky individuals in each generation find technology appropriate to their needs. For my father 90 years ago, technology was a motorcycle. He was an impoverished young musician growing up in England in the years before World War I, and the motorcycle came to him as a liberation. He was a working-class boy in a country dominated by the snobberies of class and accent. He learned to speak like a gentleman, but he did not belong in the world of gentlemen. The motorcycle was a great equalizer. On his motorcycle, he was the equal of a gentleman. He could make the grand tour of Europe without having inherited an upper-class income. He and three of his friends bought motorcycles and rode them all over Europe.

My father fell in love with his motorcycle and with the technical skills that it demanded. He understood, 60 years before Robert Pirsig wrote *Zen and the Art of Motorcycle Maintenance*, the spiritual quality of the motorcycle. In my father's day, roads were bad and repair shops few and far between. If you intended to travel any long distance, you needed to carry your own tool kit and spare parts and be prepared to take the machine apart and put it back together again. A breakdown of the machine in a remote place often required major surgery. It was as essential for a rider to understand the anatomy and physiology of the motorcycle as it was for a surgeon to understand the anatomy and physiology of a patient. It sometimes happened that my father and his friends would arrive at a village where no motorcycle had ever been seen before. When this happened, they would give rides to the village children and hope to be rewarded with a free supper at the village inn. Technology in the shape of a motorcycle was comradeship and freedom.

Fifty years after my father, I discovered joyful technology in the shape of a nuclear fission reactor. That was in 1956, in the first intoxicating days of peaceful nuclear energy, when the technology of reactors suddenly emerged from wartime secrecy and the public was invited to come and play with it. This was an invitation that I could not refuse. It looked then as if nuclear energy would be the great equalizer, providing cheap and abundant energy to rich and poor alike, just as 50 years earlier the motorcycle gave mobility to rich and poor alike in class-ridden England.

I joined the General Atomic Company in San Diego, where my friends were playing with the new technology. We invented and built a little reactor which we called the TRIGA, designed to be inherently safe. Inherent safety meant that it would not misbehave even if the people operating it were grossly incompetent. The company has been manufacturing and selling TRIGA reactors for 40 years and is still selling them today, mostly to hospitals and medical centres, where they produce short-lived isotopes for diagnostic purposes. They have never misbehaved or caused any danger to the people who used them. They have only run into trouble in a few places where the neighbours objected to their presence on ideological grounds, no matter how safe they might be. We were successful with the TRIGA because it was designed to do a useful job at a price that a big hospital could afford. The price in 1956 was a quarter of a million dollars. Our work with the TRIGA was joyful because we finished it quickly, before the technology became entangled with politics and bureaucracy, before it became clear that nuclear energy was not and never could be the great equalizer.

Forty years after the invention of the TRIGA, my son George found another joyful and useful technology, the technology of CAD-CAM, computer-aided design and computer-aided manufacturing. CAD-CAM is the technology of the postnuclear generation, the technology that succeeded after nuclear energy failed. George is a boat-builder. He designs seagoing kayaks. He uses modern materials to reconstruct the ancient craft of the Aleuts, who perfected their boats by trial and error over thousands of years and used them to travel prodigious distances across the northern Pacific. His boats are fast and rugged and seaworthy. When he began his boat-building 25 years ago, he was a nomad, travelling up and down the north Pacific coast, trying to live like an Aleut, and he built his boats like an Aleut, shaping every part of each boat and stitching them together with his own hands. In those days he was a nature-child, in love with the wilderness, rejecting the urban society in which he had grown up. He built boats for his own use and for his friends, not as a commercial business.

As the years went by George made a graceful transition from the role of rebellious teenager to the role of solid citizen. He married, raised a

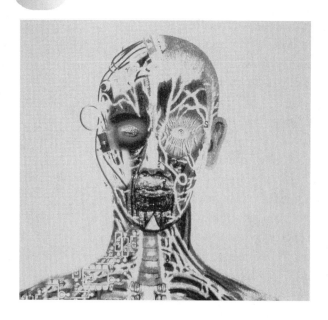

daughter, bought a house in the city of Bellingham, and converted an abandoned tavern by the waterfront into a well-equipped workshop for his boats. His boats are now a business. And he discovered the joys of CAD-CAM.

His workshop now contains more computers and software than sewing needles and hand tools. It is a long time since he made the parts of a boat by hand. He now translates his designs directly into CAD-CAM software and transmits them electronically to a manufacturer who produces the parts. George collects the parts and sells them by mail order to his regular customers with instructions for assembling them into boats. Only on rare occasions, when a wealthy customer pays for a custom-built job, does George deliver a boat assembled in the workshop. The boat business occupies only a part of his time. He also runs a historical society concerned with the history and ethnography of the north Pacific. The technology of CAD-CAM has given George resources and leisure, so that he can visit the Aleuts in their native islands and reintroduce to the young islanders the forgotten skills of their ancestors.

Forty years into the future, which joyful new technology will be enriching the lives of our grandchildren? Perhaps they will be designing their own dogs and cats. Just as the technology of CAD-CAM began in the production lines of large manufacturing companies and later became accessible to individual citizens like George, the technology of genetic engineering may soon spread out from the biotechnology companies and agricultural industries and become accessible to our grandchildren. Designing dogs and cats in the privacy of a home may become as easy as designing boats in a waterfront workshop.

Instead of CAD-CAM we may have CAS-CAR, computer-aided selection and computer-aided reproduction. With the CAS-CAR software, you first program your pet's colour scheme and behaviour, and then transmit the program electronically to the artificial fertilization laboratory for implementation. Twelve weeks later, your pet is born, satisfaction guaranteed by the software company. When I recently described these possibilities in a public lecture at a children's museum in Vermont, I was verbally assaulted by a young woman in the audience. She accused me of violating the rights of animals. She said I was a typical scientist, one of those cruel people who spend their lives torturing animals for fun. I tried in vain to placate her by saying that I was only speaking of possibilities, that I was not actually myself engaged in designing dogs and cats. I had to admit that she had a legitimate complaint. Designing dogs and cats is an ethically dubious business. It is not as innocent as designing boats.

When the time comes, when the CAS-CAR software is available, when anybody with access to the software can order a dog with pink and purple spots that can crow like a rooster, some tough decisions will have to be made. Shall we allow private citizens to create dogs who will be objects of contempt and ridicule, unable to take their rightful place in dog society? And if not, where shall we draw the line between legitimate animal breeding and illegitimate creation of monsters? These are difficult questions that our children and grandchildren will have to answer. Perhaps I should have spoken to the audience in Vermont about designing roses and orchids. Vegetables, it seems, do not have rights. Dogs and cats are too close to being human. They have feelings like ours. If our grandchildren are allowed to design their own dogs and cats, the next step will be using the CAS-CAR software to design their own babies. Before that next step is reached, they ought to think carefully about the consequences.

What can we do today, in the world as we find it at the end of the 20th century, to turn the evil consequences of technology into good? The ways in which science may work for good or evil in human society are many and various. As a general rule, to which there are many exceptions, science works for evil when its effect is to provide toys for the rich, and works for good when its effect is to provide necessities for the poor. Cheapness is an essential virtue. The motorcycle worked for good because it was cheap enough for a poor schoolteacher to own. Nuclear energy worked mostly for evil because it remained a toy for rich governments and rich companies to play with. "Toys for the rich" means not only toys in the literal sense but technological conveniences that are available to a minority of people and make it harder for those excluded to take part in the economic and cultural life of the community. "Necessities for the poor" include not only food and shelter but adequate public health services, adequate public transportation, and access to decent education and jobs.

The scientific advances of the 19th century and the first half of the 20th were generally beneficial to society as a whole, spreading wealth to rich and poor alike with some degree of equity. The electric light, the telephone, the refrigerator, radio, television, synthetic fabrics, antibiotics, vitamins, and vaccines were social equalizers, making life easier and more comfortable for almost everybody, tending to narrow the gap between rich and poor rather than to widen it. Only in the second half of [the 20th] century has the balance of advantage shifted. During the last 40 years, the strongest efforts in pure science have been concentrated in highly esoteric fields remote from contact with everyday problems. Particle physics, low-temperature physics, and extragalactic astronomy are examples of pure sciences moving further and further away from their origins. The intensive pursuit of these sciences does not do much harm, or much good, either to the rich or the poor. The main social benefit provided by pure science in esoteric fields is to serve as a welfare program for scientists and engineers.

At the same time, the strongest efforts in applied science have been concentrated upon products that can be profitably sold. Since the rich can be expected to pay more than the poor for new products, market-driven applied science will usually result in the invention of toys for the rich. The laptop computer and the cellular telephone are the latest of the new toys. Now that a large fraction of high-paying jobs are advertised on the Internet, people excluded from the Internet are also excluded from access to jobs. The failure of science to produce benefits for the poor in recent decades is due to two factors working in combination: the pure scientists have become more detached from the mundane needs of humanity, and the applied scientists have become more attached to immediate profitability.

Although pure and applied science may appear to be moving in opposite directions, there is a single underlying cause that has affected them both. The cause is the power of committees in the administration and funding of science. In the case of pure science, the committees are composed of scientific experts performing the rituals of peer review. If a committee of scientific experts selects research projects by majority vote, projects in fashionable fields are supported while those in unfashionable fields are not. In recent decades, the fashionable fields have been moving further and further into specialized areas remote from contact with things that we can see and touch. In the case of applied science, the committees are composed of business executives and managers. Such people usually give support to products that affluent customers like themselves can buy.

Only a cantankerous man like Henry Ford, with dictatorial power over his business, would dare to create a mass market for automobiles by arbitrarily setting his prices low enough and his wages high enough that his workers could afford to buy his product. Both in pure science and in applied science, rule by committee discourages unfashionable and bold ventures. To bring about a real shift of priorities, scientists and entrepreneurs must assert their freedom to promote new technologies that are more friendly than the old to poor people and poor countries. The ethical standards of scientists must change as the scope of the good and evil caused by science has changed. In the long run, as Haldane and Einstein said, ethical progress is the only cure for the damage done by scientific progress.

The nuclear arms race is over, but the ethical problems raised by nonmilitary technology remain. The ethical problems arise from three "new ages" flooding over human society like **tsunamis**. First is the Information Age, already arrived and here to stay, driven by computers and digital memory. Second is the Biotechnology Age, due to arrive in full force early in the 21st century, driven by DNA sequencing and genetic engineering. Third is the Neurotechnology Age, likely to arrive later in this century, driven by neural sensors and exposing the inner workings of human emotion and personality to manipulation. These three new technologies are profoundly disruptive. They offer liberation from ancient drudgery in factory, farm, and office. They offer healing of ancient diseases of body and mind. They offer wealth and power to the people who possess the skills to understand and control them. They destroy industries based on older technologies and make people trained in older skills useless. They are likely to bypass the poor and reward the rich. They will tend, as Hardy said over 80 years ago, to accentuate the inequalities in the existing distribution of wealth, even if they do not, like nuclear technology, more directly promote the destruction of human life.

tsunamis
large tidal waves caused by underwater earthquakes

The poorer half of humanity needs cheap housing, cheap health care, and cheap education, accessible to everybody, with high quality and high aesthetic standards. The fundamental problem for human society in this century is the mismatch between the three new waves of technology and the three basic needs of poor people. The gap between technology and needs is wide and growing wider. If technology continues along its present course, ignoring the needs of the poor and showering benefits upon the rich, the poor will sooner or later rebel against the tyranny of technology and turn to irrational and violent remedies. In the future, as in the past, the revolt of the poor is likely to impoverish rich and poor together.

The widening gap between technology and human needs can only be filled by ethics. We have seen in the last 30 years many examples of the power of ethics. The worldwide environmental movement, basing its power on ethical persuasion, has scored many victories over industrial wealth and technological arrogance. The most spectacular victory of the environmentalists was the downfall of nuclear industry in the United States and many other countries, first in the domain of nuclear power and more recently in the domain of weapons. It was the environmental movement that closed down factories for making nuclear weapons in the United States, from plutonium-producing Hanford to warhead-producing Rocky Flats. Ethics can be a force more powerful than politics and economics.

Unfortunately, the environmental movement has so far concentrated its attention upon the evils that technology has done rather than upon the good that technology has failed to do. It is my hope that the attention of the Greens will shift in this century from the negative to the positive. Ethical victories putting an end to technological follies are not enough. We need ethical victories of a different kind, engaging the power of technology positively in the pursuit of social justice.

If we can agree with Thomas Jefferson that these truths are self-evident, that all men are created equal, that they are endowed with certain inalienable rights, that among these are life, liberty, and the pursuit of happiness, then it should also be self-evident that the abandonment of millions of people in modern societies to unemployment and destitution is a worse defilement of the earth than nuclear power stations. If the ethical force of the environmental movement can defeat the manufacturers of nuclear power stations, the same force should also be able to foster the growth of technology that supplies the needs of impoverished humans at a price they can afford. This is the great task for technology in this century.

The free market will not by itself produce technology friendly to the poor. Only a technology positively guided by ethics can do it. The power of ethics must be exerted by the environmental movement and by concerned scientists, educators, and entrepreneurs working together. If we are wise, we shall also enlist in the common cause of social justice the enduring power of religion. Religion has in the past contributed mightily to many good causes, from the building of cathedrals and the education of children to the abolition of slavery. Religion will remain in the future a force equal in strength to science and equally committed to the long-range improvement of the human condition.

In the world of religion, over the centuries, there have been prophets of doom and prophets of hope, with hope in the end predominating. Science also gives warnings of doom and promises of hope, but the yearnings and promises of sciences cannot be separated. Every honest scientific prophet must mix the good news with the bad. Haldane was an honest prophet, showing us the evil done by science not as inescapable fate but as a challenge to be overcome. He wrote in his book *Daedalus* in 1923, "We are at present almost completely ignorant of biology, a fact which often escapes the notice of biologists, and renders them too presumptuous in their estimates of the present condition of their science, too modest in their claims for its future." Biology has made amazing progress since 1923, but Haldane's statement is still true.

We still know little about the biological processes that affect human beings most intimately—the development of speech and social skills in infants, the interplay between moods and emotions and learning and understanding in children and adults, the onset of aging and mental deterioration at the end of life. None of these processes will be understood within the next decade, but all of them might be understood within the . . . century. Understanding will then lead to new technologies that offer hope of preventing tragedies and **ameliorating** the human condition. Few people believe any longer in the romantic dream that human beings are perfectible. But most of us still believe that human beings are capable of improvement.

ameliorating
making better

In public discussions of biotechnology today, the idea of improving the human race by artificial means is widely condemned. The idea is repugnant because it conjures up visions of Nazi doctors sterilizing Jews and killing defective children. There are many good reasons for condemning enforced sterilization and euthanasia. But the artificial improvement of human beings will come, one way or another, whether we like it or not, as soon as the progress of biological understanding makes it possible. When people are offered technical means to improve themselves and their children, no matter what they conceive improvement to mean, the offer will be accepted. Improvement may mean better health, longer life, a more cheerful disposition, a stronger heart, a smarter brain, the ability to earn more money as a rock star or baseball player or business executive. The technology of improvement may be hindered or delayed by regulation, but it cannot be permanently suppressed. Human improvement, like abortion today, will be officially disapproved, legally discouraged, or forbidden, but widely practised. It will be seen by millions of citizens as a liberation from past constraints and injustices. Their freedom to choose cannot be permanently denied.

Two hundred years ago, William Blake engraved *The Gates of Paradise,* a little book of drawings and verses. One of the drawings, with the title "Aged Ignorance," shows an old man wearing professorial eyeglasses and holding a large pair of scissors. In front of him, a winged child is running naked in the light from a rising sun. The old man sits with his back to the sun. With a self-satisfied smile he opens his scissors and clips the child's wings. With the picture goes a little poem:

> In Time's Ocean falling drown'd,
> In Aged Ignorance profound,
> Holy and cold, I clip'd the Wings
> Of all Sublunary Things.

This picture is an image of the human condition in the era that is now beginning. The rising sun is biological science, throwing light of ever-increasing intensity onto the processes by which we live and feel and think. The winged child is human life, becoming for the first time aware of itself and its potentialities in the light of science. The old man is our existing human society, shaped by ages of past ignorance. Our laws, our loyalties, our fears and hatreds, our economic and social injustices, all grew slowly and are deeply rooted in the past. Inevitably the advance of biological knowledge will bring clashes between old institutions and new desires for human self-improvement. Old institutions will clip the wings of new desires. Up to a point, caution is justified and social constraints are necessary. The new technologies will be dangerous as well as liberating. But in the long run, social constraints must bend to new realities. Humanity cannot live forever with clipped wings. The vision of self-improvement, which William Blake and Samuel Gompers in their different ways proclaimed, will not vanish from the earth.

The Truth about the Environment

Bjorn Lomborg

Ecology and economics should push in the same direction. After all, the "eco" part of each word derives from the Greek word for "home," and the protagonists of both claim to have humanity's welfare as their goal. Yet environmentalists and economists are often at loggerheads. For economists, the world seems to be getting better. For many environmentalists, it seems to be getting worse.

These environmentalists, led by such veterans as Paul Ehrlich of Stanford University, and Lester Brown of the Worldwatch Institute, have developed a sort of "litany" of four big environmental fears:

- Natural resources are running out.

- The population is ever growing, leaving less and less to eat.

- Species are becoming extinct in vast numbers: forests are disappearing and fish stocks are collapsing.

- The planet's air and water are becoming ever more polluted.

Human activity is thus defiling the earth, and humanity may end up killing itself in the process.

The trouble is, the evidence does not back up this litany. First, energy and other natural resources have become more abundant, not less so since the Club of Rome published *The Limits to Growth* in 1972. Second, more food is now produced per head of the world's population than at any time in history. Fewer people are starving. Third, although species are indeed becoming extinct, only about 0.7% of them are expected to disappear in the next 50 years, not 25–50%, as has so often been predicted. And finally, most forms of environmental pollution either appear to have been exaggerated, or are transient—associated with the early phases of industrialisation and therefore best cured not by restricting economic growth, but by accelerating it. One form of pollution—the release of greenhouse gases that causes global warming—does appear to be a long-term phenomenon, but its total impact is unlikely to pose a devastating problem for the future of humanity. A bigger problem may well turn out to be an inappropriate response to it.

Can Things Only Get Better?

Take these four points one by one. First, *the exhaustion of natural resources.* The early environmental movement worried that the mineral resources on which modern industry depends would run out. Clearly, there must be some limit to the amount of fossil fuels and metal ores that can be extracted from the earth: the planet, after all, has a finite mass. But that limit is far greater than many environmentalists would have people believe.

Reserves of natural resources have to be located, a process that costs money. That, not natural scarcity, is the main limit on their availability. However, known reserves of all fossil fuels, and of most commercially important metals, are now larger than they were when *The Limits to Growth* was published. In the case of oil, for example, reserves that could be extracted at reasonably competitive prices would keep the world economy running for about 150 years at present consumption rates. Add to that the fact that the price of solar energy has fallen by half in every decade for the past 30 years, and appears likely to continue to do so into the future, and energy shortages do not look like a serious threat either to the economy or to the environment.

The development for non-fuel resources has been similar. Cement, aluminium, iron, copper, gold, nitrogen and zinc account for more than 75% of global expenditure on raw materials. Despite an increase in consumption of these materials of between two- and ten-fold over the past 50 years, the number of years of available reserves has actually grown. Moreover, the increasing abundance is reflected in an ever-decreasing price: *The Economist*'s index of prices of industrial raw materials has dropped some 80% in inflation-adjusted terms since 1845.

Next, the *population explosion* is also turning out to be a bugaboo. In 1968, Dr. Ehrlich predicted in his best-selling book, *The Population Bomb*, that "the battle to feed humanity is over. In the course of the 1970s the world will experience starvation of tragic proportions— hundreds of millions of people will starve to death."

That did not happen. Instead, according to the United Nations, agricultural production in the developing world has increased by 52% per person since 1961. The daily food intake in poor countries has increased from 1,932 calories, barely enough for survival, in 1961 to 2,650 calories in 1998, and is expected to rise to 3,020 by 2030. Likewise, the proportion of people in developing countries who are starving has dropped from 45% in 1949 to 18% today, and is expected to decline even further to 12% in 2010 and just 6% in 2030. Food, in other words, is becoming not scarcer but ever more abundant. This is reflected in its price. Since 1800 food prices have decreased by more than 90%, and in 2000, according to the World Bank, prices were lower than ever before.

Modern Malthus

Dr. Ehrlich's prediction echoed that made 170 years earlier by Thomas Malthus. Malthus claimed that, if unchecked, human population would expand exponentially, while food production could increase only linearly, by bringing new land into cultivation. He was wrong. Population growth has turned out to have an internal check: as people grow richer and healthier, they have smaller families. Indeed, the growth rate of the human population reached its peak, of more than 2% a year, in the early 1960s. The rate of increase has been declining ever since. It is now 1.26%, and is expected to fall to 0.46% in 2050. The United Nations estimates that most of the world's population growth will be over by 2100, with the population stabilising at just below 11 billion (see Figure 1).

Malthus also failed to take account of developments in agricultural technology. These have squeezed more and more food out of each hectare of land. It is this application of human ingenuity that has boosted food production, not merely in line with, but ahead of, population growth. It has also, incidentally, reduced the need to take new land into cultivation, thus reducing the pressure on biodiversity.

Third, that *threat of biodiversity loss* is real, but exaggerated. Most early estimates used simple island models that linked a loss in habitat with a loss of biodiversity. A rule-of-thumb indicated that loss of 90% of forest

Figure 1

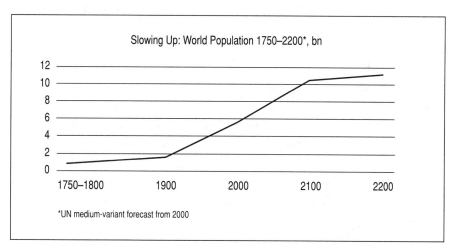

Source: UNPD

Figure 2

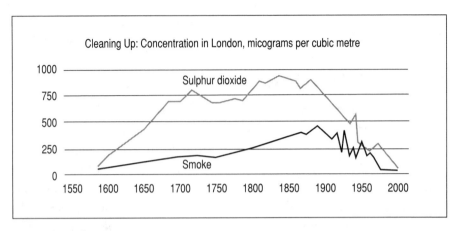

Source: B. Lomborg

meant a 50% loss of species. As rainforests seemed to be cut at alarming rates, estimates of annual species loss of 20,000–100,000 abounded. Many people expected the number of species to fall by half globally within a generation or two.

However, the data simply does not bear out these predictions. In the eastern United States, forests were reduced over two centuries to fragments totalling just 1–2% of their original area, yet this resulted in the extinction of only one forest bird. In Puerto Rico, the primary forest area has been reduced over the past 400 years by 99%, yet "only" seven of 60 species of bird have become extinct. All but 12% of the Brazilian Atlantic rainforest was cleared in the 19th century, leaving only scattered fragments. According to the rule-of-thumb, half of all its species should have become extinct. Yet, when the World Conservation Union and the Brazilian Society of Zoology analysed all 291 known Atlantic forest animals, none could be declared extinct. Species, therefore, seem more resilient than expected. And tropical forests are not lost at annual rates of 2–4%, as many environmentalists have claimed: the latest UN figures indicate a loss of less than 0.5%.

Fourth, *pollution* is also exaggerated. Many analyses show that air pollution diminishes when a society becomes rich enough to be able to afford to be concerned about the environment. For London, the city for which the best data are available, air pollution peaked around 1890 (see Figure 2). Today, the air is cleaner than it has been since 1585. There is good reason to believe that this general picture holds true for all developed countries. And, although air pollution is increasing in many developing countries, they are merely replicating the development of the industrialised countries. When they grow sufficiently rich they, too, will start to reduce their air pollution.

All this contradicts the litany. Yet opinion polls suggest that many people, in the rich world, at least, nurture the belief that environmental standards are declining. Four factors cause this disjunction between perception and reality.

Always Look on the Dark Side of Life

One is the lopsidedness built into scientific research. Scientific funding goes mainly to areas with many problems. That may be wise policy, but it will also create an impression that many more potential problems exist than is the case.

Secondly, environmental groups need to be noticed by the mass media. They also need to keep the money rolling in. Understandably, perhaps, they sometimes exaggerate. In 1997, for example, the Worldwide Fund for Nature issued a press release entitled, "Two-thirds of the world's forests lost forever." The truth turns out to be nearer 20%.

Though these groups are run overwhelmingly by selfless folk, they nevertheless share many of the characteristics of other lobby groups. That would matter less if people applied the same degree of scepticism to environmental lobbying as they do to lobby groups in other fields. A trade organization arguing for, say, weaker pollution controls is instantly seen as self-interested. Yet a green organisation opposing such a weakening is seen as altruistic, even if a dispassionate view of the controls in question might suggest they are doing more harm than good.

A third source of confusion is the attitude of the media. People are clearly more curious about bad news than good. Newspapers and broadcasters are there to provide what the public wants. That, however, can lead to significant distortions of perception. An example was America's encounter with El Niño in 1997 and 1998. This climatic phenomenon was accused of wrecking tourism, causing allergies, melting the ski-slopes and causing 22 deaths by dumping snow in Ohio.

A more balanced view comes from a recent article in the *Bulletin of the American Meteorological Society*. This tries to count up both the problems and the benefits of the 1997-98 Niño. The damage it did was estimated at $4 billion. However, the benefits amounted to some $19 billion. These came from higher winter temperatures (which saved an estimated 850 lives, reduced heating costs and diminished spring floods caused by meltwaters), and from the well-documented connection between past Niños and fewer Atlantic hurricanes. In 1998, America experienced no big Atlantic hurricanes and thus avoided huge losses. These benefits were not reported as widely as the losses.

The fourth factor is poor individual perception. People worry that the endless rise in the amount of stuff everyone throws away will cause the world to run out of places to dispose of waste. Yet, even if America's trash output continues to rise as it has done in the past, and even if the American population doubles by 2100, all the rubbish America produces through the entire 21st century will still take up only the area of a square, each of whose sides measures 28km (18 miles). That is just one-12,000th of the area of the entire United States.

Ignorance matters only when it leads to faulty judgments. But fear of largely imaginary environmental problems can divert political energy from dealing with real ones. The table [on the next page], showing the cost in the United States of various measures to save a year of a person's life, illustrates the danger. Some environmental policies, such as reducing lead in petrol and sulfur-dioxide emissions from fuel oil, are very cost-effective. But many of these are already in place. Most environmental measures are less cost-effective than interventions aimed at improving safety (such as installing air-bags in cars) and those involving medical screening and vaccination. Some are absurdly expensive.

Yet a false perception of risk may be about to lead to errors more expensive even than controlling the emission of benzene at tire plants. Carbon-dioxide emissions are causing the planet to warm. The best estimates are that the temperature will rise by some 2°-3°C in this century, causing considerable problems, almost exclusively in the developing world, at a total cost of $5,000 billion. Getting rid of global warming would thus seem to be a good idea. The question is whether the cure will actually be more costly than the ailment.

Despite the intuition that something drastic needs to be done about such a costly problem, economic analyses clearly show that it will be far more expensive to cut carbon-dioxide emissions radically than to pay the costs of adaptation to the increased temperatures. The effect of the Kyoto Protocol on the climate would be minuscule, even if it were implemented in full. A model by Tom Wigley, one of the main authors of the reports of the UN Climate Change Panel, shows how an expected temperature increase of 2.1°C in 2100 would be diminished by the treaty to an increase of 1.9°C instead. Or, to put it another way, the temperature increase that the planet would have experienced in 2094 would be postponed to 2100.

So the Kyoto agreement does not prevent global warming, but merely buys the world six years. Yet, the cost of Kyoto, for the United States

The Price of a Life: Cost of Saving One Year of One Person's Life, 1993	$
Passing laws to make seatbelt use mandatory	69
Sickle-cell anaemia screening for black newborns	240
Mammography for women aged 50	810
Pneumonia vaccination for people aged over 65	2,000
Giving advice on stopping smoking to people who smoke more than one packet a day	9,800
Putting men aged 30 on a low-cholesterol diet	19,000
Regular leisure-time physical activity, such as jogging for men aged 35	38,000
Making pedestrians and cyclists more visible	73,000
Installing air-bags (rather than manual lap belts) in cars	120,000
Installing arsenic emission-control at glass-manufacturing plants	51,000,000
Setting radiation emission standards for nuclear-power plants	180,000,000
Installing benzene emission control at rubber-tire manufacturing plants	20,000,000,000

Table 1

Source: T. Tengs et al, Risk Analysis, June 1995

alone, will be higher than the cost of solving the world's single most pressing health problem: providing universal access to clean drinking water and sanitation. Such measures would avoid 2 [million] deaths every year, and prevent half a billion people from becoming seriously ill.

And that is the best case. If the treaty were implemented inefficiently, the cost of Kyoto could approach $1 trillion, or more than five times the cost of worldwide water and sanitation coverage. For comparison, the total global-aid budget today is about $50 billion a year.

To replace the litany with facts is crucial if people want to make the best possible decisions for the future. Of course, rational environmental management and environmental investment are good ideas—but the costs and benefits of such investments should be compared to those of similar investments in all the other important areas of human endeavour. It may be costly to be overly optimistic—but more costly still to be too pessimistic.

Is Humanity Suicidal?

Edward O. Wilson

Imagine that on an icy moon of Jupiter—say, Ganymede—the space station of an alien civilization is concealed. For millions of years its scientists have closely watched the earth. Because their law prevents settlement on a living planet, they have tracked the surface by means of satellites equipped with sophisticated sensors, mapping the spread of large assemblages of organisms, from forests, grasslands and tundras to coral reefs and the vast planktonic meadows of the sea. They have recorded millennial cycles in the climate, interrupted by the advance and retreat of glaciers and scattershot volcanic eruptions.

The watchers have been waiting for what might be called the Moment. When it comes, occupying only a few centuries and thus a mere tick in geological time, the forests shrink back to less than half their original cover. Atmospheric carbon dioxide rises to the highest level in 100,000 years. The ozone layer of the stratosphere thins, and holes open at the poles. Plumes of nitrous oxide and other toxins rise from fires in South America and Africa, settle in the upper troposphere and drift eastward across the oceans. At night the land surface brightens with millions of pinpoints of light, which coalesce into blazing swaths across Europe, Japan and eastern North America. A semicircle of fire spreads from gas flares around the Persian Gulf.

It was all but inevitable, the watchers might tell us if we met them, that from the great diversity of large animals, one species or another would eventually gain intelligent control of Earth. That role has fallen to Homo sapiens, a primate risen in Africa from a lineage that split away from the chimpanzee line five to eight million years ago. Unlike any creature that lived before, we have become a geophysical force, swiftly changing the atmosphere and climate as well as the composition of the world's fauna and flora. Now in the midst of a population explosion, the human species has doubled to 5.5 billion during the past 50 years. It is scheduled to double again in the next 50 years. No other single species in evolutionary history has even remotely approached the sheer mass in protoplasm generated by humanity.

Darwin's dice have rolled badly for Earth. It was misfortune for the living world in particular, many scientists believe, that a carnivorous primate and not some more benign form of animal made the breakthrough. Our species retains hereditary traits that add greatly to our destructive impact. We are tribal and aggressively territorial, intent on private space beyond minimal requirements and oriented by selfish sexual and reproductive drives. Cooperation beyond the family and tribal levels comes hard.

Worse, our liking for meat causes us to use the sun's energy at low efficiency. It is a general rule of ecology that (very roughly) only about 10 percent of the sun's energy captured by photosynthesis to produce plant tissue is converted into energy in the tissue of herbivores, the animals that eat the plants. Of that amount, 10 percent reaches the tissue of the carnivores feeding on the herbivores. Similarly, only 10 percent is transferred to carnivores that eat carnivores. And so on for another step or two. In a wetlands chain that runs from marsh grass to grasshopper to warbler to hawk, the energy captured during green production shrinks a thousandfold.

In other words, it takes a great deal of grass to support a hawk. Human beings, like hawks, are top carnivores, at the end of the food chain whenever they eat meat, two or more links removed from the plants; if chicken, for example, two links, and if tuna, four links. Even with most societies confined today to a mostly vegetarian diet, humanity is gobbling up a large part of the rest of the living world. We appropriate between 20 and 40 percent of the sun's energy that would otherwise be fixed into the tissue of natural vegetation, principally by our consumption of crops and timber, construction of buildings and roadways and the creation of wastelands. In the relentless search for more food, we have reduced animal life in lakes, rivers and now, increasingly, the open ocean. And everywhere we pollute the air and water, lower water tables and extinguish species.

The human species is, in a word, an environmental abnormality. It is possible that intelligence in the wrong kind of species was foreordained to be a fatal combination for the biosphere. Perhaps a law of evolution is that intelligence usually extinguishes itself.

This admittedly dour scenario is based on what can be termed the juggernaut theory of human nature, which holds that people are programmed by their genetic heritage to be so selfish that a sense of global responsibility will come too late. Individuals place themselves first, family second, tribe third and the rest of the world a distant fourth. Their genes also predispose them to plan ahead for one or two generations at most. They fret over the petty problems and conflicts of their daily lives and respond swiftly and often ferociously to slight challenges to their status and tribal security. But oddly, as psychologists have discovered, people also tend to underestimate both the likelihood and impact of such natural disasters as major earthquakes and great storms.

The reason for this myopic fog, evolutionary biologists contend, is that it was actually advantageous during all but the last few millennia of the two million years of existence of the genus Homo. The brain evolved into its present form during this long stretch of evolutionary time, during which people existed in small, preliterate hunter-gatherer bands. Life was precarious and short. A premium was placed on close attention to the near future and early reproduction, and little else. Disasters of a magnitude that occur only once every few centuries were forgotten or transmuted into myth. So today the mind still works comfortably backward and forward for only a few years, spanning a period not exceeding one or two generations. Those in past ages whose genes inclined them to short-term thinking lived longer and had more children than those who did not. Prophets never enjoyed a Darwinian edge.

The rules have recently changed, however. Global crises are rising in the life span of the generation now coming of age, a foreshortening that may explain why young people express more concern about the environment than do their elders. The time scale has contracted because of the exponential growth in both the human population and technologies impacting the environment. Exponential growth is basically the same as the increase of wealth by compound interest. The larger the population, the faster the growth; the faster the growth, the sooner the population becomes still larger. In Nigeria, to cite one of our more fecund nations, the population is expected to double from its 1988 level to 216 million by the year 2010. If the same rate of growth were to continue to 2110, its population would exceed that of the entire present population of the world.

With people everywhere seeking a better quality of life, the search for resources is expanding even faster than the population. The demand is being met by an increase in scientific knowledge, which doubles every 10 to 15 years. It is accelerated further by a parallel rise in environment-devouring technology. Because Earth is finite in many resources that determine the quality of life—including arable soil, nutrients, fresh water and space for natural ecosystems—doubling of consumption at constant time intervals can bring disaster with shocking suddenness. Even when a nonrenewable resource has been only half used, it is still only one interval away from the end. Ecologists like to make this point with the French riddle of the lily pond. At first there is only one lily pad in the pond, but the next day it doubles, and thereafter each of its descendants doubles. The pond completely fills with lily pads in 30 days. When is the pond exactly half full? Answer: on the 29th day.

Yet, mathematical exercises aside, who can safely measure the human capacity to overcome the perceived limits of Earth? The question of central interest is this: Are we racing to the brink of an abyss, or are we just gathering speed for a takeoff to a wonderful future? The crystal ball is clouded; the human condition baffles all the more because it is both unprecedented and bizarre, almost beyond understanding.

In the midst of uncertainty, opinions on the human prospect have tended to fall loosely into two schools. The first, exemptionalism, holds that since humankind is transcendent in intelligence and spirit, so must our species have been released from the iron laws of ecology that bind all other species. No matter how serious the problem, civilized human beings, by ingenuity, force of will and—who knows—divine dispensation, will find a solution.

Population growth? Good for the economy, claim some of the exemptionalists, and in any case a basic human right, so let it run. Land shortages? Try fusion energy to power the desalting of sea water, then reclaim the world's deserts. (The process might be assisted by towing icebergs to coastal pipelines.) Species going extinct? Not to worry. That is nature's way. Think of humankind as only the latest in a long line of exterminating agents in geological time. In any case, because our species has pulled free of old-style, mindless Nature, we have begun a different order of life. Evolution should now be allowed to proceed along this new trajectory. Finally, resources? The planet has more than enough resources to last indefinitely, if human genius is allowed to address each new problem in turn, without alarmist and unreasonable restrictions imposed on economic development. So hold the course, and touch the brakes lightly.

The opposing idea of reality is environmentalism, which sees humanity as a biological species tightly dependent on the natural world. As formidable as our intellect may be and as fierce our spirit, the argument goes, those qualities are not enough to free us from the constraints of the natural environment in which our human ancestors evolved. We cannot draw confidence from successful solutions to the smaller problems of the past. Many of Earth's vital resources are about to be exhausted, its atmospheric chemistry is deteriorating and human populations have already grown dangerously large. Natural ecosystems, the wellsprings of a healthful environment, are being irreversibly degraded.

At the heart of the environmentalist world view is the conviction that human physical and spiritual health depends on sustaining the planet in a relatively unaltered state. Earth is our home in the full, genetic sense, where humanity and its ancestors existed for all the millions of years of their evolution. Natural ecosystems—forests, coral reefs, marine blue waters—maintain the world exactly as we would wish it to be maintained. When we debase the global environment and extinguish the variety of life, we are dismantling a support system that is too complex to understand, let alone replace, in the foreseeable future. Space scientists theorize the existence of a virtually unlimited array of other planetary environments, almost all of which are uncongenial to human life. Our own Mother Earth, lately called Gaia, is a specialized conglomerate of organisms and the physical environment they create on a day-to-day basis, which can be destabilized and turned lethal by careless activity. We run the risk, conclude the environmentalists, of beaching ourselves upon alien shores like a great confused pod of pilot whales.

If I have not done so enough already by tone of voice, I will now place myself solidly in the environmentalist school, but not so radical as to wish a turning back of the clock, not given to driving spikes into Douglas firs to prevent logging and distinctly uneasy with such hybrid movements as ecofeminism, which holds that Mother Earth is a nurturing home for all life and should be revered and loved as in premodern (paleolithic and archaic) societies and that ecosystematic abuse is rooted in androcentric—that is to say, male-dominated—concepts, values and institutions.

Still, however soaked in androcentric culture, I am radical enough to take seriously the question heard with increasing frequency: Is humanity suicidal? Is the drive to environmental conquest and self-propagation embedded so deeply in our genes as to be unstoppable?

My short answer—opinion if you wish—is that humanity is not suicidal, at least not in the sense just stated. We are smart enough and have time enough to avoid an environmental catastrophe of civilization-threatening dimensions. But the technical problems are sufficiently formidable to require a redirection of much of science and technology, and the ethical issues are so basic as to force a reconsideration of our self-image as a species.

There are reasons for optimism, reasons to believe that we have entered what might someday be generously called the Century of the Environment. The United Nations Conference on Environment and Development, held in Rio de Janeiro in June 1992, attracted more than 120 heads of government, the largest number ever assembled, and helped move environmental issues closer to the political center stage; on Nov. 18, 1992, more than 1,500 senior scientists from 69 countries issued a "Warning to Humanity," stating that overpopulation and environmental deterioration put the very future of life at risk. The greening of religion has become a global trend, with theologians and religious leaders addressing environmental problems as a moral issue. In May 1992, leaders of most of the major American denominations met with scientists as guests of members of the United States Senate to formulate a "Joint Appeal by Religion and Science for the Environment." Conservation of biodiversity is increasingly seen by both national governments and major landowners as important to their country's future. Indonesia, home to a large part of the native Asian plant and animal species, has begun to shift to land-management practices that conserve and sustainably develop the remaining rain forests. Costa Rica has created a National Institute of Biodiversity. A pan-African institute for biodiversity research and management has been founded, with headquarters in Zimbabwe.

Finally, there are favorable demographic signs. The rate of population increase is declining on all continents, although it is still well above zero almost everywhere and remains especially high in sub-Saharan Africa. Despite entrenched traditions and religious beliefs, the desire to use contraceptives in family planning is spreading. Demographers estimate that if the demand were fully met, this action alone would reduce the eventual stabilized population by more than two billion.

In summary, the will is there. Yet the awful truth remains that a large part of humanity will suffer no matter what is done. The number of people living in absolute poverty has risen during the past 20 years to nearly one billion and is expected to increase another 100 million by the end of the decade. Whatever progress has been made in the developing countries, and that includes an overall improvement in the average standard of living, is threatened by a continuance of rapid population growth and the deterioration of forests and arable soil.

Our hopes must be chastened further still, and this is in my opinion the central issue, by a key and seldom-recognized distinction between the nonliving and living environments. Science and the political process can be adapted to manage the nonliving, physical environment. The human hand is now upon the physical homeostat. The ozone layer can be mostly restored to the upper atmosphere by elimination of CFC's, with these substances peaking at six times the present level and then subsiding during the next half century. Also, with procedures that will prove far more difficult and initially expensive, carbon dioxide and other greenhouse gases can be pulled back to concentrations that slow global warming.

The human hand, however, is not upon the biological homeostat. There is no way in sight to micromanage the natural ecosystems and the millions of species they contain. That feat might be accomplished by generations to come, but then it will be too late for the ecosystems—and perhaps for us. Despite the seemingly bottomless nature of creation, humankind has been chipping away at its diversity, and Earth is destined to become an impoverished planet within a century if present trends continue. Mass extinctions are being reported with increasing frequency in every part of the world. They include half the freshwater fishes of peninsular Malaysia, 10 birds native to Cebu in the Philippines, half the 41 tree snails of Oahu, 44 of the 68 shallow-water mussels of the Tennessee River shoals, as many as 90 plant species growing on the Centinela Ridge in Ecuador, and in the United States as a whole, about 200 plant species, with another 680 species and races now classified as in danger of extinction. The main cause is the destruction of natural habitats, especially tropical forests. Close behind, especially on the Hawaiian archipelago and other islands, is the introduction of rats, pigs, beard grass, lantana and other exotic organisms that outbreed and extirpate native species.

The few thousand biologists worldwide who specialize in diversity are aware that they can witness and report no more than a very small percentage of the extinctions actually occurring. The reason is that they have facilities to keep track of only a tiny fraction of the millions of species and a sliver of the planet's surface on a yearly basis. They have devised a rule of thumb to characterize the situation: that whenever careful studies are made of habitats before and after disturbance, extinctions almost always come to light. The corollary: the great majority of extinctions are never observed. Vast numbers of species are apparently vanishing before they can be discovered and named.

There is a way, nonetheless, to estimate the rate of loss indirectly. Independent studies around the world and in fresh and marine waters have revealed a robust connection between the size of a habitat and the amount of biodiversity it contains. Even a small loss in area reduces the number of species. The relation is such that when the area of the habitat is cut to a tenth of its original cover, the number of species eventually drops by roughly one-half. Tropical rain forests, thought to harbor a majority of Earth's species (the reason conservationists get so exercised about rain forests), are being reduced by nearly that magnitude. At the present time they occupy about the same area as that of the 48 coterminous United States, representing a little less than half their original, prehistoric cover, and they are shrinking each year by about 2 percent, an amount equal to the state of Florida. If the typical value (that is, 90 percent area loss causes 50 percent eventual extinction) is applied, the projected loss of species due to rain forest destruction worldwide is half a percent across the board for all kinds of plants, animals and microorganisms.

When area reduction and all the other extinction agents are considered together, it is reasonable to project a reduction by 20 percent or more of the rain forest species by the year 2020, climbing to 50 percent or more by midcentury, if nothing is done to change current practice. Comparable erosion is likely in other environments now under assault, including many coral reefs and Mediterranean-type heathlands of Western Australia, South Africa and California.

The ongoing loss will not be replaced by evolution in any period of time that has meaning for humanity. Extinction is now proceeding thousands of times faster than the production of new species. The average life span of a species and its descendants in past geological eras varied according to group (like mollusks or echinoderms or flowering plants) from about 1 to 10 million years. During the past 500 million years, there have been five great extinction spasms comparable to the one now being inaugurated by human expansion. The latest, evidently caused by the strike of an asteroid, ended the Age of Reptiles 66 million years ago. In each case it took more than 10 million years for evolution to completely replenish the biodiversity lost. And that was in an otherwise undisturbed natural environment. Humanity is now destroying most of the habitats where evolution can occur.

The surviving biosphere remains the great unknown of Earth in many respects. On the practical side, it is hard even to imagine what other species have to offer in the way of new pharmaceuticals, crops, fibers, petroleum substitutes and other products. We have only a poor grasp of the ecosystem services by which other organisms cleanse the water, turn soil into a fertile living cover and manufacture the very air we breathe. We sense but do not fully understand what the highly diverse natural world means to our esthetic pleasure and mental well-being.

Scientists are unprepared to manage a declining biosphere. To illustrate, consider the following mission they might be given. The last remnant of a rain forest is about to be cut over. Environmentalists are stymied. The contracts have been signed, and local landowners and politicians are intransigent. In a final desperate move, a team of biologists is scrambled in an attempt to preserve the biodiversity by extraordinary means. Their assignment is the following: collect samples of all the species of organisms quickly, before the cutting starts; maintain the species in zoos, gardens and laboratory cultures or else deep-freeze samples of the tissues in liquid nitrogen, and, finally, establish the procedure by which the entire community can be reassembled on empty ground at a later date, when social and economic conditions have improved.

The biologists cannot accomplish this task, not if thousands of them came with a billion-dollar budget. They cannot even imagine how to do it. In the forest patch live legions of species: perhaps 300 birds, 500 butterflies, 200 ants, 50,000 beetles, 1,000 trees, 5,000 fungi, tens of thousands of bacteria and so on down a long roster of major groups. Each species occupies a precise niche, demanding a certain place, an exact microclimate, particular nutrients and temperature and humidity cycles with specified timing to trigger phases of the life cycle. Many, perhaps most, of the species are locked in symbioses with other species; they cannot survive and reproduce unless arrayed with their partners in the correct idiosyncratic configurations.

Even if the biologists pulled off the taxonomic equivalent of the **Manhattan Project**, sorting and preserving cultures of all the species, they could not then put the community back together again. It would be like unscrambling an egg with a pair of spoons. The biology of the microorganisms needed to reanimate the soil would be mostly unknown. The pollinators of most of the flowers and the correct timing of their appearance could only be guessed. The "assembly rules," the sequence in which species must be allowed to colonize in order to coexist indefinitely, would remain in the realm of theory.

In its neglect of the rest of life, exemptionalism fails definitively. To move ahead as though scientific and entrepreneurial genius will solve each crisis that arises implies that the declining biosphere can be similarly manipulated. But the world is too complicated to be turned into a garden. There is no biological homeostat that can be worked by humanity; to believe otherwise is to risk reducing a large part of Earth to a wasteland.

The environmentalist vision, prudential and less exuberant than exemptionalism, is closer to reality. It sees humanity entering a bottleneck unique in history, constricted by population and economic pressures. In order to pass through to the other side, within perhaps 50 to 100 years, more science and entrepreneurship will have to be devoted to stabilizing the global environment. That can be accomplished, according to expert consensus, only by halting population growth and devising a wiser use of resources than has been accomplished to date. And wise use for the living world in particular means preserving the surviving ecosystems, micromanaging them only enough to save the biodiversity they contain, until such time as they can be understood and employed in the fullest sense for human benefit.

Manhattan Project
name for the American effort to develop the atomic bomb during WWII

When Doctors Make Mistakes

Atul Gawande

I—Crash Victim

At 2 A.M. on a crisp Friday in winter, I was in sterile gloves and gown, pulling a teenage knifing victim's abdomen open, when my pager sounded. "Code trauma, three minutes," the operating-room nurse said, reading aloud from my pager display. This meant that an ambulance would be bringing another trauma patient to the hospital momentarily, and, as the surgical resident on duty for emergencies, I would have to be present for the patient's arrival. I stepped back from the table and took off my gown. Two other surgeons were working on the knifing victim: Michael Ball, the attending (the staff surgeon in charge of the case), and David Hernandez, the chief resident (a general surgeon in his last of five years of training). Ordinarily, these two would have come later to help with the trauma, but they were stuck here. Ball, a dry, imperturbable forty-two-year-old Texan, looked over to me as I headed for the door. "If you run into any trouble, you call, and one of us will peel away," he said.

I did run into trouble. In telling this story, I have had to change significant details about what happened (including the names of the participants and aspects of my role), but I have tried to stay as close to the actual events as I could while protecting the patient, myself, and the rest of the staff. The way that things go wrong in medicine is normally unseen and, consequently, often misunderstood. Mistakes do happen. We think of them as aberrant; they are anything but.

The emergency room was one floor up, and, taking the stairs two at a time, I arrived just as the emergency medical technicians wheeled in a woman who appeared to be in her thirties and to weigh more than two hundred pounds. She lay motionless on a hard orange plastic spinal board—eyes closed, skin pale, blood running out of her nose. A nurse directed the crew into Trauma Bay 1, an examination room outfitted like an O.R., with green tiles on the wall, monitoring devices, and space for portable X-ray equipment. We lifted her onto the bed and then went to work. One nurse began cutting off the woman's clothes. Another took vital signs. A third inserted a large-bore intravenous line

"When Doctors Make Mistakes" from the *New Yorker*, February 1, 1999, by Atul Gawande.

into her right arm. A surgical intern put a Foley catheter into her blad-der. The emergency-medicine attending was Samuel Johns, a gaunt, Ichabod Crane-like man in his fifties. He was standing to one side with his arms crossed, observing, which was a sign that I could go ahead and take charge.

If you're in a hospital, most of the "moment to moment" doctoring you get is from residents—physicians receiving specialty training and a small income in exchange for their labor. Our responsibilities depend on our level of training, but we're never entirely on our own: there's always an attending, who oversees our decisions. That night, since Johns was the attending and was responsible for the patient's immediate management, I took my lead from him. But he wasn't a surgeon, and so he relied on me for surgical expertise.

"What's the story?" I asked.

An E.M.T. rattled off the details: "Unidentified white female unre-strained driver in high-speed rollover. Ejected from the car. Found unresponsive to pain. Pulse a hundred, B.P. a hundred over sixty, breath-ing at thirty on her own . . ."

As he spoke, I began examining her. The first step in caring for a trauma patient is always the same. It doesn't matter if a person has been shot eleven times or crushed by a truck or burned in a kitchen fire. The first thing you do is make sure that the patient can breathe without difficulty. This woman's breaths were shallow and rapid. An oximeter, by means of a sensor placed on her finger, measured the oxygen satu-ration of her blood. The "O_2 sat" is normally more than ninety-five per cent for a patient breathing room air. The woman was wearing a face mask with oxygen turned up full blast, and her sat was only ninety per cent.

"She's not oxygenating well," I announced in the flattened-out, wake-me-up-when-something-interesting-happens tone that all surgeons have acquired by about three months into residency. With my fingers, I verified that there wasn't any object in her mouth that would obstruct her airway; with a stethoscope, I confirmed that neither lung had collapsed. I got hold of a bag mask, pressed its clear facepiece over her nose and mouth, and squeezed the bellows, a kind of balloon with a one-way valve, shooting a litre of air into her with each compression. After a minute or so, her oxygen came up to a comfortable ninety-eight per cent. She obviously needed our help with breathing. "Let's tube her," I said. That meant putting a tube down through her vocal cords and into her trachea, which would insure a clear airway and allow for mechanical ventilation.

Johns, the attending, wanted to do the intubation. He picked up a Mac 3 laryngoscope, a standard but fairly primitive-looking L-shaped metal instrument for prying open the mouth and throat, and slipped the shoehornlike blade deep into her mouth and down to her larynx. Then he yanked the handle up toward the ceiling to pull her tongue out of the way, open her mouth and throat, and reveal the vocal cords, which sit like fleshy tent flaps at the entrance to the trachea. The patient didn't wince or gag: she was still out cold.

"Suction!" he called. "I can't see a thing."

He sucked out about a cup of blood and clot. Then he picked up the endotracheal tube—a clear rubber pipe about the diameter of an index finger and three times as long—and tried to guide it between her cords. After a minute, her sat started to fall.

"You're down to seventy per cent," a nurse announced.

Johns kept struggling with the tube, trying to push it in, but it banged vainly against the cords. The patient's lips began to turn blue.

"Sixty per cent," the nurse said.

Johns pulled everything out of the patient's mouth and fitted the bag mask back on. The oximeter's luminescent-green readout hovered at sixty for a moment and then rose steadily, to ninety-seven per cent. After a few minutes, he took the mask off and again tried to get the tube in. There was more blood, and there may have been some swelling, too: all the poking down the throat was probably not helping. The sat fell to sixty per cent. He pulled out and bagged her until she returned to ninety-five per cent.

When you're having trouble getting the tube in, the next step is to get specialized expertise. "Let's call anesthesia," I said, and Johns agreed. In the meantime, I continued to follow the standard trauma protocol: completing the examination and ordering fluids, lab tests, and X-rays. Maybe five minutes passed as I worked.

The patient's sats drifted down to ninety-two per cent—not a dramatic change but definitely not normal for a patient who is being manually ventilated. I checked to see if the sensor had slipped off her finger. It hadn't. "Is the oxygen up full blast?" I asked a nurse.

"It's up all the way," she said.

I listened again to the patient's lungs—no collapse. "We've got to get her tubed," Johns said. He took off the oxygen mask and tried again.

Somewhere in my mind, I must have been aware of the possibility that her airway was shutting down because of vocal-cord swelling or blood. If it was, and we were unable to get a tube in, then the only chance she'd have to survive would be an emergency tracheostomy:

cutting a hole in her neck and inserting a breathing tube into her trachea. Another attempt to intubate her might even trigger a spasm of the cords and a sudden closure of the airway—which is exactly what did happen.

If I had actually thought this far along, I would have recognized how ill-prepared I was to do an emergency "trache." Of the people in the room, it's true, I had the most experience doing tracheostomies, but that wasn't saying much. I had been the assistant surgeon in only about half a dozen, and all but one of them had been non-emergency cases, employing techniques that were not designed for speed. The exception was a practice emergency trache I had done on a goat. I should have immediately called Dr. Ball for backup. I should have got the trache equipment out—lighting, suction, sterile instruments—just in case. Instead of hurrying the effort to get the patient intubated because of a mild drop in saturation, I should have asked Johns to wait until I had help nearby. I might even have recognized that she was already losing her airway. Then I could have grabbed a knife and started cutting her a tracheostomy while things were still relatively stable and I had time to proceed slowly. But for whatever reasons—**hubris**, inattention, wishful thinking, hesitation, or the uncertainty of the moment—I let the opportunity pass.

Johns hunched over the patient, intently trying to insert the tube through her vocal cords. When her sat once again dropped into the sixties, he stopped and put the mask back on. We stared at the monitor. The numbers weren't coming up. Her lips were still blue. Johns squeezed the bellows harder to blow more oxygen in.

"I'm getting resistance," he said.

The realization crept over me: this was a disaster. "Damn it, we've lost her airway," I said. "Trache kit! Light! Somebody call down to O.R. 25 and get Ball up here!"

People were suddenly scurrying everywhere. I tried to proceed deliberately, and not let panic take hold. I told the surgical intern to get a sterile gown and gloves on. I took a bactericidal solution off a shelf and dumped a whole bottle of yellow-brown liquid on the patient's neck. A nurse unwrapped the tracheostomy kit—a sterilized set of drapes and instruments. I pulled on a gown and a new pair of gloves while trying to think through the steps. This is simple, really, I tried to tell myself. At the base of the thyroid cartilage, the Adam's apple, is a little gap in which you find a thin, fibrous covering called the cricothyroid membrane. Cut through that and—voilà! You're in the trachea. You slip through the hole a four-inch plastic tube shaped like a plumber's elbow

hubris
pride

joint, hook it up to oxygen and a ventilator, and she's all set. Anyway, that was the theory.

I threw some drapes over her body, leaving the neck exposed. It looked as thick as a tree. I felt for the bony prominence of the thyroid cartilage. But I couldn't feel anything through the rolls of fat. I was beset by uncertainty—where should I cut? should I make a horizontal or a vertical incision?—and I hated myself for it. Surgeons never dithered, and I was dithering.

"I need better light," I said.

Someone was sent out to look for one.

"Did anyone get Ball?" I asked. It wasn't exactly an inspiring question.

"He's on his way," a nurse said.

There wasn't time to wait. Four minutes without oxygen would lead to permanent brain damage, if not death. Finally, I took the scalpel and cut. I just cut. I made a three-inch left-to-right swipe across the middle of the neck, following the procedure I'd learned for elective cases. I figured that if I worked through the fat I might be able to find the membrane in the wound. Dissecting down with scissors while the intern held the wound open with retractors, I hit a vein. It didn't let loose a lot of blood, but there was enough to fill the wound: I couldn't see anything. The intern put a finger on the bleeder. I called for suction. But the suction wasn't working; the tube was clogged with the clot from the intubation efforts.

"Somebody get some new tubing," I said. "And where's the light?"

Finally, an orderly wheeled in a tall overhead light, plugged it in, and flipped on the switch. It was still too dim; I could have done better with a flashlight.

I wiped up the blood with gauze, then felt around in the wound with my fingertips. This time, I thought I could feel the hard ridges of the thyroid cartilage and, below it, the slight gap of the cricothyroid membrane, though I couldn't be sure. I held my place with my left hand.

James O'Connor, a silver-haired, seen-it-all anesthesiologist, came into the room. Johns gave him a quick rundown on the patient and let him take over bagging her.

Holding the scalpel in my right hand like a pen, I stuck the blade down into the wound at the spot where I thought the thyroid cartilage was. With small, sharp strokes—working blindly, because of the blood and the poor light—I cut down through the overlying fat and tissue until I felt the blade scrape against the almost bony cartilage. I searched with the tip of the knife, walking it along until I felt it reach a gap. I hoped it was the cricothyroid membrane, and pressed down firmly. Then I felt the tissue suddenly give, and I cut an inch-long opening.

When I put my index finger into it, it felt as if I were prying open the jaws of a stiff clothespin. Inside, I thought I felt open space. But where were the sounds of moving air that I expected? Was this deep enough? Was I even in the right place?

"I think I'm in," I said, to reassure myself as much as anyone else.

"I hope so," O'Connor said. "She doesn't have much longer."

I took the tracheostomy tube and tried to fit it in, but something seemed to be blocking it. I twisted it and turned it, and finally jammed it in. Just then, Ball, the surgical attending, arrived. He rushed up to the bed and leaned over for a look. "Did you get it?" he asked. I said that I thought so. The bag mask was plugged onto the open end of the trache tube. But when the bellows were compressed the air just gurgled out of the wound. Ball quickly put on gloves and a gown.

"How long has she been without an airway?" he asked.

"I don't know. Three minutes."

Ball's face hardened as he registered that he had about a minute in which to turn things around. He took my place and summarily pulled out the trache tube. "God, what a mess," he said. "I can't see a thing in this wound. I don't even know if you're in the right place. Can we get better light and suction?" New suction tubing was found and handed to him. He quickly cleaned up the wound and went to work.

The patient's sat had dropped so low that the oximeter couldn't detect it anymore. Her heart rate began slowing down—first to the sixties and then to the forties. Then she lost her pulse entirely. I put my hands together on her chest, locked my elbows, leaned over her, and started doing chest compressions.

Ball looked up from the patient and turned to O'Connor. "I'm not going to get her an airway in time," he said. "You're going to have to try from above." Essentially, he was admitting my failure. Trying an oral intubation again was pointless—just something to do instead of watching her die. I was stricken, and concentrated on doing chest compressions, not looking at anyone. It was over, I thought.

And then, amazingly, O'Connor: "I'm in." He had managed to slip a pediatric-size endotracheal tube through the vocal cords. In thirty seconds, with oxygen being manually ventilated through the tube, her heart was back, racing at a hundred and twenty beats a minute. Her sat registered at sixty and then climbed. Another thirty seconds and it was at ninety-seven per cent. All the people in the room exhaled, as if they, too, had been denied their breath. Ball and I said little except to confer about the next steps for her. Then he went back downstairs to finish working on the stab-wound patient still in the O.R.

We eventually identified the woman, whom I'll call Louise Williams; she was thirty-four years old and lived alone in a nearby suburb. Her alcohol level on arrival had been three times the legal limit, and had probably contributed to her unconsciousness. She had a concussion, several lacerations, and significant soft-tissue damage. But X-rays and scans revealed no other injuries from the crash. That night, Ball and Hernandez brought her to the O.R. to fit her with a proper tracheostomy. When Ball came out and talked to family members, he told them of the dire condition she was in when she arrived, the difficulties "we" had had getting access to her airway, the disturbingly long period of time that she had gone without oxygen, and thus his uncertainty about how much brain function she still possessed. They listened without protest; there was nothing for them to do but wait.

11—The Banality of Error

To much of the public—and certainly to lawyers and the media—medical error is a problem of bad physicians. Consider some other surgical mishaps. In one, a general surgeon left a large metal instrument in a patient's abdomen, where it tore through the bowel and the wall of the bladder. In another, a cancer surgeon biopsied the wrong part of a woman's breast and thereby delayed her diagnosis of cancer for months. A cardiac surgeon skipped a small but key step during a heart-valve operation, thereby killing the patient. A surgeon saw a man racked with abdominal pain in the emergency room and, without taking a C.T. scan, assumed that the man had a kidney stone; eighteen hours later, a scan showed a rupturing abdominal aortic aneurysm, and the patient died not long afterward.

How could anyone who makes a mistake of that magnitude be allowed to practice medicine? We call such doctors "incompetent," "unethical," and "negligent." We want to see them punished. And so we've wound up with the public system we have for dealing with error: malpractice lawsuits, media scandal, suspensions, firings.

There is, however, a central truth in medicine that complicates this tidy vision of misdeeds and misdoers: *all* doctors make terrible mistakes. Consider the cases I've just described. I gathered them simply by asking respected surgeons I know—surgeons at top medical schools—to tell me about mistakes they had made just in the past year. Every one of them had a story to tell.

ubiquity
presence everywhere

In 1991, *The New England Journal of Medicine* published a series of landmark papers from a project known as the Harvard Medical Practice Study—a review of more than thirty thousand hospital admissions in New York State. The study found that nearly four per cent of hospital patients suffered complications from treatment which prolonged their hospital stay or resulted in disability or death, and that two-thirds of such complications were due to errors in care. One in four, or one per cent of admissions, involved actual negligence. It was estimated that, nationwide, a hundred and twenty thousand patients die each year at least partly as a result of errors in care. And subsequent investigations around the country have confirmed the **ubiquity** of error. In one small study of how clinicians perform when patients have a sudden cardiac arrest, twenty-seven of thirty clinicians made an error in using the defibrillator; they may have charged it incorrectly or lost valuable time trying to figure out how to work a particular model. According to a 1995 study, mistakes in administering drugs—giving the wrong drug or the wrong dose, say—occur, on the average, about once for every hospital admission, mostly without ill effects, but one per cent of the time with serious consequences.

If error were due to a subset of dangerous doctors, you might expect malpractice cases to be concentrated among a small group, but in fact they follow a uniform, bell-shaped distribution. Most surgeons are sued at least once in the course of their careers. Studies of specific types of error, too, have found that repeat offenders are not the problem. The fact is that virtually everyone who cares for hospital patients will make serious mistakes, and even commit acts of negligence, every year. For this reason, doctors are seldom outraged when the press reports yet another medical horror story. They usually have a different reaction: *That could be me.* The important question isn't how to keep bad physicians from harming patients; it's how to keep good physicians from harming patients.

Medical-malpractice suits are a remarkably ineffective remedy. Troyen Brennan, a Harvard professor of law and public health, points out that research has consistently failed to find evidence that litigation reduces medical-error rates. In part, this may be because the weapon is so imprecise. Brennan led several studies following up on the patients in the Harvard Medical Practice Study. He found that fewer than two per cent of the patients who had received substandard care ever filed suit. Conversely, only a small minority among the patients who did sue had in fact been the victims of negligent care. And a patient's likelihood of winning a suit depended primarily on how poor his or her outcome was, regardless of whether that outcome was caused by disease or unavoidable risks of care.

The deeper problem with medical-malpractice suits, however, is that by demonizing errors they prevent doctors from acknowledging and discussing them publicly. The tort system makes adversaries of patient and physician, and pushes each to offer a heavily slanted version of events. When things go wrong, it's almost impossible for a physician to talk to a patient honestly about mistakes. Hospital lawyers warn doctors that, although they must, of course, tell patients about complications that occur, they are never to intimate that they were at fault, lest the "confession" wind up in court as damning evidence in a black-and-white morality tale. At most, a doctor might say, "I'm sorry that things didn't go as well as we had hoped."

There is one place, however, where doctors can talk candidly about their mistakes, if not with patients, then at least with one another. It is called the Morbidity and Mortality Conference—or, more simply, M. & M.—and it takes place, usually once a week, at nearly every academic hospital in the country. This institution survives because laws protecting its proceedings from legal discovery have stayed on the books in most states, despite frequent challenges. Surgeons, in particular, take the M. & M. seriously. Here they can gather behind closed doors to review the mistakes, complications, and deaths that occurred on their watch, determine responsibility, and figure out what to do differently next time.

III—Show and Tell

At my hospital, we convene every Tuesday at five o'clock in a steep, plush amphitheatre lined with oil portraits of the great doctors whose achievements we're meant to live up to. All surgeons are expected to attend, from the interns to the chairman of surgery; we're also joined by medical students doing their surgery "rotation." An M. & M. can include almost a hundred people. We file in, pick up a photocopied list of cases to be discussed, and take our seats. The front row is occupied by the most senior surgeons: terse, serious men, now out of their scrubs and in dark suits, lined up like a panel of senators at a hearing. The chairman is a leonine presence in the seat closest to the plain wooden podium from which each case is presented. In the next few rows are the remaining surgical attendings; these tend to be younger, and several of them are women. The chief residents have put on long white coats and usually sit in the side rows. I join the mass of other residents, all of us in short white coats and green scrub pants, occupying the back rows.

For each case, the chief resident from the relevant service—cardiac, vascular, trauma, and so on—gathers the information, takes the podium, and tells the story. Here's a partial list of cases from a typical week (with a few changes to protect confidentiality): a sixty-eight-year-old man who bled to death after heart-valve surgery; a forty-seven-year-old woman who had to have a reoperation because of infection following an arterial bypass done in her left leg; a forty-four-year-old woman who had to have bile drained from her abdomen after gallbladder surgery; three patients who had to have reoperations for bleeding following surgery; a sixty-three-year-old man who had a cardiac arrest following heart-bypass surgery; a sixty-six-year-old woman whose sutures suddenly gave way in an abdominal wound and nearly allowed her intestines to spill out. Ms. Williams's case, my failed tracheostomy, was just one case on a list like this. David Hernandez, the chief trauma resident, had subsequently reviewed the records and spoken to me and others involved. When the time came, it was he who stood up front and described what had happened.

Hernandez is a tall, rollicking, good old boy who can tell a yarn, but M. & M. presentations are bloodless and compact. He said something like: "This was a thirty-four-year-old female unrestrained driver in a high-speed rollover. The patient apparently had stable vitals at the scene but was unresponsive, and brought in by ambulance unintubated. She was G.C.S. 7 on arrival." G.C.S. stands for the Glasgow Coma Scale, which rates the severity of head injuries, from three to fifteen. G.C.S. 7 is in the comatose range. "Attempts to intubate were made without success in the E.R. and may have contributed to airway closure. A cricothyroidotomy was attempted without success."

These presentations can be awkward. The chief residents, not the attendings, determine which cases to report. That keeps the attendings honest—no one can cover up mistakes—but it puts the chief residents, who are, after all, underlings, in a delicate position. The successful M. & M. presentation inevitably involves a certain elision of detail and a lot of passive verbs. No one screws up a cricothyroidotomy. Instead, "a cricothyroidotomy was attempted without success." The message, however, was not lost on anyone.

Hernandez continued, "The patient arrested and required cardiac compressions. Anesthesia was then able to place a pediatric E.T. tube and the patient recovered stable vitals. The tracheostomy was then completed in the O.R."

So Louise Williams had been deprived of oxygen long enough to go into cardiac arrest, and everyone knew that meant she could easily have suffered a disabling stroke or been left a vegetable. Hernandez concluded with the fortunate aftermath: "Her workup was negative for permanent cerebral damage or other major injuries. The tracheostomy was removed on Day 2. She was discharged to home in good condition on Day 3." To the family's great relief, and mine, she had woken up in the morning a bit woozy but hungry, alert, and mentally intact. In a few weeks, the episode would heal to a scar.

But not before someone was called to account. A front-row voice immediately thundered, "What do you mean, 'A cricothyroidotomy was attempted without success?'" I sank into my seat, my face hot.

"This was my case," Dr. Ball volunteered from the front row. It is how every attending begins, and that little phrase contains a world of surgical culture. For all the talk in business schools and in corporate America about the virtues of "flat organizations," surgeons maintain an old-fashioned sense of hierarchy. When things go wrong, the attending is expected to take full responsibility. It makes no difference whether it was the resident's hand that slipped and lacerated an aorta; it doesn't matter whether the attending was at home in bed when a nurse gave a wrong dose of medication. At the M. & M., the burden of responsibility falls on the attending.

Ball went on to describe the emergency attending's failure to intubate Williams and his own failure to be at her bedside when things got out of control. He described the bad lighting and her extremely thick neck, and was careful to make those sound not like excuses but merely like complicating factors. Some attendings shook their heads in sympathy. A couple of them asked questions to clarify certain details. Throughout, Ball's tone was objective, detached. He had the air of a CNN newscaster describing unrest in Kuala Lumpur.

As always, the chairman, responsible for the over-all quality of our surgery service, asked the final question. What, he wanted to know, would Ball have done differently? Well, Ball replied, it didn't take long to get the stab-wound patient under control in the O.R., so he probably should have sent Hernandez up to the E.R. at that point or let Hernandez close the abdomen while he himself came up. People nodded. Lesson learned. Next case.

At no point during the M. & M. did anyone question why I had not called for help sooner or why I had not had the skill and knowledge that Williams needed. This is not to say that my actions were seen as acceptable. Rather, in the hierarchy, addressing my errors was Ball's role. The day after the disaster, Ball had caught me in the hall and taken me aside. His voice was more wounded than angry as he went through my specific failures. First, he explained, in an emergency tracheostomy it might have been better to do a vertical neck incision; that would have kept me out of the blood vessels, which run up and down—something I should have known at least from my reading. I might have had a much easier time getting her an airway then, he said. Second, and worse to him than mere ignorance, he didn't understand why I hadn't called him when there were clear signs of airway trouble developing. I offered no excuses. I promised to be better prepared for such cases and to be quicker to ask for help.

Even after Ball had gone down the fluorescent-lit hallway, I felt a sense of shame like a burning ulcer. This was not guilt: guilt is what you feel when you have done something wrong. What I felt was shame: *I* was what was wrong. And yet I also knew that a surgeon can take such feelings too far. It is one thing to be aware of one's limitations. It is another to be plagued by self-doubt. One surgeon with a national reputation told me about an abdominal operation in which he had lost control of bleeding while he was removing what turned out to be a benign tumor and the patient had died. "It was a clean kill," he said. Afterward, he could barely bring himself to operate. When he did operate, he became tentative and indecisive. The case affected his performance for months.

Even worse than losing self-confidence, though, is reacting defensively. There are surgeons who will see faults everywhere except in themselves. They have no questions and no fears about their abilities. As a result, they learn nothing from their mistakes and know nothing of their limitations. As one surgeon told me, it is a rare but alarming thing to meet a surgeon without fear. "If you're not a little afraid when you operate," he said, "you're bound to do a patient a grave disservice."

The atmosphere at the M. & M. is meant to discourage both attitudes—self-doubt and denial—for the M. & M. is a cultural ritual that inculcates in surgeons a "correct" view of mistakes. "What would you do differently?" a chairman asks concerning cases of avoidable complications. "Nothing" is seldom an acceptable answer.

In its way, the M. & M. is an impressively sophisticated and human institution. Unlike the courts or the media, it recognizes that human error is generally not something that can be deterred by punishment. The M. & M. sees avoiding error as largely a matter of will—of staying sufficiently informed and alert to anticipate the myriad ways that things can go wrong and then trying to head off each potential problem before it happens. Why do things go wrong? Because, doctors say, making them go right is hard stuff. It isn't damnable that an error occurs, but there is some shame to it. In fact, the M. & M.'s **ethos** can seem paradoxical. On the one hand, it reinforces the very American idea that error is intolerable. On the other hand, the very existence of the M. & M., its place on the weekly schedule, amounts to an acknowledgment that mistakes are an inevitable part of medicine.

But why do they happen so often? Lucian Leape, medicine's leading expert on error, points out that many other industries—whether the task is manufacturing semiconductors or serving customers at the Ritz-Carlton—simply wouldn't countenance error rates like those in hospitals. The aviation industry has reduced the frequency of operational errors to one in a hundred thousand flights, and most of those errors have no harmful consequences. The buzzword at General Electric these days is "Six Sigma," meaning that its goal is to make product defects so rare that in statistical terms they are more than six standard deviations away from being a matter of chance—almost a one-in-a-million occurrence.

Of course, patients are far more complicated and idiosyncratic than airplanes, and medicine isn't a matter of delivering a fixed product or even a catalogue of products; it may well be more complex than just about any other field of human endeavor. Yet everything we've learned in the past two decades—from cognitive psychology, from "human factors" engineering, from studies of disasters like **Three Mile Island** and **Bhopal**—has yielded the same insights: not only do all human beings err but they err frequently and in predictable, patterned ways. And systems that do not adjust for these realities can end up exacerbating rather than eliminating error.

The British psychologist James Reason argues, in his book *Human Error*, that our propensity for certain types of error is the price we pay for the brain's remarkable ability to think and act intuitively—to sift quickly through the sensory information that constantly bombards us without wasting time trying to work through every situation anew. Thus systems that rely on human perfection present what Reason calls "latent errors"—errors waiting to happen. Medicine teems with examples. Take writing out a prescription, a rote procedure that relies on memory and attention, which we know are unreliable. Inevitably, a physician will sometimes specify the wrong dose or the wrong drug. Even when the prescription is written correctly, there's a risk that it will be misread. (Computerized ordering systems can almost eliminate errors of this kind, but only a small minority of hospitals have adopted them.) Medical equipment, which manufacturers often build without human operators in mind, is another area rife with latent errors: one reason physicians are bound to have problems when they use cardiac defibrillators is that the devices have no standard design. You can also make the case that onerous workloads, chaotic environments, and inadequate team communication all represent latent errors in the system.

James Reason makes another important observation: disasters do not simply occur, they evolve. In complex systems, a single failure rarely leads to harm. Human beings are impressively good at adjusting when an error becomes apparent, and systems often have built-in defenses. For example, pharmacists and nurses routinely check and counter-check physicians' orders. But errors do not always become apparent, and backup systems themselves often fail as a result of latent errors. A pharmacist forgets to check one of a thousand prescriptions. A machine's alarm bell malfunctions. The one attending trauma surgeon available gets stuck in the operating room. When things go wrong, it is usually because a series of failures conspire to produce disaster.

The M. & M. takes none of this into account. For that reason, many experts see it as a rather shabby approach to analyzing error and improving performance in medicine. It isn't enough to ask what a clinician could or should have done differently so that he and others may learn for next time. The doctor is often only the final actor in a chain of events that set him or her up to fail. Error experts, therefore, believe that it's the process, not the individuals in it, which requires closer examination and correction. In a sense, they want to industrialize medicine. And they can already claim one success story: the specialty of anesthesiology, which has adopted their precepts and seen extraordinary results.

IV—Nearly Perfect

At the center of the emblem of the American Society of Anesthesiologists is a single word: "Vigilance." When you put a patient to sleep under general anesthesia, you assume almost complete control of the patient's body. The body is paralyzed, the brain rendered unconscious, and machines are hooked up to control breathing, heart rate, blood pressure—all the vital functions. Given the complexity of the machinery and of the human body, there are a seemingly infinite number of ways in which things can go wrong, even in minor surgery. And yet anesthesiologists have found that if problems are detected they can usually be solved. In the nineteen-forties, there was only one death resulting from anesthesia in every twenty-five hundred operations, and between the nineteen-sixties and the nineteen-eighties the rate had stabilized at one or two in every ten thousand operations.

But Ellison (Jeep) Pierce had always regarded even that rate as unconscionable. From the time he began practicing, in 1960, as a young anesthesiologist out of North Carolina and the University of Pennsylvania, he had maintained a case file of details from all the deadly anesthetic accidents he had come across or participated in. But it was one case in particular that galvanized him. Friends of his had taken their eighteen-year-old daughter to the hospital to have her wisdom teeth pulled, under general anesthesia. The anesthesiologist inserted the breathing tube into her esophagus instead of her trachea, which is a relatively common mishap, and then failed to spot the error, which is not. Deprived of oxygen, she died within minutes. Pierce knew that a one-in-ten-thousand death rate, given that anesthesia was administered in the United States an estimated thirty-five million times each year, meant thirty-five hundred avoidable deaths like that one.

In 1982, Pierce was elected vice-president of the American Society of Anesthesiologists and got an opportunity to do something about the death rate. The same year, ABC's "20/20" aired an exposé that caused a considerable stir in his profession. The segment began, "If you are going to go into anesthesia, you are going on a long trip, and you should not do it if you can avoid it in any way. General anesthesia [is] safe most of the time, but there are dangers from human error, carelessness, and a critical shortage of anesthesiologists. This year, six thousand patients will die or suffer brain damage." The program presented several terrifying cases from around the country. Between the small crisis that the show created and the sharp increases in physicians' malpractice-insurance premiums at that time, Pierce was able to mobilize the Society of Anesthesiologists around the problem of error.

He turned for ideas not to a physician but to an engineer named Jeffrey Cooper, the lead author of a groundbreaking 1978 paper entitled "Preventable Anesthesia Mishaps: A Study of Human Factors." An unassuming, fastidious man, Cooper had been hired in 1972, when he was twenty-six years old, by the Massachusetts General Hospital bioengineering unit, to work on developing machines for anesthesiology researchers. He gravitated toward the operating room, however, and spent hours there observing the anesthesiologists, and one of the first things he noticed was how poorly the anesthesia machines were designed. For example, a clockwise turn of a dial decreased the concentration of potent anesthetics in about half the machines but increased the concentration in the other half. He decided to borrow a technique called "critical incident analysis"—which had been used since the nineteen-fifties to analyze mishaps in aviation—in an effort to learn how equipment might be contributing to errors in anesthesia. The technique is built around carefully conducted interviews, designed to capture as much detail as possible about dangerous incidents: how specific accidents evolved and what factors contributed to them. This information is then used to look for patterns among different cases.

Getting open, honest reporting is crucial. The Federal Aviation Administration has a formalized system for analyzing and reporting dangerous aviation incidents, and its enormous success in improving airline safety rests on two cornerstones. Pilots who report an incident within ten days have automatic immunity from punishment, and the reports go to a neutral, outside agency, NASA, which has no interest in using the information against individual pilots. For Jeffrey Cooper, it was probably an advantage that he was an engineer, and not a physician, so that anesthesiologists regarded him as a discreet, unthreatening interviewer.

The result was the first in-depth, scientific look at errors in medicine. His detailed analysis of three hundred and fifty-nine errors provided a view of the profession unlike anything that had been seen before. Contrary to the prevailing assumption that the start of anesthesia ("takeoff") was the most dangerous part, anesthesiologists learned that incidents tended to occur in the middle of anesthesia, when vigilance waned. The most common kind of incident involved errors in maintaining the patient's breathing, and these were usually the result of an undetected disconnection or misconnection of the breathing tubing, mistakes in managing the airway, or mistakes in using the anesthesia machine. Just as important, Cooper enumerated a list of contributory factors, including inadequate experience, inadequate familiarity with equipment, poor communication among team members, haste, inattention, and fatigue.

The study provoked widespread debate among anesthesiologists, but there was no concerted effort to solve the problems until Jeep Pierce came along. Through the anesthesiology society at first, and then through a foundation that he started, Pierce directed funding into research on how to reduce the problems Cooper had identified, sponsored an international conference to gather ideas from around the world, and brought anesthesia-machine designers into safety discussions.

It all worked. Hours for anesthesiology residents were shortened. Manufacturers began redesigning their machines with fallible human beings in mind. Dials were standardized to turn in a uniform direction; locks were put in to prevent accidental administration of more than one anesthetic gas; controls were changed so that oxygen delivery could not be turned down to zero.

Where errors could not be eliminated directly, anesthesiologists began looking for reliable means of detecting them earlier. For example, because the trachea and the esophagus are so close together, it is almost inevitable that an anesthesiologist will sometimes put the breathing tube down the wrong pipe. Anesthesiologists had always checked for this by listening with a stethoscope for breath sounds over both lungs. But Cooper had turned up a surprising number of mishaps—like the one that befell the daughter of Pierce's friends—involving undetected esophageal intubations. Something more effective was needed. In fact, monitors that could detect this kind of error had been available for years, but, in part because of their expense, relatively few anesthesiologists used them. One type of monitor could verify that the tube was in the trachea by detecting carbon dioxide being exhaled from the lungs. Another type, the pulse oximeter, tracked blood-oxygen levels, thereby providing an early warning that something was wrong with the patient's breathing system. Prodded by Pierce and others, the anesthesiology society made the use of both types of monitor for every patient receiving general anesthesia an official standard. Today, anesthesia deaths from misconnecting the breathing system or intubating the esophagus rather than the trachea are virtually unknown. In a decade, the over-all death rate dropped to just one in more than two hundred thousand cases—less than a twentieth of what it had been.

And the reformers have not stopped there. David Gaba, a professor of anesthesiology at Stanford, has focussed on improving human performance. In aviation, he points out, pilot experience is recognized to be invaluable but insufficient: pilots seldom have direct experience with serious plane malfunction anymore. They are therefore required to undergo yearly training in crisis simulators. Why not doctors, too?

Gaba, a physician with training in engineering, led in the design of an anesthesia-simulation system known as the Eagle Patient Simulator. It is a life-size, computer-driven mannequin that is capable of amazingly realistic behaviour. It has a circulation, a heartbeat, and lungs that take in oxygen and expire carbon dioxide. If you inject drugs into it or administer inhaled anesthetics, it will detect the type and amount, and its heart rate, its blood pressure, and its oxygen levels will respond appropriately. The "patient" can be made to develop airway swelling, bleeding, and heart disturbances. The mannequin is laid on an operating table in a simulation room equipped exactly like the real thing. Here both residents and experienced attending physicians learn to perform effectively in all kinds of dangerous, and sometimes freak, scenarios: an anesthesia-machine malfunction, a power outage, a patient who goes into cardiac arrest during surgery, and even a cesarean-section patient whose airway shuts down and who requires an emergency tracheostomy.

Though anesthesiology has unquestionably taken the lead in analyzing and trying to remedy "systems" failures, there are signs of change in other quarters. The American Medical Association, for example, set up its National Patient Safety Foundation in 1997 and asked Cooper and Pierce to serve on the board of directors. The foundation is funding research, sponsoring conferences, and attempting to develop new standards for hospital drug-ordering systems that could substantially reduce medication mistakes—the single most common type of medical error.

Even in surgery there have been some encouraging developments. For instance, operating on the wrong knee or foot or other body part of a patient has been a recurrent, if rare, mistake. A typical response has been to fire the surgeon. Recently, however, hospitals and surgeons have begun to recognize that the body's bilateral symmetry makes these errors predictable. Last year, the American Academy of Orthopedic Surgeons endorsed a simple way of preventing them: make it standard practice for surgeons to initial, with a marker, the body part to be cut before the patient comes to surgery.

The Northern New England Cardiovascular Disease Study Group, based at Dartmouth, is another success story. Though the group doesn't conduct the sort of in-depth investigation of mishaps that Jeffrey Cooper pioneered, it has shown what can be done simply through statistical monitoring. Six hospitals belong to this consortium, which tracks deaths and complications (such as wound infections, uncontrolled bleeding, and stroke) arising from heart surgery and tries to identify various risk factors. Its researchers found, for example, that there were relatively high death rates among patients who developed anemia after bypass surgery, and that anemia developed most often in small patients. The fluid used to "prime" the heart-lung machine caused the anemia, because it diluted a patient's blood, so the smaller the patient (and his or her blood supply) the greater the effect. Members of the consortium now have several promising solutions to the problem. Another study found that a group at one hospital had made mistakes in "handoffs"—say, in passing preoperative lab results to the people in the operating room. The study group solved the problem by developing a pilot's checklist for all patients coming to the O.R. These efforts have introduced a greater degree of standardization, and so reduced the death rate in those six hospitals from four per cent to three per cent between 1991 and 1996. That meant two hundred and ninety-three fewer deaths. But the Northern New England cardiac group, even with its narrow focus and techniques, remains an exception; hard information about how things go wrong is still scarce. There is a hodgepodge of evidence that latent errors and systemic factors may contribute to surgical errors: the lack of standardized protocols, the surgeon's inexperience, the hospital's inexperience, inadequately designed technology and techniques, thin staffing, poor teamwork, time of day, the effects of managed care and corporate medicine, and so on and so on. But which are the major risk factors? We still don't know. Surgery, like most of medicine, awaits its Jeff Cooper.

V—Getting It Right

It was a routine gallbladder operation, on a routine day: on the operating table was a mother in her forties, her body covered by blue paper drapes except for her round, antiseptic-coated belly. The gallbladder is a floppy, finger-length sac of bile like a deflated olive-green balloon tucked under the liver, and when gallstones form, as this patient had learned, they can cause excruciating bouts of pain. Once we removed her gallbladder, the pain would stop.

There are risks to this surgery, but they used to be much greater. Just a decade ago, surgeons had to make a six-inch abdominal incision that left patients in the hospital for the better part of a week just recovering from the wound. Today, we've learned to take out gallbladders with a minute camera and instruments that we manipulate through tiny incisions. The operation, often done as day surgery, is known as laparoscopic cholecystectomy, or "lap chole." Half a million Americans a year now have their gallbladders removed this way; at my hospital alone, we do several hundred lap choles annually.

When the attending gave me the go-ahead, I cut a discreet inch-long semicircle in the wink of skin just above the belly button. I dissected through fat and fascia until I was inside the abdomen, and dropped into place a "port," a half-inch-wide sheath for slipping instruments in and out. We hooked gas tubing up to a side vent on the port, and carbon dioxide poured in, inflating the abdomen until it was distended like a tire. I inserted the miniature camera. On a video monitor a few feet away, the woman's intestines blinked into view. With the abdomen inflated, I had room to move the camera, and I swung it around to look at the liver. The gallbladder could be seen poking out from under the edge.

We put in three more ports through even tinier incisions, spaced apart to complete the four corners of a square. Through the ports on his side, the attending put in two long "graspers," like small-scale versions of the device that a department-store clerk might use to get a hat off the top shelf. Watching the screen as he maneuvered them, he reached under the edge of the liver, clamped onto the gallbladder, and pulled it up into view. We were set to proceed.

Removing the gallbladder is fairly straightforward. You sever it from its stalk and from its blood supply, and pull the rubbery sac out of the abdomen through the incision near the belly button. You let the carbon dioxide out of the belly, pull out the ports, put a few stitches in the tiny incisions, slap some Band-Aids on top, and you're done. There's one looming danger, though: the stalk of the gallbladder is a branch off the liver's only conduit for sending bile to the intestines for the digestion of fats. And if you accidentally injure this main bile duct, the bile backs up and starts to destroy the liver. Between ten and twenty per cent of the patients to whom this happens will die. Those who survive often have permanent liver damage and can go on to require liver transplantation. According to a standard textbook, "injuries to the main bile duct are nearly always the result of misadventure during operation and are therefore a serious reproach to the surgical profession." It is a true surgical error, and, like any surgical team doing a lap chole, we were intent on avoiding this mistake.

Using a dissecting instrument, I carefully stripped off the fibrous white tissue and yellow fat overlying and concealing the base of the gallbladder. Now we could see its broad neck and the short stretch where it narrowed down to a duct—a tube no thicker than a strand of spaghetti peeking out from the surrounding tissue, but magnified on the screen to the size of major plumbing. Then, just to be absolutely sure we were looking at the gallbladder duct and not the main bile duct, I stripped away some more of the surrounding tissue. The attending and I stopped at this point, as we always do, and discussed the anatomy. The neck of the gallbladder led straight into the tube we were eying. So it had to be the right duct. We had exposed a good length of it without a sign of the main bile duct. Everything looked perfect, we agreed. "Go for it," the attending said.

I slipped in the clip applier, an instrument that squeezes V-shaped metal clips onto whatever you put in its jaws. I got the jaws around the duct and was about to fire when my eye caught, on the screen, a little globule of fat lying on top of the duct. That wasn't necessarily anything unusual, but somehow it didn't look right. With the tip of the clip applier, I tried to flick it aside, but, instead of a little globule, a whole layer of thin unseen tissue came up, and, underneath, we saw that the duct had a fork in it. My stomach dropped. If not for that little extra fastidiousness, I would have clipped off the main bile duct.

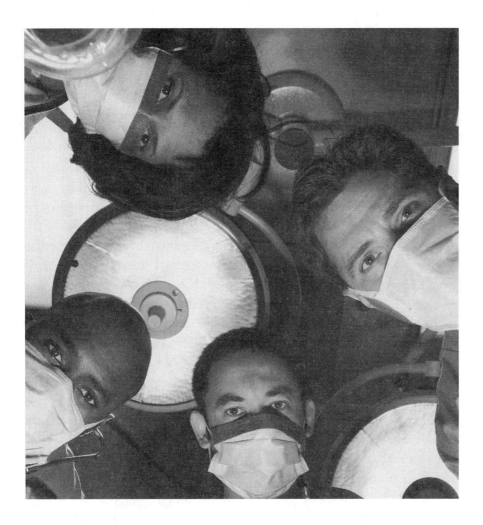

Here was the paradox of error in medicine. With meticulous technique and assiduous effort to insure that they have correctly identified the anatomy, surgeons need never cut the main bile duct. It is a paradigm of an avoidable error. At the same time, studies show that even highly experienced surgeons inflict this terrible injury about once in every two hundred lap choles. To put it another way, I may have averted disaster this time, but a statistician would say that, no matter how hard I tried, I was almost certain to make this error at least once in the course of my career.

But the story doesn't have to end here, as the cognitive psychologists and industrial-error experts have demonstrated. Given the results they've achieved in anesthesiology, it's clear that we can make dramatic improvements by going after the process, not the people. But there are distinct limitations to the industrial cure, however necessary its emphasis on systems and structures. It would be deadly for us, the individual actors, to give up our belief in human perfectibility. The statistics may say that someday I will sever someone's main bile duct, but each time I go into a gallbladder operation I believe that with enough will and effort I can beat the odds. This isn't just professional vanity. It's a necessary part of good medicine, even in superbly "optimized" systems. Operations like that lap chole have taught me how easily error can occur, but they've also showed me something else: effort does matter; diligence and attention to the minutest details can save you.

This may explain why many doctors take exception to talk of "systems problem," "continuous quality improvement," and "process reëngineering." It is the dry language of structures, not people. I'm no exception: something in me, too, demands an acknowledgment of my autonomy, which is also to say my ultimate culpability. Go back to that Friday night in the E.R., to the moment when I stood, knife in hand, over Louise Williams, her lips blue, her throat a swollen, bloody, and suddenly closed passage. A systems engineer might have proposed some useful changes. Perhaps a backup suction device should always be at hand, and better light more easily available. Perhaps the institution could have trained me better for such crises, could have required me to have operated on a few more goats. Perhaps emergency tracheostomies are so difficult under any circumstances that an automated device could have been designed to do a better job. But the could-haves are infinite, aren't they? Maybe Williams could have worn her seat belt, or had one less beer that night. We could call any or all of these factors latent errors, accidents waiting to happen.

But although they put the odds against me, it wasn't as if I had no chance of succeeding. Good doctoring is all about making the most of the hand you're dealt, and I failed to do so. The indisputable fact was that I hadn't called for help when I could have, and when I plunged the knife into her neck and made my horizontal slash my best was not good enough. It was just luck, hers and mine, that Dr. O'Connor somehow got a breathing tube into her in time.

There are all sorts of reasons that it would be wrong to take my license away or to take me to court. These reasons do not absolve me. Whatever the limits of the M. & M., its fierce ethic of personal responsibility for errors is a formidable virtue. No matter what measures are taken, medicine will sometimes falter, and it isn't reasonable to ask that it achieve perfection. What's reasonable is to ask that medicine never cease to aim for it.

The Tale of the Ancient Molecule

Paul Davies

Inside each and every one of us lies a message. It is inscribed in an ancient code, its beginnings lost in the mists of time. Decrypted, the message contains instructions on how to make a human being. Nobody wrote the message; nobody invented the code. They came into existence spontaneously. Their designer was Mother Nature herself, working only within the scope of her immutable laws and capitalizing on the vagaries of chance. The message isn't written in ink or type, but in atoms, strung together in an elaborately arranged sequence to form DNA, short for deoxyribonucleic acid. It is the most extraordinary molecule on Earth.

Human DNA contains many billions of atoms, linked in the distinctive form of two coils entwined in mutual embrace. This famous double helix is in turn bundled up in a very **convoluted** shape. Stretch out the DNA in just one cell of your body and it would make a thread two meters long. These are big molecules indeed.

convoluted
intricately winding

Although DNA is a material structure, it is pregnant with meaning. The arrangement of the atoms along the helical strands of your DNA determines how you look and even, to a certain extent, how you feel and behave. DNA is nothing less than a blueprint—or, more accurately, an algorithm or instruction manual—for building a living, breathing, thinking human being.

We share this magic molecule with almost all other life forms on Earth. From fungi to flies, from bacteria to bears, organisms are sculpted according to their respective DNA instructions. Each individual's DNA differs from others in the same species (with the exception of identical twins), and differs even more from that of other species. But the essential structure—the chemical makeup, the double-helix architecture—is universal.

DNA is incredibly, unimaginably ancient. It almost certainly existed three and a half billion years ago. It makes nonsense of the phrase "as old as the hills": DNA was here long before any surviving hills on Earth. Nobody knows how or where the first DNA molecule formed. Some scientists even speculate that it is an alien invader, a molecule from Mars perhaps, or from a wandering comet. But however the first strand of DNA came to exist, our own DNA is very probably a direct descendent of it. For the crucial quality of DNA, the property that sets it apart from other big organic molecules, is its ability to replicate itself. Put simply, DNA is in the business of making more DNA, generation after generation, instruction manual after instruction manual, cascading down through the ages from microbes to man in an unbroken chain of copying.

Of course, copying as such produces only more of the same. Perfect replication of DNA would lead to a planet knee-deep in identical single-celled organisms. However, no copying process is totally reliable. A photocopier may create stray spots, a noisy telephone line will garble a fax transmission, and a computer glitch can spoil data transferred from hard disk to a floppy. When errors occur in DNA replication, they can manifest themselves as mutations in the organisms that inherit them. Mostly a mutation is damaging, just as a random word change in a Shakespeare sonnet would likely mar its beauty. But occasionally, quite by chance, an error might produce a positive benefit, conferring an advantage on the mutant. If the advantage is life-preserving, enabling the organism to reproduce itself more efficiently, then the miscopied DNA will out-replicate its competitors and come to predominate. Conversely, if the copying error results in a less well-adapted organism, the mutant strain will probably die out after a few generations, eliminating this particular DNA variant.

This simple process of replication, variation, and elimination is the basis of Darwinian evolution. Natural selection—the continual sifting of mutants according to their fitness—acts like a ratchet, locking in the advantageous errors and discarding the bad. Starting with the DNA of some primitive ancestor microbe, bit by bit, error by error, the increasingly lengthy instructions for building more complex organisms came to be constructed.

Some people find the idea of an instruction manual that writes itself simply by accumulating chance errors hard to swallow, so let me go over the argument once more, using a slightly different metaphor. Think of the information in human DNA as the score for a symphony. This is a grand symphony indeed, a mighty orchestral piece with hundreds of musicians playing thousands of notes. By comparison, the DNA of the ancient ancestor microbe is but a simple melody. How does a melody turn into a symphony?

Suppose a scribe is asked to copy the original tune as a musical score. Normally the copying process is faithful, but once in a while a **quaver**

quaver
an eighth note

becomes a **crotchet**, a C becomes a D. A slip of the pen introduces a slight change of tempo or pitch. Occasionally a more serious error leads to a major flaw in the piece, an entire bar omitted or repeated perhaps. Mostly these mistakes will spoil the balance or harmony, so that the score is of no further use: nobody would wish to listen to its musical rendition. But very occasionally the scribe's slip of the pen will add an imaginative new sound, a pleasing feature, a successful addition or alteration, quite by chance. The tune will actually improve, and be approved for the future. Now imagine this process of improvement and elaboration continuing though trillions of copying procedures. Slowly but surely, the tune will acquire new features, develop a richer structure, evolve into a sonata, even a symphony.

crotchet
a quarter note

The crucial point about this metaphor, and it cannot be stressed too strongly, is that the symphony comes into being without the scribe's ever having the slightest knowledge of, or interest in, music. The scribe might have been deaf from birth and know nothing whatever of melodies. It doesn't matter, because the scribe's job is not to compose the music but to copy it. Where the metaphor fails is in the selection process. There is no cosmic musician scrutinizing the score of life and exercising quality control. There is only nature, red in tooth and claw, applying a simple and brutal rule: if it works, keep it; if it doesn't, kill it. And "works" here is defined by one criterion and one criterion only, which is replication efficiency. If the mistake results in more copies made, then, by definition, without any further considerations, it works. If A out-replicates B, even by the slightest margin, then, generations on, there will be many more A's than B's. If A and B have to compete for space or resources, it's a fair bet that A will soon eliminate B entirely. A survives, B dies.

Darwinism is the central principle around which our understanding of biology is constructed. It offers an economical explanation of how a relatively simple genetic message elaborates itself over the eons to create molecules of DNA complex enough to produce a human being. Once the basic manual, the precursor DNA, existed in the first place, random errors and selection might gradually be able to evolve it. Good genes are kept, bad genes are discarded. . . . Obviously Darwinian evolution can operate only if life of some sort already exists (strictly, it requires not life in its full glory, only replication, variation, and selection). Darwinism can offer absolutely no help in explaining that all-important first step: the origin of life. But if the central principle of life fails to explain the origin of life, we are left with a problem. What other principle or principles might explain how it all began?

To solve this problem, we must seek clues. Where can we look for clues about the origin of life? A good place to begin is to ask where life itself began. If we discover the place where life started, we may be able to guess the physical conditions that accompanied its genesis. Then we can set about studying the chemical processes that occur in such conditions, and build up an understanding of the prebiotic phase bit by bit.

Finding Darwin's God

Kenneth R. Miller

The great hall of the Hynes Convention Center in Boston looks nothing like a church. And yet I sat there, smiling amid an audience of scientists, shaking my head and laughing to myself as I remembered another talk, given long ago, inside a church to an audience of children.

Without warning, I had experienced one of those moments in the present that connects with the scattered recollections of our past. Psychologists tell us that [these] things happen all the time. Five thousand days of childhood are filed, not in chronological order, but as bits and pieces linked by words, or sounds, or even smells that cause us to retrieve them for no apparent reason when something "refreshes" our memory. And just like that, a few words in a symposium on developmental biology had brought me back to the day before my first communion. I was eight years old, sitting with the boys on the right side of our little church (the girls sat on the left), and our pastor was speaking.

Putting the finishing touches on a year of preparation for the sacrament, Father Murphy sought to impress us with the reality of God's power in the world. He pointed to the altar railing, its polished marble gleaming in sunlight, and firmly assured us that God himself had fashioned it. "Yeah, right," whispered the kid next to me. Worried that there might be the son or daughter of a stonecutter in the crowd, the good Father retreated a bit. "Now, he didn't carve the railing or bring it here or cement it in place . . . but God himself *made* the marble, long ago, and left it for someone to find and make into part of our church."

I don't know if our pastor sensed that his description of God as craftsman was meeting a certain tide of skepticism, but no matter. He had another trick up his sleeve, a can't-miss, sure-thing argument that, no doubt, had never failed him. He walked over to the altar and picked a flower from the vase.

"Look at the beauty of a flower," he began. "The Bible tells us that even Solomon in all his glory was never arrayed as one of these. And do you know what? Not a single person in the world can tell us what makes a flower bloom. All those scientists in their laboratories, the ones

Kenneth R. Miller, "Finding Darwin's God," *Brown Alumni Magazine*, Volume 100, Number 2/ November–December, 1999. Copyright © 1999 by *Brown Alumni Magazine*. Reprinted with permission.

who can split the atom and build jet planes and televisions, well, not one of them can tell you how a plant makes flowers." And why should they be able to? "Flowers, just like you, are the work of God."

I was impressed. No one argued, no one wisecracked. We filed out of the church like good little boys and girls, ready for our first communion the next day. And I never thought of it again, until this symposium on developmental biology. Sandwiched between two speakers working on more fashionable topics in animal development was Elliot M. Meyerowitz, a plant scientist at Caltech. A few of my colleagues, uninterested in research dealing with plants, got up to stretch their legs before the final talk, but I sat there with an ear-to-ear grin on my face. I jotted notes furiously; I sketched the diagrams he projected on the screen and wrote additional speculations of my own in the margins. Meyerowitz, you see, had explained how plants make flowers.

The four principal parts of a flower—sepals, petals, stamens, and pistils—are actually modified leaves. This is one of the reasons why plants can produce reproductive cells just about anywhere, while animals are limited to a very specific set of reproductive organs. Your little finger isn't going to start shedding reproductive cells anytime soon. But in springtime, the tip of any branch on an apple tree may very well blossom and begin scattering pollen. Plants can produce new flowers anywhere they can grow new leaves. Somehow, however, the plant must find a way to "tell" an ordinary cluster of leaves that they should develop into floral parts. That's where Meyerowitz's lab took over.

Several years of patient genetic study had isolated a set of mutants that could only form two or three of the four parts. By crossing the various mutants, his team was able to identify four genes that had to be turned on or off in a specific pattern to produce a normal flower. Each of these genes, in turn, sets off a series of signals that "tell" the cells of a brand new bud to develop as sepals or petals rather than ordinary leaves. The details are remarkable, and the interactions between the genes are fascinating. To me, sitting in the crowd thirty-seven years after my first communion, the scientific details were just the icing on the cake. The real message was "Father Murphy, you were wrong." God doesn't make a flower. The floral induction genes do.

Our pastor's error, common and widely repeated, was to seek God in what science has not yet explained. His assumption was that God is best found in territory unknown, in the corners of darkness that have not yet seen the light of understanding. These, as it turns out, are exactly the wrong places to look.

Searching the Shadows

By pointing to the process of making a flower as proof of the reality of God, Father Murphy was embracing the idea that God finds it necessary to cripple nature. In his view, the blooming of a daffodil requires not a self-sufficient material universe, but direct intervention by God. We can find God, therefore, in the things around us that lack material, scientific explanations. In nature, elusive and unexplored, we will find the Creator at work.

The creationist opponents of evolution make similar arguments. They claim that the existence of life, the appearance of new species, and, most especially, the origins of mankind have not and cannot be explained by evolution or any other natural process. By denying the self-sufficiency of nature, they look for God (or at least a "designer") in the deficiencies of science. The trouble is that science, given enough time, generally explains even the most baffling things. As a matter of strategy, creationists would be well-advised to avoid telling scientists what they will never be able to figure out. History is against them. In a general way, we really do understand how nature works.

And evolution forms a critical part of that understanding. Evolution really does explain the very things that its critics say it does not. Claims disputing the antiquity of the earth, the validity of the fossil record, and the sufficiency of evolutionary mechanisms vanish upon close inspection. Even to the most fervent anti-evolutionists, the pattern should be clear—their favorite "gaps" are filling up: the molecular mechanisms of evolution are now well-understood, and the historical record of evolution becomes more compelling with each passing season. This means that science can answer their challenges to evolution in an obvious way. Show the historical record, provide the data, reveal the mechanism, and highlight the convergence of theory and fact.

There is, however, a deeper problem caused by the opponents of evolution, a problem for religion. Like our priest, they have based their search for God on the premise that nature is *not* self-sufficient. By such logic, only God can make a species, just as Father Murphy believed only God could make a flower. Both assertions support the existence of God *only* so long as these assertions are true, but serious problems for religion emerge when they are shown to be false.

If we accept a *lack* of scientific explanation as proof for God's existence, simple logic would dictate that we would have to regard a successful scientific explanation as an argument *against* God. That's why creationist reasoning, ultimately, is much more dangerous to religion than to science. Elliot Meyerowitz's fine work on floral induction suddenly becomes a threat to the divine, even though common sense tells us it should be nothing of the sort. By arguing, as creationists do, that nature cannot be self-sufficient in the formation of new species, the creationists forge a logical link between the limits of natural processes to accomplish biological change and the existence of a designer (God). In other words, they show the proponents of atheism exactly how to disprove the existence of God—show that evolution works, and it's time to tear down the temple. This is an offer that the enemies of religion are all too happy to accept.

Putting it bluntly, the creationists have sought God in darkness. What we have not found and do not yet understand becomes their best—indeed their only—evidence for the divine. As a Christian, I find the flow of this logic particularly depressing. Not only does it teach us to fear the acquisition of knowledge (which might at any time disprove belief), but it suggests that God dwells only in the shadows of our understanding. I suggest that, if God is real, we should be able to find him somewhere else—in the bright light of human knowledge, spiritual and scientific.

Faith and Reason

Each of the great Western monotheistic traditions sees God as truth, love, and knowledge. This should mean that each and every increase in our understanding of the natural world is a step toward God and not, as many people assume, a step away. If faith and reason are both gifts from God, then they should play complementary, not conflicting, roles in our struggle to understand the world around us. As a scientist and as a Christian, that is exactly what I believe. True knowledge comes only from a combination of faith and reason.

A nonbeliever, of course, puts his or her trust in science and finds no value in faith. And I certainly agree that science allows believer and nonbeliever alike to investigate the natural world through a common lens of observation, experiment, and theory. The ability of science to transcend cultural, political, and even religious differences is part of its genius, part of its value as a way of knowing. What science cannot do is assign either meaning or purpose to the world it explores. This leads some to conclude that the world as seen by science is devoid of meaning and absent of purpose. It is not. What it does mean, I would suggest, is that our human tendency to assign meaning and value must transcend science and, ultimately, must come from outside it. The science that results can thus be enriched and informed from its contact with the values and principles of faith. The God of Abraham does not tell us which proteins control the cell cycle. But he does give us a reason to care, a reason to cherish that understanding, and above all, a reason to prefer the light of knowledge to the darkness of ignorance.

As more than one scientist has said, the truly remarkable thing about the world is that it actually does make sense. The parts fit, the molecules interact, the darn thing works. To people of faith, what evolution says is that nature is complete. Their God fashioned a material world in which truly free and independent beings could evolve. He got it right the very first time.

To some, the murderous reality of human nature is proof that God is absent or dead. The same reasoning would find God missing from the unpredictable branchings of an evolutionary tree. But the truth is deeper. In each case, a deity determined to establish a world that was truly independent of his whims, a world in which intelligent creatures would face authentic choices between good and evil, would have to fashion a distinct, material reality and then let his creation run. Neither the self-sufficiency of nature nor the reality of evil in the world mean God is absent. To a religious person, both signify something quite different—the strength of God's love and the reality of our freedom as his creatures.

The Weapons of Disbelief

As a species, we like to see ourselves as the best and brightest. We are the intended, special, primary creatures of creation. We sit at the apex of the evolutionary tree as the ultimate products of nature, self-proclaimed and self-aware. We like to think that evolution's goal was to produce us.

In a purely biological sense, this comforting view of our own position in nature is false, a product of self-inflating distortion induced by the imperfect mirrors we hold up to life. Yes, we are objectively among the most complex of animals, but not in every sense. Among the systems of the body, we are the hands-down winners for physiological complexity in just one place—the nervous system—and even there, a nonprimate (the dolphin) can lay down a claim that rivals our own.

More to the point, any accurate assessment of the evolutionary process shows that the notion of one form of life being more highly evolved than another is incorrect. Every organism, every cell that lives today, is the descendant of a long line of winners, of ancestors who used successful evolutionary strategies time and time again, and therefore lived to tell about it—or, at least, to reproduce. The bacterium perched on the lip of my coffee cup has been through as much evolution as I have. I've got the advantage of size and consciousness, which matter when I write about evolution, but the bacterium has the advantage of numbers, of flexibility, and most especially, of reproductive speed. That single bacterium, given the right conditions, could literally fill the world with its descendants in a matter of days. No human, no vertebrate, no animal could boast of anything remotely as impressive.

What evolution tells us is that life spreads out along endless branching pathways from any starting point. One of those tiny branches eventually led to us. We think it remarkable and wonder how it could have happened, but any fair assessment of the tree of life shows that our tiny branch is crowded into insignificance by those that bolted off in a thousand different directions. Our species, *Homo sapiens*, has not "triumphed" in the evolutionary struggle any more than has a squirrel, a dandelion, or a mosquito. We are all here, now, and that's what matters. We have all followed different pathways to find ourselves in the present. We are all winners in the game of natural selection. *Current* winners, we should be careful to say.

That, in the minds of many, is exactly the problem. In a thousand branching pathways, how can we be sure that one of them, historically and unavoidably, would lead for sure to us? Consider this: we mammals now occupy, in most ecosystems, the roles of large, dominant land animals. But for much of their history, mammals were restricted to habitats in which only very small creatures could survive. Why? Because another group of vertebrates dominated the earth—until, as Stephen Jay Gould has pointed out, the cataclysmic impact of a comet or asteroid drove those giants to extinction. "In an entirely literal sense," Gould has written, "we owe our existence, as large and reasoning animals, to our lucky stars."

So, what if the comet had missed? What if our ancestors, and not dinosaurs, had been the ones driven to extinction? What if, during the Devonian period, the small tribe of fish known as rhipidistians had been obliterated? Vanishing with them would have been the possibility of life for the first tetrapods. Vertebrates might never have struggled onto the land, leaving it, in Gould's words, forever "the unchallenged domain of insects and flowers."

Surely this means that mankind's appearance on this planet was *not* pre-ordained, that we are here not as the products of an inevitable procession of evolutionary success, but as an afterthought, a minor detail, a happenstance in a history that might just as well have left us out. What follows from this, to skeptic and true believer alike, is a conclusion whose logic is rarely challenged—that no God would ever have used such a process to fashion his prize creatures. How could he have been sure that leaving the job to evolution would lead things to working out the "right" way? If it was God's will to produce us, then by showing that we are the products of evolution, we would rule God as Creator. Therein lies the value or the danger of evolution.

Not so fast. The biological account of lucky historical contingencies that led to our own appearance on this planet is surely accurate. What does not follow is that a perceived lack of inevitability translates into something that we should regard as incompatibility with a divine will. To do so seriously underestimates God, even as this God is understood by the most conventional of Western religions.

Yes, the explosive diversification of life on this planet was an unpredictable process. But so were the rise of Western civilization, the collapse of the Roman Empire, and the winning number in last night's lottery. We do not regard the indeterminate nature of any of these events in human history as antithetical to the existence of a Creator; why should we regard similar events in natural history any differently? There is, I would submit, no reason at all. If we can view the contingent events in the families that produced our individual lives as consistent with a Creator, then certainly we can do the same for the chain of circumstances that produced our species.

The alternative is a world where all events have predictable outcomes, where the future is open neither to chance nor to independent human action. A world in which we would always evolve is a world in which we would never be free. To a believer, the particular history leading to us shows how truly remarkable we are, how rare is the gift of consciousness, and how precious is the chance to understand.

Certainty and Faith

One would like to think that all scientific ideas, including evolution, would rise or fall purely on the basis of the evidence. If that were true, evolution would long since have passed, in the public mind, from controversy into common sense, which is exactly what has happened within the scientific community. This is, unfortunately, not the case—evolution remains, in the minds of much of the American public, a dangerous idea, and for biology educators, a source of never-ending strife.

I believe much of the problem is the fault of those in the scientific community who routinely enlist the findings of evolutionary biology in support [of] their own philosophical pronouncements. Sometimes these take the form of stern, dispassionate pronouncements about the meaninglessness of life. Other times we are lectured that the contingency of our presence on this planet invalidates any sense of human purpose. And very often we are told that the raw reality of nature strips the authority from any human system of morality.

As creatures fashioned by evolution, we are filled, as the biologist E. O. Wilson has said, with instinctive behaviors important to the survival of our genes. Some of these behaviors, though favored by natural selection, can get us into trouble. Our desires for food, water, reproduction, and status, our willingness to fight, and our tendencies to band together into social groups, can all be seen as behaviors that help ensure evolutionary success. Sociobiology, which studies the biological basis of social behaviors, tells us that in some circumstances natural selection will favor cooperative and nurturing instincts—"nice" genes that help us get along together. Some circumstances, on the other had, will favor aggressive self-centered behaviors, ranging all the way from friendly competition to outright homicide. Could such Darwinian ruthlessness be part of the plan of a loving God?

Yes, it could. To survive on this planet, the genes of our ancestors, like those of any other organism, had to produce behaviors that protected, nurtured, defended, and ensured the reproductive successes of the individuals that bore them. It should be no surprise that we carry such passions within us, and Darwinian biology cannot be faulted for giving their presence a biological explanation. Indeed, the Bible itself gives ample documentation of such human tendencies, including pride, selfishness, lust, anger, aggression, and murder.

Darwin can hardly be criticized for pinpointing the biological origins of these drives. All too often, in finding the sources of our "original sins," in fixing the reasons why our species displays the tendencies it does, evolution is misconstrued as providing a kind of justification for the worst aspects of human nature. At best, this is a misreading of the scientific lessons of sociobiology. At worst, it is an attempt to misuse biology to abolish any meaningful system of morality. Evolution may explain the existence of our most basic biological drives and desires, but that does not tell us that it is always proper to act on them. Evolution has provided me with a sense of hunger when my nutritional resources are running low, but evolution does not justify my clubbing you over the head to swipe your lunch. Evolution explains our biology, but it does not tell us what is good, or right, or moral. For those answers, however informed we may be by biology, we must look somewhere else.

What Kind of World?

Like it or not, the values that any of us apply to our daily lives have been affected by the work of Charles Darwin. Religious people, however, have a special question to put to the reclusive naturalist of Down House. Did his work ultimately contribute to the greater glory of God, or did he deliver human nature and destiny into the hands of a professional scientific class, one profoundly hostile to religion? Does Darwin's work strengthen or weaken the idea of God?

The conventional wisdom is that whatever one may think of his science, having Mr. Darwin around certainly hasn't helped religion very much. The general thinking is that religion has been weakened by Darwinism and has been constrained to modify its view of the Creator in order to twist doctrine into conformity with the demands of evolution. As Stephen Jay Gould puts it, with obvious delight, "Now the conclusions of science must be accepted *a priori*, and religious interpretations must be finessed and adjusted to match unimpeachable results from the **magisterium** of natural knowledge!" Science calls the tune, and religion dances to its music.

magisterium
proper realm

This sad specter of a weakened and marginalized God drives the continuing opposition to evolution. This is why the God of the creationists requires, above all, that evolution be shown not to have functioned in the past and not to be working now. To free religion from the tyranny of Darwinism, creationists need a science that shows nature to be incomplete; they need a history of life whose events can only be explained as the result of supernatural processes. Put bluntly, the creationists are committed to finding permanent, intractable mystery in nature. To such minds, even the most perfect being we can imagine would not have been perfect enough to fashion a creation in which life would originate and evolve on its own. Nature must be flawed, static, and forever inadequate.

Science in general, and evolutionary science in particular, gives us something quite different. It reveals a universe that is dynamic, flexible, and logically complete. It presents a vision of life that spreads across the planet with endless variety and intricate beauty. It suggests a world in which our material existence is not an impossible illusion propped up by magic, but the genuine article, a world in which things are exactly what they seem. A world in which we were formed, as the Creator once told us, from the dust of the earth itself.

It is often said that a Darwinian universe is one whose randomness cannot be reconciled with meaning. I disagree. A world truly without meaning would be one in which a deity pulled the string of every human puppet, indeed of every material particle. In such a world, physical and biological events would be carefully controlled, evil and suffering could be minimized, and the outcome of historical processes strictly regulated. All things would move toward the Creator's clear, distinct, established goals. Such control and predictability, however, comes at the price of independence. Always in control, such a Creator would deny his creatures any real opportunity to know and worship him—authentic love requires freedom, not manipulation. Such freedom is best supplied by the open contingency of evolution.

One hundred and fifty years ago it might have been impossible not to couple Darwin to a grim and pointless determinism, but things look different today. Darwin's vision has expanded to encompass a new world of biology in which the links from molecule to cell and from cell to organism are becoming clear. Evolution prevails, but it does so with a richness and subtlety its original theorist may have found surprising and could not have anticipated.

We know from astronomy, for example, that the universe had a beginning, from physics that the future is both open and unpredictable, from geology and paleontology that the whole of life has been a process of change and transformation. From biology we know that our tissues are not impenetrable reservoirs of vital magic, but a stunning matrix of complex wonders, ultimately explicable in terms of biochemistry and molecular biology. With such knowledge we can see, perhaps for the first time, why a Creator would have allowed our species to be fashioned by the process of evolution.

ex nihilo
out of nothing

If he so chose, the God whose presence is taught by most Western religions could have fashioned anything, ourselves included, ***ex nihilo***, from his wish alone. In our childhood as a species, that might have been the only way in which we could imagine the fulfillment of a divine will. But we've grown up, and something remarkable has happened: we have begun to understand the physical basis of life itself. If a string of constant miracles were needed for each turn of the cell cycle or each flicker of a cilium, the hand of God would be written directly into every living thing—his presence at the edge of the human sandbox would be unmistakable. Such findings might confirm our faith, but they would also undermine our independence. How could we fairly choose between God and man when the presence and the power of the divine so obviously and so literally controlled our every breath? Our freedom as his creatures requires a little space and integrity. In the material world, it requires self-sufficiency and consistency with the laws of nature.

Evolution is neither more nor less than the result of respecting the reality and consistency of the physical world over time. To fashion material beings with an independent physical existence, any Creator would have had to produce an independent material universe in which our evolution over time was a contingent possibility. A believer in the divine accepts that God's love and gift of freedom are genuine—so genuine that they include the power to choose evil and, if we wish, to freely send ourselves to Hell. Not all believers will accept the stark conditions of that bargain, but our freedom to act has to have a physical and biological basis. Evolution and its sister sciences of genetics and molecular biology provide that basis. In biological terms, evolution is the only way a Creator could have made us the creatures we are—free beings in a world of authentic and meaningful moral and spiritual choices.

Those who ask from science a final argument, an ultimate proof, an unassailable position from which the issue of God may be decided will always be disappointed. As a scientist I claim no new proofs, no revolutionary data, no stunning insight into nature that can tip the balance in one direction or another. But I do claim that to a believer, even in the most traditional sense, evolutionary biology is not at all the obstacle we often believe it to be. In many respects, evolution is the key to understanding our relationship with God.

When I have the privilege of giving a series of lectures on evolutionary biology to my freshman students, I usually conclude those lectures with a few remarks about the impact of evolutionary theory on other fields, from economics to politics to religion. I find a way to make clear that I do not regard evolution, properly understood, as either antireligious or antispiritual. Most students seem to appreciate those sentiments. They probably figure that Professor Miller, trying to be a nice guy and doubtlessly an agnostic, is trying to find a way to be **unequivocal** about evolution without offending the University chaplain.

unequivocal
clear and definitive

There are always a few who find me after class and want to pin me down. They ask me point-blank: "Do you believe in God?"

And I tell each of them, "Yes."

Puzzled, they ask: "What kind of God?"

Over the years I have struggled to come up with a simple but precise answer to that question. And, eventually I found it. I believe in Darwin's God.

UNIT 5

Arts and Culture

The purpose of art is the lifelong construction of a state of wonder.

Glenn Gould

As an artist, one is not a citizen of society. An artist is bound to explore every aspect of human experience, the darkest corners—not necessarily—but if that is where one is led, that's where one must go. You cannot worry about what the structure of your own particular segment of society considers bad behaviour, good behaviour; good exploration, bad exploration. So, at the time you're being an artist, you're not a citizen. You don't have the social responsibility of a citizen. You have, in fact, no social responsibility whatsoever.

David Cronenberg

I cannot praise a fugitive and cloistered virtue, unexercised and unbreathed, that never sallies out and sees her adversary but slinks out of the race.

Milton

Fantasies are more than substitutes for unpleasant realities, they are also dress rehearsals. All acts performed in the world begin in the imagination.

Barbara Grizzuti Harrison

Confronted with a story, any story, we immediately seek to fathom it out, to know it, even though we realize that if we succeed it will no longer be interesting, it will die. Oddly, then, the greatest pleasure we can get from a story only comes when the smaller satisfaction of having explained it away is thwarted. The mind discards, as it were, the chaff of the explicable to find real repose, or real excitement, in a kernel of enigma.

Tim Parks

Introduction

Throughout the course of *The Human Project*, reason has helped us to examine some thorny and fundamental problems. You may recall the question of the possibility of freedom in Unit 1, the collision of inevitable change and the persistence of old attitudes in Unit 2, the possibility that human nature itself imposes limits on our hopes for political solutions in Unit 3, the concern that the technological offspring of science may cause us to lose our way in the search for a better world in Unit 4. For answers to these and other questions, we have relied on reason and the methods of various disciplines such as psychology, sociology, philosophy, politics and science. In Unit 5, we shift emphasis, not in the sense of turning away from reason and method, but in the sense of adding a certain openness to imagination and a receptivity to pleasure. For the arts are about the significance of a parallel and imagined universe in the mind, a place where the real world may be reflected and criticized perhaps, but where the chief motive to explore is pleasure.

The problem that occurs when that parallel and imagined universe is produced primarily by another country is explored by John Steckley in "A Canadian Lament." Canadians are avid consumers of American culture, so much so that it is rare for Canadians to read, see or hear their own stories in novels, film or music. On one hand, this phenomenon is understandable: we have a small population, we live next door to the most vibrant producer of popular culture in the world and, consequently, it is quite normal to be fascinated by American culture, as, indeed, are the citizens of every other country in the world. On the other hand, if we don't develop our own voice and our own story as a counterbalance to American culture, we forego a vital tool for self-understanding and will be compelled to see the problems of growing up, finding a mate, facing danger and growing old through Californian eyes.

Ian Baird, in "One More Time: Our Ongoing Dialogue with Popular Music," takes an altogether more appreciative stance of the power of American popular music to reflect social realities, to console those who suffer the injuries caused by inequality and, moreover, to encourage the "transgression" needed to express both an outrage at injustice and an insistence on freedom. He traces the origin of much popular music to the blues, with its haunting mix of the sacred and the profane. The story of how the blues influenced British musicians of the 60s, who then exported the blues back to America, is an intriguing example of cultural migration. Today, we see similar migrations, as the music of the ghetto forms the beat at every suburban party. The blues has an authenticity that popular music at its best aspires to, but frequently fails to deliver, as it gets caught up in the understandable drive for commercial success.

In "Serious Pleasure: The Role of the Arts," Clive Cockerton engages in the same kinds of questions from a more philosophical perspective. Specifically, he explores the Platonic view that art has the power to seduce people to think and do things they shouldn't and, therefore, ought to be banned from society. In his rejection of the Platonic view, Cockerton argues that aesthetic pleasure is intrinsically valuable, that artistic insights can facilitate self-reflection, and, finally, that artistic experience helps to create a sense of community. Rather than diminishing us, Cockerton argues, art substantially enhances our lives.

The question of whether we can learn anything reliable from art is the focus of Cockerton's "Objectivity and Subjectivity." If we agree with the philosopher Nietzsche that there are no facts independent of interpretation, does that mean that all interpretations are of equivalent value or that some interpretations are more helpful and illuminating than others? If we see art through the lens of our personal circumstances, our gender, our social and economic class and our ethnic and cultural background, do we each see something different according to the specifics of our personal history? If the answer is yes, then there really doesn't seem to be much to talk about in art, other than to exchange highly personal, cultural and gendered interpretations. Thomas Lux's poem, "The Voice You Hear When You Read Silently," explores the weight of personal experience—the way the voice in your head "never says anything neutrally." And yet it is undeniable that artworks produced in different times, by people of different genders and classes still speak to us. That is why, for instance, so many white, middle-class, educated people living in relative luxury in contemporary Europe and North America still find something irresistible in the blues songs that express the suffering and reflect the harsh realities of blacks living in Mississippi and Chicago over eighty years ago. It seems hard to deny that there is something in art that can break through the differences that divide us.

It is difficult to talk about art as an abstraction without talking about specific works of art. For this reason, a number of poems, thoughtfully introduced by George Byrnes, and a narrative excerpt are included in this unit as lively examples of artworks that illustrate some of the more general points made in the essays. As the Russian novelist Alexander Solzhenitsyn wrote, "The sole substitute for an experience that we have not ourselves lived through is art and literature." The excerpt entitled

"Us or Me" from Ian McEwan's novel *Enduring Love* tells a frightening tale of human failure in the face of the forces of nature. This compelling story grasps our attention because the author has created an immediacy around the threat of sudden death. It is a threat that we all understand on one level, but none of us really fully grasp until we face it ourselves. Our own death we can barely consider, even though we know it will come. So we look for clues in the untimely ends of others: we gaze with fascination at automobile accidents, eagerly consume violent movies and listen hard to horrific tales. It's as if we have to flirt with the death of others in order to prepare for our own. McEwan's horrific tale tells us that there are moments, "pinpricks on the time map," which, in a rush, accumulate wild significance and lethal threat. After these moments, we are never the same; we can never go back to what we were before. We may rationalize our behaviour or analyze what would have been the right strategy, but both approaches merely attempt to avoid the brutal realization that there is sometimes a stupidity in the unfolding of events that leads to tragedy. At such times, we sense our vulnerability in an undeniable way.

A Canadian Lament

John Steckley

Can You Hear Me?

You live in Toronto, the largest city in Canada. Yet if I asked you to come up with a song that mentioned the name of your city, could you do it? Hard, isn't it? How about I make it easier and ask you to come up with a song that mentions any place in Canada. It's still a difficult task. If you know a lot about music and have a good memory—and it helps to have lived a long time—you might be able to come up with old songs by Gordon Lightfoot, Neil Young and, of course, anything by Stompin' Tom Connors of "Bud the Spud" and "Sudbury Saturday Night" fame. If you're younger, you might bring to mind something by Blue Rodeo, the Tragically Hip, I Mother Earth or maybe a song about the Black experience in Toronto, by one of our rap deejays.

Want something easier? Try thinking of a song that mentions a place in the United States. New York, Los Angeles, San Francisco and Chicago, and if you like country, Nashville, Memphis, the states of California, Carolina (North or South), Arkansas or Kentucky, and just about every place in Texas spring to mind pretty fast.

Canadians such as Shania Twain, Alanis Morissette, Céline Dion, Avril Lavigne and Bryan Adams are among the biggest musical stars in North America. But do they ever sing about where they are from? Will Shania ever mention her hometown of Timmins, as she has Arkansas in her song "Home's Not Where His Heart Is Anymore"? Will Alanis sing about how ironic it is to be raised in Ottawa? Will the lyrics of a Céline Dion song ever mention Québec when she sings in English? Will Avril Lavigne sing about a "SK8R Boi" who plays hockey in her hometown of Napanee? When he is singing with big stars such as Pavarotti, Streisand or Tina Turner, will Bryan Adams ever suggest that they sing about Vancouver? Don't hold your breath.

While we are on the subject of music, think of the big-name musicals that make so much money and play so long in Toronto. They all have a setting that is outside of this country: *Ragtime* (United States), *Sunset Boulevard* (Hollywood), *Evita* (Argentina), *Phantom of the Opera* (Paris), *Les Misérables* (Paris), *Cats* (London), *Joseph and the Amazing*

"A Canadian Lament" is by John Steckley of the Humber College Institute of Technology and Advanced Learning. Used by permission.

Technicolour Dreamcoat (Egypt), *Jane Eyre* (England), *Showboat* (United States), *Beauty and the Beast* (France) and *Damn Yankees* (about the New York baseball team). Don't ever expect to see and hear a production of *How About Those Jays?*

Can You See Me?

Move now to the television screen. A substantial number of television shows are filmed in Vancouver and Toronto, but those cities don't exist in those shows. Licence plates are always obscured in some way. You don't see distinctive features such as the CN Tower or the Lion's Gate Bridge. "Due South" was shot in Toronto, but took place in Chicago (with introductory stock footage of recognizable Chicago features). "The X-Files" was originally shot in Vancouver, but the main characters were FBI agents who travelled around the United States looking for signs of aliens (not ones wearing toques, hockey sweaters and eating doughnuts—my spell check doesn't like the word "toques"). Think of American place names in television shows, past and present: "Boston Public," "L.A. Law," "LAPD," "Streets of San Francisco," "Dallas," "Beverly Hills 90210," "Hawaii Five-0," "Miami Vice," "The Fresh Prince of Bel Air," "New York Undercover," "CSI—Miami" . . .

What about the big screen, movies? American domination is almost complete here; Canada is barely a player. Our films are like our milk: 2 per cent of the movies shown in our theatres is Canadian. Compare that with 45 per cent domestically produced films in France (a figure that, they fear, shows American domination) and 11 per cent in Australia. How many movies have you watched in the last year, two years, 11 years, that took place *officially* (complete with licence plates, names and recognizable landmarks) in Canada? Can you think of the names of any Canadian movies? *Hard Core Logo, Dance Me Outside, Jesus of Montreal, The Sweet Hereafter,* and *The Decline of the American Empire* probably don't sound familiar to you. Count up all the different times you've seen someone play the part of the president of the United States in a movie. Now try to remember whether you've ever seen

American domination of movies tends to block out Canadian voices.

anyone play the prime minister of Canada. No wonder so many children believe that the leader of our country is a president.

Canadian stories don't get told. Bring to mind all the baseball movies that have been made. *It Happens Every Spring, Ty Cobb, Angels in the Outfield, Bull Durham,* A *League of Their Own, Major League, Field of Dreams,* and *The Babe* are but a few. Now think of the teams involved: New York Yankees, California Angels, Cleveland Indians, Chicago Cubs and minor league teams in the United States. What do you feel are the chances that you'll ever see a movie that features the Toronto Blue Jays (twice World Series champs) or the Montreal Expos? There have been many movies made concerning other sports: boxing, basketball and football especially. But what about hockey? There's *Slapshot,* with Canadian actors and a very Canadian story (about a one-industry town and its hockey team) but with an American star and an American location. The *Mighty Ducks* movies serve as not-so-subtle Disney movie advertisements for a Disney-owned team. There is a flood of Canadian books out now about hockey, particularly focused in on the two greatest Canadian sports franchises of all time: the Montreal Canadiens and the Toronto Maple Leafs. There are a good number of movie-inspiring stories in those books, but they will most likely remain on the printed page. My childhood heroes—Eddie Shack, Bobby Baun, Tim Horton, Frank Mahovlich and, even, grudgingly as a Leaf fan, "Rocket" Richard, "Boom Boom" Geoffrion and Jean Béliveau—will probably never be seen in the movies.

Didn't it seem strange in *Wayne's World* to see people playing road hockey—the youthful experience of most Canadian males and a growing number of Canadian females? I didn't realize how Canadian an experience that is until I lived a year in Scotland. One day I heard the sound of wood scraping on pavement and I ran out of my house to see whether it was the sound of someone playing road hockey. Mike Myers (Wayne) of course is Canadian. But in the movies he played road hockey in a suburb of Chicago, and, even that quintessentially Canadian landmark, the doughnut shop, was named after a player for an American team, Chicago's Stan Mikita. Mike Myers grew up in Scarborough and recreated that place in Chicago, and later in San Francisco, with the Scottish family in *So I Married an Axe Murderer.* His story felt so familiar that I felt I had met his dad when I grew up in Don Mills, right next door to Scarborough, but the location was wrong. I doubt if it was a San Francisco story; the expatriate Scottish presence is so much stronger in Canada than in the United States.

There is a recent exception to my "Canadian stories don't get told" declaration. In 1996 the movie *Fly Away Home* came out to some success, and as I write it is the movie with the most copies in my video rental store. It is based on Bill Lishman's autobiography *Father Goose*, which is the story of how a man who earns his living making metal sculptures such as the famous "Autohenge" (a Stonehenge made out of car wrecks) pursued a lifelong dream to fly with the birds. The story is deeply rooted in southern Ontario. He grew up near Oshawa; his first commissioned sculpture was for the opening of Yorkdale shopping mall in Toronto; he made front page news with the sculpture of a metal horse that he left, as a publicity stunt, outside of Toronto City Hall; he was one of the most conspicuous figures in the opposition to the construction of the airport in Pickering during the 1970s; his art adorns Canada's Wonderland and Marineland. In the early 1990s he fought Ottawa (actually a federal bureaucrat with a strong need to control) to fly in an ultralight plane largely of his own design with a group of Canada geese to the southern coastal states, first Virginia, then North Carolina. The geese had "imprinted" on him, taking him and his planes to be their parents. It was not only an experiment to benefit the geese, who may have to change their migration paths due to the destruction of habitat and overhunting, but it was also an experiment that may lead some day to his working with endangered species such as the whooping crane and the trumpeter swan.

Now I liked the movie. It touched the emotions without manipulating them too much. There were good shots of the southern Ontario farmers' fields and woodlots that are dear to my heart. And if I could live with the southern Californian accent of Kevin Costner when he played the role of the Englishman Robin Hood, I suppose I can deal with the southern accent of Jeff Daniels in the part of Canadian Bill Lishman and the New Zealand accent of Anna Paquin as the heroine Amy who had been brought up by her mother in New Zealand. I didn't very much mind them changing the story so that a young girl was the one who the geese imprinted onto. And I found it humorous that to make sure people knew that the film was taking place in Canada, pictures of the Queen were featured prominently. But somehow something was lost for me. Maybe it was the sense of place that you get about American locations in recent movies such as *Fargo* and *Leaving Las Vegas*, and pretty much any movie based in L.A. or New York. Maybe so few movies present Canadian stories, that I was hungry in this exception for more representation of where I was raised.

Can You Read About Me?

There is constant political and economic pressure coming from the United States to further weaken our media by overturning the cultural protection statements in the North American Free Trade Agreement of 1994. Should American magazines such as *Sports Illustrated* and *Reader's Digest* be treated as "Canadian" because they have some Canadian content? The World Trade Organization, based in Geneva, tentatively answered this question with a "yes," and it has the political power to enforce that answer. "Treated as Canadian" means they would have no import taxes put on them and that Canadian companies could claim certain tax concessions when advertising in these publications. "Treated as Canadian" means that these "split-run" magazines (they have a "run" or slightly different publication in more than one place over the same publication period) could charge less for advertising. In 1993, when *Sports Illustrated* tried this, it charged $6250 for a full-page ad, while *Maclean's*, a Canadian magazine, charged $25 400 for the same full-page ad. Most of a magazine's revenue, some 70 per cent, comes from those advertisements. These Canadian-American split runs can offer cheaper rates because they ride on the money spent on the American publication. They don't have to pay a significant amount for their writers, editors or illustrators as, for the most part, that is paid for in the American run. The extra money the Canadian magazines charge for advertising comes from paying for Canadian writers, editors, illustrators and such. When people argue that there should be a "level playing field," with no government "interference," they speak not knowing that, as we have seen, there is no level playing field to begin with. The American side of the field is much higher because of their size and economic power. Government restriction would make the field more level, not less.

The American magazines were successful in obtaining the rights from the World Trade Organization to make split-runs. Canadian Heritage Minister Sheila Copps countered in December 1999 with the Canadian Magazine Fund, $150 million to be made available to Canadian-owned magazines having 80 per cent Canadian content. If this move does not prove effective, Canadian magazines will be muscled off the stands by more powerful American magazines. Fewer Canadian stories will be told, and of those that are, fewer will be written by Canadians. It could lead to other "cultural industries" being put in the same situation.

The aggressive attitude that at least some highly placed Americans have taken can be seen in former U.S. Trade Representative Charlene Barshefsky's comments:

> We cannot allow Canadian entities to use "culture" as an excuse to provide commercial advantages to Canadian products or to evict U.S. firms from the Canadian market.[1]

I agree with Peter C. Newman's opinion that the issue is not just about magazines; it is about how two different societies view their national cultures—one aggressively international, the other geared more toward national survival and understanding:

> To Americans, culture is their most successful export; they thrive on influencing the minds, fashions, manners and outlooks of a world tuned into their movies, television, clothes, books and heroes.
>
> Canadian culture is a far more subtle and fragile commodity, involving scattered truths about our past history, current hopes and future aspirations—about why we hold our ground in this cold land with empty horizons. . . . [I]ts many expressions—including Canadian magazines—must continue to find a market in order to give it voice and shape.[2]

Can Anything Be Done About It?
Canadian Content Rules and Government Involvement

One way of fighting this American arts domination is through government regulations requiring that Canadian content make up a fixed percentage of what is heard and seen on radio and television—30 per cent for the former and 50 per cent for the latter. Should we try this with movies as well, in order to increase the impact of Canadian content laws? There are complications involved. How do you define something as Canadian? How many Canadians involved make something Canadian rather than American or British? If a band had two Canadians and two Americans, does it qualify? A few years ago a Bryan Adams album was determined not to be Canadian because of the number of non-Canadians involved in the production. But then, Bryan might not have become the big star he is today if he hadn't had Canadian content rules to give his early material air play.

Sometimes artistically silly situations develop. A Toronto radio station was previewing a new U2 album. They could not play the whole CD in one hour because that would violate 30 per cent Canadian content rules. So, strangely, Canadian songs were intermixed among those of the U2 CD. The radio station had been burned the year before when it had aired a top 1000 greatest hits playlist and had to do the last 15 songs a day after the weekend was over, so as not to violate "the rules." On the other side of the coin, we see cynical stations that play Canadian tunes during the wee hours and the weekends when listenership is down, a practice referred to as the "beaver bin." "And, now, insomniacs, we have the all-Rita-McNeil hour."

There is a similar practice with television stations. The Canadian Radio-Television and Telecommunications Commission (CRTC) set the rule that during the "prime time" hours of six to midnight, there must be 50 per cent Canadian content. Both the two big private networks use what is called the "bookends" approach. They show news, which qualifies as Canadian content, from six to seven and eleven to midnight. Thus, they don't have to show much entertainment that is Canadian. In a recent study (valid for early 1997), during the crucial seven-to-eleven slot during weekdays, CTV showed only two hours of Canadian production out of a possible twenty, and Global showed five (three hours of which was hockey). The CBC had all but half an hour filled with Canadian content. No wonder that the former Minister of Heritage, Sheila Copps, suggested that Ottawa exclude television news and sports from the 50 per cent. The private networks responded to her suggestion by saying that they don't have the money to produce more Canadian content. In the words of Guy Maavera, CTV's programming vice-president:

> There isn't going to be more Canadian drama created as a result of that kind of change, because there isn't going to be any more money in the system for it. All we will be doing is giving up advertising revenue from American programs.[3]

One suggested way to increase the money spent on shows with Canadian content was for a cap to be put on the amounts that private Canadian broadcasters could bid for non-Canadian shows. The thinking was that it would free up money for those broadcasters to spend on Canadian prime-time shows. That suggestion was not implemented.

There is a significant amount of economic and political pressure brought to bear to reduce or eliminate Canadian content rules. We saw its effects when the cable networks took an American country music station out of the general package and substituted a Canadian one, which presented a higher percentage of Canadian country performers. The main sponsor for the American station, General Electric, was very upset, and made some pretty significant economic threats about what it might do if the American station was not returned to its former status.

Finally, a compromise was achieved. Both networks, Canadian and American, became part of the general cable package.

One further comment on Canadian content rules is needed. They do not guarantee that our stories are told, our voice is heard. Much that qualifies as Canadian content is what is termed "industrial Canadian." It qualifies as Canadian because of the number of Canadians hired, but the story it tells has really nothing to do with this country. Would you say that "X-Files," when it was filmed in British Columbia, made a Canadian statement? The same negative response would come concerning "F/X" and "Nikita," both of which were mostly American-clone, fashion-statement style with good-looking Australian stars, no Canadian substance.

Government is involved beyond making Canadian content rules. The federal government, through Telefilm Canada and the Cable Fund, invests something in the neighbourhood of $250 million a year to create independently produced Canadian TV movies and dramatic series. Then there is the CBC. In addition, the federal government and some provincial governments, including Ontario, provide production-investor tax relief and tax benefits for those who advertise on Canadian stations. Canadian-produced films and television shows have benefitted from such efforts. Export sales of Canadian-produced films and television programming in 1995 amounted to about $1.4 billion, a significant increase from earlier years. This gain could be threatened in the future by American political and economic pressure, and by moves made by the World Trade Organization to restrict "unfair trading practices."

The Problem of Attitude

Another part of the problem relates to our attitude. Many seem to feel that if a work is Canadian, then there is something wrong with it, that to be successful we have to copy what someone else does. One exception that we are proud of is the work of the Group of Seven, visual artists who are "very Canadian" in what they portray. But they too had to confront and overcome this attitude. A.Y. Jackson, one of the Group of Seven, when faced with severe criticism from Canadian critics, came up with some good advice in 1922:

> A little less skepticism regarding the work of our own artists and a little more towards a lot of foreign work which floods our market would seem a more intelligent attitude to take. The only things to be ashamed about in Canadian art are the scarcity of people who appreciate it, and the limited and obvious views that prevail as to what a work of art should be.[4]

The CEO of Alliance, a major Canadian film and TV producer (close your eyes and see the triangle that appears as their logo), spoke the words of the self-imposed Canadian anthem of defeat when he said:

> We don't make popcorn movies. . . . We have to stay out of the main-stream. Attempting to compete can only lead to failure because of what we are up against.[5]

It is wrong simply to U.S.-bash and cry in the one thing that remains Canadian—our beer. When something is given away, it can hardly be thought of as stolen. Americans have a strong sense of their own culture that has much to be admired. We should exhibit a similar passion. We can't blame them for wanting to shout out who they are, nor for their desire to "start spreading the word" (as it says in the song "New York, New York"). We could take a page from their book, or maybe their magazine, which may be the only kind of magazine we read soon.

Canadians involved with the arts often seem to think that Canada won't sell, either to Canadians or Americans. But think back to the 1980s, when Bob and Doug McKenzie, the hosers (my spell check now includes that word as well as toques) from the Great White North, with their toques, their back bacon and their beer, were so popular. (Now you remember another Canadian movie, *Strange Brew*.) Part of their success in Canada was not just the jokes, but that it felt so good to see something even remotely like ourselves on television. The "Red Green Show" has repeated that success with many of the same images. The popularity of both shows in the United States should convince us that Canadians showing Canada can sell.

We do have well-established traditions concerning songs about ourselves. One common feature among Canada's Native peoples was for people to own songs. You might receive a song in a vision, or have one presented to you as a precious gift that only you could sing. Angela Sydney, the last speaker of Tagish, gave her son returning from World War II the clan-owned song of a man who was lost for years at sea after being stranded on the ice while hunting seal. It was a song of return-ing back to the people after coming close to death. There were also death songs that would give you strength when you knew or suspected that you were going to die soon. Our whole landscape was filled with song when this was Native land only. Many, many rivers, rapids, lakes, hills, valleys and sacred spots were described in song. It helped to connect people with the land. Travel across that land now and there are few songs that sing to it.

The Atlantic provinces provide other examples. Living in Newfoundland, I discovered a rich heritage of songs about the people, their history and culture. I was raised on the down-home music of Don Messer and his Islanders on CBC, my mother being from Prince Edward Island. The first Canadian international star in country music, Hank Snow, would often sing of his "Nova Scotia Home."

Then there is Québec. There is no shortage of passionate songs about Québécois life, nor plays, nor movies, nor television shows. And we have had singing Canadian "cowboys" too, not afraid to sing about where they were from. Wilf Carter and Ian Tyson spring immediately to my mind. Let's hope that cowboy-hatted "New Country" stars Terri Clarke and Paul Brandt follow suit.

Perhaps other Canadian actors can follow Dan Ackroyd's lead. In January 1997, he played in a two-part mini-series about the Avro Arrow, an important Canadian story about the collapse of an ambitious fighter plane project during the late 1950s. He helped give the production star credibility when investors were looked for and did so for a third of his usual salary. It seems to me that he has set a standard by which other Canadian stars should be judged.

This does not mean that Canadians should tell only Canadian stories. Michael Ondaatje's enormously successful book *The English Patient* has British heroes and takes place in North Africa and Italy. It is important that Canadian writers have the freedom to tell such stories. Still, it felt good when I went to see the movie and heard key supporting characters say that they were from Montreal and when someone asked, "Is there anybody from Picton?" It was rather like seeing the face of someone you know on the TV screen.

What I am talking about is more than just hearing names of places and teams that are Canadian. It is about the Canadian voice. What is this? I've never heard a definition of "voice" that I like, but I know it is about a people's capacity to tell about who they are through TV, movies, books, magazines, music and art. When your voice is taken away from you, you cannot be heard, no one gets to hear your story. It is as if you don't exist.

Notes

[1] As cited in Marci McDonald's "Menacing Magazines," *Maclean's*, March 24, 1977, p. 54.

[2] Peter C. Newman, "The Canadian Dream Loses a Big Round," *Maclean's*, January 27, 1997, p. 56.

[3] As quoted in Sid Adilman's "TV Bosses Slam CanCon Ideas," *Toronto Star*, March 1, 1997, p. L5.

[4] Charles C. Hill, *The Group of Seven: Art for a Nation* (Ottawa: National Gallery of Canada in association with McLelland & Stewart, 1995), p. 134.

[5] As cited in Brian Johnson's "The Canadian Patient," *Maclean's*, March 24, 1997.

One More Time: Our Ongoing Dialogue with Popular Music

Ian Baird

The musician sat curled over his guitar, long brown fingers orbiting deftly atop the soundboard as if pulled by a force of gravity from the vibrating strings. A bottle of whiskey sat on the floor next to him and a fedora perched precariously on his head. As thick shrouds of cigarette smoke swirled around, people smacked their knees and thighs to the music, hooting and hollering and whistling. A couple of people got up and shuffled their feet, swirled their hips, twirled their bodies. Hard-working, dead-tired sharecroppers who were all gathered for a few hours of freedom and joy and laughter on a Saturday night in this small, rough-hewn room: the local juke joint. Maybe they'd get lucky in a card game tonight or get squeezed tight by a welcoming pair of limbs. They would listen to some soul-stirring or foot-stomping blues music: "Terraplane Blues," or "Preachin' Blues," or "Trouble in Mind." The musician shouted "have mercy!" with a deep, raspy laugh between songs, took a drink, and started into a new song, his fingers once again thrumming the guitar strings, his feet tapping against the worn hard floor.

Through the night and into the morning the bluesman sang and preached about trouble and the blues. He sang that trouble was a steady companion for the black man in the American South. He sang that sometimes life could become so gloomy, so lonesome, and so hard, that a person just did not know how to go on. Then he preached that if that person picked up a guitar and sang the blues and told the entire world how he had the blues, then maybe that person could get by for a just little bit longer. He sang:

> *Trouble in mind, I'm blue*
> *But I won't be blue always,*
> *'Cause the sun's gonna shine in my backdoor some day.*[1]

The music of the guitar twanged and the smell of whiskey and dance sweat filled the room. And for a time the listeners forgot about the pain of the past week in their backs and bones, the bitter hopelessness of poverty, the lashing brutality of racism. Until the next week when the cruel bossman and dire poverty and misfortune would come back for a long, long visit.

"Preachin' Blues": Popular Music and Its Dialogue with Religion

The scene described above might have taken place in any juke joint in the Mississippi Delta or in Texas or Louisiana in the 1920s or 30s or 40s. Many music historians say that the blues evolved out of a combination

---

"One More Time: Our Ongoing Dialogue with Popular Music" is by Ian Baird of the Humber College Institute of Technology and Advanced Learning. Used by permission.

of work hollers sung in the cotton fields and hymns sung in Protestant churches. Work hollers consisted of one group of slaves in a field calling out a musical phrase that was then answered by another group in an adjacent field. Named "call and response," this musical form was like a conversation connecting the different groups of workers in the fields. I will suggest in this article that popular music has pretty much done the same thing over the years: engaged in an ongoing, resonant dialogue with other forms of music, other musicians and audiences, and many other facets of human experience.

To begin, let us consider the intense spiritual character of the blues and how it created a fairly involved dialogue with religion in early 20th-century America. Like religion, the blues deals with things like sin, danger, hunger, fear, oppression and disaster. Back then, Black people could not really protect themselves from all these bad things—except in two ways. They could go to church on Sundays and go down on their knees and pray to God and ask Him to forgive their sins—but then they might have to wait until the next world for deliverance. Or they could go to the juke joint on a Saturday night and thumb their noses at bad luck and trouble and even the devil himself, and listen to a blues musician sing and preach the blues. Now the blues would not stop devastating floods or fires or the boweevil eating the cotton crop or the plantation owner taking away a sharecropper's wife. But it could make people feel a lot better, and unless they drank some bad whiskey or lost all their money at cards or got into a bad knife fight—they were not any worse off after a night at the juke joint than before.

The preachers, naturally, did not like it when people went to the juke joint at night because they spent all their money on whiskey and cards and sex and had none left Sunday morning for the collection plate. So they started calling the blues "devil music." There were other good reasons for this too, such as the church's opinion of many of the common topics of blues songs: fighting, guns, murder, crime, drunkenness, gambling and hoodoo (magic). But there always remained a strong if ambivalent link between the blues and gospel music, and between the juke joint and the church. A lot of the time it was the same musicians who played and sang both gospel and the blues. In the case of some blues musicians, like Skip James, their fathers were preachers, and some blues musicians even became preachers themselves.

For a Black person in the American South in the early 20th century, there were not a lot of choices to be made. There were not too many things he or she could do to alleviate injustice and suffering. African-Americans in those times could not vote, hold political office, go to college, or own a plantation or a store. But what they *could* do was pray and sing: anybody could pray and sing: because nobody could stop you from praying and singing unless they killed you. And if they did, someone else might sing about it later, like the great singer Billie Holliday did in the song, "Strange Fruit," about the horrors of lynching.

"Blue Suede Shoes": Popular Music and Its Dialogue with Class

French sociologist Pierre Bourdieu proposes that one of the main differences between the upper classes and the working classes is one of detachment from cultural experience: what he calls "distinction." "The detachment of the pure gaze," he argues, is an "active distance" attained from not having to provide for the necessities of life, from living a "life of ease."[2]

In music and in many other areas, the distinction Bourdieu is talking about is one of "taste." You either have good taste or you don't. Refinement and sophistication are the trademarks of distinction. And while it can be learned to a certain extent, mostly you must be raised in the "proper" environment to achieve it.

Equally important is the idea that, as a cultured person, one also remains "distinct" from the art one encounters. For a spectator, maintaining a "pure gaze" is extremely important. The eye of the "pure gaze" is refined but cool and unemotional, aloof, and even indifferent to the experience of art and culture. You never get your hands dirty and actually "touch" the art you are receiving.

With so-called "low culture," in contrast, you do the exact opposite. You engage extensively and intimately with the art or music you experience. That is why the working classes generally prefer art forms like music where you can use your whole body and get "down and dirty." You move your limbs, tap your feet, hum, sing and dance around. You experience the whole thing as direct and intense involvement.

In many senses, when listening to and experiencing popular music we actually *become* the music, taking it into our bodies and letting it course through our muscles and lungs and into the toes of our blue suede shoes. If opera glasses in a theatre box high up above the rabble are the symbol of upper-class distinction, then the mosh pit is the symbol of the working-class musical immediacy of the body.

One reason why the song "My Generation" by the Who was such a huge hit in the 1960s was because lead vocalist Roger Daltry not only sang about generational alienation, but also about youth seeking to find a voice in a very literal sense, which he dramatized through his violent stutter on the word "my" of the lyric "talkin' about my generation." He seemed hardly to be able to get the word out. This stuttering reflected the frustration of his powerlessness, of being silenced and having nothing to represent who he was. But when the word finally burst out of his mouth, it changed everything. Youth suddenly had a clear, strong voice and an identity and a means of expression.

The Who became famous for trashing their hotel rooms when they were on the road and for wrecking their expensive guitars on stage. This seemingly irrational destruction was related to the same kind of intense physical involvement with music. They were also thumbing their noses at our obsession with material possession. Naturally, the ne'er-do-wells and the wrong-side-of-the-tracks clique ate it all up—but so did hordes of middle-class kids from the trim lawns of suburban America.

Hip-hop and "gangsta" rap have a different but equally belligerent take on materialism. Hip-hop videos, with all their gold, cognac and expensive cars, constitute an impolite flaunting of "taste," to say the least. But there is more: all those flashing arms and hand signs and extreme close-ups of petulant, defiant black faces create a very physical kind of music and language (in rap, language has physical robustness that most regular lyrics lack) that gives those in power the heebie-jeebies. (Tattoos, belly rings and tongue piercings are also very physical engagements with culture.)

During the 60s, the Who, the Beatles and the Rolling Stones were all bands made up of British boys from working-class neighbourhoods. Ironically, rock stardom was all about not really working, about escaping work and the chains of the working class. The blue-collar dream of striking it rich through rock was not so much about breaking the bonds of class difference as taking them to their extreme and riding them all the way to fame and fortune.

In North America a similar phenomenon occurred, but here a somewhat different genre of blue-collar rock emerged. Singers like Bob Seger, Bruce Springsteen, John Mellancamp, Joe Walsh and even Canada's own Neil Young sang anthems of the working man, the small-town man, the farming man: he was "like a rock," "born in the U.S.A.," in a "small town," taking the "Rocky Mountain way," driving "an Econoline." Popular music in general has always had its ties to the working man and working woman. Even back hundreds of years ago when princes and archdukes hired musicians as servants to write music for the glory of their courts, musicians (sometimes the very same ones) were also in the streets, playing the music of the taverns and street corners and singing about the needs and urges of the emotional and physical self. One might say that for a long time there has been a touch of rebellion, with or without a cause, in many forms of popular music and in many centuries of singing about getting "no satisfaction."

And like the blues did on the plantations of the Delta close to a hundred years before, in the 1980s and 90s, hip-hop and rap emerged from the trouble of inner-city America, where trouble now came in the form of dire poverty, hunger, violence, drug addiction, lack of education and disease. Private desperation and individual tragedy became transformed into collective experience as musicians yet again filled the role of giving a voice to people visited by trouble in all its guises. Rap musicians like Public Enemy, Ice-T and Ice Cube inspired young African-Americans who were "used, abused without clues" to become politically active and, like "hoochie-coochie man" Muddy Waters in Chicago decades earlier, stressed that "brothers of the same mind" were "here" and ready to "mess with you" in order to have their voices heard. Later, rap musicians like Tupac Shakur, Snoop Dogg and Biggy Smallz would continue to express to new generations of black and white listeners in musical and lyrical terms the effort it took to survive and rise above a drive-by adolescence spent in inner-city ghettos.

Over time the early political activism of rap's origins has given way to an infatuation with the trappings of materialism. Enjoying the current heady days of extreme wealth and mainstream success, today's rap musicians are concerned less with resistance and more with marketing "street cred" to the huge white audiences who download hip-hop music in digital droves and buy baggy bundles of hip-hop clothing at middle-class suburban malls. But this change—this move into "da club," as 50 Cent puts it—is perhaps not entirely a sell-out. Just like political revolution, abundance for the disadvantaged has been a long-time transcultural symbol of giving the bird to "the breaks," no matter how fleeting or momentary that abundance may ultimately be. So despite the bling-bling and bluster of a 50 Cent or an Eminem, "don't believe the hype," necessarily.

"Thunder Road": Popular Music and Its Dialogue with Time and Space

By its very makeup, music is about time. Its very identity is time: tracks, beats, measures, rhythms, whole notes, quarter notes, sixteenth notes. Music is also about the time it takes to experience it and when in time we listen to it: Sunday morning hymns, the Friday Sabbath cantor, the morning call to prayer from the minaret; Saturday night in the juke joint, the local pub, the corner bar, the nightclub, or standing in line all night to get tickets to a concert by the Next Big Thing; conversely, Saturday night at the opera, or the symphony, or using your Gold Visa card over your cell phone to buy front-row tickets to a Broadway show.

We have music during the times of weddings, funerals, births, first communion parties and bar mitzvahs; Christmas, Ramadan, Diwali, Chinese New Year, Canada Day, potlatches and rain dances. We listen to Sesame Street when we're young, the Rat Pack when we're old. Music is cool, hip, hot, a new release, top forty, cutting edge, groundbreaking. Or it's old, retro, remastered, re-released, nostalgic, classic.

But that is not all. Music is about space too. About strings on guitars being physically bent to create the blue notes out of the Western scale: the flatted 3rd, 5th and 7th steps of the scale. About, too, walls of amplified sound, Hammond organs, fuzz pedals, tremolo bars, synthesizer racks, double bass drums, Hendrix's white Stratocaster, turntables, Midi cables, MP3 and WAV files: all examples of music as physical space (huge or minuscule).

Moreover, we expect to hear music in different places. Indeed, place has been as crucial an element as any in the development of music. There is music for the campfire, the temple, the chapel; different music for the tavern, the pub, the town square; different music again for the palace, the court and the concert hall.

When music changes in terms of time, space or place, it changes its musical language as well. Its response to a musical "call" is a response that is contained within it own time and space while still responding to other times and spaces. It speaks with its own unique voice, but in answer to a chorus of other voices over other times, spaces and places. Music in history is music that changes, develops, evolves, goes forward and backward. But it is always in conversation with the music and musicians who have come before.

Look at the blues. It began in the Deep South, in the fields and then the juke joints, at crossroads and on dusty highways. Then it took a train up to the north and moved onto the killing floors of the Chicago slaughterhouses and into the noisy, smoke-filled bars of the South Side. Crowds grew bigger, the drinking got heavier, knives were exchanged for guns and the noises of the night grew louder and more varied. So the blues musicians started using electric guitars and sped up the music. They still used the same 12-bar pattern derived from Christian hymns and the AAB pattern derived from the work hollers, but now they consistently added drums and bass all the time. Bluesmen like Muddy Waters and Willie Dixon simplified the lyrics and the range of song themes so people didn't have to listen as hard or stay sober enough to remember them.

And the speeded-up blues travelled everywhere across America and was whitewashed and sequined up and taken into white dance halls and performed by white musicians. Now they simply called it rock and roll: Bill Hailey and the Comets, Buddy Holly, Elvis Presley.

The new media of radio and television made the music ever-present. Kids listened to "Top 40" tunes on transistor radios and carried them to the beach, school, and the cottage. Television brought Beatlemania and Jim Morrison lighting his fire into our living rooms on Sunday nights. And perhaps as representative as any development in the coming of age of rock and roll in the 1950s and 60s, popular music came into our cars. There were songs about cars, tunes specifically written to be listened to in cars: low-ridin', chicken-playin', hot-roddin', pedal-to-the-metal music. Let the rich listen in their elegant salons and concert halls: "born to run," working-class youth would take their music for a ride onto the "thunder roads" of America.

But still the blues did not stop moving. It boarded a plane and flew to England and aspiring English musicians such as Eric Clapton, Keith Richards and Eric Burden crowded around blues legends such as Muddy Waters and Sonny Boy Williamson. Musicians who, according to Sonny Boy, "wanted to play the blues so bad and played it SO bad!"

Blues was wedded with the power rock of distortion pedals and amplifier stacks. It became hard rock or acid rock. Jimi Hendrix electrified England, and power groups like Cream and Led Zeppelin took the airwaves by storm. Then, as blues and rock and roll met again at the crossroads at the midnight hour, heavy metal was spawned. A cartoonish, *Tales-from-the-Crypt* comic book version of the blues, the music of Black Sabbath and Judas Priest nonetheless harkened back to the hellhounds and devils of blues singers such as Robert Johnson and Skip James. Bands such as Metallica, Slayer, Slipknot and Queens of the Stone Age followed over the coming decades.

Stadium rock bands and hair bands, on the other hand, simply added eyeliner and hairspray to rock and roll and the blues in the 1980s. The themes of songs—once reflective of the pain of injustice, misfortune and poverty—now often became trite, narrow and flattened out. So too did the music: repetitive, unimaginative, overproduced and designed more to provide photo ops for through-the-air-leaping, longhaired lead singers in tight leather pants. Politicized music about suffering and injustice now became self-indulgent, sexualized music about lust and infidelity. Oh well, the same thing happened to the blues in Chicago in the 1950s and then to rap in Hollywood during the 1990s.

Rock and roll went into the recording studio and further new sounds emerged. Live music became one thing, studio albums something else.

While bands like the Grateful Dead steadfastly stuck to the road and concentrated on their distinctive live shows (retinues of Deadheads following along), producer George Martin re-engineered the post–*Sgt. Pepper* Beatles as the purveyors of multi-track electronic and orchestral studio wizardry and Ravi Shanker-influenced canned musical mysticism. Some bands in the 70s did both—for example, Pink Floyd and Emerson Lake and Palmer, with their huge shows and highly produced studio albums. Later, DJs would continue an extended conversation with live and studio music by mixing and remixing past, present and future.

There were conversations and often arguments that arose between North and South (Neil Young and Lynyrd Skynyrd regarding the southern men of Alabama), or East and West. Even before the hip-hop battle between Biggy Smallz and Tupac Shakur ended in the deaths of both, there was Woodstock versus Altamont in 1969. The children of the Age of Aquarius tumbled about a huge anthill in New York State celebrating free love, rock and roll, and hallucinogenic wonderment. A few months later an edgy, petulant, nasty crowd at the Altamont Speedway in California erupted into violence that ended in death while the Rolling Stones performed.

Then MTV came on the scene like a strident interior designer wired on cocaine and began wallpapering musical sound as visual candy. Video changed how music was not only heard, but also written and produced. Today the virtual spaces of the Internet and digital downloads are rewriting the face of music yet again. Is the old-fashioned record store soon going to experience its final death throes?

Just as the physical experience of popular music is of huge importance to its character and role, time and space are crucial to anyone's engagement with popular music of every kind. Whether sacred or profane, lofty or lowly, passed on as manna from heaven or bubbling up from the sewers, popular music is something we feel in our bones as it travels around us in the very air we breathe.

"Where the Streets Have No Name":
Popular Music and Its Dialogue with Freedom

As Clive Cockerton points out in "Serious Pleasure: The Role of the Arts," the Greek philosopher Plato thought that art was corrupting. The ancient Greeks believed that music, being mathematical, was generally a little better than other forms of art, but when it got people going physically—singing, dancing, shaking their booties so to speak—thinkers like Plato despised it too. Music then became too sensual and irrational. Popular music was a drug for the masses, a placebo, a way of keeping everyone under the thumb of tyranny. Just give people a little rock and roll and everything will be fine.

And that is the question, is it not? Did rock and roll actually liberate youth in the 50s, challenge the conformity of suburbia and confront the atomic juggernaut of the cold war? Or was it instead just about working class kids in blue suede shoes being neatly packed away in a 45-rpm vinyl warehouse of the status quo? Elvis as hip-grinding rebel; but Elvis too as soldier boy and good-ol' boy: Sequins R Us, God Bless America and I'm all shnooked up.

The rebellious spirit seemed to grow more defined and focused during the 1960s. Rock and roll became idealistic and politically activated; a new age seemed right around the corner. The Establishment was already tottering on its corrupt foundations. So what happened then? Did rock and roll simply sell out? At Woodstock, for example, the Aquarian dream seemed to sparkle vibrantly, yet at the same time to be on the eve of its own destruction. Despite the earnestness of the words and music of protest, the helicopters that flew in artists like Joplin sounded (whup, whup, whup, whup) eerily like those taking working-class boys and Black boys to their deaths in the Vietnam War. Meanwhile, the ubiquitous sound towers that emerged like giants from among the sea of bodies resembled the guard towers of the coming explosion of the American industrial-prison complex in the 1980s during the "war on drugs."

So—one more time—was rock and roll a new vision, a talisman of freedom that 60s rockers could wear with their beads, their long hair and the flags they sewed onto their Levis? Or were these rock music fans all just dupes, the blind slaves of the record company bosses, the easy riding politicians who were laughing all the way to the bank? In the same vein, is rap today still truly about resistance and black identity, or is it simply about selling overpriced basketball shoes and clothing and showing off your bling-bling?

Either way, it seems to be clear that one of the main roles that popular music plays is that of transgression: of crossing boundaries, testing limits. Whether it be the "princes of darkness" of heavy metal, androgynous stars like Michael Jackson or Marilyn Manson or the "gangstas" of hip hop, musicians often take on the task of pushing a particular society's standards to the margins of acceptability.

Indeed, in many cultures, musicians have traditionally fulfilled the role of the trickster—a figure who says one thing and means another, who frequently disguises his true meaning behind a false pose. The bluesman was equal parts saint and sinner, and you never really knew which role

he would be playing at any given time. He could make you lose your soul one night and then he could turn around and hand it right back to you all polished up, squeaky clean and as good as new the very next day. This was a special kind of power: the freedom to change things, most of all the self.

Without the ambiguity of the trickster, the troubling inconsistencies of a Robert Johnson, John Lennon, Kurt Cobain, Madonna or Tupac Shakur, perhaps we would never see beyond the ordinary, the mundane, the dry indifference of official "taste." The very fact that we do not know their intentions, their meaning, their relevance *for sure* is the one thing that keeps us always questioning, and keeps our engagement and dialogue with music open and unfixed, and consequently, at least some-what democratic.

Transgressing norms, conventions and social propriety is necessary in any culture that strives to entertain freedom and resist domination. Transgression is essential to any idea of change, of redefining bound-aries, of understanding difference and of recognizing multiple levels of meaning. Without transgression we simply do not know where we stand or who we are. The powers that be might give us Eden, and it might very well be perfection, but knowing nothing of our nakedness limits the depth of our collective experience.

At the other end of the scale, transgression can simply become a bad cartoon, breaking rules for its own sake, destroying meaning and value because everything becomes permissible and there remains no sense of the reason for transgressing to begin with. When transgression becomes the standard and the law, then it devolves into the conformity of debauchery and violence: Woodstock becomes Altamont, John Lennon becomes Charles Manson. Worse, in the final analysis, transgression may actually work to bolster the status quo by making money for capitalism and distracting its audience from the real political issues of freedom and human rights in favour of a little titillation and some bling-bling.

The price of popular music is its very populism, which has been a tool for tyrants since ancient times. But it may be the price we have to pay for the not insignificant possibilities for an open society that the experience of popular music offers. The primarily uncertain and un-official status of popular music is also its main means of disturbing the status quo, of offering at least some alternatives to the conventional and often unjust activities of the powers that be. Moreover, it cannot be forgotten that true innovation in popular music has always emerged from the unpredictable margins and never from the overproduced, controlled and controlling centre, even if these innovations are hijacked and appropriated later on. And the rock-and-roll activism of the 60s is certainly not dead. Groups like Public Enemy, U2 and Rage Against the Machine have been powerfully engaged with politics and justice. Trickster as rock star does not always mean self-absorbed rogue with no interest in the rest of the world. That role is just as likely to be filled by the disengaged elitist art collector as by any rule-breaking, profanity-spewing, trash-talking rapper.

So perhaps the answer to all of the above questions is a very tricksterly yes, yes, yes, and yes again. Popular music simply contains both the "good" *and* the "bad" (and sometimes the plain "butt ugly") in its calls and responses. That is the very characteristic and value of dialogue as a demo-cratic principle: its openness to a variety of responses means that we can never entirely predict or control the responses we might elicit over time and space. On the one hand, popular music gives voice to the marginal-ized, validates the emotion and the body, raises the spirits of all and encourages dialogue between the past and the present, between black and white, north, south, east, and west. On the other hand, it lowers the bar, encourages mediocrity, validates appearances in place of substance, incites gratuitous violence, promotes ignorance and inhibits tolerance. But in the end, popular music simply just IS, in all its mishmash, and in all its extremes, from aspiring to sublime, liberating visions to choking to death on its own vomit (a final pastime of many a rock star).

To ask popular music always to give us the same response, whether marvellous or ludicrous, is simply asking too much of it. Popular music responds to our changing calls and, as such, it is as brilliant and dreary as we are at any given time and shares our good points equally with our failings. And perhaps that is not such a bad quality for a cultural form that has the potential to express so fully our diverse, uncertain and all-too-human condition.

Notes

[1] R.M. Jones, "Trouble in Mind," MCA Music, a Division of MCA Inc., ASCAP.

[2] Pierre Bourdieu, *Distinction: A Social Critique of the Judgement of Taste* (London: Routledge, 1984).

Serious Pleasure: The Role of the Arts

Clive Cockerton

In many people's eyes, the arts are the toy department of life—occasionally amusing, perhaps, but in the long run a waste of time for men and women of action and purpose. The Greek philosopher Plato (427–347 BCE) argued that art was a distraction we would be better off without. According to Plato, art was a distraction for the following reasons:

1. Art deals with images, not truth; it doesn't advance knowledge, it doesn't discover anything, it only seems to understand.

2. Art imitates reality; to learn about reality it is much better to study reality itself rather than a pale imitation.

3. Art is sensual and distracts us from the more important quests (such as moral or spiritual quests). In its arousal of basic instincts, in its stimulation/simulation of violence and lust, it is anarchic, a force for disorder in the community.

In short—empty, imitative and corrupting.

Since Plato, many moralists have branched off from these arguments and urged us to consider that bright colour and decoration are immoral because they call attention to the self instead of singing the praises of God, or that "realistic" novels were too shocking for the delicate sensibilities of young women, or that rock 'n' roll would corrupt and deprave youth with its primitive rhythms. At a much less passionate level, many business people are skeptical of the arts, except where they can be trained to serve the purpose of promoting consumption of goods and services in advertising. Politicians frequently see the arts as "frills," and in a time of recession the artistic community is the first to feel the cuts of government support. All of these views, whether held by philosophers, moralists, business people or politicians, have in common the conviction that art is not serious.

This doesn't mean that the effects of art can't be serious. Plato was concerned that literature and art were disruptive and corrupting. Stories need sinners to be interesting. Tales of people who always do the right thing are predictable, preachy and boring. Yet stories that embrace all that

"Serious Pleasure: The Role of the Arts" is by Clive Cockerton of the Humber College Institute of Technology and Advanced Learning. Used by permission.

is human, the sinners as well as the saints, compel us to accept the humanity of those who lie, cheat, betray, of those who are greedy, lustful and cruel. Not just accept the humanity of others, but also recognize those very qualities in ourselves. Moralists worry that this recognition and acceptance are subversive and undermine moral authority. Whenever we encounter an argument that says that a certain film or type of music will inflame or deprave, or that violence on TV will lead to violent children, we are dealing with an offshoot of Plato's original concern.

Aristotle, a student of Plato, developed a counter-argument that suggested that the symbolic experience of violence in the arts was actually helpful and worked like a safety valve for our violent sides. Through the emotion raised in watching a story unfold, we achieve *catharsis*, a cleansing and purging of destructive emotion in a safe and contained way. For Aristotle, nothing was to be gained from denying our destructive urges. Indeed, the opportunity to face our sometimes violent and immoral nature in a story lessened the threat that our urges might become reality. In other words, when watching a violent and terrifying story, we rehearse the emotion along with the actors and are released from having to act it out. However, recent psychological tests on children exposed to violent television suggest that some harmful results do occur. There's no simple, mechanical process whereby children watch violent acts and then always re-enact them. It's a more subtle process of shifting the atmosphere, of weakening the inhibition to violence that over time can result in changed behaviour. However, Aristotle couldn't predict Saturday morning TV and its impact on children. His insights were an attempt to describe adult responses to serious drama, and they remain useful as reflections on how the adult mind responds. Even adults have terrors and nightmares, and the arts enable us to face what horrifies us and move beyond it as well.

But can art have a harmful impact on sane, responsible adults? Recently, the Canadian legal system seemed to be saying that citizens needed to be protected from their own reactions when it seized paintings by Eli Langer of children in potentially sexual positions. This action was curiously directed at the paintings themselves rather than at the painter. The clear suggestion is that some subject matter cannot be explored, a suggestion that most artists would resist. Society clearly has interests at stake, and probably should find ways to protect itself from exploitation of sensational subject matter, but there is a great deal of difference between the sleazy exploitation of the pornographer and the serious exploration of the artist. The courts, however, have not found a reliable way of measuring that difference. Should the failure of the courts and the anxieties of moralists keep us from discussing controversial subjects? Is the danger from the arts real? As Plato writes:

> Much is at stake, more than most people suppose; it is a choice between becoming a good man or a bad; poetry, no more than wealth or power or honours, poetry can tempt us to be careless of justice and virtue. (*The Republic*)

Although Plato refers to poetry here, this fear of temptation would apply equally to other arts, because the seductive power of all arts threatens the rule of reason. Elsewhere, Plato argues that drama

> waters the growth of passions which should be allowed to wither away and sets them up in control although the goodness and happiness of our lives depend on their being held in subjection.

This idea may seem exaggerated and extreme to a modern audience, but for Plato our happiness depended on leading a good life, and a good life depended on control of the emotions by reason.

Plato's second objection, that art imitates reality, reflects his concern that we could be deceived by the distortions and exaggerations of the story-telling process. Put crudely, a film such as *Disclosure*, which presents the story of a man who is sexually harassed by his female employer, however worthwhile the story may be in artistic terms, could lead the viewer to gross misperceptions about the nature of sexual harassment and power in the workplace. Clearly, the social reality has been that men have been the dominant gender in terms of business power and are far more likely to harass employees than women. Yet the fictional story may be compelling because it touches our emotions or thrills us, and we may be tempted to think of the film as a realistic and likely representation of what really goes on in business. The reality becomes apparent when we think about it, but for Plato we are always in danger when we succumb to the pleasurable pull of a story that could lead us down a rhetorical path to error. Of course, we are all aware and a little bit wary of the common lies of film—the couple overcoming all obstacles to their love and riding off into the sunset and the hero triumphing against seemingly impossible odds. However, the creators of these stories could defend their stories by saying that they don't have to be likely, just plausible, and that the preference for heroic triumph over dismal failure is an understandable and universal audience choice.

My favourite distortion is the glaring omission that very few characters in film worry about who pays, and no screen time is consumed with the

Scene from *Disclosure*

practical issues of getting and saving money that take up so much time in the actual world. Writers and filmmakers could respond that all stories necessarily involve compression, and that compression involves eliminating superfluous detail, leaving the essential story to stand out boldly, without being submerged in the minute and tedious chores of everyday life. I'm just not sure that our relationship to money is always so inessential.

Perhaps Plato's most intellectually interesting objection is the first one—that art involves an inevitable illusion. What we see in film is not reality; when we read fiction, we enter a world that is entirely made up. For Plato, the fact that we see images and enter into fantasy worlds means that we are turning away from truth. After reading a novel, can we say we know anything about the real world? We may think we know something of the human situation described in the plot of the novel, but have we acquired any verifiable concepts, as we might have if we had read a psychology textbook instead?

Well, perhaps not verifiable in the same controlled, scientific, experimental way, and maybe not full-blown concepts, but I would argue that, yes, novels provide us with genuine insights into human behaviour and situations. And these insights are verifiable, at least in a comparative way. When we finish a novel, we compare the truth of what we have read with our experience of the truth. In this way, every reading is some kind of experiment, some kind of verification. The fact that Hamlet or Falstaff are made-up characters in Shakespeare's plays does not prevent us from learning a great deal about ourselves and other people from them. They may be literally non-existent, but it makes no sense to refer to them in this way because their creation enriches our understanding of the real. So, too, does the imaginative testing of possibilities involved in any serious novel. And since every testing of fictional possibilities is verified or rejected by every reader, novels that are read and endorsed by many readers probably have a lot to say to us. Perhaps novels are the most insightful artistic medium, but surely the same comparative experience operates with certain kinds of realistic film. In *American Beauty*, for instance, the film clearly tries to capture something of the mood of suburban North America. The audience naturally compares its own attitudes to the attitudes toward money, work, family and sexuality depicted in the film and almost immediately looks for answers to some interesting questions. Is the film credible? Does it fit with my own experience, or is it at least plausible, given the fictional characters and situation? When we see a film that affects us, we reflect on what we have seen, we search for verification in our own lives.

We experience stories as we experience the world—from a perspective, a point of view that is both emotional and rational. Plato was wary of our emotional natures; he believed that they were not to be denied perhaps, but kept in strict control. In our day, despite the enormous success of science, we generally don't experience life as detached observers. Indeed, detachment seems too clinical, and the perspective of the scientist lacks the engagement with experience that a fulfilled life seems to require. Instead we grope about through our lives, using bits of knowledge and lots of emotion in a constantly shifting understanding—as we do in novels. We discover that emotion can be as reliable a guide to right conduct and behaviour as ideas and concepts. Some actions just don't feel right. Others, despite what we might have been taught to believe, feel liberating and joyful. Literature helps us to feel more acutely and generously as it guides us through the ever-expanding repertoire of human situations contained in its pages. It involves a passionate way of knowing, different from, but not inferior to, the relentless rationality of the philosopher or the precise observation of the scientist.

Still, literature is the most intellectual art form. Ideas are undeniably present in great works; even if they are never explicitly described, or talked about, they hover in the background. The consequences of ideas are revealed, are shown to be valuable or not, but not directly in argument form. Ideas are produced by scientists, philosophers, academics, by all of us. It is in literature that ideas are given flesh, tested not in debate, but in a re-creation of life. The cold, abstract and theoretical position is abandoned and replaced with a vantage point that is passionately considered and grounded in particular lives. As the philosopher Lorraine Code writes:

> The claim that literature is a source of knowledge rests upon a belief in the value of understanding the particular. It implies that a minute and inward understanding of particulars has the capacity to go beyond itself, to show something more general . . . (*Epistemic Responsibility*)

Why do some particular characters' lives seem to speak to all of us, when clearly not all of our lives resemble the particular character? The writer creates an image of human complexity that draws us into the fictional world, convinces us of its reality and at the same time throws light onto the real world. Theoretical understanding may be an essential element to knowledge, but unless it is grounded in the particular, theoretical understanding seems bloodless. *The Insider* examines a number of complicated issues such as the ethics of whistle-blowing, corporate control of the media and the compromises people face in the workplace. The narrative of *The Insider* takes us inside these complicated legal and ethical issues by presenting it as personal experience, thereby making it intimate. And it is precisely this intimate knowledge that might elude a purely historical perspective.

The great American poet Wallace Stevens wrote a poem whose title, "Not Ideas about the Thing, but the Thing Itself," contains the ambition most writers have to deliver directly an intimate understanding of the world. For this intimacy to be achieved, characters can't just be mouthpieces of ideas or virtues, but instead must convince us of their full individuality and their real humanity. Our lives are shaped by diverse combinations of ideas and experience, whether we are conscious of them or not. Fiction provides a means of becoming more conscious, of constantly examining and testing these ideas and experiences. Through this fictional process, we learn which ideas are useful, not just as ideas but as guiding principles.

When we read a novel, we may come to know a situation or a character very well; indeed, we may know all the significant details about a person's life (thoughts as well as actions). It's possible to know fictional characters better than our close friends. By providing us with all the information we need and by coming to a conclusion, novels present a complete vision. This completeness necessarily lacks some of life's random quality. Novels conclude, life goes on. By concluding, novels ask us to stop and think. By focusing on some of the most fundamental issues (growth, independence, love, pain, death) that we encounter in the real world, novels ask us to reflect on our own lives. But they don't just ask: they seduce us with pleasure, with worlds spun from word-magic. They extend the promise of intimacy, they leave us with insight.

Whenever it occurs, the combination of pleasure, beauty and insight is life-affirming. While pleasure and beauty are frequently found on the shimmering surface of art—in the form of delight in a turn of phrase or in intensity of vision—the insight cuts to the heart of issues, toward a deeper understanding of people and human experience. The answer to Plato's desire to rid his world of art lies in the value of pleasure and insight to the individual reader and viewer. Rather than being opposed to the quest for a rational life, perhaps the arts are complementary to it, providing a testing board for the different ideas that call out to us. At any rate, art's value doesn't stop with beneficial experiences for the individual, but extends to a community. Indeed, the shared experience of art helps to create a sense of community. Many cold winds blow through an individual's life, but the arts tell you that you're not alone, that others have cried as hard, laughed as loudly and loved as deeply. There's pleasure in that—in the community with others that the arts magically bring to us. Serious pleasure.

Objectivity and Subjectivity

Clive Cockerton

When we attempt to choose a movie for Saturday night, we might begin by poring over the newspaper, scanning the listings, reading the reviews. This film is an "absolute delight," that film is "irresistible," this one "touching and sensitive." Choices, choices. How does one sort the good from the bad in such a list? Add to the questions of the intrinsic worth of the film the problem of the individual's mood. Sometimes "touching and sensitive" just doesn't stand a chance against "frivolous and fun."

In fact, most of the decisions we might make when choosing a film are subjective. After all, how can one effectively compare a musical to a thriller except on the basis of how one feels at the moment? In choosing a film we make decisions based on content that is suitable to our mood and a faith that the form of the film will measure up to its content. Once we have seen the film, however, we usually wish to weigh the success of our choice. Our conclusions usually fall into two categories:

1. "I really like the film because..."

2. "That is a good film because..."

These statements are really very different from each other: the first statement records a *subjective preference* while the second attempts an *objective evaluation*. Preference tends to be more content-oriented, as in, "I really liked the ending," or "It was a great love story," while attempts to prove the worth of the film tend to be more form-oriented, as in, "The photography was beautiful" or "The pace was exciting."

For most of us, whether or not we like a film is much more important than whether the film is any good. As well, it is clearly possible to like a film we know we cannot defend as a good film. Our preference may be formed because of the presence of a favourite actor, a locale such as Africa or New York that fascinates us, or moments such as steamy love scenes or violent car chases that we find irresistible. The presence of these elements in no way forms a criterion for excellence, and the absence of these elements does not indicate a bad film. Indeed,

"Objectivity and Subjectivity" is by Clive Cockerton of the Humber College Institute of Technology and Advanced Learning. Used by permission.

our preference for these elements declares a lot about ourselves and our own feelings, but says virtually nothing about the film. As well, it is quite possible to dislike a film that we know fulfills all the requirements of a good film for strictly personal reasons, such as the fact that the film reminds us of unpleasant or painful moments in our own lives.

Although there is clearly no possibility of argument or contradiction regarding personal feelings about an art object (they just simply are what they are), it is also clear that we can change our minds about works of art. A painting can look shapeless and disorganized to us until someone more expert reveals a previously overlooked organizing principle. A novel can sometimes seem obscure and difficult until we become familiar with its language and worldview. We might condemn a film as confusing and subsequently read an interview with the director in which he states that he wants his audience to feel confused. If the film achieves its aim, how can we condemn it? These examples happen frequently and point to the fact that proper artistic evaluation is more than just a subjective statement about our perspective at the moment. It is not simply a case of thinking one thing on Monday and another on Friday. We replace the first view with the second because we think that the second view more accurately and objectively describes the art. It is as if at first glance we perceive a frog, but after consultation with experts we begin to discern the prince hiding within. Of course, there are many more frogs than princes, and we are more frequently deceived by art works that initially seem good but over time don't stand up to close examination.

Experts attempt to engage our minds in the task of analyzing the aesthetic emotion. They teach us to analyze the art work, to look separately at its elements, and to establish standards or criteria by which to evaluate the elements. The use of this largely mental process can help us to understand more about the art work independent of our own subjective bias. Aristotle identified three criteria based on his study of Greek poetry and drama: unity, clarity and integrity. Unity (of mood, of time and place among others) as a criterion didn't have the longevity of the other two: Aristotle couldn't anticipate the successful mixing of comic and tragic mood that would take place in Shakespeare's plays and other later works. However, clarity of expression seems as useful a standard by which to judge as any. Integrity, in the relationship of the parts of the play or poem to the whole and in the relationship of the whole to reality, forms the basis of much critical judgement. If we substitute simplicity of design, or perhaps more appropriately, focus for the concept of unity, we have a starting point in our discussion of criteria.

However, in our search for objective criteria by which to judge art objects, it must be admitted that no criteria will work for all art objects. We praise the playful fantasy in the paintings of Henri Rousseau, yet we do not condemn the paintings of Edvard Munch for lacking that quality; indeed, we praise Munch for his graphic rendering of inner torment. We appreciate one novel's realistic depiction of character and delight in another's cartoon-like parodies. We appreciate the grim honesty of films like *Trainspotting* and at the same time are charmed by the simple beauty of films like *The Black Stallion*. Yet on occasion films displaying "simple beauty" or "grim honesty" lack other qualities, and we find them unsatisfactory. The fact that no one criterion or element guarantees a work's value makes the job of appraisal that much more difficult. One thing is clear: On different occasions we judge by different criteria. Moreover, the skilled and open-minded consumer of art lets the individual work of art dictate the criteria by which it is to be judged.

Some contemporary critics suggest that in a modern consumer society we are so overwhelmed with artistic experiences and images that the task of sorting them into piles of good and bad is a hopeless one. These critics see a rough equality of banality in all objects, and find that wit and beauty come from the perspective of the audience, and are not necessarily contained in the art. It is how you see a TV program, for instance, not the TV program itself that makes the experience lively and intelligent or dull and stupid. Some of these critics would go so far as to say that a book has no meaning by itself, that an unread book is a vacuum, and that the reader is the one who provides the meaning. Since every reader's experience is shaped by their gender, their class and cultural background, there can be no universal objective meaning, only a collection of diverse and subjective impressions. As one critic, Frank Lentricchia, writes of his relationship to literature:

> I come to the text with specific hangups, obsessions, worries, and I remake the text, in a sense, for me, for my times. . . . The moment you start talking about it, you have injected interpretation. The text is not speaking; you are speaking for the text. You activate the text.

Still other critics focus on the possibility of consensus (among informed observers) operating as a kind of objectivity. This agreement by experts operates as a kind of "rough guide" to truth. However, these "agreements by experts" do not always have the shelf life that one would expect. It is clear that some art works do not seem to travel well from one historical period to the next. The novels of Sir Walter Scott (*Ivanhoe*, *The Heart of Midlothian*) were extremely popular in the nineteenth century and are hardly read today. In the last hundred years, the literary reputation of Ernest Hemingway was extraordinarily high in the '20s and '30s, but today Hemingway is more often seen as an interesting but minor writer.

One historical period may form an aesthetic preference for certain artistic qualities, preferring, for instance, clean and simple elegance to the previous generation's taste for exuberant and stylized decoration. When watching old films on television, we can be initially struck by what now seems bizarre fashion and style. Our experience of these films can be even more seriously undermined by outmoded attitudes, particularly sexist and racist ones. Everything that has happened to form our present consciousness stands as an obstacle to the appreciation of these films.

Even within an historical period, critics sometimes disagree about the value of an individual work. Recently, films such as *Titanic*, *Gladiator*, *The Passion of the Christ* and *Erin Brockovich* have received very diverse reviews. All the critics may agree, for instance, that pace in editing and structure is a very important element in a film's success. They may all agree that pace is a problem in any particular film. But some critics will find that the other elements of the film compensate for the weakness in pace and will give the film an overall high evaluation. Some of the disagreement can be explained by the fact that, despite agreement in theory on the importance of pace, in practice many critics habitually weigh some criteria more than others. Therefore, those critics who

Scene from *Gladiator*, 2000

regard editing as the most essential creative act in film will habitually favour films that possess skillful editing in spite of other problems that may exist in the film. Other critics may habitually value elements of script, acting or cinematography more highly than editing and refuse to accept that the obvious virtues in editing make up for the perceived weakness in acting. When a preference is habitual, we can be pretty sure that its origin is rooted deeply in our own personality and experience.

In spite of the effort of art critics to focus on the art rather than themselves, to analyze and evaluate the elements of art rather than narrate their own experiences, it remains obvious that elements of personality can't always be transcended. Perhaps the relationship between art and our experience of art is circular. The more we possess the inner experience, the more we grow curious about that external art object. The more we learn about art, the more we learn about what makes us who we are. That moment on Saturday night when the theatre goes dark, we watch the slowly brightening screen and wonder what this film world will be like. At the end of the film, if we have been moved by the film, our natural instinct is to be quiet, to digest our own experience before surfacing to the workaday world. But watching movies is a social activity, and it's irresistible to turn to our friends and ask, "What do you think? Wasn't it good? I really liked the part where . . ." We share our delight, and we compare experiences. Our view becomes larger.

Ultimately, the question is much larger than whether our statements about art are objective or not. The question applies not only to art. It's about the world. It's just that art is a convenient place to begin the argument. If we cannot agree on the meaning of a single art object, with its known borders, its beginnings, middle and end, with its human author, how can we make statements about a limitless universe—a universe not divided into neat stages of development, ending in closure, but a universe constantly evolving, stretching out to infinity, and a universe whose author is either unknown or not available to interview.

Is the external world totally independent of us, or, as the ancient Greek philosopher Protagoras held, is it us and our perceptions that are the measure of all things? Even if we grant the existence of the external world, it doesn't seem possible to get beyond our perceptions of it. Scientists have their protocol, the scientific method, which is meant to banish subjective interpretation. In the search for the underlying principles of things as they are, science took over from religion the chief role of establishing truth. And what a magnificent job science has done. In revealing the structure of sub-atomic particles, in determining the epicentre and strength of an earthquake, in isolating a deadly virus and developing vaccines, and in improving the quality of life for millions, science can lay claim to being humanity's most successful enterprise.

Think of the surgeon holding a human heart in his or her hands, repairing a faulty valve and placing it back into the person's chest, giving the patient 20 more years of life. All of the knowledge, the complex theory and practical skill that go into a successful operation rest on a physician's informed judgement that an operation is called for. That judgement is fallible, as are all human judgements. For the history of science is full of examples of misreadings, of scientists finding only what they were looking for and not finding what they weren't, of finding solutions to problems that fit not only their hypotheses but also the prevailing ideology. Ultimately, scientists too must depend on their very fallible senses (or their high-tech extensions) to draw conclusions. Yet the role of the scientist confers no immunity to normal human pressures, the ego needs, the economic necessity to succeed, the political compulsion to research in certain directions. Scientists may be the most objective amongst us, but even in this highly trained class of people, subjective considerations colour many perceptions.

The truth about the world, the final objective Truth, is getting harder to find, yet meaning, subjective meaning, is everywhere. A single rational explanation for the universe and all it contains may no longer be possible. Our knowledge (scientific and otherwise) has grown and grown until it has reached a point beyond which any one individual can comprehend the whole. To see the whole domain of our knowledge we need to climb a very high mountain; we haven't found the mountain yet (although on several occasions we thought we had) and are beginning to doubt whether it exists.

Instead of the overview from the mountain, what we have is the microview of the specialist. What we have are fragments of the whole: knowledge and insight from the physicist, the philosopher, the biologist, the historian, the psychologist, the literary critic, the political economist. The fragments don't cohere into one magnificent interpretation of the universe. They exist as beams of light that illuminate the darkness for a certain time, as probes that reveal something about the world, and as a point of view.

We both rely on and are suspicious of experts. We rely on them, for their fragmentary understanding of the world is the best insight that we've got. But in a deeper sense we know them to be fallible. No political thinker predicted the collapse of communism in Eastern Europe, yet we continue to tune into the TV to hear what those experts have to say. Young parents read everything they can get their hands on about child rearing, yet are highly selective about the ideas they apply to their own children. We may listen with interest to the reasoned arguments of the nuclear power experts, but when they tell us that we have nothing to fear the shadow of **Chernobyl** falls over the discussion.

Every discipline of study is currently racked with conflict, with dissenting voices. If even the experts can't agree, are the rest of us just gambling on what and whom we choose to believe? It becomes so difficult to judge the worth of arguments that threaten to go beyond the realm of our expertise. The difficulty causes many of us to give up the task of sifting through the ideas, adopting instead a weary and cynical assumption that all views are equal. Many of us come from school systems that value self-expression as the highest good. It doesn't matter what gets expressed (all views are roughly equal anyway); just so long as a view gets expressed, the system will applaud. This emphasis involves a radical turning away from the searching after truth that has so long inspired our education. If there's no truth to search for, why struggle so hard?

If there's no truth, then what we have left are competing views, subjective perceptions. My view becomes as valuable as yours because there's no way to measure them against each other. On the surface, there's an increase in tolerance as we all recognize that what may be true for me may not be true for you. But beneath the surface lurks the urge for dominance, the recognition that the prevailing view belongs to the loudest, most powerful voice.

And so we have the competition of interests and perspectives: Québec, the West, free trade, feminists, unionists, Native peoples, Blacks, environmentalists. The competition is healthy, the diversity of views enriching. But without truth as a goal, the contest of ideas has no referee; it's too easy for reason to become a weapon to beat your opponent with, not a tool to dig for understanding. Still, we're in the middle of a huge process in our relationship to the world and each other. If fragmentation into competing perspectives and specialized bits of knowledge is the current mode, perhaps all we need to do is wait for the emergence of new and better ideas that might reconcile some of the conflicts and satisfy our yearning for something to believe in. The competition of ideas has been evident throughout this text: Are we free or determined? in Unit 1; What changes and what remains the same? in Unit 2; Do we have the sense to cooperate with each other or are

Chernobyl
site of a nuclear accident in Ukraine

we doomed to conflict? in Unit 3; Can science provide the solutions to the problems it creates? in Unit 4. Do we have to make a choice? Do we have to run to the comfort of certainty? Or do we have to learn to love the paradox—to see in contradiction the breathing in, the breathing out of ideas?

The arts, particularly narrative arts such as film and the novel, may have a role to play in helping us to reconcile apparent contradictions. By successfully creating a fictional world that recreates the real world, the artist sets artificial boundaries around what is included in the story, how many characters, subplots and themes. Fictionalizing the world tells us everything we need to know; the artist creates a vision of life that is remarkable in its completeness. The sharing of this vision creates a sense of community between artist and audience and holds out the possibility of consensus. We are not alone; others see the same world, sometimes with great clarity and undeniable insight. It's as if the film or novel creates a fictional mountain from which we can finally see the human truth stretched out below in all its complexity and contradiction. It is just a glimpse, but it is reassuring. In the midst of the darkest night-time thunderstorm, the lightning can suddenly illuminate our world in a flash of brilliant light, letting us know that the world is still there, under the cover of darkness.

The Story: An Introduction

Clive Cockerton

The psychiatrist Adam Philips makes the point that the implicit wish of flirtation is to sustain the life of desire. It does so in a potentially dangerous way. When we flirt with another person, we're trying out the notion that we really could be different, that our identity is not fixed, that our commitments don't tell all there is to know about us. Flirting rehearses the idea that life could be completely different, but the usual end of flirtation is the reinforcement of commitment, as we turn back to our partner and our regular life. If we don't return, then the flirtation becomes something else: it crosses a line, ceases to be flirtation and transforms into an affair. This play of commitment, resistance to commitment and reinforcement of commitment acknowledges that we are ever evolving. Whenever we flirt, we flirt with possibility, and the mind can become intoxicated with the richness of that possibility.

Literature, among many other things, also plays with possibility, as it explores imaginative worlds at least as complex as our own experience. Freud acknowledged the psychological significance of this exploration when he commented that our need for plurality in our lives was adequately met only in literature. This is why stories exert such a powerful hold on us, from those first stories that are read to us by our parents to the latest film. What would it be like to live another life? It's an irresistible mental experiment.

Ezra Pound, the great American poet, once defined poetry as language charged with meaning to the utmost degree. The same definition works for the best prose as well. In Ian McEwan's "Us or Me," language is used with great precision and power. When he writes, "We were running towards a catastrophe, which itself was a kind of furnace in whose heat identities and fates would buckle into new shapes," he captures the transformative power of events with a clarifying simplicity. Since most of what we know about the world comes to us through the use of language, when we are in the presence of a master the words themselves take on, in Pound's sense, a special charge.

Still, we read most stories to find out what happens in the end—who gets the girl, does the killer get away—and, in this way, all stories are

"The Story: An Introduction" is by Clive Cockerton of the Humber College Institute of Technology and Advanced Learning. Used by permission.

mystery stories. The mystery isn't just how it ends up —who is married or who dies—but rather the mystery of all the possibilities that life contains and what is or isn't closed off to us. In "Us or Me," we desperately want to know what happens, but in a deeper sense we are rehearsing our vulnerability before the ruthlessness of events.

Us or Me

Ian McEwan

The beginning is simple to mark. We were in sunlight under a turkey oak, partly protected from a strong, gusty wind. I was kneeling on the grass with a corkscrew in my hand, and Clarissa was passing me the bottle—a 1987 Daumas Gassac. This was the moment, this was the pinprick on the time map: I was stretching out my hand, and as the cool neck and the black foil touched my palm, we heard a man's shout. We turned to look across the field and saw the danger. Next thing, I was running towards it. The transformation was absolute: I don't recall dropping the corkscrew, or getting to my feet, or making a decision, or hearing the caution Clarissa called after me. What idiocy, to be racing into this story and its labyrinths, sprinting away from our happiness among the fresh spring grasses by the oak. There was the shout again, and a child's cry, enfeebled by the wind that roared in the tall trees along the hedgerows. I ran faster. And there, suddenly, from different points around the field, four other men were converging on the scene, running like me.

I see us from three hundred feet up, through the eyes of the buzzard we had watched earlier, soaring, circling and dipping in the tumult of currents: five men running silently towards the centre of a hundred-acre field. I approached from the south-east, with the wind at my back. About two hundred yards to my left two men ran side by side. They were farm labourers who had been repairing the fence along the field's southern edge where it skirts the road. The same distance beyond them was the motorist, John Logan, whose car was banked on the grass verge with its door, or doors, wide open. Knowing what I know now, it's odd to evoke the figure of Jed Parry directly ahead of me, emerging from a line of beeches on the far side of the field a quarter of a mile away, running into the wind. To the buzzard Parry and I were tiny forms, our white shirts brilliant against the green, rushing towards each other like lovers, innocent of the grief this entanglement would bring. The encounter that would unhinge us was minutes away, its enormity disguised from us not only by the barrier of time but by the colossus in the centre of the field that drew us in with the power of a terrible ratio that set fabulous magnitude against the puny human distress at its base.

What was Clarissa doing? She said she walked quickly towards the centre of the field. I don't know how she resisted the urge to run. By the time it happened—the event I am about to describe, the fall—she had almost caught us up and was well placed as an observer, unencumbered by participation, by the ropes and the shouting, and by our fatal lack of co-operation. What I describe is shaped by what Clarissa saw too, by what we told each other in the time of obsessive re-examination that followed: the aftermath, an appropriate term for what happened in a field waiting for its early summer mowing. The aftermath, the second crop, the growth promoted by that first cut in May.

I'm holding back, delaying the information. I'm lingering in the prior moment because it was a time when other outcomes were still possible; the convergence of six figures in a flat green space has a comforting geometry from the buzzard's perspective, the knowable, limited plane of the snooker table. The initial conditions, the force and the direction of the force, define all the consequent pathways, all the angles of collision and return, and the glow of the overhead light bathes the field, the baize and all its moving bodies, in reassuring clarity. I think that while we were still converging, before we made contact, we were in a state of mathematical grace. I linger on our dispositions, the relative distances and the compass point—because as far as these occurrences were concerned, this was the last time I understood anything clearly at all.

What were we running towards? I don't think any of us would ever know fully. But superficially the answer was, a balloon. Not the nominal space that encloses a cartoon character's speech or thought, or, by analogy, the kind that's driven by mere hot air. It was an enormous balloon filled with helium, that elemental gas forged from hydrogen in the nuclear furnace of the stars, first step along the way in the generation of multiplicity and variety of matter in the universe, including our selves and all our thoughts.

We were running towards a catastrophe, which itself was a kind of furnace in whose heat identities and fates would buckle into new shapes. At the base of the balloon was a basket in which there was a boy, and by the basket, clinging to a rope, was a man in need of help.

Even without the balloon the day would have been marked for memory, though in the most pleasurable of ways, for this was a reunion after a separation of six weeks, the longest Clarissa and I had spent apart in our seven years. On the way out to Heathrow I had made a detour into Covent Garden and found a semi legal place to park, close to Carluccio's. I went in and put together a picnic whose centre-piece was a great ball of mozzarella which the assistant fished out of an earthenware vat with a wooden claw. I also bought black olives, mixed salad and focaccia. Then I hurried up Long Acre to Bertram Rota's to take delivery of Clarissa's birthday present. Apart from the flat and our car, it was the most expensive single item I had ever bought. The rarity of this little book seemed to give off a heat I could feel through the thick brown wrapping paper as I walked back up the street.

Forty minutes later I was scanning the screens for arrival information. The Boston flight had only just landed and I guessed I had a half-hour wait. If one ever wanted proof of Darwin's contention that the many expressions of emotion in humans are universal, genetically inscribed, then a few minutes by the arrivals gate in Heathrow's Terminal Four should suffice. I saw the same joy, the same uncontrollable smile, in the faces of a Nigerian earth mama, a thin-lipped Scottish granny and a pale, correct Japanese businessman as they wheeled their trolleys in and recognized a figure in the expectant crowd. Observing human variety can give pleasure, but so too can human sameness. I kept hearing the same sighing sound on a downward note, often breathed through a name as two people pressed forward to go into their embrace. Was it a major second, or a minor third, or somewhere in between? Pa-pa! Yolan-ta! Ho-bi! Nz-e! There was also a rising note, crooned into the solemn, wary faces of babies by long-absent fathers or grandparents, cajoling, beseeching an immediate return of love. Han-nah? Tom-ee? Let me in!

The variety was in the private dramas: a father and teenage son, Turkish perhaps, stood in a long silent clinch, forgiving each other, or mourning a loss, oblivious to the baggage trolleys jamming around them; identical twins, women in their fifties, greeted each other with clear distaste, just touching hands and kissing without making contact; a small American boy, hoisted on to the shoulders of a father he did not recognize, screamed to be put down, provoking a fit of temper in his tired mother.

But mostly it was smiles and hugs, and in thirty-five minutes I experienced more than fifty theatrical happy endings, each one with the appearance of being slightly less well acted than the one before, until I began to feel emotionally exhausted and suspected that even the children were being insincere. I was just wondering how convincing I myself could be now in greeting Clarissa when she tapped me on the shoulder, having missed me in the crowd and circled round. Immediately my detachment vanished, and I called out her name, in tune with all the rest.

Less than an hour later we were parked by a track that ran through beech woods in the Chiltern Hills, near Christmas Common. While Clarissa changed her shoes I loaded a backpack with our picnic. We set off down our path arm in arm, still elated by our reunion; what was familiar about her—the size and feel of her hand, the warmth and tranquillity in her voice, the Celt's pale skin and green eyes—was also novel, gleaming in an alien light, reminding me of our very first meetings and the months we spent falling in love. Or, I imagined, I was another man, my own sexual competitor, come to steal her from me. When I told her she laughed and said I was the world's most complicated simpleton, and it was while we stopped to kiss and wondered aloud whether we should not have driven straight home to bed that we glimpsed through the fresh foliage the helium balloon drifting dreamily across the wooded valley to our west. Neither the man nor the boy was visible to us. I remember thinking, but not saying, that it was a precarious form of transport when the wind, rather than the pilot, set the course. Then I thought that perhaps this was the very nature of its attraction. And instantly the idea went out of my mind.

We went through College Wood towards Pishill, stopping to admire the new greenery on the beeches. Each leaf seemed to glow with an internal light. We talked about the purity of this colour, the beech leaf in spring, and how looking at it cleared the mind. As we walked into the wood the wind began to get up and the branches creaked like rusted machinery. We knew this route well. This was surely the finest landscape within an hour of central London. I loved the pitch and roll of the fields and their scatterings of chalk and flint, and the paths that dipped across them to sink into the darkness of the beech stands, certain neglected, badly drained valleys where thick iridescent mosses covered the rotting tree trunks and where you occasionally glimpsed a muntjak blundering through the undergrowth.

For much of the time as we walked westwards we were talking about Clarissa's research—John Keats dying in Rome in the house at the foot of the Spanish Steps where he lodged with his friend Joseph Severn. Was it possible there were still three or four unpublished letters of Keats' in existence? Might one of them be addressed to Fanny Brawne? Clarissa had reason to think so and had spent part of a sabbatical term travelling around Spain and Portugal, visiting houses known to Fanny Brawne and to Keats' sister Fanny. Now she was back from Boston where she had been working in the Houghton Library at Harvard, trying to trace correspondence from Severn's remote family connections. Keats' last known letter was written almost three months before he died to his old friend Charles Brown. It's rather stately in tone, and typical in throwing out, almost as parenthesis, a brilliant description of artistic creation— "the knowledge of contrast, feeling for light and shade, all that information (primitive sense) necessary for a poem are great enemies to the recovery of the stomach." It's the one with the famous farewell, so piercing in its reticence and courtesy: "I can scarcely bid you goodbye, even in a letter. I always made an awkward bow. God bless you! John Keats." But all the biographies agree that Keats was in remission from tuberculosis when he wrote this letter, and remained so for a further ten days. He visited the Villa Borghese, and strolled down the Corso. He listened with pleasure to Severn playing Haydn, he mischievously tipped his dinner out the window in protest at the quality of the cooking, and he even thought about starting a poem. If letters existed from this period why would Severn or, more likely, Brown, have wanted to suppress them? Clarissa thought she had found the answer in a couple of references in correspondence between distant relations of Brown's written in the 1840s, but she needed more evidence, different sources.

"He knew he'd never see Fanny again," Clarissa said. "He wrote to Brown and said that to see her name written would be more than he could bear. But he never stopped thinking about her. He was strong enough those days in December, and he loved her so hard. It's easy to imagine him writing a letter he never intended to send."

I squeezed her hand and said nothing. I knew little about Keats or his poetry, but I thought it possible that in his hopeless situation he would not have wanted to write precisely because he loved her so much. Lately I'd had the idea that Clarissa's interest in these hypothetical letters had something to do with our own situation, and with her conviction that love that did not find its expression in a letter was not perfect. In the months after we met, and before we bought the apartment, she had written me some beauties, passionately abstract in their exploration of the ways our love was different from and superior to any that had ever existed. Perhaps that's the essence of a love letter, to celebrate the unique. I had tried to match hers, but all that sincerity would permit me were the facts, and they seemed miraculous enough to me: a beautiful woman loved and wanted to be loved by a large, clumsy, balding fellow who could hardly believe his luck.

We stopped to watch the buzzard as we were approaching Maidensgrove. The balloon may have re-crossed our path while we were in the woods that cover the valleys around the nature reserve. By the early afternoon we were on the Ridgeway Path, walking north along the line of the escarpment. Then we struck out along one of those broad fingers of land that project westwards from the Chilterns into the rich farmland below. Across the Vale of Oxford we could make out the outlines of the Cotswold Hills and beyond them, perhaps, the Brecon Beacons rising in a faint blue mass. Our plan had been to picnic right out on the end where the view was best, but the wind was too strong by now. We went back across the field and sheltered among the oaks along the northern side. And it was because of these trees that we did not see the balloon's descent. Later I wondered why it had not been blown miles away. Later still I discovered that the wind at five hundred feet was not the same that day as the wind at ground level.

The Keats conversation faded as we unpacked our lunch. Clarissa pulled the bottle from the bag and held it by its base as she offered it to me. As I have said, the neck touched my palm as we heard the shout. It was a baritone, on a rising note of fear. It marked the beginning and, of course, an end. At that moment a chapter, no, a whole stage of my life closed. Had I known, and had there been a spare second or two, I might have allowed myself a little nostalgia. We were seven years into a child-less marriage of love. Clarissa Mellon was also in love with another man, but with his two hundredth birthday coming up he was little trou-ble. In fact he helped in the combative exchanges that were part of our equilibrium, our way of talking about work. We lived in an art deco apartment block in North London with a below average share of worries—a money shortage for a year or so, an unsubstantiated cancer scare, the divorces and illnesses of friends, Clarissa's irritation with my occasional and manic bouts of dissatisfaction with my kind of work—but there was nothing that threatened our free and intimate existence.

What we saw when we stood from our picnic was this: a huge gray balloon, the size of a house, the shape of a tear drop, had come down in the field. The pilot must have been half way out of the passenger basket as it touched the ground. His leg had become entangled in a rope that was attached to an anchor. Now, as the wind gusted, and pushed and lifted the balloon towards the escarpment, he was being half dragged, half carried across the field. In the basket was a child, a boy of about ten. In a sudden lull, the man was on his feet, clutching at the basket, or at the boy. Then there was another gust, and the pilot was on his back, bumping over the rough ground, trying to dig his feet in for purchase, or lunging for the anchor behind him in order to secure it in the earth. Even if he had been able, he would not have dared disentangle himself from the anchor rope. He needed his weight to keep the balloon on the ground, and the wind could have snatched the rope from his hands.

As I ran I heard him shouting at the boy, urging him to leap clear of the basket. But the boy was tossed from one side to another as the balloon lurched across the field. He regained his balance and got a leg over the edge of the basket. The balloon rose and fell, thumping into a hummock, and the boy dropped backwards out of sight. Then he was up again, arms stretched out towards the man and shouting something in return—words or inarticulate fear, I couldn't tell.

I must have been a hundred yards away when the situation came under control. The wind had dropped, the man was on his feet, bending over the anchor as he drove it into the ground. He had unlooped the rope from his leg. For some reason, complacency, exhaustion or simply because he was doing what he was told, the boy remained where he was. The towering balloon wavered and tilted and tugged, but the beast was tamed. I slowed my pace, though I did not stop. As the man straightened, he saw us—or at least the farm workers and me—and he waved us on. He still needed help, but I was glad to slow to a brisk walk. The farm labourers were also walking now. One of them was coughing loudly. But the man with the car, John Logan, knew something we didn't and kept on running. As for Jed Parry, my view of him was blocked by the balloon that lay between us.

The wind renewed its rage in the treetops just before I felt its force on my back. Then it struck the balloon which ceased its innocent comical wagging and was suddenly stilled. Its only motion was a shimmer of strain that rippled out across its ridged surface as the contained energy accumulated. It broke free, the anchor flew up in a spray of dirt, and balloon and basket rose ten feet in the air. The boy was thrown back, out of sight. The pilot had the rope in his hands and was lifted two feet clear off the ground. If Logan had not reached him and taken hold of one of the many dangling lines the balloon would have carried the boy away. Instead, both men were now being pulled across the field, and the farm workers and I were running again.

I got there before them. When I took a rope, the basket was above head height. The boy inside it was screaming. Despite the wind, I caught the smell of urine. Jed Parry was on a rope seconds after me, and the two farm workers, Joseph Lacey and Toby Greene, caught hold just after him. Greene was having a coughing fit, but he kept his grip. The pilot was shouting instructions at us, but too frantically, and no one was listening. He had been struggling too long, and now he was exhausted and emotionally out of control. With five of us on the lines the balloon was secured. We simply had to keep steady on our feet and pull hand over hand to bring the basket down, and this, despite whatever the pilot was shouting, was what we began to do.

By this time we were standing on the escarpment. The ground dropped away sharply at a gradient of about twenty-five percent, and then levelled out into a gentle slope towards the bottom. In winter this is a favourite tobogganning spot for local kids. We were all talking at once. Two of us, myself and the motorist, wanted to walk the balloon away from the edge. Someone thought the priority was to get the boy out. Someone else was calling for the balloon to be pulled down so that we could anchor it firmly. I saw no contradiction, for we could be pulling the balloon down as we moved back into the field. But the second opinion was prevailing. The pilot had a fourth idea, but no one knew or cared what it was.

I should make something clear. There may have been a vague communality of purpose, but we were never a team. There was no chance, no time. Coincidences of time and place, a predisposition to help, had brought us together under the balloon. No one was in charge —or everyone was, and we were in a shouting match. The pilot, red-faced, bawling and sweating, we ignored. Incompetence came off him like heat. But we were beginning to bawl our own instructions too. I know that if I had been uncontested leader the tragedy would not have happened. Later I heard some of the others say the same thing about themselves. But there was not time, no opportunity for force of character to show. Any leader, any firm plan would have been preferable to none. No human society, from the hunter-gatherer to the post-industrial, has come to the attention of anthropologists that did not have its leaders and the led; and no emergency was ever dealt with effectively by democratic process.

It was not so difficult to bring the passenger basket down low enough for us to see inside. We had a new problem. The boy was curled up on the floor. His arms covered his face and he was gripping his hair tightly. "What's his name?" we said to the red-faced man.

"Harry."

"Harry!" we shouted. "Come on Harry. Harry! Take my hand, Harry. Get out of there Harry!"

But Harry curled up tighter. He flinched each time we said his name. Our words were like stones thrown down at his body. He was in paralysis of will, a state known as learned helplessness, often noted in laboratory animals subjected to unusual stress; all impulses to problem-solving disappear, all instinct for survival drains away. We pulled the basket down to the ground and managed to keep it there, and we were just leaning in to try and lift the boy out when the pilot shouldered us aside and attempted to climb in. He said later that he told us what he was trying to do. We heard nothing but our own shouting and swearing. What he was doing seemed ridiculous, but his intentions, it turned out, were completely sensible. He wanted to deflate the balloon by pulling a cord that was tangled in the basket.

"Yer great pillock!" Lacey shouted. "Help us reach the lad out."

I heard what was coming two seconds before it reached us. It was as though an express train were traversing the treetops, hurtling towards us. An airy, whining, whooshing sound grew to full volume in half a second. At the inquest the Met office figures for wind speeds that day were part of the evidence, and there were some gusts, it was said, of seventy miles an hour. This must have been one, but before I let it reach us, let me freeze the frame—there's a security in stillness—to describe our circle.

To my right the ground dropped away. Immediately to my left was John Logan, a family doctor from Oxford, forty-two years old, married to a historian, with two children. He was not the youngest of our group, but he was the fittest. He played tennis to county level, and belonged to a mountaineering club. He had done a stint with a mountain rescue team in the Western Highlands. Logan was a mild, reticent man apparently, otherwise he might have been able to force himself usefully on us as a leader. To his left was Joseph Lacey, sixty-three, farm labourer, odd job man, captain of his local bowls team. He lived with his wife in Watlington, a small town at the foot of the escarpment. On his left was his mate, Toby Greene, fifty-eight, also a farm labourer, unmarried, living with his mother at Russell's Water. Both men worked for the Stonor estate. Greene was the one with the smoker's cough. Next around the circle, trying to get into the basket, was the pilot, James Gadd, fifty-five, an executive in a small advertising company who lived in Reading with his wife and one of their grown-up children who was mentally handicapped. At the inquest Gadd was found to have breached half a dozen basic safety procedures which the coroner listed tonelessly. Gadd's ballooning licence was withdrawn. The boy in the basket was Harry Gadd, his grandson, ten years old, from Camberwell, London. Facing me, with the ground sloping away to his left, was Jed Parry. He was twenty-eight, unemployed, living on an inheritance in Hampstead.

This was the crew. As far as we were concerned, the pilot had abdicated his authority. We were breathless, excited, determined on our separate plans, while the boy was beyond participating in his own survival. He lay in a heap, blocking out the world with his forearms. Lacey, Greene and

I were attempting to fish him out, and now Gadd was climbing over the top of us. Logan and Parry were calling out their own suggestions. Gadd had placed one foot by his grandson's head, and Greene was cussing him when it happened. A mighty fist socked the balloon in two rapid blows, one-two, the second more vicious than the first. And the first was vicious. It jerked Gadd right out of the basket on to the ground, and it lifted the balloon five feet or so, straight into the air. Gadd's considerable weight was removed from the equation. The rope ran through my grip, scorching my palms, but I managed to keep hold, with two feet of line spare. The others kept hold too. The basket was right above our heads now, and we stood with arms upraised like Sunday bell ringers. Into our amazed silence, before the shouting could resume, the second punch came and knocked the balloon up and westwards. Suddenly we were treading the air with all our weight in the grip of our fists.

Those one or two ungrounded seconds occupy as much space in memory as might a long journey up an uncharted river. My first impulse was to hang on in order to keep the balloon weighted down. The child was incapable, and was about to be borne away. Two miles to the west were high-voltage power lines. A child alone and needing help. It was my duty to hang on, and I thought we would all do the same.

Almost simultaneous with the desire to stay on the rope and save the boy, barely a neuronal pulse later, came other thoughts in which fear and instant calculations of logarithmic complexity were fused. We were rising, and the ground was dropping away as the balloon was pushed westwards. I knew I had to get my legs and feet locked around the rope. But the end of the line barely reached below my waist and my grip was slipping. My legs flailed in the empty air. Every fraction of a second that passed increased the drop, and the point must come when to let go would be impossible or fatal. And compared to me Harry was safe curled up in the basket. The balloon might well come down safely at the bottom of the hill. And perhaps my impulse to hang on was nothing more than a continuation of what I had been attempting moments before, simply a failure to adjust quickly.

And again, less than one adrenally incensed heartbeat later, another variable was added to the equation: someone let go, and the balloon and its hangers-on lurched upwards another several feet.

I didn't know, nor have I ever discovered, who let go first. I'm not prepared to accept that it was me. But everyone claims not to have been first. What is certain is that if we had not broken ranks, our collective weight would have brought the balloon to earth a quarter of the way down the slope a few seconds later as the gust subsided. But as I've said, there was no team, there was no plan, no agreement to be broken. No failure. So can we accept that it was right, every man for himself? Were we all happy afterwards that this was a reasonable course? We never had that comfort, for there was a deeper covenant, ancient and automatic, written in our nature. Co-operation—the basis of our earliest hunting successes, the force behind our evolving capacity for language, the glue of our social cohesion. Our misery in the aftermath was proof that we knew we had failed ourselves. But letting go was in our nature too. Selfishness is also written on our hearts. This is our mammalian conflict—what to give to the others, and what to keep for yourself. Treading that line, keeping the others in check, and being kept in check by them, is what we call morality. Hanging a few feet above the Chilterns escarpment, our crew enacted morality's ancient, irresolvable dilemma: us, or me.

Someone said *me*, and then there was nothing to be gained by saying *us*. Mostly, we are good when it makes sense. A good society is one that makes sense of being good. Suddenly, hanging there below the basket, we were a bad society, we were disintegrating. Suddenly the sensible choice was to look out for yourself. The child was not my child, and I was not going to die for it. The moment I glimpsed a body fall away— but whose?—and I felt the balloon lurch upwards, the matter was settled; altruism had no place. Being good made no sense. I let go and fell, I reckon, about twelve feet. I landed heavily on my side and got away with a bruised thigh. Around me—before or after, I'm not so sure—bodies were thumping to the ground. Jed Parry was unhurt. Toby Greene broke his ankle. Joseph Lacey, the oldest, who had done his National Service with a paratroop regiment, did no more than wind himself.

By the time I got to my feet the balloon was fifty yards away, and one man was still dangling by his rope. In John Logan, husband, father, doctor and mountain rescue worker, the flame of altruism must have burned a little stronger. It didn't need much. When four of us let go, the balloon, with six hundred pounds shed, must have surged upwards. A delay of one second would have been enough to close his options. When I stood up and saw him, he was a hundred feet up, and rising, just where the ground itself was falling. He wasn't struggling, he wasn't kicking or trying to claw his way up. He hung perfectly still along the line of the rope, all his energies concentrated in his weakening grip. He was already a tiny figure, almost black against the sky. There was no sight of the boy. The balloon and its basket lifted away and westwards, and the smaller Logan became, the more terrible it was, so terrible it was funny, it was a stunt, a joke, a cartoon, and a frightened laugh heaved out of my chest. For this was preposterous, the kind of thing that happened to Bugs Bunny, or Tom, or Jerry, and for an instant, I thought it wasn't true, and that only I could see right through the joke, and that my utter disbelief would set reality straight and see Dr. Logan safely to the ground.

I don't know whether the others were standing, or sprawling. Toby Greene was probably doubled up over his ankle. But I do remember the silence into which I laughed. No exclamations, no shouted instructions as before. Mute helplessness. He was two hundred yards away now, and perhaps three hundred feet above the ground. Our silence was a kind of acceptance, a death warrant. Or it was horrified shame, because the wind had dropped, and barely stirred against our backs. He had been on the rope so long that I began to think he might stay there until the balloon drifted down, or the boy came to his senses and found the valve that released the gas, or until some beam, or god, or some other impossible cartoon thing came and gathered him up. Even as I had that hope we saw him slip down right to the end of the rope. And still he hung there. For two seconds, three, four. And then he let go. Even then, there was a fraction of time when he barely fell, and I still thought there was a chance that a freak physical law, a furious thermal, some phenomenon no more astonishing than the one we were witnessing would intervene and bear him up. We watched him drop. You could see the acceleration. No forgiveness, no special dispensation for flesh, or bravery, or kindness. Only ruthless gravity. And from somewhere, perhaps from him, perhaps from some indifferent crow, a thin squawk cut through the stilled air. He fell as he had hung, a stiff little black stick. I've never seen such a terrible thing as that falling man.

Are Poems Puzzles?

George Byrnes

Why is poetry so difficult to read? Why can't poets just say what they mean instead of writing in ways that obscure their meaning? Before I try to answer these questions, I want you to stop reading for a moment (you will find this article more interesting if you really do try this exercise) and try an experiment in writing a poem yourself, by following these three steps:

Step 1:
Arrange the letters of your name vertically on the lines below or on a separate, lined piece of paper, with one letter per line.

Step 2:
Choose a word that begins with each letter in your name. Do this for all of the letters in your name.

Step 3:
Use each word in a phrase or sentence; your poem should have at least the same number of lines as the letters in your name.

Poets, of course, do not normally use mechanical methods such as this to create poetry. In completing this exercise, however, you necessarily made some of the same decisions that poets make concerning three important elements of modern poetry: *word choice, line arrangement* and *theme.* You will find the poems included in this unit more interesting if you keep these elements in mind.

Now let's look at my results to examine how word choice, line arrangement and theme function together:

"Are Poems Puzzles?" is by George Byrnes of the Humber College Institute of Technology and Advanced Learning. Used by permission.

Step 1:	Step 2:	Step 3:
G	Giant	**G**iant lizards fly at the sun
E	Eyes	My **E**yes can only watch
O	Orange	the **O**range hue of nothing.
R	Revolver	I would reach for a **R**evolver
G	Ganges	or glide into the **G**anges.
E	End	It will **E**nd sometime.

As you were using your imagination in Step 3 to use the words chosen in Step 2 in a phrase, you will have realized that the words themselves filtered the kinds of connections you were able to imagine. Some words or images that came to mind would have been rejected for some reason—fish thrown back into the pond of your mind because they did not connect fruitfully with the other words in the previous or subsequent line. In poetry, perhaps more than in any other literary form, words are not just used for communicating ideas or actions; the connections created between the words *are* the poem.

Sometimes words can have symbolic or associative value, that is, layers of meaning beyond their literal definition. For example, the maple leaf is a symbol of Canada, and the eagle is a symbol of the United States; each symbol implies characteristics about each country. Poems can certainly be enriched by symbols, as symbols are an economical way to express what would take a prose writer many pages to say. But not all poems rely on symbols, and none of the poems included in this unit do.

In the example above, the word "Orange" connects with "sun" from the first line, as orange is a colour associated with the setting sun; a setting sun, furthermore, is an image associated with death or with something ending. "Orange" thus takes on a number of meanings that go beyond its basic meaning and also serves to connect "sun" with another image of death or ending: "revolver." While "Ganges" is a powerful symbol of fertility and spiritual cleansing, if you only read this word as the name of a river, not much is lost. In fact, the symbolic value of this word was not even a concern of mine when I chose it. I only recognized it later when I became a reader of my poem.

As a rule, when first reading a poem, read to understand its literal level—the everyday meaning of its words. Once you have established the literal level, you can later look for other levels that may be implied by the words.

Next, you needed to make some decisions about whether the words on one line should continue on to the next line or whether they should be read as a unit separated from the next line. Unlike sentences in narratives which continually move the reader forward, each line in a poem contributes to the poem's rhythm and meaning in many ways. In the example above, the punctuation indicates that the first and last lines are to be read as single lines. What effect does this have on the meaning of these lines? How would the poem change if you split the lines that are meant to be read together into separate lines?

Finally, you were probably aware as you tried to make connections for each letter in your name that you also wanted to find a way to draw all the lines together, so the words, images, lines form a whole that begins with the first word and is fully expressed by the last word. This is the role of theme—it connects the many elements of a literary work and unifies the poem. In the example above, the words "nothing," "revolver," and "end" suggest a theme of death or suicide. If this were a short story, we would probably learn why the speaker of the poem feels this way, but here we are only given the sense of the speaker's passiveness, eyes that "watch . . . nothing," a speaker who is unable or unwilling to, like the lizards, "fly at the sun." What themes did you develop in your experiment?

Obviously, my experiment above did not generate a great poem. Perhaps you had more luck. The experiment, however, did produce something that is best understood if we read it not as an accidental grouping of words, but as a poem: *a literary form that dramatizes theme through the choice and arrangement of words into lines.*

Now let's next apply these concerns to the poems included in this unit. Philip Larkin's "This Be the Verse" begins with a sensational first line that might shock you at first ("They fuck you up, your mum and dad"). We do not expect to see expletives in poetry, but expletives are just words— powerful words, to be sure, but words nevertheless. Just as you did in the above experiment, Larkin chose a word consistent with the state of mind of the speaker of the poem—its persona.[1] If we go a bit deeper, we will see the choice to use an expletive actually derives from the structural and thematic principles of the poem itself; the poem deals with the persona's anger at his own upbringing and his sense of the pointlessness of having children. For this poem, the expletive simply fits into the poem better than any other word, and its placement at the beginning of the poem sets the tone of the poem in terms we all can understand.

Sharon Olds's poem "I Go Back to May 1937" dramatizes a theme similar to "This Be the Verse," and both poems are written in the first person. Olds's poem, however, is remarkably different. There are several reasons for this. Larkin's poem is relatively simple in theme and method, but startling because of its attitude and diction. Olds's poem is more complex in its narrative framework and its theme, but more conventional in its diction and point of view. Unlike Larkin's tightly structured poem (four lines per stanza, rhyming in alternate lines: abab), Olds uses an open, descriptive technique that allows the "speaker" to weave together her image of her parents before they were married and portray her anger at being the child of what appears to have been a less-than-fulfilled marriage.

Perhaps the most distinctive feature of Olds's poem is how she shapes each line. Note how often the speaker uses repeated words at the beginning of lines (I, they, you, his, her) and starts new sentences in the middle or even at the end of lines ("but I don't do it. I want to live. I")—a syntax that resembles the give-and-take of an argument. As well, note the tonal difference between the passages in which the parents are described ("they are kids, they are dumb . . .") and the more urgent lines that reflect the speaker's emotional point of view: "I want to go up to them and say Stop. . . ." The last line of a poem is always important to its meaning. What do you make of the speaker's attitude at the end? How does this line redirect the poem from being merely a complaint about the effect parents have on their children to a poem that says something about poetry itself?

A poem that says something about poetry itself is exactly the point of Thomas Lux's "The Voice You Hear When You Read Silently." Just as in Olds's poem where the shape of the lines makes significant contributions to the meaning of the poem, Lux's poem plays with the form of a line—using the first line to continue the idea begun in the title:

> The Voice You Hear When You Read Silently is not silent, it is a
> speaking-out-loud voice in your head; it is spoken

As with the inclusion of an expletive in Larkin's poem, the effect of this approach may be a bit disorienting at first, but it is an effect that has a purpose: it creates a sense of a poem that begins even before the reader makes it begin by reading. For Lux, this kind of playing with words is one way to get beyond words as mere communication, as mere representation of external reality.

Through the rest of the poem, Lux continues to play with the meanings of "silence" and "speaking" to explore how the reader charges any literary work with his or her own voice, changing "barn" into "a barn you know or knew," into "what you know by feeling." Lux's poem is not a poem about something out there; its theme is how literature is created within us, through us, and that its meaning cannot be separated from us.

The last poem, Walt Whitman's "A Noiseless Patient Spider," is the only non-contemporary poem included in this unit. It was written in the 19th century. As a result, you will notice a difference in the use of word choice, line arrangement and theme.

Walt Whitman was an American poet who believed a poem was really an occasion to sing, not just to speak, and to sing loudly with a confidence that may seem unusual or even inappropriate today when so much of literature involves irony and presents challenges to traditional values and ideas, as in the Larkin and Olds poems. Even Lux's poem, which links the idea of "voice" with one's essential self, does not risk using the word "soul," a concept that carries with it many religious and philosophical associations,[2] as Whitman does without reservation:

And you O my soul where you stand,
Surrounded, detached, in measureless oceans of space,

The arrangement of Whitman's poem also supports his song-like affirmation of the soul's search for meaning in the universe. The poem is divided into two stanzas, each of which is equivalent to a single sentence, but note that the second stanza begins with "And," so the poem really runs uninterrupted from its beginning ("A noiseless patient spider") to its end ("O my soul"). Whitman's lines also do not have a fixed length like Larkin's poem, or the narrow, blocked-in look of the poems by Olds and Lux; Whitman's lines are stretched to accommodate the vibrant rhythm and imagery of the song:

It launch'd forth filament, filament, filament, out of itself,
Ceaselessly musing, venturing, throwing, seeking the spheres to
connect them,

For each of these poets, poems are not puzzles designed to mystify the uninitiated. Poets play with words and line configurations in very creative ways, but they do this to dramatize theme. Unlike the mechanical approach you adopted to write a poem at the beginning of this article, contemporary poets write in the open space between their talent and their experience where the shape of a poem, while sensed early, is always the last thing known. Robert Frost, an American poet, described it as playing tennis with the net down, a game much harder than it would at first appear because what is "in" or "over" still has to be judged.

Concerns about the difficulty in reading poetry are not unusual. Even the American poet William Carlos Williams felt that what poetry had to offer people had become imperilled by a poetics that relied on esoteric symbols and allusions. He wrote in one of his poems:

It is difficult
to get the news from poems
yet men die miserably every day
for lack
of what is found there.[3]

Sensitivity to how poems mean—through word choice, arrangement of words into lines and theme—will allow you to enter into poems and return with the "news" that matters to you.[4]

Notes

[1] Do not always assume that the poet and a poem's persona are one and the same person. Larkin's poem is better read as spoken by someone other than Larkin; Olds's poem, however, is better read as expressing her experience and point of view. Sometimes it doesn't matter who the speaker is, as in the poems by Lux and Whitman.

[2] Compare B.F. Skinner's views in "Can Science Help?" (Unit 1), where he argues that society should abandon "the traditional philosophy of human nature" in favour of a scientific model.

[3] William Carlos Williams, from "Asphodel, That Greeny Flower," *Collected Poems, Volume II, 1939–1962* (Carcanet, 1989).

[4] Dana Gioia, in an article titled "Can Poetry Matter," writes, "Williams understood poetry's human value but had no illusions about the difficulties his contemporaries faced in trying to engage the audience that needed the art most desperately. To regain poetry's readership one must begin by meeting Williams's challenge to find what 'concerns many men,' not simply what concerns poets." Originally published in *The Atlantic Monthly,* May 1991. www.theatlantic.com/unbound/poetry/gioia/gioia.htm (Accessed March 25, 2004).

This Be the Verse

Philip Larkin

They fuck you up, your mum and dad.
They may not mean to, but they do.
They fill you with the faults they had
And add some extra, just for you.

But they were fucked up in their turn
By fools in old-style hats and coats,
Who half the time were soppy-stern
And half at one another's throats.

Man hands on misery to man.
It deepens like a coastal shelf.
Get out as early as you can,
And don't have any kids yourself.

"This Be the Verse" is reprinted by permission of Philip Larkin and Faber and Faber Ltd.

I Go Back to May 1937

Sharon Olds

I see them standing at the formal gates of
    their colleges,
I see my father strolling out
under the ochre sandstone arch, the
red tiles glinting like bent
plates of blood behind his head, I
see my mother with a few light books at
    her hip
standing at the pillar made of tiny bricks
    with the
wrought-iron gate still open behind her, its
sword-tips black in the May air,
they are about to graduate, they are about
    to get married,
they are kids, they are dumb, all they know is
    they are
innocent, they would never hurt anybody.
I want to go up to them and say Stop,
don't do it—she's the wrong woman,
he's the wrong man, you are going to do things
you cannot imagine you would ever do,
you are going to do bad things to children,
you are going to suffer in ways you never
    heard of,
you are going to want to die. I want to go
up to them there in the late May sunlight
    and say it,
her hungry pretty blank face turning to me,
her pitiful beautiful untouched body,
his arrogant handsome blind face turning to me,
his pitiful beautiful untouched body,
but I don't do it. I want to live. I
take them up like the male and female
paper dolls and bang them together
at the hips like chips of flint as if to
strike sparks from them, I say
Do what you are going to do, and I will
    tell about it.

"I Go Back to May 1937" is reprinted with permission from the author.

The Voice You Hear When You Read Silently

Thomas Lux

is not silent, it is a speaking-
out-loud voice in your head; it is *spoken*,
a voice is *saying* it
as you read. It's the writer's words,
of course, in a literary sense
his or her "voice" but the sound
of that voice is the sound of *your* voice.
Not the sounds your friends know
or the sound of a tape played back
but your voice
caught in the dark cathedral
of your skull, your voice heard
by an internal ear informed by internal abstracts
and what you know by feeling,
having felt. It is your voice
saying, for example, the word "barn"
that the writer wrote
but the "barn" you say
is a barn you know or knew. The voice
in your head, speaking as you read,
never says anything neutrally—some people
hated the barn they knew,
some people love the barn they know
so you hear the word loaded
and a sensory constellation
is lit: horse-gnawed stalls,
hayloft, black heat tape wrapping
a water pipe, a slippery
spilled *chirrr* of oats from a split sack,
the bony, filthy haunches of cows . . .
And "barn" is only a noun—no verb
or subject has entered into the sentence yet!
The voice you hear when you read to yourself
is the clearest voice: you speak it
speaking to you.

A Noiseless Patient Spider

Walt Whitman

A noiseless patient spider,
I mark'd where on a little promontory it stood isolated,
Mark'd how to explore the vacant vast surrounding,
It launch'd forth filament, filament, filament, out of itself,
Ever unreeling them, ever tirelessly speeding them.

And you O my soul where you stand,
Surrounded, detached, in measureless oceans of space,
Ceaselessly musing, venturing, throwing, seeking the spheres to connect
    them,
Till the bridge you will need be form'd, till the ductile anchor hold,
Till the gossamer thread you fling catch somewhere, O my soul.

From *Leaves of Grass* (Philadelphia: David McKay, 1891–92.

APPENDIX

StudyDesk

To help you understand the many topics covered in *The Human Project*, we have included a computer study guide with the textbook. The StudyDesk program contains the following elements for each unit of the textbook:

- **Unit Overview:** a brief introduction to the main themes and issues of each unit;
- **Learning Outcomes:** a list of activities you will be able to complete at the end of each unit;
- **Key Concepts:** a quick way to review essential concepts you should understand, unit by unit;
- **Unit Review:** a complete list, on an article-by-article basis, of all terms and historical figures mentioned;
- **Terms and Concepts:** definitions and commentary of over 150 terms and concepts;
- **Biographical Sketches:** background information on over 80 historical figures mentioned in the textbook;
- **Summaries of Textbook Articles:** point-form summaries of each textbook article; and
- **Reading Room:** a selection of representative works by authors cited in the textbook along with reference materials.

The StudyDesk program uses your Internet browser to display on your computer. The StudyDesk screen is split into two panes. An expandable Table of Contents appears on the left side of the screen. To view the topics contained in each unit, just click the "book" icon next to the unit number. Similarly, to hide the topics from view, click the "book" icon again. To read the information contained in any topic, click the topic name. The topic information will then appear on the right side of the screen as demonstrated in the graphic shown here.

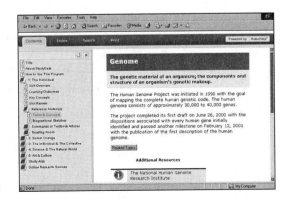

If you have ever used a web browser to view pages on the Internet, you will be familiar with the basic format of StudyDesk: clicking hotlinks calls up new pages that contain additional information. StudyDesk, however, uses a special form of web page. Most of the pages are contained in the program itself, while others are available only when you are online. The online pages are clearly identified by a special graphic: 🛈.

Unlike the textbook, the pages of which are usually read in order, with StudyDesk you use the mouse to call information to the screen in the order that serves your needs. You control what you read simply by clicking the mouse on a hotword (words in blue font or graphics that contain links) to activate a "jump" or a popup of a new page. When a jump occurs, new information will appear in place of what you were reading. When a popup occurs, new information appears on top of what you are reading in a scrollable window.

StudyDesk also includes several function buttons at the top of the screen:

- **Contents:** displays the expandable/collapsible Table of Contents in the left panel of the StudyDesk screen;
- **Index:** displays an alphabetic list of topics contained within StudyDesk;
- **Search:** displays a dialog field in the left panel of the screen in which you can type search words; the results of the search are then displayed in the left panel; and
- **Print:** allows you to print the currently displayed topic.

How to Start StudyDesk

StudyDesk runs directly from the CD-ROM that accompanies the textbook. A web page should appear when you insert the CD-ROM. If it does not, navigate to the CD-ROM drive, and click the file named "start-here.htm." This page contains additional information about the program and a link to start StudyDesk.

Minimum System Requirements

Computer: Pentium level PC, Mac OS X
RAM: 32mb
CD-ROM Drive
Browser: All major browsers supported
Plugin: Macromedia Flash 6.0 or later (installable from CD-ROM)

Humber Contributors

Ian Baird ("One More Time: Our Ongoing Dialogue with Popular Music") teaches humanities and sociology at the Humber College Institute of Technology and Advanced Learning. He has also worked as a professional musician for a number of years and is currently working on a novel that features rock and blues musicians.

George Bragues ("The Economics of Social Change"; "The Game We Call Politics: A Primer") teaches humanities, politics, philosophy, and economics at the Humber College Institute of Technology and Advanced Learning and politics and economics at the University of Guelph-Humber. He has also been a regular contributor to the *National Post* since 1999, writing opinion pieces on financial, economic, and political issues of the day in the paper's financial section. His research interests include 18th-century moral and political philosophy and classical liberalism along with topics in which the concerns of economics and philosophy intersect. His academic publications include articles in *The Independent Review* and *Business Ethics Quarterly* (forthcoming, 2005).

George Byrnes (StudyDesk CD-ROM; "Are Poems Puzzles?") teaches humanities and other online courses at the Humber College Institute of Technology and Advanced Learning. He is also a regular facilitator in judicial writing seminars held across Canada.

Melanie Chaparian (general editor; "Am I Free or Determined?") is the Program Coordinator of Humanities at the Humber College Institute of Technology and Advanced Learning, where she has taught humanities and philosophy since 1990.

Clive Cockerton (general editor; "Serious Pleasure: The Role of the Arts"; "Objectivity and Subjectivity"; "The Story: An Introduction") is the Associate-Dean of General Education at the Humber College Institute of Technology and Advanced Learning.

Mitchell Lerner ("On Inhumanity") has taught sociology at York University and humanities and sociology at Humber College. While pursuing an active business career, he remains an articulate voice on contemporary issues.

Greg Narbey ("Can We All Just Get Along?") teaches humanities and politics at the Humber College Institute of Technology and Advanced Learning, where he has taught for over 10 years.

Wendy O'Brien ("From Biology to Biography: A Brief History of the Self") teaches philosophy at the Humber College Institute of Technology and Advanced Learning and the University of Guelph–Humber.

Morton Ritts ("Politics in the Life of the Individual"; "Soul Force versus Physical Force") teaches humanities and history at the Humber College Institute of Technology and Advanced Learning.

Suzanne Senay ("Making Sense of the Universe") teaches humanities and philosophy at the Humber College Institute of Technology and Advanced Learning. Her interests include the history of modern philosophy, epistemology, and ethics.

John Steckley ("A Canadian Lament") teaches humanities, anthropology, and sociology at the Humber College Institute of Technology and Advanced Learning, where he has been a teacher for more than 20 years. He has published six books on Aboriginal peoples and is a specialist in the Huron language, culture, and history. He is also an above-average bar-band drummer.

PHOTO CREDITS

"AS IS" LICENSE AGREEMENT AND LIMITED WARRANTY

READ THIS LICENSE CAREFULLY BEFORE OPENING THIS PACKAGE. BY OPENING THIS PACKAGE, YOU ARE AGREEING TO THE TERMS AND CONDITIONS OF THIS LICENSE. IF YOU DO NOT AGREE, DO NOT OPEN THE PACKAGE. PROMPTLY RETURN THE UNOPENED PACKAGE AND ALL ACCOMPANYING ITEMS TO THE PLACE YOU OBTAINED THEM. THESE TERMS APPLY TO ALL LICENSED SOFTWARE ON THE DISK EXCEPT THAT THE TERMS FOR USE OF ANY SHAREWARE OR FREEWARE ON THE DISKETTES ARE AS SET FORTH IN THE ELECTRONIC LICENSE LOCATED ON THE DISK:

1. GRANT OF LICENSE and OWNERSHIP: The enclosed computer programs and any data ("Software") are licensed, not sold, to you by Pearson Education Canada Inc. ("We" or the "Company") in consideration of your adoption of the accompanying Company textbooks and/or other materials, and your agreement to these terms. You own only the disk(s) but we and/or our licensors own the Software itself. This license allows instructors and students enrolled in the course using the Company textbook that accompanies this Software (the "Course") to use and display the enclosed copy of the Software for academic use only, so long as you comply with the terms of this Agreement. You may make one copy for back up only. We reserve any rights not granted to you.

2. USE RESTRICTIONS: You may not sell or license copies of the Software or the Documentation to others. You may not transfer, distribute or make available the Software or the Documentation, except to instructors and students in your school who are users of the adopted Company textbook that accompanies this Software in connection with the course for which the textbook was adopted. You may not reverse engineer, disassemble, decompile, modify, adapt, translate or create derivative works based on the Software or the Documentation. You may be held legally responsible for any copying or copyright infringement which is caused by your failure to abide by the terms of these restrictions.

3. TERMINATION: This license is effective until terminated. This license will terminate automatically without notice from the Company if you fail to comply with any provisions or limitations of this license. Upon termination, you shall destroy the Documentation and all copies of the Software. All provisions of this Agreement as to limitation and disclaimer of warranties, limitation of liability, remedies or damages, and our ownership rights shall survive termination.

4. DISCLAIMER OF WARRANTY: THE COMPANY AND ITS LICENSORS MAKE NO WARRANTIES ABOUT THE SOFTWARE, WHICH IS PROVIDED "AS-IS." IF THE DISK IS DEFECTIVE IN MATERIALS OR WORKMANSHIP, YOUR ONLY REMEDY IS TO RETURN IT TO THE COMPANY WITHIN 30 DAYS FOR REPLACEMENT UNLESS THE COMPANY DETERMINES IN GOOD FAITH THAT THE DISK HAS BEEN MISUSED OR IMPROPERLY INSTALLED, REPAIRED, ALTERED OR DAMAGED. THE COMPANY DISCLAIMS ALL WARRANTIES, EXPRESS OR IMPLIED, INCLUDING WITHOUT LIMITATION, THE IMPLIED WARRANTIES OF MERCHANTABILITY AND FITNESS FOR A PARTICULAR PURPOSE. THE COMPANY DOES NOT WARRANT, GUARANTEE OR MAKE ANY REPRESENTATION REGARDING THE ACCURACY, RELIABILITY, CURRENTNESS, USE, OR RESULTS OF USE, OF THE SOFTWARE.

5. LIMITATION OF REMEDIES AND DAMAGES: IN NO EVENT, SHALL THE COMPANY OR ITS EMPLOYEES, AGENTS, LICENSORS OR CONTRACTORS BE LIABLE FOR ANY INCIDENTAL, INDIRECT, SPECIAL OR CONSEQUENTIAL DAMAGES ARISING OUT OF OR IN CONNECTION WITH THIS LICENSE OR THE SOFTWARE, INCLUDING, WITHOUT LIMITATION, LOSS OF USE, LOSS OF DATA, LOSS OF INCOME OR PROFIT, OR OTHER LOSSES SUSTAINED AS A RESULT OF INJURY TO ANY PERSON, OR LOSS OF OR DAMAGE TO PROPERTY, OR CLAIMS OF THIRD PARTIES, EVEN IF THE COMPANY OR AN AUTHORIZED REPRESENTATIVE OF THE COMPANY HAS BEEN ADVISED OF THE POSSIBILITY OF SUCH DAMAGES. SOME JURISDICTIONS DO NOT ALLOW THE LIMITATION OF DAMAGES IN CERTAIN CIRCUMSTANCES, SO THE ABOVE LIMITATIONS MAY NOT ALWAYS APPLY.

6. GENERAL: THIS AGREEMENT SHALL BE CONSTRUED AND INTERPRETED ACCORDING TO THE LAWS OF THE PROVINCE OF ONTARIO. This Agreement is the complete and exclusive statement of the agreement between you and the Company and supersedes all proposals, prior agreements, oral or written, and any other communications between you and the company or any of its representatives relating to the subject matter.

Should you have any questions concerning this agreement or if you wish to contact the Company for any reason, please contact in writing: Editorial Manager, Pearson Education Canada, 26 Prince Andrew Place, Don Mills, Ontario, M3C 2T8.